RESEMBLANCE & DISGRACE

RESEMBLANCE

 ## DISGRACE

Alexander Pope
and the
Deformation of Culture

HELEN DEUTSCH

Harvard University Press
Cambridge, Massachusetts, and London, England
1996

Library of Congress Cataloging in Publication Data

Deutsch, Helen, 1961–
Resemblance and disgrace : Alexander Pope and the deformation
of culture / Helen Deutsch.
p. cm.
Includes bibliographical references and index.
ISBN 0-674-76489-7 (alk. paper)
1. Pope, Alexander, 1688–1744—Criticism and interpretation.
2. Literature and society—England—History—18th century.
3. Verse satire, English—History and criticism. 4. Abnormalities, Human,
in literature. 5. Pope, Alexander, 1688–1744—Health. 6. Imitation in
literature. 7. Monsters in literature. 8. Health in literature.
I. Title.
PR3634.D48 1996
821'.5—dc20 95-31183

For my grandfather,
Frederick Deutsch,
with love and gratitude

Preface

Thine is just such an Image of *his* Pen,
As thou thy Self art of the Sons of Men:
Where our own Species in Burlesque we trace,
A Sign-Post Likeness of the Noble Race;
That is at once Resemblance and Disgrace.

Verses Address'd to the Imitator of the First
Satire of the Second Book of Horace

This book has its roots in my long fascination with the imitative originality of
Alexander Pope's poetry, and its written origins in an Amherst College honors
thesis on the evolution of the epic simile from Homer through Pope's mock-
epic. My gradual move from the propriety of a traditional reading of Pope in
his classical context to the impropriety of my current focus on deformity, seems
to me now to have been determined by the poetry itself. Pope's habits of mind
have conditioned and challenged my own.

When doctoral research first led me to the words of my epigraph and title,
they shocked me not just by their cruelty, but also by their descriptive power.
Pope's poetry, while indebted to a variety of authorial models, is above all about
himself and his particular version of authorship. Pope himself, in his own writings and those of his readers, singularly embodies imitative originality. To write
about deformity in relation to Pope is not simply to point to the great poet's
weakness, but to discern what makes his life's work unique.

I try in what follows to bring freshly posed questions of the embodiment
of authorship, identity, and originality to the reading of Pope, and thereby to
make Pope's case available to a larger field of literary and cultural inquiry. While
I am greatly indebted to recent criticism of this poet in delineating such a field,
it seems to me that the pleasures of Pope's texts have often been lost in the
process of reframing them. *Resemblance and Disgrace* incorporates recent per-

spectives on Pope into a revision of both the poetic particulars and the person of the poet on which it depends.

Verses Address'd to the Imitator . . . of Horace is hardly alone in its attempt to mortify Pope by reducing him to an object of visible derision. Preserved in the British Museum is a four volume bound set of pamphlet attacks on Pope documenting the flood of published abuse the poet alludes to in his *Epistle to Arbuthnot* as "the libel'd Person and the pictur'd Shape" (353). Inscribed in the first volume are the words, "Job, Chapt. 31, Vers. 35": "Behold it is my desire, that my adversary had written a book. Surely I would take it on my shoulder and bind it as a crown unto me." This gesture exemplifies the paradoxes of agency that Pope's deformity enables. Pope himself had these pamphlets collected and bound; the reference to Job is his own. He rewrites Job's metaphor as a literal "beholding" of bound book and burdened body. The poet has indeed taken his adversary's "book" on his shoulder: by fashioning a crown of heroism out of the cruelest of attacks he authors such a book himself. His abused person becomes the sign he proudly displays, his shoulder hunched by the weight of injustice. The writer at the mercy of his readers' derision becomes a self-made spectacle, inviting his audience to view the proof of his moral integrity. Pope has "authored," one might say, both his adversary's book and the public image that such a book documents.

In this book I read deformity as a poetics. While Pope's poetry abounds with aberrant creatures (Thersites in his *Iliad* translation, the Cave of Spleen in *The Rape of the Lock,* and the "jumbled Race" of the Dunces' monstrous creation come to mind), such literal monsters are not the focus of a project that attempts to outline a monstrous methodology. Pope himself mocks and deplores those sycophants in his *Epistle to Arbuthnot:*

> . . . who to my Person pay their court,
> I cough like *Horace,* and tho' lean, am short,
> *Ammon's* great Son one shoulder had too high,
> Such *Ovid's* nose, and "Sir! you have an *Eye*—"
> Go on, obliging Creatures, make me see
> All that disgrac'd my Betters, met in me.   (115–120)

I distinguish myself from such company by distinguishing Pope from his "Betters" in keeping with his own poetic project. Pope makes clear in these lines that his person is not a simple point of comparison or "resemblance." I hope to show that the resulting "disgrace" becomes in this poet's hands a unique form of distinction.

Preface

As this book went through many metamorphoses it incurred many debts. At Amherst College Frederick Griffiths, David Sofield, and William H. Pritchard first inspired and encouraged my reading of Pope and interest in literary imitation. At the University of California, Berkeley, John Traugott—who brought me into the eighteenth century—William S. Anderson, Richard Feingold, Steven Knapp, and Florence Verducci provided invaluable guidance and insight as I wrote the dissertation that contained the germ of this book. Neil Hertz's early questions and criticisms got me started and kept me going. Lowell Bowditch, Linda Charnes, Heather James, Ann Kibbie, William Taliaferro, and Evelyn Tribble all read parts of the dissertation and provided both dialogue and support. At Northwestern Larry Lipking and Nicola Watson worked with me for years in the trenches of the eighteenth century, asked crucial questions, and along with Martin Mueller read and critiqued early pieces of a new project focusing exclusively on Pope, while Joseph Roach and Christopher Herbert provided essential votes of confidence. A 1992–93 postdoctoral year at the UCLA Center for Seventeenth- and Eighteenth-Century Studies and the William Andrews Clark Memorial Library provided me with the time, leisure, resources, and intellectual community that enabled me to write most of this book. To the Clark Professors who brought me to UCLA that year—Anne K. Mellor, Sara Melzer, and Kathryn Norberg, to the director of the Center, Peter Reill, and to the librarians and staff at the Clark Memorial Library and the Center, I will be forever grateful. Lindsay Waters of Harvard University Press had faith in the manuscript, and Alison Kent and Kate Brick saw me through its production with unfailing competence and cheer. David B. Morris and Susan Staves helped to give the book its final shape. Kimberly Baldus and Jennifer Michael provided crucial help with final details. A subvention grant from the University Research Grants Council at Northwestern allowed me to include the illustrations. Eric Sundquist and the Department of English at UCLA believed enough in the book to make a California dream a reality. Permission has been granted to reprint " 'The Truest Copies' and the 'Mean Original': Pope, Deformity, and the Poetics of Self-Exposure," *Eighteenth-Century Studies* 27, 1 (Fall 1993): 1–26, which appears in expanded form in Chapter 1.

A few friends have been so essential that they elude any narrative frame for the book's development. Diane Furtney and Jeredith Merrin have been the ideal readers who transformed my writing life; with them as audience I know that the risks are worth taking. The intellectual generosity and constant friendship of Eva Cherniavsky first helped me to handle an unruly group of Berkeley undergraduates and have been indispensable ever since. I owe more than I can

ix

say to Julia Stern's brilliant reading, conversation, correspondence, open heart, and unflagging assistance in matters emotional and practical (including the loan of a computer at the last moment). Sharon Achinstein and Wendy Wall were more like sisters than colleagues; along with Jules Law and Chuck Wasserburg they were the best of friends. Deanna Kreisel made the most difficult of transitions into *Thelma and Louise* with a happy ending. Heidi Gilpin and Nancy Salzer made Los Angeles feel like home, and Jayne Lewis's gift of original engagement and genuine friendship began a new era for me there. Ruthanne Deutsch, Betty Capaldi, and Frederick Deutsch always believed in me and this book with love. The best this book brought me, and who made this book its best, I save for last—my partner in work and life, my inspiration, Michael Meranze.

Contents

Illustrations

Introduction

When first young *Maro* in his boundless Mind
A work t'outlast Immortal *Rome* design'd,
Perhaps he seem'd *above* the Critick's Law,
And but from *Nature's Fountains* scorn'd to draw:
But when t'examine ev'ry Part he came,
Nature and *Homer* were, he found, the *same:*
Convinc'd, amaz'd, he checks the bold Design,
And Rules as strict his labour'd Work confine,
As if the *Stagyrite* o'erlook'd each Line.
Learn hence for Ancient *Rules* a just Esteem;
To copy *Nature* is to copy *Them.*

An Essay on Criticism, 130–140.

All Nature is but Art, unknown to thee;
All Chance, Direction, which thou canst not see;
All Discord, Harmony, not understood;
All partial Evil, universal Good:
And, spite of Pride, in erring Reason's spite,
One truth is clear, "Whatever IS, is RIGHT."

An Essay on Man, I, 289–294.

Alexander Pope's body was deformed, and with that fact my book begins. Trampled by a cow when he was a child, Pope suffered from Pott's disease, or tuberculosis of the spine, which resulted in a curvature that grew worse with time. The eighteenth century's most prominent poet, who described the life of a wit as "a warfare upon Earth,"[1] endured a continual and painful war between an active mind in a beautiful head and what he called "this scurvy tenement of my body."[2] When full-grown he was barely four and a half feet tall. Voltaire described him as "protuberant before and behind," and in an early self-mocking

I

moment the poet described himself anonymously as "a lively little Creature, with long Arms and Legs: A Spider is no ill Emblem of him."[3] Pope's physical being, his physical pain, and his vulnerability to the cruelty of the public gaze deprived him of self-control and alienated him from his body. It also made him painfully unique.

When Pope chooses the spider as his "Emblem," he makes corporeal reality the basis for a metaphor of authorial identity. The spider, so brilliantly brought to life in Pope's friend Jonathan Swift's *Battle of the Books* (1710), boasts that he is "a domestick Animal, furnisht with a Native Stock within my self," whose home "is all built with my own Hands, and the Materials extracted altogether out of my own Person." His rival the bee describes such self-sufficiency differently: the spider is a creature "which by a lazy Contemplation of four Inches round; by an over-weening Pride, which feeding and engendering on it self, turns all into Excrement and Venom; producing nothing at last, but Fly-bane and a Cobweb."[4] Productive independence is recast by a potential victim as wasteful solipsism. Pope waged a similar war with a contemporary reading (and lampooning) public of unprecedented size and power, as well as with a host of classical predecessors, for the power of self-representation, self-possession, and authorial integrity. Pope's ironic self-designation demonstrates in miniature his attempts to mediate, and thereby to appropriate, the battle between ancients and moderns that Swift's text satirizes. Throughout the continuous revision that distinguished his poetic career, Pope marked culturally current material with his deformity's singular contradictions.

For Pope, whether the medium be text or landscape, poetic form was most indisputably exemplified by the heroic couplet. In his hands the couplet achieved its apotheosis; it conceived and ordered a world. I attempt in what follows to explicate what can be thought of as Pope's ultimate couplet of public form and personal deformity.[5]

The power of Pope's poetry is contained and displayed by its focus on the visible, its adherence to the material world of particular objects that it teaches readers how to imagine and use.[6] Pope's use of detail provides a literary example of what Ronald Paulson has termed an aesthetic of difficulty that renders visual and verbal inseparable.[7] This poetic attention to sometimes ugly particulars is embodied by the author himself. His physical deformity becomes a vehicle for self-reflection, self-representation, and self-legitimation. The poet's body is both a trademark of his poetry's invisible property, and a sign of his own vulnerable visibility, rendering him at once an inimitable original and a faulty imitation.

Deformity frames the power of Pope's vision with its reminder of the observer's gaze.

This conjunction of form with deformity suggests complicated questions about the poet's relation both to his authorial self-representations and to history, evoking different facets of agency and authorship.[8] Deformity compromises authorship both spatially and temporally, rendering transcendence impossible, whether in the form of literary monument or timeless truth. What it offers instead is a conjunction of the spatial with the temporal, a *discordia concors* in which each realm of potential abstraction defines and limits the other. Pope's couplet is refined for the orderly discord of paradox; for the conjoining of opposites in delicate balance; for the linking of disparate realms of meaning through analogy, zeugma, and oxymoron; for the strong antipathies of satire. The protean nature of such poetry makes it difficult to locate Pope "himself" in historical relation to the changing world in which he lived, a world of burgeoning empire and emergent capitalism, enlivened and feminized (in a view Pope helped to define) by its elite's appetite for an ever-increasing variety of objects.[9] As a Catholic, as the most prominent literary businessman of his time, and as a powerful political spokesman for the Opposition, Pope made his mark at once in the center and on the margins of a historical moment he both celebrated and deplored.

Many recent critical accounts portray Pope as an "arch-negator," who rejects the so-called feminine realm of the grotesque body, the marketplace, and the mob, and thus becomes the inverse reflection of what he fears.[10] This Pope enlists classical sources in the service of a bourgeois entrepreneurship which he endeavors to recast as cultural authority; driven by his unconscious fear of a feminine disorder and instability in which he is complicit, this Pope is undermined by the complexity of both his classical originals (texts more consciously ambivalent about the cost of empire) and his own poetry.[11] Pope's couplet thus reduces historical and textual irresolution to the obdurately blindered "strong Antipathy of Good to Bad."[12] Such accounts are invaluable because they implicate Pope in the unruly historical particulars—unruly in their challenge to traditional distinctions of value, class, and gender—which they condemn him for rejecting.

The still-enduring portraits of Pope which preceded these, most notably Reuben Brower's Horatian champion of moral integrity and Maynard Mack's civic-minded inheritor of a literary and political tradition of retirement, are enriched—if perhaps defaced—by an awareness of how such masculine poetic integrity is compromised by its resemblance to the worldly corruption it attacks.[13] One of the most historically nuanced readings of this earlier tradition is William Dowling's recent study of the Augustan verse epistle. Dowling describes poetry such as Pope's as "ideological intervention," more radical than conservative in its critique of emergent capitalism, but radical in a way that is "retrospective" and nostalgic.[14] Such poetry speaks for a landed gentry which was losing economic power while reinforcing mythic power; it attempts to recreate an imaginary community based on classical models as an alternative to what it perceives as potentially solipsistic social disintegration. In this portrait, Pope is again blindly dedicated to the poetic project of restoring an aristocracy that would eliminate both himself and his audience. But in the tradition of those sympathetic readers of the great Tory satirists, and despite his admirable attempt to argue for the "reality" and ideological importance of literary worlds, Dowling is uninterested in how Pope's particular poetic attempts to literally recreate and possess such community signal his conscious affinity for the very materialist society his poetry condemns.[15]

What both schools of Pope criticism have in common is their own blindness to the way in which deformity for Pope is both a biographical fact and a literary method, a mode of conceiving. Whether recent readers blame Pope for socioeconomic hypocrisy or praise him for moral and political heroism, only one side of the couplet of form and deformity is acknowledged. And in both cases, whether the critic reveals Pope's deformity as if it were the return of the repressed, or represses it on the poet's behalf, deformity as a self-consciously created figure for Pope's poetics patterned after the poet's own person is lost from sight.[16]

In this book I attempt to read Pope against the background of what Barbara Stafford has described as a "metaphorology" of the body in the eighteenth century.[17] By situating Pope in relation to a cultural collage of images and interpretations of monstrosity, of which deformity was often read (not least of all by Pope's attackers) as a visible sign, I hope to make legible Pope's deployment of his person, and to show how such deployment questions eighteenth-century definitions of nature and art. Both defending and confounding such definitions, Pope's method gives particular form to a cultural obsession.

Monstrosity was a conceptual couplet for the eighteenth century, at once contemporary science's proof of natural origins and a reminder of earlier ideas of the supernatural.[18] The history of this concept tells a story of gender and power. Renaissance theories of monstrosity blamed the mother's impressionable and desirous imagination for imprinting the embryo with an image other than the father's, while Enlightenment thinking replaced the mother's unnatural and licentious mimicking of art with the scientist's paternal and natural law.[19] When rationality prevailed over monstrosity, no longer describing it but regulating it, female agency was excluded and monstrosity's duplicity was repressed: "the irregular submits to the rule, the prodigy to the predictable."[20]

In Pope's time, deformity could still be read as obstructing the succession of a chain of being based on transparent analogy, as an unnatural originality that obscured the light of universal truth. As Stafford writes:

> The monster began and ended in the incorrect image, in the indelibility of the flawed, strange, and incongruous impression. Its verbal cognates were . . . barbarisms . . . Irrational and perverted image-word copulations were falsely modeled on the simultaneity of pictures, and thus denied the correct sequentiality of language. They included those hybrids that Neo-classical criticism deemed wrongful nonrepresentations: allegorical obscurities, distorted grotesques, and jumbled nonsense. The monster . . . interrupts, through glaring excess or defect, the plenitude of succession.[21]

As Marie-Hélène Huet puts it, "monstrosity always reveals a truth," however disruptive or unwelcome.[22] The genre which by the close of the century was designated the appropriate visual forum for deformity—namely caricature—tells the material and ephemeral truth of a body in pain.[23] Such truth is portrayed not as disembodied abstraction but as "minutely elaborated pains and pleasures impertinently and obtrusively wandering around on their own."[24] While eighteenth-century arbiters of taste declared that "monsters are for natural history cabinets, & not for painting galleries," caricaturists restored to monstrosity its ancient mystery, its subjectivity, its magical power of sympathy.[25] The art of caricature, as Stafford puts it, "relied not on reason but on the emotional potency of fetishes . . . It attempted to objectify, and give texture to, raw bodily experience lying beyond words and behind shape . . . [It] selected tangible signs or visible tokens possessing marvelous ornamental or singular qualities."[26] Stafford describes the fetishistic quality of caricature in the late eighteenth century as a kind of atavism, "an irrational element of popular culture appearing at the end of a long rationalistic tradition."[27] In this discussion monstrosity's binaries—now conceived in terms of class—of high and low culture are thereby also located historically, before and after the advent of print. My reading of Pope examines a moment at which such binaries are not yet fully distinct, when the rationalistic tradition epitomized by the linguistic practice of nominalism and classification, and the print medium that made it possible, were just beginning to come into their own.[28] At this moment, caricature's disorder and the law of reason could coexist; Pope's poetry provides one example of how they formed a symbiosis.[29]

As this brief discussion shows, the theory of generation, which in the eighteenth century was also a theory of property, "has always been a theory of art."[30] And the definition of "conception," originated by Aristotle and perpetuated through the Renaissance as "the male having an idea in the female body," linked intellectual with physical procreation by a gendered division: masculine intellectual property is made visible by feminine corporeality.[31] Deformity and monstrosity expose the complicity of such oppositions and therefore pose questions of the gendering of authorship, the power of paternity, and the stability of inheritance; the resolutions were in part played out in the arena of art and aesthetic theory.

Such questions preoccupied Pope at the dawn of a literary career in which he endeavored to define the modern author as both producer and proprietor of his literary estate, while delineating an aesthetic of self-effacement that he would heroically resist. In a milieu of literary production which has been described as a field of socioeconomic "monstrous contingency," otherwise known as Grub Street, such an effort at self-possession was difficult indeed.[32] At the intersection of the imitative art of the maternal imagination and the paternal truth of nature's law—of ancient knowledge and modern reason, divine portent and collectable curiosity, duncely impropriety and polished refinement, feminizing commodification and masculine self-possession—deformity within and without Pope's work signified the liminality of knowledge, the mystery of origins, and the difficulties of inheritance and ownership.

By reading for deformity, I want to restore the familiar passages quoted as epigraphs, two of Pope's most notoriously conservative statements, to some of their original strangeness, and thus to gesture toward a narrative of Pope's career. This narrative begins with a celebration of the hierarchy of literary succession in which self-effacement is equivalent to self-assertion. It then moves toward a reframing of obscure deformity as a vehicle for imagining an invisible order, and ends with a portrait of a poet whose vision continually exceeds the very conditions of its possibility.

The *Essay on Criticism* (1711) delineates a luminous chain of literary inheritance which bases authority on inventive refinement and filial propriety. In the first passage's monitory Oedipal fable of the fall from authorial innocence, Virgil's error is to attempt to render Homer invisible by envisioning an unmediated originality. He imagines Homer as an obstacle to his view of Nature, rather than as identical to Nature itself. The Roman poet here mirrors the author of the *Essay* both in his ambition and in his indebtedness to his originals.[33] His naively arrogant trust in the boundlessness of his own mind is belied by the labored nature of his final product. Virgil's fantasy of a transparent view of Nature necessitates the denial of his artistic fathers' surveillance.

What unite Nature and Homer, and make them both visible and legible, are the "Ancient Rules" that bind critics and poets. Virgil, the prototype for most Western poets after Homer, learns to write as if Aristotle were looking over his shoulder; he conflates nature and art, and confines an ambitious imagination by reminding himself that his work was envisioned by another. In keeping with this emphasis on vision, Pope's famous claim that "true Wit is Nature to Advantage dresst" (297), a comparison that this poem carries to great lengths, equates fashion with both social and poetic decorum, proper style with filial devotion to literary fathers.[34] The young Pope's virtuoso performance constructs transparent correspondences, illuminated by what the poem calls Nature's "*clear, unchang'd,* and *Universal* Light" (71), between authors, poems, and worldly propriety, equating self-effacement with self-assertion, visibility with authority.

While Pope's wit illuminates art's transparency in *An Essay on Criticism,* in *An Essay on Man* (1733–34) he enlists wit in the recreation of nature's obscurity, hoping above all to achieve a "steering betwixt the extremes of doctrines seemingly opposite."[35] The *Essay on Man* thereby provides a poetic equivalent of the art of caricature, punning on disorder and deformity by its injunctions toward multiple perspectives. What seems to me most monstrous about this poem for its critics is its defacement of invisible truth with visible metaphors. In this controversy, as in the medical debate over the genesis of monsters, monstrosity is ultimately equated with the embodiment of human intellectual conception, an embodiment imagined as a fall into obscurity and a vision of limitation.

Considering "*Man* in the abstract, his *Nature* and his *State,*" the anonymous yet enormously popular and controversial *Essay on Man* rewrites the question of monstrosity as part of what Pope termed the "Anatomy of the Mind" and of man's place in the divine order.[36] With aphoristic concision, this poem negotiates the opposing perspectives of poetry and philosophy as it considers the individual manifestations of human nature. Pope's contemporary defender and editor William Warburton described his method in the *Essay* as "the art of converting Poetical Ornaments into Philosophical Reasoning," while Maynard Mack has termed it "the rational passing over into mystery."[37] In his book *The Rape of the Text* Harry Solomon restores the rich intellectual context of what readers since the poem's first influential opponent, the logician and theologian Jean Paul de Crousaz, have considered its "unnatural couplings" of beauty with truth.[38] By linking Pope's *Essay* to a rich and anti-dogmatic tradition of academic discourse that began with Cicero's debt to Socrates, and which, in the manner of Socrates, achieves a kind of negative knowledge through an eclectic questioning of received tenets, Solomon restores Pope's seemingly unequivocal "Whatever IS, is RIGHT," to its original and paradoxical ambiguity. In such a context, this declarative statement becomes not descriptive but rather directive, a "hypothetical 'rule of life,' " whose language demands that the reader envision the invisible.[39]

Pope's friend and later his bookseller, the footman-turned-poet Robert Dodsley, describes reading the *Essay on Man* as a process of difficult and gradual enlightenment, a labor to achieve a vision modeled on but transcending the human body. He describes this vision as both self-knowledge and acknowledgment of authorial power:

> So when at first I view'd thy wond'rous Plan,
> Leading thro' all the winding Maze of Man;
> Bewilder'd, weak, unable to pursue,
> My Pride would fain have laid the Fault on You.
> This false, That ill-expresst, this Thought not good,
> And all was wrong which I misunderstood.
> But reading more attentive, soon I found,
> The Diction nervous, and the Doctrine sound.
> Saw Man, a Part of that stupendous Whole,
> *Whose Body Nature is, and God the Soul.*
> Saw in the Scale of Things his middle State,
> And all his Powers adapted just to That.
> Saw Reason, Passion, Weakness, how of use,
> How all to Good, to Happiness conduce.
> Saw my own Weakness, thy Superior Power,
> And still the more I read, admire the more.[40]

Samuel Johnson, who translated Crousaz's attack on the *Essay* from the original French into English, believed strongly in the dangerously feminine power of the *Essay*'s poetry to masquerade as philosophy while reducing it to nonsense:

> This *Essay* affords us an egregious instance of the predominance of genius,
> the dazzling splendor of imagery, and the seductive powers of eloquence.
> Never were penury of knowledge and vulgarity of sentiment so happily

disguised. The reader feels his mind full, though he learns nothing; and when he meets it in its new array no longer knows the talk of his mother and his nurse . . .

Surely a man of no very comprehensive search may venture to say that he has heard all this before, but it was never till now recommended by such a blaze of embellishment or such sweetness of melody.[41]

The same eloquence which, for Dodsley, reveals the light of truth along with his own shortcomings of vision, for Johnson obscures the nugatory chaos of that which is too close to home. The "dazzling splendor" and "seductive powers" of the *Essay*'s imagery and eloquence conceal the homely talk of mother and nurse.[42] In the same way that Johnson, in his angry response to the *Essay on Criticism*, demands that Pope's "true wit" be separated from the dress of expression, in his reading of the *Essay on Man* he mandates that the poem be viewed "disrobed of its ornaments." From this vantage point, nothing remains. Dodsley's vision of man's place in an ineffable whole is countered by Johnson's recognition of an unattainable originality whose essence is feminine reiteration.[43]

These two accounts of reading *An Essay on Man* demonstrate the impossibility of distinguishing ornament from substance, vision from text, poetry from philosophy, that renders Pope's most abstract text a monstrous embodiment of the invisible. These responses differ in the speaker's degree of resistance to seeing himself as an object in another author's plan. Such a difference in perspective determines whether monstrosity is envisioned as an aberration or as part of an invisible whole. From the authorial perspective, monstrosity is restored to a paradoxical order, which Montaigne, one of Pope's many influences in the *Essay on Man,* describes in his essay "On a Monstrous Child":

What we call monsters are not so to God, who sees in the immensity of his work the infinity of forms that he has comprised in it; and it is for us to believe that this figure that astonishes us is related and linked to some other figure of the same kind unknown to man. From his infinite wisdom there proceeds nothing but that is good and ordinary and regular; but we do not see its arrangement and relationship. *What he sees often, he does not wonder at, even if he does not know why it is. If something happens which he has not seen before, he thinks it is a prodigy.* [Cicero, *On Divination*].[44]

This difference defines the *trompe l'oeil* effect of reading for deformity, an effect created by the vacillations of the reader and writer between the positions of subject and object. In this study I examine such effects as they transpire in the overlapping object-worlds of the curiosity, the commodity, the portrait, the garden, the literary imitation, and the original composition.

What I hope will become visible in the process is the function of Pope's deformity as a sign of the monstrosity of imitative authorship, a phenomenon which caused Lady Mary Wortley Montagu to brand both the poet's body and his printed book "at once Resemblance and Disgrace" of originals both artificial and natural.[45] But such humiliating visibility also marks this author as a rightful owner of literary property and legislator of culture, who comes to display his own deformity as the evidence of his moral heroism.

The
"Truest Copies"
of a
"Mean Original"

Few proficients have a greater genius for Monsters than myself.

"To a Lady from her Brother,"
10 February 1714/15?, *Correspondence,* vol. 1, p. 277.

In this chapter I determine how Alexander Pope's body remains outside, yet inexorably connected to, the orderly mirroring of his couplets. My book thus begins by shifting its focus from the poet's polished lines to the author's distorted body. This body beyond the poetry's frame becomes the central figure for both this poet's life-work, and for the cultural imagination of authorship at a transitional moment when the profession of letters in England, not yet fully formed, under constant and embattled negotiation, is a matter of "monstrous contingency."[1] Pope's body lends its shape to an era during which:

> it was no simple matter to delineate the person of the expressive author in contrast to that of the artisanal book producer, to differentiate the economic interests of writers from those of publishers, or to determine the relation between a writer's legal personality (as a copyright holder or as responsible for obscene libel) and his or her ethical or aesthetic personality (as creator or moral authority).[2]

In the context of such contestation, Pope's indelibly marked body functions not as his work's coherent metaphor, nor as its effect or cause, nor as its repressed opposite, but rather as its distinguishing mark; a mark which Pope's recent critics have learned to disavow but with which his contemporaries were fascinated. The metaphor of portraiture points to the way in which the image of the author in Pope's time takes the place of both the concept of authorship, and the chaotic social milieu which gives it life. Such an image, whether in print or in paint, is constructed in relation to the codes that give the social body meaning, that attempt to keep it whole. Portraiture, like literature, was a booming business in eighteenth-century England, and like literature drew an unprecedentedly large and various audience by benefit of mass reproduction. Just as the author's individuality stands in marked disjunction from the texts he imitates, from the system that markets him, and from the confused orders of those who read him, so the idea of the particular likeness, of "portraiture as a concept thus stands in a contradictory relationship to the mythic unified body which is rationalized and re-presented in portrait depictions."[3] The original portrait, in other words, like the original author, is for the eighteenth-century public something of a paradox.

Alexander Pope, the most frequently portrayed individual of his generation, particularly embodies this paradox.[4] Eighteenth-century codes of bodily representation privileged the head, and more specifically the face, as the site of character, reading the image of the face "in symbolic relation to the subject, not in representation of it."[5] As Deidre Lynch argues, "the legible face indexed character: a social norm, a determinate place on the ethical map where every person had a proper place and where distinction was contained within limits. Recognizing a face, or putting a name to a face, was thus an allegory for . . . discriminating and weighing samenesses and differences."[6] Pope's unique body, by its deviation from the norm and by the improper attention it calls to itself, disrupts these somatic and symbolic economies by refusing to be read.

Reconsidering the authorial body that has been constructed as monstrous, and which in its obviousness has remained paradoxically invisible to later readers, enables us to see both how meaning is figured at a particular cultural moment, and where meaning has its limits. To read Pope's deformity is to delineate the limits of form itself for his cultural field; it is to see the reflection of his poetry's finished surface, the roots of his hard-won Augustan "originality," the marks of his monumental cultural entrepreneurship and self-possession, in illicit ambiguity.[7] At the intersection of the general and the particular, public gaze and personal display, social metaphor and individual metonymy, when this authorial body is made visible, it is uniquely deformed.

Pope's body is above all a body of contradictions, and Pope a figure of personal and historical liminality. Called both the last Renaissance poet and the first modern author, he shrewdly negotiated the historical transition from patronage to mass publication by his active solicitation of subscriptions in translating the *Iliad*. The first professional author to also be *de facto* his own publisher was both the product and a shaping presence of an era in which, as Mark Rose writes, the "work was now above all the objectification of a personality." While "readers increasingly approached literary texts as theologians had long approached the book of nature, seeking to find the marks of the divine author's personality in his works," the mortal author became a text at the mercy of his readers, a text readers tried to control by depicting.[8] Reauthorizing a celebrity both courted and compulsory, Pope does not transform his body through his work, nor does he try to write himself out of his body, rather he silences his audience by making his body visible. Throughout his career, Pope struggled for control over this authorial image.

The first, and earliest, of such images was composed by a well-known contemporary of Pope's, the critic John Dennis, in response to a perceived libel in the form of an unidentified "Imitation of Horace." Entitled "A True Character of Mr. Pope, and His Writings,"[9] Dennis's tirade, one of his few exercises in the genre descended from Horace and Samuel Butler, centers on the ambiguity of "character"—iterable printed mark, (in)decipherable letter, or ineffable moral substance—and gives that ambiguity the shape of a monster. Signalling uneasiness about originality, claiming to have written a private letter rather than an essay, Dennis begins with an anonymous "character within a character" that allows him to ventriloquize the harshest of his attacks:

> That he is one, whom God and Nature have mark'd for want of Common Honesty, and his own Contemptible Rhimes for want of Common Sense, that those Rhimes have found great Success with the Rabble, which is a Word almost as comprehensive as Mankind; but that the Town, which supports him, will do by him, as the Dolphin did by the Ship-wrack'd *Monkey,* drop him as soon as it finds him out to be a Beast, whom it fondly now mistakes for a Human Creature. 'Tis, *says he,* a very little but very comprehensive Creature, in whom all Contradictions meet, and all Contrarieties are reconcil'd; when at one and the same time, like the Ancient *Centaurs,* he is a Beast and a Man, a Whig and a Tory, a virulent *Papist* and yet forsooth, a Pillar of the Church of *England,* a Writer at one and the same time, of GUARDIANS and of EXAMINERS, an assertor of Liberty and of the Dispensing Power of Kings; a Rhimester without Judgment or Reason, and a Critick without Common Sense; a Jesuitical Professor of Truth, a base and a foul Pretender to Candour; a Barbarous Wretch, who is perpetually boasting of Humanity and Good Nature, a lurking way-laying Coward, and a Stabber in the Dark; who is always pretending to Magnanimity, and to sum up all Villains in one, a Traytor-Friend, one who has betrayed all Mankind.[10]

Pope's literary villainy, his betrayal of "all Mankind," takes on his body's unnatural shape, a shape initially described as that of a beast, but ultimately fixed as undefinable ("like the Ancient *Centaurs,* he is a Beast and a Man"). The unclassifiability which Pope himself will later point to repeatedly as the sign of his political integrity—"Tories call me Whig, and Whigs a Tory"[11]—here signals physical and moral abjection. Dennis writes Pope "himself" in the perverse image of his future poetry; this portrait of a "very comprehensive Creature, in whom all Contradictions meet, and all Contrarieties are reconcil'd," for whom the ultimate opposition (as it is in the *Epilogue to the Satires* and the fourth book of the *Dunciad*) is between himself and all mankind (an opposition which Dennis, like Pope, marks as originating from a literary model), resembles nothing more than Pope's couplet art. Dennis takes the analogy one step further by identifying Pope's monstrous origins with the embodiment of the genre that Pope will ultimately transform into his own image (a genre whose etymological origins were, fittingly enough, considered dubious): "The grosser part of his gentle Readers believe the Beast to be more than Man; as Ancient Rusticks took his Ancestors for those Demy-Gods they call *Fauns* and *Satyrs.*"[12]

Dennis's pun here seems prescient, since in 1716 Pope was still a respectful imitator of classical fathers, rather than an embattled satiric hero whose greatest opponents were the originals who gave him form. And it is Pope's expertise at imitation which occasions some of Dennis's most extreme virulence:

> As he is in Shape a *Monkey,* is so in his every Action; in his senseless Chattering, and his merry Grimaces, in his doing hourly Mischief and hiding himself, in the variety of his Ridiculous Postures, and his continual Shiftings, from Place to Place, from Persons to Persons, from Thing to Thing. But whenever he Scribbles, he is emphatically a *Monkey,* in his awkward servile Imitations . . .
>
> Thus for fifteen years together this Ludicrous Animal has been a constant *Imitator.* Yet he has rather mimick'd these great Genius's, than he has Imitated them. He has given a False and a Ridiculous Turn to all their good and their great Qualities, and has, as far as in him lies, Burlesqu'd them without knowing it.[13]

Dennis's portrayal once again slides imperceptibly from the bestial form of the author to his literary style, a style which is itself "awkward," "servile," and ultimately unrecognizable even by Pope himself: "He has . . . Burlesqu'd them without knowing it." Imitation is so much in Pope's nature, that in Dennis's terms he is a mere mimicry.

Yet what makes Pope an "original" in Dennis's portrait is identical to that which marks him as a cheap imitation. Defending himself against possible charges against "our upbraiding him with his Natural Deformity, which did not come upon him as his own Fault, but seems to be the Curse of God upon him," Dennis circuitously argues that his attack on Pope's person "is intended to lead . . . to an Exact Knowledge of the Truth by a very little enlarging upon it."[14]

> We desire that Person to consider, that this little Monster has upbraided People with their Calamities and their Diseases, and Calamities and Diseases, which are either false or past, or which he himself gave them by adminstring Poison to them; we desire that Person to consider, that Calamities and Diseases, if they are neither false nor past, are common to all Men; that a Man can no more help his Calamities and his Diseases, than a Monster can his Deformity; that there is no Misfortune, but what the Generality of Mankind are liable too, and that there is no one Disease, but what all the rest of Mankind are Subject too; whereas the Deformity of this Libeller, is Visible, Present, Lasting, Unalterable, and Peculiar to himself. 'Tis the mark of God and Nature upon him, to give us warning that we should hold no Society with him, as a Creature not of our Original, nor of our Species . . . Thus, Sir, I return you Truth for Slander, and a just Satire for an Extravagant Libel, which is therefore ridiculously call'd an Imitation of *Horace*.[15]

From building a sympathetic analogy between the helpless Pope and the victims of his unjust satire, Dennis abruptly shifts to an opposition that objectifies the satirist and places him in an abjectly visible contrast to an invisible generality. The ultimate difference is between the uniformity of "the rest of Mankind" and the "Visible, Present, Lasting, Unalterable, and Peculiar" mark of Pope's deformity, a mark which distinguishes him from and deprives him of "Society," and which enables Dennis to distinguish "Truth" from "Slander," "Satire" from "Libel." Should readers still object to such a construction of the author, Dennis argues, he need only point to Pope's text (the original of which has yet to be found) for further proof:

> When they behold [Horace] thus miserably mangled, and reflect at once with Contempt and Horrour, upon this Barbarous Usage of him, [they] will not be able to refrain from exclaiming in the most vehement Manner.
> *Qualis adest, Quantum mutatus ab illo, &c*[16]

In a dizzying regress of allusion in which form mimics content, Dennis quotes Satan's opening speech in *Paradise Lost,* which begins the narrative of Milton's epic with a moment at which recognition and misrecognition unite in an acknowledgment of degradation. Satan speaks to his second in command, Beelzebub:

> If thou beest hee; but O how fall'n! how changed
> From him, who in the happy Realms of Light
> Cloth'd with transcendent brightness didst outshine
> Myriads though bright: (I, 84–87)

but the reader hears at once an allusion to Isaiah XIV.12: "How art thou fallen from heaven, oh Lucifer," and an echo of a pagan lament for lost heroism in Virgil's *Aeneid* II, 275–276: "ei mihi, qualis erat! quantum mutatatus ab illo/ Hectore."[17] These two super-imposed narratives of the loss of an ideal, themselves forming a third narrative of historical loss, frame Satan's recognition of another's sad change as a misrecognition of himself. Performing a similar shift from subject to object, James Ralph (among others) brings Dennis's description of Pope's Horace to bear on Pope himself, juxtaposing the phrase as the epigraph to his poem *Sawney* (1728) with Pope's own words from the *Essay on the Dunciad* "Now Farce and Epic get a jumbled Race." (Pope himself used the phrase to describe the end of Villiers in the third of the *Moral Essays*.)[18] This line enables the lampooners to imagine both Pope and his text in corporeal form and literary context. Pointing to the authorial body as visibly marked by its fall from an original wholeness, these words nevertheless, burdened by their hyper-referentiality, themselves exemplify the failure of such transparent visibility inherent in attempts at literary originality. In Dennis's case, the question of agency takes on particular importance. What Dennis perceives as Pope's violence to his Horatian original exculpates his own violence to the imitator. What distinguishes Dennis's aggression from Pope's is the extent to which that violence is made visible (and therefore self-evident) and the author to whom such violence is attributed (Pope himself or "God and Nature"). For Dennis, Pope's mistake is, like Lucifer, to have presumed to be his own author.

Dennis's portrait sets the tone and the terms for a plethora of exercises in the same genre, the greatest number inspired by the provocation of Pope's *Dunciad*. One factor remains consistent: the origin of such portraits of the author is always, as the borrowing from Milton indicates, a matter of vexed indebtedness.[19] The image of Pope on a pedestal bearing the insignia "His Holiness and his Prime Minister" (an ass respectfully attends the author, who is rapt in thought as he pens "The Dunciad with Notes Variorum") is in many ways the visual equivalent of Dennis' verbal picture. Pope wears a papal miter, his Catholicism, as the Dennis lampoon also shows, a sign of his marginality and moral indeterminacy, rendering him both supreme and abject.[20] Pope's face is a realistic representation copied from a portrait by Kneller authorized by the poet; his body a fantastic hybrid of ape and rat, complete with humped hairy shoulders and hairless tail. Both visually and verbally, then, the image is a pastiche of past "originals." The pamphlet version of this engraving, identical but for the miter and the words on the pedestal, goes to greater lengths to emphasize the Babel-like dimensions of this portrait's textual reflections. Following the frontispiece (see Figure 1) are the texts of four "INSCRIPTIONS graven on the four sides of the Pedestal, whereon is erected the Busto of Martinus Scriblerus, from which Original the Effigies pre-fixed to this Work was taken."[21] The author explains, "as all Criminals who fly from Justice are executed in *Effigie*, his Figure is exposed, and four Inscriptions under it, on the several Sides of the Pedestal, in *Greek, Latin, Spanish,* and *English* . . . This curious image communicated to me [by a Dunce] I thought it proper to take a cut from it."[22] Whether by "curious image," the writer refers to Pope, the pedestal, or the inscriptions themselves (the texts of which are neither translated nor commented upon in the body of the pamphlet) is unclear. What remains is the ambiguity of the image itself (human head on animal body) and the juxtaposition of image with text.

Beneath the frontispiece is a brief blank verse poem, explicating either the image or its title, "The PHIZ and CHARACTER of the Hyper-critick and Commentator" ("phiz" here ambiguously distinguished from the "character" it is meant to represent):

> Nature herself shrunk back when thou wert born,
> And cry'd the Works not mine—
> The Midwife stood agast; and when she saw
> Thy Mountain back and thy distorted legs,
> Thy face half minted with the Stamp of Man,
> And half ore'come with Beast stood doubting long,
> Whose right in thee were more.

Pope's monstrosity in this portrait is that he is author-less; his character, quite literally the visual imprint of his identity, leaves him a coin of indeterminate value that no one, least of all maternal Nature, will own.

PORTRAYAL AND SELF-POSSESSION

As these examples show, the portrait poses problems of truth and "truth to life," of identity conceived as visual stasis rather than narrative movement, of original

Figure 1.

Frontispiece to *Pope Alexander's Supremacy and Infallibility Examined*
(London: *Monthly Chronicle*, 1729).

subjects and faithful representations, that consume both Pope and his reading
public. Satan's words in the mouths of Pope's lampooners portray Pope's descent
from a semi-divine originality and his fall into narrative as a moment of stasis
made visible by his deformity. Pope's satire abounds in portraits—one thinks of
Timon in *Epistle to Burlington*, Sporus in *To Arbuthnot*, or the poetic portrait
gallery of *Epistle to a Lady* (suggestively subtitled "Of the Characters of
Women"), among many others—which confound the visual with the verbal.

Such confabulation, as Dennis's remarks on Pope's "Imitation of Horace" also indicate, is crucially related to Pope's career-long endeavor to base poetic originality on literary imitation of classical models. The genre of the satiric portrait or character, in which literature takes painting as its model, conflates the visual with the textual through its reliance on the frame. As Roland Barthes states in his discussion of the portrait of the aging castrato in *S/Z:* "Every literary description is a *view.* It could be said that the speaker, before describing, stands at the window, not so much to see, but to establish what he sees by its very frame."[23] The frame which creates the possibility of such a vision excludes as much as it includes; as it establishes what is both visible and "natural," it ultimately creates "a *supplementary* meaning (accessory and atopical): that of the human body: the figure is not the sum, the frame, or the support of the meanings; it is an additional meaning, a kind of diacritical paradigm."[24]

Barthes accounts for the effect of the "natural" in literary portraiture as the product of the artificial and incomplete coincidence, the "disparity," of different codes of representation. In the process of reading the portrait, that which is initially figured as the object of the frame, the body, becomes itself the subject, "the semantic space," that establishes meaning. For Barthes, the body's meaning is supplementary, excessive, ornamental, and finally, diacritical. By that final adjective, Barthes indicates that the meaning of the portrayed body resides both inside and outside the text of which the portrait is a part: the diacritical is that which separates, or indicates distinction; as a grammatical mark it is that which, according to the *O.E.D.,* is "applied to signs or marks used to distinguish different sounds or values of the same letter." The verbally portrayed body, therefore, inflects and informs our reading of the space which it adorns and which gives it shape; it comes to mean as we come to see it, at once (and neither) visual space and (nor) verbal text. It is with the unnatural origins of such a "diacritical paradigm" that the figure of Pope's body confronts us.

In a cultural confounding of the visual with the textual, the market for Pope's poetry was inseparable from a thriving market for images of the poet. Portraying Pope was something of a national pastime. When Voltaire came to England, he was convinced of the esteem with which the British held the arts by observing that "the picture of the prime minister hangs over the chimney of his own closet, but I have seen that of Mr. Pope in twenty noblemen's houses."[25] As with his literary work, Pope made it his task to authorize these images, thereby compelling readers to claim them for themselves. Here, for example, in 1742, two years before Pope's death, the young Joshua Reynolds, later to become a great portraitist of authors, first sees this most self-conscious of subjects. The setting, aptly enough, is a marketplace: Lord Oxford's auction of paintings, including three portraits of Pope, at Covent Garden:

> The room was much crowded. Pope came in. Immediately it was mentioned he was there, a lane was made for him to walk through. [He soon heard the name of Mr. Pope, Mr. Pope, whispered from every mouth . . . Immediately every person drew back to make a free passage for the distinguished poet, and all those on each side held out their hands for him to touch as he passed.] Everyone in the front rows by a kind of enthusiastic impulse shook hands with him. Reynolds did likewise with the rest and was very happy in having that opportunity. Pope was seldom seen in public, so it was a great sight to see him. [He was, according to Sir Joshua's account, about four feet six high; very humpbacked and deformed; he wore a black coat; and according to the fashion of that time, had on a little sword. Sir Joshua adds that he had a large and very fine eye, and a long handsome nose; his mouth had those peculiar marks which always are found in the mouths of crooked persons; and the muscles which run across the cheek were so strongly marked as to appear like small cords. Roubilliac, the statuary, who made a bust of him from life, observed that his countenance was that of a person who had been much afflicted with headache, and he should have known the fact from the contracted appearance of the skin between his eyebrows, though he had not been otherwise apprised of it. This bust of Roubilliac is now (1791) in possession of Mr. Bindley, Commissioner of Stamps.] Sir Joshua said he had an extraordinary face, not an everyday countenance—a pallid, studious look; not merely a sharp, keen countenance, but something grand, like Cicero's. It was like what Petronius Arbiter says [grandiaque indomiti verba Ciceronis]. He said there was an appearance about his mouth which is found only in the deformed, and from which he could have known him to be deformed.[26]

This portrait is initially remarkable for its layers of self-referentiality: it is a portrait not so much of Pope but of a portraitist seeing Pope through superimposed mirrors of reputation and relation. The now famous painter recollects for the biographer of a celebrated mutual friend his youthful encounter with an already canonical poet. He has told the story before, but his memory of Pope's celebrity and the ineffable marks of Pope's deformity (not the body itself but the legible marks of bodily distortion on the poet's face) unite the two accounts. Within Reynolds' narrative, the living image of Pope's person, by virtue of his efforts to keep himself out of circulation, becomes a tautology of value, an alluring commodity: "Pope was seldom seen in public, so it was a great sight to see him."

But Pope's image is also excessively familiar. Overly exposed in print and in portraits, the poet's face is an open book to a classically educated and dutifully inquisitive audience. What he provides in person is supplemental, art's proof, its diacritical mark.

Pope's face is exceptional, one might say "legible," to Sir Joshua because of its "pallid, studious look"; like his body (as other portraits of Pope will show), his face is marked by, and therefore a mark of, his zeal for literary labor. Sir Joshua has learned to decipher this face through reading both visual and verbal texts. The sculptor Roubiliac, "who made a bust of him from life" (see Figure 2), provides Reynolds with the authority to support his reading of Pope's pained countenance, and reinforces our awareness of that countenance as collectable commodity, a sculpted imprimatur in the possession of the Minister of Stamps. The account collapses the distinction between the bust and the living head. Similarly, when Reynolds searches for a metaphor for Pope's distinctive face, he comes up with one from the realm of literature. Perhaps it is the classical content of Pope's painstaking and pain-inducing literary labors that reminds the younger artist of Cicero, another self-made literary man. But even more interestingly, Reynolds is reminded not of Cicero "himself," nor his oratory, but of a textual construction of Cicero, Petronius's verbal portrait not of the orator/author but of his *language:* "the sublime words of indomitable Cicero." This curiously verbal vision portrays a contaminating collusion of literature and life: Pope's voracious reading distorts his face; his face resembles heroic oratory described in writing. The English poet himself becomes a walking classical imitation, formed after and read by virtue of Latin models of self-creation, a text whose most immediately decipherable feature is the mark of deformity.

Such marks remind us that the struggle for definition of the modern author is a struggle for ownership of meaning. If, as Mark Rose argues, "the distinguishing characteristic of the modern author . . . is that he is a proprietor, that he is conceived as the originator and therefore the owner of a special kind of commodity, the 'work,' "[27] the case of Pope demonstrates particularly clearly how the author is formed, and deformed, in that work's image. Francis Hargrave's *Argument in Defense of Literary Property* could serve as the explicatory text for Reynolds' portrait: "a literary work *really* original, like the human face, will always have some singularities, some lines, some features, to characterize it, and to fix and establish its identity."[28] The creation of such an identity paradoxically excludes the agency of the author himself.

Pope's figure is a text both ineffably original—that which, like the mark of deformity, stands only for itself, rarely seen and therefore a sight to see—and

Figure 2.

Terra-cotta bust of Alexander Pope,
by L. F. Roubiliac, ca. 1738.

recognizably derivative; the poet whose literary career was one long exercise in imitation of the classics himself embodies translation. When a less sympathetic although equally proficient reader of both Pope and the classics, Lady Mary Wortley Montagu, responds to Pope's pointed attacks on herself as Sappho in the *First Satire of the Second Book of Horace Imitated,* her distaste for classical imitation couples with a disgusted exposure of the imitator's monstrosity. In her *Verses address'd to the Imitator of . . . Horace by a Lady of London,* she describes Pope's "motly Page" as a kind of monstrous hybrid of "Roman Wit" and "English Rage," "modern Scandal" and "ancient Sense" which distorts Horace beyond recognition. As Pope's text is to Horace's on the space of the page, so the poet's body is to the divine original:

> Thine is just such an Image of *his* [Horace's] Pen,
> As thou thy Self art of the Sons of Men:
> Where our own Species in Burlesque we trace,
> A Sign-Post Likeness of the Noble Race;
> That is at once Resemblance and Disgrace. (11–15)[29]

If Pope's text is a monstrous distortion, then Pope himself is a monster. Dennis's attack on the young Pope haunts this lampoon: a singular burlesque of the original species, the poet physically embodies the genre of imitation; he is a distorted sign of the natural. Just as the poetry's conjunction of what Dr. Johnson labelled "irreconcilable dissimilitude," its yoking of "Roman images" with "English manners," produces something "uncouth and party-colored, neither original nor translated, neither ancient nor modern," so the threat of the poet's deformity is its indeterminacy, its weakening of natural distinction.[30] But imitation's ambiguous form also provides Pope with the means to bind his unnatural figure to the most correct art. Thus Lady Mary, like scores of other attackers after her, staves off such unnatural confusion by marking Pope's body out:

> When God created Thee, one would believe,
> He said the same as to *the Snake of Eve;*
> *To human Race Antipathy declare,*
> *Twixt them and Thee be everlasting War* . . . (54–57)
> And with the Emblem of thy Crooked Mind,
> Mark'd on thy Back, like *Cain,* by God's own Hand;
> Wander like him, accursed through the Land. (110–112)

Pope's attacker here reacts against the monstrous ambiguity of both Pope and his text by asserting a fixed binary opposition between the deformed poet and the human race, and a transparent analogy, one with the guarantee of a divine Author, between the crooked back and the crooked mind. A walking emblem, Pope's body explicates the evil within. Lady Mary turns her libeller into a morally decipherable divine text as she turns the divine text against her libeller: Pope becomes a thing both written and written upon.[31]

In Pope's literary self-fashioning, this lampoon shows, deformity and poetic form create the ultimate couplet, guaranteeing the author, if not possession of his text, at least a kind of patent on it. Literary imitation's complex balance of readerly fidelity and authorial originality repels Lady Mary and causes her to identify Pope with his unnatural text. Yet such a balance, and an ability to anticipate and manipulate such responses, inform Pope's career-long strategies of self-authorization through literary imitation.

23

THE DISEASE OF TRANSLATION

Even the most libertine of imitators must suffer from what Dryden called "the disease of translation" that both frees him from and binds him to his own authority.[32] The disease of translation from which Pope suffers can be read as a dramatization of the paradox of his own physical affliction. King Mezentius in Virgil's *Aeneid* invented a torture whereby living victims were bound to corpses and left to die. Pope, who spoke of his own body as "the wretched carcase I am annexed to," turns the torture of his physical existence into an image of his art.[33] The poet translates the battleground of the active mind within the wasted frame which his deformity makes of him into his particular brand of literary imitation; like Mezentius' torture, Pope's work binds art inexorably to the physical reality we expect it to transcend. In all of its correctness, Pope's art has something of the monstrous and the illicit in it.

Edward Young, in his *Conjectures on Original Composition* (1759), a seminal work in the creation of the modern author, explicitly excludes his model and predecessor Pope from the ranks of the original: "An *Original* may be said to be of a *vegetable* nature; it rises spontaneously from the vital root of genius; it *grows,* it is not *made: Imitations* are often a sort of manufacture wrought up by those *mechanics, art* and *labour,* out of pre-existent materials not their own."[34] The poet who speaks of himself in his imitation of Horace's *Epistle II, ii* as "that unweary'd Mill / That turn'd ten thousand Verses" (78–79), faces the potential threat of becoming a poetry machine; incapable of the gentlemanly "True Ease in Writing" which conceals its art, the poet of more mechanical than natural genius risks being both unoriginal and inhuman.[35]

So comprehensive is Pope's "Ars Poetica" that it eliminates any trace of its natural origins. Virtually all critical searches for the true Pope begin and end in literary self-consciousness. "Even as a child," David Morris writes, Pope was "never wholly outside the world of literature."[36] Whether he is claiming in the *Epistle to Arbuthnot* that he "lisped in Numbers, for the Numbers came" (128), breaking his health by doing "nothing but writ[ing] and read[ing]," performing for his father by producing "good rhymes," giving the gardener a starring part in his first dramatic effort, writing a lampoon on his schoolmaster, making a pilgrimage to Will's Coffee House at age twelve to get a good look at John Dryden, or writing at that age an "Horatian poem without an original"—his "Ode on Solitude"—where, as Morris puts it, Pope "seemed to pass directly from infancy to middle age or its literary equivalent," the young Pope is represented as already in debt to the author he was to become.[37]

Such all-encompassing art defines all literary endeavors as inherently imitative. By imitation I refer to contemporary definitions of the freest of translations, what Dryden dubbed one step beyond the golden mean of "paraphrase," and marked as the opposite extreme of literalist "metaphrase," namely "this libertine way of rendering authors . . . where the translator (if now he has not lost that name) assumes the liberty not only to vary from words and sense, but to foresake them both as he sees occasion."[38] Samuel Johnson opines in his *Life of Dryden* that a translator "is to exhibit his author's thoughts in such a dress of diction as the author would have given them had his language been English: rugged magnificence is not to be softened; hyperbolical ostentation is not to be repressed, nor sententious affectation to have its points blunted. A translator is to be like his author: it is not his business to excel him."[39] Johnson's translator is not so much a creator as a linguistic transvestite; his work is judged by "its effect as an English poem," but the body clothed is that of the original author.[40] Thus the translator paradoxically frees himself from responsibility for a deviant original by fidelity to its deviations. In just this way, as David Morris points out, Horace's Latin originals provide Pope with a "ready-made structure" which is itself inchoate, affording the English poet an escape from his audience's expectation of more coherent forms.[41]

Both Johnson and Dryden leave the question of what is behind the dress, what of substance makes the work unique, largely unanswered. Sliding out of a verbal trap into a visual metaphor, Dryden's translator becomes in a later essay a portraitist, capable of creating "a double sort of likeness, a good one and a bad. 'Tis one thing to draw the outlines true, the features like, the proportions exact, the colouring itself perhaps tolerable, and another thing to make all these graceful, by the posture, the shadowings, and chiefly by the spirit which animates the whole."[42] Dryden's model translator is ultimately a life-bestowing god, while a failed copyist is termed a narcissist who studies "himself more than those who sat to him," and thereby commits a kind of murder: "A good poet is no more like himself in a dull translation, than his carcass would be to his living body."[43] By an act of complete self-effacement the ideal translator here asserts his own originality by bringing the dead to life. But for a translator to display himself through imitation is a kind of profane exhibitionism: "to state it fairly, imitation of an author is the most advantageous way for a translator to show himself, but the greatest wrong which can be done to the memory and reputation of the dead."[44]

Pope's friend and patron Lord Bolingbroke inverts the paradox when he recommends, after Boileau, that rather than translating an ancient author "servilely" and literally, "a good writer will *jouster contre l'original,* rather imitate than translate, and rather emulate than imitate: he will transfuse the sense and spirit of the original into his own work, and will endeavor to write as the ancient author would have wrote, had he writ in the same language."[45] For Bolingbroke, rebellious self-assertion is the highest brand of fidelity. The translator's own work is paramount; the original is not a passive subject but rather an active adversary against whom the imitator must compete in a mock-heroic battle. The imitator becomes an actor playing a role, and finally, an author creating a character who is and is not himself.

The questions of authority which this brief discussion of literary imitation raises, the complex negotiations between servility and freedom, fidelity and originality, natural genius and mechanical servility, sincere fidelity to the original and self-interested theatricality, which comprise the genre, are keys to any investigation of Pope's self-fashioning. Pope is perhaps his own most original act of literary imitation. The originals against whom he plays the part of Pope are not only classical models but also earlier or conflicting versions of himself. (The voice of "F." [friend] in the *Epilogue to the Satires,* for example, is a conventionally Horatian Pope speaking.) In translating his own person into Horace's persona, in displaying his living self dressed in dead letters, Pope becomes neither dead nor alive, neither entirely authentic nor completely artificial, but possessed of a trademark in the form of his particular body.[46]

Pope himself comments on the immoral aspects of imitation when he publishes his anonymous imitation of Horace's notoriously bawdy Satire 1.2 on sexual mores, calling it *Sober Advice from Horace Imitated from his Second Sermon in the Manner of Mr. POPE* (1734). Warmly dedicating the work to himself, the poet proceeds to take liberties with Horace, himself, his friends (whose sexual exploits along with those of his enemies are ridiculed in the text) and the renowned Richard Bentley, whose Latin text and emendations he reprints verbatim, and whose morally outraged and pruriently precise attempts to get Horace's original obscenities right are parodied in "Notae Bentleanae," the first of which is on the word "Imitated": "Why Imitated? Why not translated? . . . A Metaphrast had not turned *Tigellius,* and *Fufidius, Malchinus* and *Gargonius* (for I say *Malchinus,* not *Malthinus,* and *Gargonius,* not *Gorgonius*) into so many LADIES. *Benignus,* hic, hunc, &c all of the Masculine Gender: Every School-boy knows more than our Imitator."[47] Pope equates Bentley's obsessive concern with the proper spelling of proper names with a zeal for keeping the proper bodies in the proper places. In this parody, imitation makes Bentley uneasy because it takes liberties with gender in both its physical and grammatical senses. Indeed Bentley's fidelity to the letter has made gender a strictly grammatical construct; to turn a man into a lady is simply a matter of word endings, a diacritical proceeding indeed. The real infidelity is neither human adultery nor graphic poetry about it, but rather the imitator's adulteration of the original.

Literary imitation is Pope's generic portrait. Perhaps the paradox which makes Pope so mysterious can be put as simply as this: he wants imitation and artifice to embody the truth about himself.[48] How are we to take Pope's attempts to (as he claims in *Satire II, i*) "pour out all myself," to convince us, as Leopold Damrosch remarks, that "he has nothing to hide, so that art can freely coincide with life"?[49] Damrosch gets to the heart of Pope's duplicity when he writes that Pope "seeks to represent a self that is grounded upon lived experience, while the poems in turn serve to establish, if not actually to create, the self and the experience"[50] and, I would add, to make that experience marketable. Pope's life's work was to produce the definitive version of himself. "I *must* make a perfect edition of my works," Spence records him as saying, "and then I shall have nothing to do but to die."[51] That self's excluded reflection, its remainder, is Pope's deformity.

Yet deformity enables Pope's particular brand of imitation to go originality one better: his poetry marks itself not as original but as impossible to duplicate. What matters for Pope is not the poet who comes before but those who cannot replace him, no matter how hard they might try. Just as this chapter attempts to read Pope's figure for the form, so Pope's brand of imitation reads its original, one might say reconstructs the concept of originality, in order "to purify the original of meaning," and in Pope's unique case, in order to appropriate the form for himself.[52] Just as Pope's brand of literary imitation evolves over the course of his career from respectful transparency to embattled obstruction, so his texts are increasingly marked by his own inimitable, indecipherable form. Pope's body figures that curious interrelation of original and translation, of transparency and opacity, of nature and artifice, that teasing elusiveness of understanding, which Walter Benjamin refers to as "the essential kernel . . . definable as that in translation, which, in its turn is untranslatable."[53]

CORRESPONDING IN PERSON

Off the page such deformity gives the poet a constant audience, a fixed image against which he must rebel. Almost continually ill and almost never clean, Pope refers to his person in his personal letters as that which "may properly at this time be called a human structure."[54] Small wonder that such personal correspondence was written with an audience in view, and that Pope schemed to have it published first through the agency of his enemy the pirate publisher Curll and subsequently in a definitive edition under his own watchful supervision.[55] Pope writes impersonally, always performing before a potentially threatening audience, because his person is not his own. Esteeming himself "the Least Thing Like a Man in England," Pope is dead to himself.[56] His body is his burden, a blight upon and distortion of the real life within, possessing him and putting him on permanent show. It is also the vehicle through which Pope takes possession of his art by exposing what that art has successfully transmuted. Pope's malformed body offsets his feats of poetic form. In the same way that an original frees a translator from authorial responsibility, Pope's body saves him from the constrictions of sincerity.[57]

Nowhere in Pope's oeuvre is sincerity more of an issue, and more connected to issues of physical presence, than in his correspondence. In a famous early letter to Lady Mary, we can see how Pope turns physical vulnerability to his own poetic advantage.[58] This initial sally into amorous combat, the publication of which twenty years later reinscribes private self-exposure in print, begins with this proviso:

> I can say little to recommend the Letters I am beginning to write to you, but that they will be the most impartial Representations of a free heart, and the truest Copies you ever saw, tho' of a very mean Original. Not a feature will be soften'd, or any advantageous Light employd to make the Ugly thing a little less hideous, but you shall find it in all respects most Horribly Like. You will do me an injustice if you look upon any thing I shall say from this instant as a Compliment either to you or to myself: whatever I write will be the real Thought of that hour, and I know you'll no more expect it of me to persevere till Death in every Sentiment or notion I now sett down, than you would imagine a man's Face should never change after his picture was once drawn.[59]

Pope's words make it impossible to determine which is the "mean Original": his body or his heart. The reader is forced to visualize the "crazy Carcase" and reinterpret it as a metaphor for an inner reality. Lady Mary must simultaneously look and read. Pope dares Lady Mary to turn away knowing that no polite reader could allow herself to expose the author of this passage as a cripple, since to do so would reveal the deformity of her own imprisoned heart. His correspondent's potential derisive disgust has been foreclosed upon by Pope himself. Ugliness guarantees verisimilitude and virtuous transparency. But at this moment of visual stasis, Pope calls attention to the vehicle of the letter, that which Richardson would later term "writing to the moment," which absolves him of any original constancy and which posits the flow of text as the closest thing to truth. The portrait metaphor is reinstated, but is now termed unreliable in its fixity.

While we might term the previous passage moral exhibitionism, what follows can be described as sentimental voyeurism. Though many readers are familiar with the opening of the following passage, few know the conclusion:

> If Momus his project had taken of having Windows in our breasts, I should be for carrying it further and making those windows Casements: that while a Man showd his Heart to all the world, he might do something more for his friends, e'en take it out, and trust it to their handling . . . But since Jupiter will not have it so, I must be content to show my taste in Life as I do my taste in Painting, by loving to have as little Drapery as possible. Not that I think every body naked, altogether so fine a sight as yourself and a few more would be: but because 'tis good to use people to what they must be acquainted with; and there will certainly come some Day of Judgment to uncover every Soul of us. We shall then see how the Prudes of this world owed all their fine Figure only to their being a little straiter-lac'd.[60]

From the metaphor of the "window in the breast," to the more blatantly physical image of the heart actually handled, Pope shifts to the image of the self as artist's nude, devoid of drapery. From there the move to imagining Lady Mary herself naked is an easy one, all under the most decent cover of the sentimental language of sincerity, and finally of divine revelation. So effective is this strategy's duplicity that to take offense—to cover herself up—would make Lady Mary guilty not just of prudery but of dishonesty and moral culpability; to be a prude in this situation is to have something ugly within to hide. It thus becomes impossible to tell whether a response of over-delicacy or hypocrisy would be the greater sin. Regardless, the potential exposer finds herself exposed.

By baring all, Pope achieves a perverse transparency by giving to art his body's peculiar shape. He thus reinterprets deformity as do the people in "those parts of India" he tells Lady Mary of in a later letter, "where they tell us the Women best like the Ugliest fellows, as the most admirable productions of nature, and look upon Deformities as the Signatures of divine Favour."[61] The signature here, however, is Pope's own.

Although Pope's baring of the soul did not produce the desired effect in Lady Mary, many critics have since compliantly submitted to his naked truth.

Dustin Griffin, for example, applauds the sincerity of this epistolary "language of the heart" created long before Pope's Horatian poems took up the cause of authorial transparency. So invested is Griffin in Pope's loaded language of self-exposure that he refers to Pope as appearing in the letters in undress. But in support of what he construes to be Pope's goal—the creation of a self free of the body's contaminating mark—this critic refuses to uncover what the metaphors themselves expose. When Griffin quotes the opening of this letter to Lady Mary, he stops before Pope mentions the "mean Original."[62] Pope's professions of transparency make him the ideal reader's ideal and every mention of imperfection—on both the physical and moral register—is suppressed. But the ideal reader's delicacy blinds him to the fact that it is exactly that imperfection, the "Spots," which prove the "Medium must be clear" and which prove Pope himself authentic.[63]

Pope's bodily metaphors curiously figure a real body which is never touched; through feats of words Pope can demand that his person be, if not desired, at least looked upon without aversion. Just as Pope can undress his female correspondents for the duration of an honest letter, so they must be forced to imagine him as a physical presence for the space of a few sentences. The game can take place because of its limits. When Pope's friend Caryll, after the publication of the *Epistle to a Lady* which was dedicated to Martha Blount, asked if the poem's conclusion hinted at marriage, Pope replied: "[Apollo] gave me long ago to Belinda, as he did Homer to Achilles, and 'tis a mercy he has not given me to more ladies, but that I am almost as little inclined to celebrate that way, as the other."[64] Art and life, like Martha and Belinda, are rendered equally fictional by mutual distortion and mutual disembodiment.

"You have all that I am worth," the young Pope wrote to Lady Mary, "that is, my Workes."[65] As Pope's body gives shape to his art, so his books give shape to his body. The letters record a vacillation between the monumental poet and his unremarkable person. "Methinks I do very ill," he writes to Martha and Teresa Blount from Oxford, "to return to the world again, to leave the only place where I make a [good] figure, and from seeing myself seated with dignity on the most conspicuous Shelves of a Library, go to contemplate this wretched person in the abject condition of lying at a Lady's feet in Bolton street."[66] When Pope edited this letter for inclusion in the official collection, he changed the phrase "contemplate this wretched person" to "put myself in the abject posture." The process by which body becomes book is exemplified by the way in which Pope edits the phrase person out of the soon-to-be-published proceedings, even if it means including the phrase myself. In the original version Pope is aloof from the action, watching his body go through abject motions; in the edited version, the poet puts himself through his paces. In both cases, the self is at its most conspicuous and most dignified when isolated between the confines of a book cover; the "person in an abject condition" is excluded from print.

While the Blounts stayed connected with Pope until his death, Lady Mary responded civilly but coolly to Pope's heated epistolary passion. The ending of their friendship is commemorated forever in Pope's vicious characterization of her as Sappho in the first of his Horatian poems, *Satire II, i* (1733), and others such as the *Epistle to a Lady* thereafter. The accounts of the connection's termination vary, but the explanation which has been elevated to the status of legend reads that Pope finally declared himself to Lady Mary in person, upon which she dissolved into a fit of laughter. Without words as his shield, the poor poet becomes a laughing stock, an emblem of the disjunction between the puny body and the printed page, known to the nineteenth century simply as *"The Rejected Poet."*[67]

In his amorous letters to women, Pope aligns the soul with the body in order to enable personal and reciprocal self-exposure. This analogy casts the crooked mind his lampooners assume his crooked body signals in a sentimental light. In his letters to men (friends and patrons), the poet recasts the soul-body analogy as heroic opposition.[68] This correspondence translates the physical into what is at one level of intensity the polite, at another the outrage of moral fervor. In translating his physical self, Pope rewrites literature into morality, correctness in its double sense. In 1730 he writes to Lord Bathurst,

> Let me tell you my life in thought and imagination is as much superior to my life in action and reality as the best soul is to the vilest body. I find the latter grows so much worse and more declining that I believe I shall soon scruple to carry it about to others; it will become almost a carcase, and as unpleasing as those which they say the spirits now and then use for vehicles to frighten folks. My health is so temporary that if I pass two days abroad it is odds but one of them I must be a trouble to any goodnatured friend and to his family; and the other, remain dispirited enough to make them no sort of amends by my languid conversation. I begin to resolve upon the whole rather to turn myself back again into myself, and apply to study as the only way I have left to entertain others, though at some expense both of my own health, and time. I really owe you and some few others some little entertainment, if I could give it them; for having received so much from them, in conscience and gratitude I ought not to go to my grave without trying at least to give them an hour or two's pleasure,

which may be as much as half the pains of my remaining life can accomplish.[69]

From the familiar generality of the soul-body analogy, Pope shifts imperceptibly to the particulars of a physical wretchedness which makes him virtually dead to the world; both dead and in debt, since his infirmity puts him at the mercy of the kindness of friends who must forgive his languid conversation.[70] In this rendition, literature replaces the social, allows the writer to entertain in the way a host entertains a guest, and permanently fills in for the evanescent companionship which the poet cannot afford. But Pope pays for this higher entertainment (we are reminded here of the vicious circle of study and deformity) with both health and time. Poetry tastefully substitutes for his physical presence, while apologizing for the trouble and distaste that presence causes. Literature permits the writer to perform gracefully while suffering in private.

By resolving to "turn myself back again into myself," Pope attempts to establish an original self outside of society, a true identity imagined in opposition to the contagious translations of the social:

> Hurry, noise, and the observances of the world, take away the power of just thinking or natural acting. A man that lives so much in the world does but translate other men; he is nothing of his own. Our customs, our tempers, our enjoyments, our distastes are not so properly effects of our natural constitution, as distempers catched by contagion. Many would live happily without any ill ones, if they lived by themselves.[71]

Retirement offers a return to the natural and the just, an escape from both physical deformity and social distemper into self-possession.[72] Pope's fantasy of a wholeness that is at once moral and physical is reminiscent of Horace's response to the desertion of the fickle goddess of fortune in Ode 3.29—"virtute mea me involvo" [I wrap myself up in my virtue]—a line Pope was fond of and used in other contexts. Horace's phrase is remarkable, I think, for the strangeness with which it literalizes an abstraction, and even more significantly, makes of an abstraction a cover for the self which by dint of the operating metaphor is envisioned as the body. (One is reminded here of Johnson's teasingly empty metaphor of the dress of literary imitation, signalling a wholeness beneath that can't be seen.) Under the cover of virtue, Pope goes beyond good manners and becomes finally heroic; so this account of his literary endeavors, written to his friend Caryll, reveals. His studies, Pope writes,

> are directed to a good end, the advancement of moral and religious vertue, and the discouragement of vicious and corrupt hearts. As to the former,

I treat it with the uttmost seriousness and respect; as to the latter, I think any means are fair and any method equal, whether preaching or laughing . . . I shall make living examples, which inforce best, and consequently put you once more upon the defence of your friend against the roar and calumny, which I expect, and am ready to suffer in so good a cause.[73]

This Pope is not merely a Grub Street producer, nor is he simply a poet: he is a warrior in the fight for the good. He is neither salesman nor dissimulator, but a servant of the Truth. This prototypical moral image emerged partly in defense of Pope's attack on particular individuals in the *Moral Essays* and poetically in *Satire II, i.* In this passage, and even more dramatically in his *Epilogue to the Satires* (1738), Pope translates social infection into solitary moral purity. The poet on show amidst a circle of onlookers becomes the sole defender of virtue, braving roar and calumny. In the Horatian poems Pope's concern with living examples, his insistence upon using particular vicious and corrupt hearts in his defense of general moral and religious virtue plays out on another level the conflict between the disembodied satirist-hero and his corruptly particular flesh.

MARKING OUT THE AUTHOR

Samuel Johnson, in an unflinchingly detailed description in his *Life of Pope,* demonstrates how readers of Pope struggle to control this economy of physical infirmity and authorial power:

> The person of Pope is well known not to have been formed by the nicest model . . . He is said to have been beautiful in his infancy; but he was of a constitution originally feeble and weak, and as bodies of a tender frame are easily distorted his deformity was probably in part the effect of his application. His stature was so low that, to bring him to a level with common tables, it was necessary to raise his seat. But his face was not displeasing, and his eyes were animated and vivid . . .
>
> Most of what can be told concerning his petty peculiarities was communicated by a female domestic of the Earl of Oxford, who knew him perhaps after the middle of life. He was then so weak as to stand in perpetual need of female attendance; extremely sensible of cold, so that he wore a kind of fur doublet under a shirt of very coarse warm linen with fine sleeves. When he rose he was invested in boddice made of stiff canvass, being scarce able to hold himself erect till they were laced, and he then put on a flannel waistcoat. One side was contracted. His legs were so slender that he enlarged their bulk with three pair of stockings, which were drawn on and off by the maid; for he was not able to dress or undress

himself, and neither went to bed nor rose without help. His weakness made it very difficult for him to be clean.[74]

In Johnson's portrait, Pope's body disempowers him, puts him eternally in a highchair, "in perpetual need of female attendance." Johnson must fix Pope's unnatural origins—the narrative of authorial self-engendering evidenced by the reader's vision of his disability—in the realm of the body now branded explicitly as feminine and feminizing.[75] He brands the poet's person a botched work of art, a poor imitation. The faultiness of the model is explained as "in part the effect of his application"; in other words, according to Johnson, Pope distorted his own body through his excessive literary efforts. Johnson here echoes a host of other writers who similarly explain Pope's deformity. Most relevant here is Spence, who cites the bifold authority of the poet's own words and his mother's nostalgic vision of a visible fall from grace preserved in a portrait of Pope as a boy "in which his face is round, plump, pretty, and of a fresh complexion. I have often heard Mrs. Pope say that he was then exactly like that picture, as I have been told by himself that it was the perpetual application he fell into, about two years afterwards, that changed his form and ruined his constitution."[76] Johnson goes on to state that the indulgence which Pope demanded in his weakness "had taught him all the unpleasing and unsocial qualities of a valetudinary man," and takes the marginalization implied by his comparison one step further: "He expected that everything should give way to his ease or humour; as a child whose parents will not hear her cry has an unresisted dominion in the nursery."[77] From infantilized invalid to female infant, Pope's authorial power takes shape in Johnson's text as bodily powerlessness. By attributing Pope's deformity to his authorial labor, Johnson paradoxically deprives Pope of any authorial power over the products of that labor, in much the same way that a translator is deprived of any authority over his original.

The cruellest kind of *ad hominem* reading can result; Pope's deformity—itself supposedly the result of his literary exertions—severs him from his own poetic forms. William Empson, commenting on the lines which close the *Epistle to Burlington* with a vision of the Golden Age, exposes Pope with cruel concision: "the relief with which the cripple for a moment identifies himself with something so strong and generous gives these two couplets an extraordinary scale."[78] The powerful voice which inspires Empson's sense of the strong and generous is here translated into and embodied in the cripple. By pointing to the stunted body behind the lofty lines, Empson excludes the poet from his prophecy of order and makes of him a spectacle. Pope is marked out, even from the vision his own words construct.

Pope's most sympathetic readers are equally unable to avoid crediting his physical imperfection for his literary genius. "Sensitive and perceptive beyond the ordinary as Pope was," Norman Ault writes, "it is only too likely that his desire for perfection sprang up and drew its miraculous growth from his bitter realization, during the formative years of adolescence, of how much he was doomed to be deprived of a man's rightful heritage, not only of health and strength and physical endurance, but also—and more tragically—of ordinary human stature and shape."[79] Whether compassionate or disgusted, critics are compelled to read Pope's body as a text in conclusive interpretation of his literary excellence. The poet's deformity becomes the center of a vicious circle of cause and effect from which Pope in his capacity as author, objectified as an infantilized and feminized cripple, is excluded. Whether readers praise the artist's use of illusion in overcoming his deformity, or exclude him as spectacle from that illusion, they must mark physical aberration as the point of origin, the boundary between art and life. Pope himself, to the letter of his deformity, becomes an ineffable original.

THE MIRROR AS SPECTACLE

Although Pope could silence potential attackers by verbal self-exposure, visual display of his body posed the possibility of loss of authorial control. Of the hundreds of portraits which Pope authorized of himself, it is not surprising that none were full-length profiles. Most portraits were Romanized busts, complete with laurel wreaths or bareheaded in the manner of Milton, nobly bodiless profiles on the faces of coins (perhaps an attempt to fix in Roman style a character fragmented by the lampoons), or splendid oil half-lengths of the poet in various reflective poses.[80]

Most full-length profiles of Pope were cruelly satiric products of the kind of morbid fascination with Pope's monstrous ambiguity evidenced in Lady Mary's attack. But not all unauthorized portraits were the work of attackers. The motivation in these rare cases—two informal sketches made in private company—seems to have been less the desire to inflict pain than an urge, like that of the critic who points beyond the page, to fix the poet's "true character."

The key to these drawings is precisely that they are self-consciously "unauthorized." One, a pen and ink sketch by Lady Burlington, shows Pope concentrating upon a game of cards.[81] A doodle resembling a parasol branching out of Pope's head places the image in a mini-narrative: a member of the party, perhaps odd woman out of the game, sketches idly and comes to focus upon one of the players. He could, like the characters in *The Rape of the Lock,* be playing ombre; but here he is too intent upon the game to be aware that someone else is composing his figure. The drawing could have been subtitled "Belinda's Revenge." It was not made public, nor identified as a portrait of Pope, until 1945.

Much more frequently reproduced, and now almost legendary, is a red chalk drawing by William Hoare, a painter of fashionable visitors to Bath who had officially painted Pope in oil. The sketch was initially published by Joseph Warton as the frontispiece to the first volume of his 1797 edition of Pope's *Works.* Warton chose to juxtapose this surreptitious full-length sketch with a Roman-type profile engraving after an oil portrait by one of Pope's most prominent portraitists and friends, Jonathan Richardson (see Figure 3). The original Richardson portrait was owned by a Dr. Richard Mead, "one of the most eminent virtuosi of his day," who had converted "his large and spacious house in Great Ormond Street . . . into a Temple of Nature, and a Repository of Time," placing Pope's portrait "near the Busts of [his] great Masters, the antient Greeks and Romans." Dr. Mead here shows himself a proper reader (and collector) of Pope's image.[82]

Turning the page in Warton's edition, however, the reader is confronted with a most improper two-page spread (see Figure 4): on the one side the poet, unaware of the viewer and engaged in conversation, his hump plainly visible, on the other an inscription (taken from the back side of the drawing) which is both an explanation and a justification:

> This is the only Portrait that was ever drawn of Mr. POPE at full Length. It was done without his knowledge, as he was deeply engaged in conversation with Mr. ALLEN in the Gallery at Prior Park, by Mr. Hoare, who sat at the other end of the Gallery.—Pope would never have forgiven the Painter had he known it—He was too sensible of the Deformity of his Person to allow the whole of it to be represented.—This Drawing is therefore exceeding valuable, as it is an Unique of this celebrated Poet.[83]

Warton's unprecedented choice of frontispieces puts on show the causal connection between Pope's canonization of himself as author and the subsequent desire on the part of his reader for "an Unique of this celebrated Poet." Pope, for better or for worse, by making himself a celebrity has made his person public property. That voyeuristic public is eager to have "the whole of it be represented."

William Hoare's unauthorized sketch thus becomes emblematic of all of Pope's efforts at self-representation. What makes the drawing worth looking at

Figure 3.

Line engraving, by T. Holloway, after an oil portrait by
Jonathan Richardson, commissioned and reproduced
here as the frontispiece to Joseph Warton's edition of
the *Works of Pope* (London, 1797), vol. 1.

is not Pope's curved back—the lampooners provided that with a vengeance—
so much as the fact that it was done in his presence but "without his knowledge." The controversy which arose about the publication of the image (one
critic, for example, complained of Warton's tactless advertising of the "Bard's
. . . pictured person and his libel'd shape"), the frequency of its reproduction as
"a favorite subject for copying by amateur draughtsmen"[84] and its popularity
in the nineteenth century, all stem from its unauthorized display of an author
whose province is self-exposure. This passage from the Reverend Robert Aris
Willmott's *Summer Time in the Country,* first published in 1849, elaborates on
the image's appeal:

> I always find it pleasanter to let [an] author . . . tell [his] own history . . .
> We catch the form and face in a looking-glass, of which the person is

Figure 4.

*T*HIS *is the only Portrait that was ever drawn of* Mr. POPE *at full Length.—It was done without his knowledge, as he was deeply engaged in converfation with* Mr. ALLEN *in the Gallery at* Prior Park, *by* Mr. HOARE, *who fat at the other end of the Gallery.—This Drawing is therefore exceedingly valuable, as it is an Unique of this celebrated Poet.*

WARTON.

Red crayon drawing by William Hoare, with the handwritten text from the back of the drawing, reproduced following the Richardson frontispiece in Warton's *Life of Pope*. Warton's name beneath the text functions as an ambiguous printed signature.

unconscious. He has no opportunity of making up his countenance, but is sketched, like Pope while in conversation with a friend in the gallery of Prior Park, and transferred to the canvas before he knows that an eye is on him—hump and all.[85]

By translating the poet's verbal professions of transparency into the visual realm of the looking glass, Wilmott puts the integrity of authorial self-representation, be it visual *or* verbal, into the balance. The author tells his own history but is unconscious of the result, which is characterized not as a text but a form and face in a looking-glass to which the image's source is strangely blind. Such unconsciousness is equated with artless sincerity because it belies authorial control; the hump surreptitiously portrayed guarantees a portrayal's truth. In his self-portrait in *Satire II, i,* Pope set the terms for this equation:

38

> I love to pour out all myself, as plain
> As downright *Shippen,* or as old *Montagne.*
> In them, as certain to be lov'd as seen,
> The Soul stood forth, nor kept a Thought within;
> In me what Spots (for Spots I have) appear,
> Will prove at least the Medium must be clear.
> In this impartial glass, my Muse intends
> Fair to expose myself, my Foes, my Friends.   (51–58)

Contrasting the lovable transparency of Shippen and Montaigne with the offputting occlusion of his own self-exposure, Pope forfeits sympathy for proof: the crooked back offsets the couplet's elegance, moral flaws make confessions more convincing, spots of ink constitute the proof of print.[86] Whether reader or author gain possession of this impartial glass, Pope's deformity imprints its vision.

As the next chapter will show, when Pope gazes at Belinda, in love with her own reflection in an extremely partial glass of his own construction, deformity strikes up an affectionately ironic affinity with femininity: an affinity based on a common love of beauty, and a common desire to author oneself. Deformity allows the poet to distinguish himself from his celebration of feminine perfection by his awareness of the contingencies of the market and of mortality, contingencies that reduce all things, however beautiful, to objects.

2

The Rape
of the Lock
a s
M i n i a t u r e   E p i c

Unnumber'd Treasures ope at once, and here
The various Off'rings of the World appear;
From each she nicely culls with curious Toil,
And decks the Goddess with the glitt'ring Spoil.
This Casket *India's* glowing Gems unlocks,
And all *Arabia* breathes from yonder Box.

The Rape of the Lock (I, 129–134)

LADIES' PLAYTHING

When Aaron Hill in his "The Progress of Wit: A Caveat" (1730) warns Alexander Pope of the dangers of his recent satirical excesses, he addresses the poet in such a way as to remind him of the feminine bases of his literary fame: "Tuneful Alexis, on the *Thame's* fair Side, / The Ladies Play-thing, and the Muses Pride."[1] One of the poem's imaginary commentators explicates Pope's fall from such social grace: "It is an Art to trifle, importantly; and even to trifle, agreeably, has its Attraction: But to trifle, unseasonably, indecently or improperly, let who will be the Trifler, must be, either, inhumane, or unguarded."[2] Hill reminds Pope that the eyes of the ladies are upon him; to disappoint or offend them would be to lose his poetic distinction.

In his glowing assessment of Pope's *Iliad*, Samuel Johnson takes a different view of Pope's debt to a female audience:

It has, however, been objected with sufficient reason that there is in the commentary too much of unseasonable levity and affected gaiety; that too many appeals are made to the ladies, and the ease which is so carefully preserved is sometimes the ease of a trifler. Every art has its terms and every kind of instruction its proper style; the gravity of common critics may be tedious, but is less despicable than childish merriment.[3]

Whether the critic be Pope's contemporary Hill or his successor Johnson, Pope is censured for an impropriety defined in relation to the proper place of trifles and, by implication, the proper power of a female audience. If, for Hill, to disregard feminine propriety is dangerous, for Johnson to perform for female pleasure is disgusting. In either case, the author's consciousness of the gaze of the female reader is crucial in determining, for good or ill, questions of literary seriousness and value.

Pope indeed translated the *Iliad* into musical couplets (which while dubbed "heroic" were perceived as less masculine than rugged blank verse)[4] and courtly commentary with a female audience in mind, and played on that audience's expectations in *The Rape of the Lock*. In this chapter I read Pope's *Iliad* against the *Rape* (and vice versa), situating both poems in relation to the potentially transformative perspective of an audience and a world of trivial things that Pope linked to the feminine. While I want to emphasize Pope's awareness of a female readership, I am interested in the way femininity functions *rhetorically* both in Pope's poetry and the critical reactions that poetry inspires. In this chapter, femininity functions as the male author's fantasy of the possibilities (both threatening and tempting) of diminishment, devaluation, and objectification inherent in what he imagines as a female reader's gaze. Epic imitation and original mock-epic thus exist in a mutual play of transformation which makes of each poem, and its author, a beautiful monstrosity, an improper trifle of eternally shifting size and scale.[5]

As an emblematic preface, I want to consider a literary curiosity more likely to be found in the archives of biomedical libraries than in canonical collections, William Hay's *Deformity: an Essay*. In line with Pope's peculiar conjoining of a rhetoric of deformity to a tradition of classical imitation, Hay's text demonstrates deformity's link to the world of heroic originals and feminine objects.

Hay's Latin epigram "DETUR PULCHRIORI" [Let it be given to the Fairest] locates the essay at the inception of an epic tradition with feminine origins. Hay designates his text as a gift to women, both compliment and trouble-maker, by referring to the golden apple of the Hesperides: the anonymous gift from Eris (Discord), the uninvited guest to the wedding of Peleus and Thetis. The apple that started the Trojan war roots the greatest of conflicts and the most masculine of genres in female vanity and rivalry over an ornament.[6] Hay's deformity exists in witty contrast to his epigram, as he attempts (in an inadvertent echo of Pope's resolution to form a "perfect edition") "by a finished piece to attone for an ill-turned person."[7] What might such a fair female audience see in Hay's text?

They might see themselves; for in Hay they have an ally. In his essay deformity allies itself with femininity in their coincident weaknesses. While Pope's assertion of his masculinity grew increasingly theatrical as his career progressed—"with pistols," he assured his family, "the least man in England was above a match for the largest"—Hay argues, in defense of deformity, that it makes him less liable to affronts which could result in duels, and concludes "on the whole . . . that Deformity is a Protection to a Man's Health and Person; which (strange as it may appear) are better defended by Feebleness than Strength."[8] In a similar fashion, Owen Ruffhead, one of Pope's first biographers in the hagiographic tradition, credits the poet's body with keeping his passions out of trouble: "his tender frame preserved him from those modes of intemperance, to which genius, in particular, has often proved a victim."[9]

For these infirm writers, as for delicate ladies, "reputations" are metonymically related to "persons," by necessity preserved from the assaults and temptations of the public realm. As is also the case with ladies, such passive virtue falls short of heroism. "But I should impose upon my reader," Hay acknowledges, "and affront Heaven, if I ascribed that to Virtue, which took its rise from Necessity."[10] Deformity writes on the body a compromise of masculine agency, a compromise Pope transforms by rewriting epic heroism in a feminine register, on the market for and with women.

Hay closes his text with two complimentary gestures. He prints a "Last Will" in which he leaves his body to science and asks that it be opened, made a biological specimen and preserved in a medical museum (part of what he wishes to display is the efficacy of a particular brand of soap for ingestion as a cure for various ills). The body which he recommends as both educational oddity and potential commodity is then playfully promoted for its beauty. Hay claims that the curved lines of his humped back make him especially desirable, since they echo those of Hogarth's *Analysis of Beauty;* his deformity gives him a place, next to the lapdog, as both a plaything and parody of female beauty, a source and object of female pleasure.[11]

Hay's playfulness rests on the fact that unlike ladies, deformed authors are not themselves beautiful objects. This difference compels and enables them to compose beautiful texts. Ruffhead proposes that "perhaps . . . the uncomeliness of [Pope's] person, might not be without some effect":

> It has been well remarked by Lord Bacon, that whoever hath any thing fixed in his person, that doth induce contempt, hath also a perpetual spur within himself, to rescue and deliver himself from scorn. This consider-

ation, therefore, might render our poet more assiduous to cultivate his mental faculties, that he might atone for the defects of an ungraceful figure, by the accomplishments of an elegant and polished mind.[12]

If the *Iliad* begins with the wrath of Achilles, by this argument a particular feminine brand of literary imitation begins with the vanity of Pope. The productions which result, elegant and polished in the extreme, make their way with both the ladies and the marketplace when more conventional means are unavailable, as alluring and potentially divisive as the golden apple. If Laura Brown is right to claim, in a moral tradition of misogynistic criticism directed at a feminized Pope which begins with John Dennis, that Pope translating the *Iliad* repeats the narcissistic idolatry of Belinda at her dressing table, then readers of the *Rape* with a stake in the integrity of epic confront an image of themselves that is similarly and playfully distorted.[13] For like the apple, Pope's feminine epics (and in inverted form the heroic satires which follow them) show that the origins of the most sublime endeavors are linked to the most trivial baubles.

William Hazlitt's estimation of Pope's achievement exemplifies what happens when readers look into his poetry's oxymoronical mirror:

> Yet within this retired and narrow circle how much, and that how exquisite, was contained! What discrimination, what wit, what delicacy, what fancy, what lurking spleen, what elegance of thought, what pampered refinement of sentiment! It is like looking at the world through a microscope, where everything assumes a new character and a new consequence, where things are seen in their minutest circumstances and slightest shades of difference; where the little becomes gigantic, the deformed beautiful, and the beautiful deformed. The wrong end of the magnifier is, to be sure, held to everything, but still the exhibition is highly curious, and we know not whether to be most pleased or surprised.[14]

In this remarkable description of the dizzying paradox of the beautiful-made-sublime, Hazlitt tries to belittle that which clearly overwhelms him: the experience, objectified as an "exhibition . . . highly curious" of reading Pope's poetry. Hazlitt frames this unsettling confrontation with strange shifts of perspective within a "retired and narrow circle"; the reader looks through a microscope, but he can dismiss what he sees since he looks through the wrong end at a scene, so Hazlitt implies, otherwise trivial, a locus of minuteness and deformity. As the context of this passage makes clear, reading Pope's poetry forces Hazlitt to look, from an inverted perspective, at a feminized world. Such a vision turns the usual view from the center inside out. Hazlitt's response encloses Pope within the bounds of a pronouncedly feminine space, and in the process constructs and belittles him in the image of woman:

> [Pope] saw nature only dressed by art; he judged of beauty by fashion; he sought for truth in the opinions of the world; he judged of the feelings of others by his own. The capacious soul of Shakespeare had an intuitive and mighty sympathy with whatever could enter into the heart of man in all possible circumstances: Pope had an exact knowledge of all that he himself loved or hated, wished or wanted. Milton has winged his daring flight from heaven to earth, through Chaos and old Night. Pope's Muse never wandered with safety, but from his library to his grotto, or from his grotto into his library back again. [Pope's] mind dwelt with greater pleasure on his own garden, than on the garden of Eden; he could describe the faultless whole-length mirror that reflected his own person, better than the smooth surface of the lake that reflects the face of heaven . . . He preferred the artificial to the natural in external objects, because he had a stronger fellow-feeling with the self-love of the maker or proprietor of a gewgaw, than admiration of that which was interesting to all mankind. He preferred the artificial to the natural in passion, because the involuntary and uncalculating impulses of the one hurried him away with a force and vehemence with which he could not grapple; while he could trifle with the conventional and superficial modifications of mere sentiment at will, laugh at or admire, put them on or off like a masquerade dress, make much or little of them, indulge them for a longer or shorter time, as he pleased . . . His mind was the antithesis of strength and grandeur; its power was the power of indifference.[15]

As in the portraits examined in chapter 1, Pope's work is here objectified and judged in the image of its author; but Hazlitt does this through a process of miniaturization which renders text and author equally feminine, trivial and interchangeable. Pope's own versions of the identity of nature and art—both the *Essay on Criticism*'s "true wit is nature to advantage dressed," and the *Essay on Man*'s "all nature is but art, unknown to thee"—haunt the opening line of this passage, and provide the basis for Hazlitt's condemnation of his narcissism. Hazlitt's passage performs a punitive version of Virgil's discovery of the impossibility of originality Pope portrays in the *Essay on Criticism*. With the loss of unmediated nature, successively figured as Shakespeare's negative capability, Milton's sublimity, and Wordsworth's affinity for true landscape ("the smooth surface of the lake that reflects the face of heaven" refers, I think, to "The Boy of Winander" passage from the *Prelude*), Pope's world is reduced to the limits of the "faultless whole-length mirror that reflected his own person." The physical flaws of that person come to mind here as they are cancelled out by the deluded self-love the passage creates and critiques. The poet's bodily deformity is elided and transformed into blind feminine vanity; his social and political marginality belittled as smug adversity to adventure. In this version of his physical and emotional confinement to himself, Pope becomes stereotypically feminine, preferring the ownership of gewgaws to the admiration of the universe, domestic perambulations to sublime flights, conventional and artificial sentiment to forceful passions; in other words, the seductive possession of the beautiful to the vertiginous thrill of the sublime.[16]

In Hazlitt's portrait, Pope's inability to escape his physical and social limitations becomes a markedly feminine unwillingness to escape himself. That self becomes by nature indifferent, and thereby inauthentic. A narcissistic woman intent on owning that which he can make in the image of his own artifice, Pope is ultimately portrayed as a coquette at her toilette, trying on emotions "like a masquerade dress," his feminine affectation forming the perfect couplet with authentic masculine "strength and grandeur." Pope has become Belinda, a self-enclosed, captivating and curious object which invites and resists this reader's appropriation.

However much I might dissent from Hazlitt's contempt for Pope, his characterization of the poetry is unusually sensitive to Pope's engagement, fascination, and complicity with the feminine; an engagement which identifies the poet, in the eyes of many critics, with the objects he produces. As Hazlitt's troubled view from the wrong end of the microscope makes clear, deformity has its beauty, its charm, its curiosity. When Pope's satiric victims fight back, they construct him as a threatening figure of monstrous ambiguity. When Pope the satirist proclaims himself a hero, he proudly displays aberration as his masculine integrity's proof. But such an offensive image (however much it haunts other representations of the poet) lacks the diminutive appeal that earned Pope the derisive sobriquet he transformed into ornament, "The Ladies' Plaything." Domesticated and miniaturized, deformity reflects in a distorted mirror a femininity defined as commodity. As Hazlitt's frustration indicates, deformity creates a peculiar kind of object that solicits, yet resists exchange; a curiosity. That same curiosity which makes Pope marginal and monstrous also renders him (at least early in his career) collectable, ornamental, and playfully familiar both with the market, and with the miniature world that is woman's place.

The Rape of the Lock began, after all, with Pope's intimacy with a small and fashionable Catholic world, with the real loss of Arabella's hair and with it the

Fermor family tranquility. And yet the poem's origins in seemingly trivial reality did more to hurt Arabella's reputation than to help it. The history of the poem's reputation, like that of an eighteenth-century lady's, takes a turn for the worse when it goes public. First circulated in manuscript, then published anonymously, contemporary readers of the *Rape* took a great deal of pleasure in identifying not just the literary sources but the contemporary models for various characters. When the anonymous two-canto version appeared, the supposed original of Sir Plume threatened Pope with physical violence, and Arabella/Belinda, initially pleased enough with the manuscript to circulate it among her own friends, protested bitterly.

The poet made amends to Arabella by printing a dedicatory epistle to the five-canto edition that continues the polite understatement of the poem's double-edged irony. Here Pope, in the style of female passivity his preface recommends, waives authorial control over the poem's publication:

> It will be in vain to deny that I have some Regard for this Piece, since I Dedicate it to You. Yet You may bear me Witness, it was intended only to divert a few young Ladies, who have good Sense and good Humour enough, to laugh not only at their Sex's little unguarded Follies, but at their own. But as it was communicated with the Air of a Secret, it soon found its Way into the World. An imperfect Copy having been offer'd to a Bookseller, You had the Good-Nature for my Sake to consent to the Publication of one more correct: This I was forc'd to before I had executed half my Design, for the *Machinery* was entirely wanting to compleat it . . .
>
> If this Poem had as many Graces as there are in Your Person, or in Your Mind, yet I could never hope it shou'd pass thro' the World so Uncensured as You have done.[17]

Neither the poem nor Arabella, both beautiful objects, passed through the world uncensured. But curiously, Arabella rejected a poetic dedication which omitted her name, and soon after 1715 had her portrait painted with a cross around her neck and Pope's famous couplet on Belinda's universal charm inscribed beneath it: "On her white Breast a sparkling *Cross* she wore / Which *Jews* might kiss, and Infidels adore" (II, 7–8).[18]

Arabella's transformation from enraged proper maiden to playful painted lady illustrates the *Rape*'s capacity to diminish the very conflict it so sneakily suggests. It also demonstrates the powerful way in which Pope's aestheticized imagination of the feminine in the *Rape* both appeals to and silences actual women. The poet's and the critic's patronizing tone knowingly diminish a rape that could or could not be more than just the loss of a lock, or a crack in a china jar. As Pope's double entendres and tricks of perspective demonstrate, such incidental fun with literary and social conventions, such proper insignificance, such aesthetic distance, such static display, are the stuff of serious epic narrative, serious violence, serious loss.

HEROIC COMMODITIES

To describe *The Rape of the Lock* as a miniature epic is to evoke a paradoxical vision of a perfect universe. For this tiny poem (tiny, at least, when viewed on the scale of the epics it mimics) offers a closure so complete that it seems to encompass empires. Both replete and hollow in its conflation of inner and outer, visual and verbal, spatial and temporal realms, this miniature epic embodies that genre of "multum in parvo" which Susan Stewart defines as "the miniaturization of language itself . . . a discourse which speaks to the human and cultural but not to the natural except to frame it . . . monumental, transcending any limited context of origin and at the same time neatly containing a universe."[19]

In *The Rape of the Lock,* Alexander Pope contains the heroic past by commodifying it. When the faithful translator of Homer pauses from his labors on the *Iliad* in order to transform Achilles' shield into Belinda's petticoat, heroic honor into drawing room chastity, what results challenges Laura Brown's characterization of this mock-epic's structure: "heroes don't own commodities."[20] Brown's failure to recognize Pope's awareness (*both* in the *Rape* and in his translation of the *Iliad*) of the ways in which transcendent classical heroism bases itself on the merely material, curiously reveals less irony and more idealism about the integrity of the classics than do Pope's imitations. Much as feminist critics are right to read Belinda as a commodity, their emphasis on Pope's monolithic construction of "woman" fails to acknowledge the pervasive femininity which the poem's irony posits at the origins of epic itself. Ellen Pollak, for example, persuasively argues that the *Rape*'s incessant synecdoches conceal beneath a critique of the beau monde's sterile materialism an endorsement of a normative objectification of woman.[21] I want to shift the focus to how Pope sees himself as compromised and objectified by a market economy, and how he uses gender to figure his own ambivalent relation to a literary market. The *Rape* itself provides the terms, terms in permanent, dazzling, and unsettling ironic play, for reading what might appear to be a binary opposition between aesthetic appreciation and satiric indignation, between heroes and commodities, as double-edged indivisibility.[22]

Such indivisibility was part of the process of composition: Pope's serious

Homeric labors ran concurrently with the writing of the *Rape,* so that it becomes impossible to tell at times which poem served as the original for the
other, rendering unattainable the possibility of originality. The play of mirrors
between serious imitation and self-conscious parody leaves neither poem's claim
to immaterial integrity intact.

The *Rape* similarly draws both on a serious epic tradition and a tradition
of epic parody which by Pope's time took Homer to task for his characters'
crudity and licentiousness. In both his *Iliad* and the *Rape,* Pope refines Homer
both poetically and morally. As Howard Weinbrot puts it, "the more characters
in *The Rape of the Lock* embrace epic values and conventions, the less pleasant
they are."[23] In his genealogy of epic diction in his *Life of Pope,* Samuel Johnson
makes such refinement a matter of consumer demand. All successors to Homer,
he argues, had to please the jaded palates of sophisticated audiences; even by
Virgil's time, "the state of the world [was] so much altered, and the demands
for elegance so much increased, that mere nature would be endured no
longer."[24]

Whether Homer is improved in his *Iliad,* or diminished and polished in
the *Rape,* Pope achieves such refinement by a process of objectification. By a
seemingly infinite repetition of a series of finite gestures whereby the ideally
proper and the immediately visual are inextricably linked, Pope gives his own
epic language a substantive quality not unlike that of Homeric formulae while
maintaining an allusive debt to the English heroic tradition most prominently
figured by Milton and Dryden. He constructs a language at once overburdened
by the past and claiming access to an immediately visible world.

Pope's version of that most exemplary of heros, Sarpedon, thus sounds
pronouncedly materialistic in his famous exhortation to battle in *Iliad* XII, the
set piece which began Pope's Homeric career in print:

> Why boast we, *Glaucus,* our extended Reign,
> Where *Xanthus'* streams enrich the *Lycian* Plain?
> Our num'rous Herds that range each fruitful Field,
> And Hills where Vines their Purple Harvest yield?
> Our foaming Bowls with gen'rous *Nectar* crown'd,
> Our Feasts enhanc'd with Musick's sprightly Sound?
> Why on those Shores are we with Joy survey'd,
> Admir'd as Heroes, and as Gods obey'd?
> Unless great Acts superior Merit prove,
> And Vindicate the bounteous Pow'rs above:
> 'Tis ours, the Dignity They give, to grace;

> The first in Valour, as the first in Place;
> That while with wondring Eyes our Martial Bands
> Behold our Deeds transcending our Commands,
> Such, they may cry, deserve the Sov'reign State,
> Whom those that Envy dare not Imitate!
> Cou'd all our Care elude the greedy Grave,
> Which claims no less the Fearful than the Brave,
> For Lust of Fame I shou'd not vainly dare
> In fighting Fields, nor urge thy Soul to War.
> But since, alas, ignoble Age must come,
> Disease, and Death's inexorable Doom;
> The Life which others pay, let Us bestow,
> And give to Fame what we to Nature owe;
> Brave, tho we fall; and honour'd, if we live;
> Or let us Glory gain, or Glory give!   (27–52)[25]

This oration exemplifies Pope's high heroic mode, and it does so, aptly enough, in miniature. Sarpedon's rhetoric, in keeping with the couplet's repetitive frame, amplifies, encloses and mirrors the original's detail. Similarly, the repetitive periphrases of heroic speech (i.e., "feathered deaths" for arrows, "fleecy care" for sheep, exemplified here by the personifications of lines 31–32) compel the reader to condense the abstract and concrete portions of each phrase into a newly imagined material whole.[26]

Sarpedon makes his plea for heroic action in a curiously static set piece. Both Pope and Homer preface the speech with a simile likening the hero to a hungry lion resolved on attack at all costs, but Pope adds a few additional lines which typically frame the speaker's words with his contemplation of a tableau:

> Resolv'd alike, Divine *Sarpedon* glows
> With gen'rous Rage, that drives him on the Foes.
> He views the Tow'rs, and meditates their Fall;
> To sure Destruction dooms the *Grecian* Wall;
> Then casting on his Friend an ardent Look,
> Fir'd with the Thirst of Glory, thus he spoke.   (21–26)

The reader views Sarpedon's meditation on the fall of the Greek camp through the lens of the ensuing fall of Troy's towers; modern fondness for melancholy ruin imposes itself upon the Homeric character's dream-vision of triumph. The speech that follows thus forecloses on narrative, offering a heroic code enhanced by its loss. Pope elaborates on Sarpedon's first question by rendering it as a landscape of privilege, each couplet elaborating a visible feature of pride of place.[27] Homer's "all men look on us as if we were immortals," escalates into the spectacle of warriors "with joy survey'd, / Admir'd as Heroes, and as Gods obey'd." For such a vision of superiority to be merited, Pope's Sarpedon argues, the audience must have ocular proof; the invisible "powers above" must become visible through "great acts," which "grace" (or visibly adorn) social "Dignity" (or worth), itself signified by material goods and position—"first in Place."

A hero's obligation (and here the lines are utterly Pope's invention) becomes by such ocular proof an original image, a marvel at the top of the hierarchy "whom those that envy dare not imitate." Pope thus rewrites the Homeric economy of heroic glory—"let us go on and win glory for ourselves, or yield it to others"—as a material economy of fame in which aristocratic largesse allies itself with art in its ability to control narrative by choosing death: "The life which others pay, let Us bestow, / And give to Fame, what we to Nature owe."

Playing with this heroic example, Pope's mock-epic art bargains unabashedly with Fame by selling Nature short. While Pope's heroic couplet elevates the concrete by linking it to the abstract, by taking the *Iliad* translation's materialism literally, the *Rape*'s heroicomical mode persistently cuts the abstract down to feminine scale. Sarpedon's spectacular economy metamorphoses into Clarissa's prudent reflections on the display of feminine value in a speech which begins the *Rape*'s fifth canto, explicitly intended "to open more clearly the MORAL of the Poem."[28] As Clarissa's advice demonstrates, in the *Rape,* from the first in "Place" to the first in "Face" is a much easier leap than it at first might have seemed.

> Say, why are Beauties prais'd and honour'd most,
> The wise Man's Passion, and the vain Man's Toast?
> Why deck'd with all that Land and Sea afford,
> Why Angels call'd, and Angel-like ador'd?
> Why round our Coaches crowd the white-glov'd Beaus,
> Why bows the Side-box from its inmost Rows?
> How vain are all these Glories, all our Pains,
> Unless good Sense preserve what Beauty gains:
> That Men may say, when we the Front-box grace,
> Behold the first in Virtue, as in Face! . . .
> But since, alas! frail Beauty must decay,
> Curl'd or uncurl'd, since Locks will turn to grey,
> Since painted, or not painted, all shall fade,
> And she who scorns a Man, must die a Maid;
> What then remains, but well our Pow'r to use,
> And keep good Humour still whate'er we lose? . . .

Beauties in vain their pretty Eyes may roll;
Charms strike the Sight, but Merit wins the Soul.   (V, 9–34)

The transformation from male honor to female ornament is here complete. While Homer's Sarpedon's consciousness of death determines his choice of glory in battle, and while Pope's Sarpedon's practicality redefines heroic glory as a matter of the material display of inimitable power, knowledge of mortality in the *Rape* would seem at first glance to resign the heroine all the more completely to her status as the visible object of male desire. With Clarissa as his mouthpiece, Pope makes this speech from a precariously ironic position which both mimics and belittles the poem's resolutely feminine perspective. The ultimate distinctions in women are made between curled or uncurled, painted or not painted. The purpose of woman's prime virtue of good sense is to preserve "what Beauty gains"; while the difference between charms and merit is similarly constructed as a quantitative rather than qualitative matter of the latter's greater effectiveness in ensnaring the enemy in love's battle.[29]

But death gives Belinda choices within the object world in which she lives. The epic hero chooses between a short and glorious and a long and undistinguished life, and thereby gains the distinction of action. The bourgeois heroine chooses between the display and the use of her beauty, between the coquette's deadly charms and the wife's virtuous productivity, and thereby gains the invisible virtue of submission. Just as Pope improves upon Homer's pagan morals, so he recommends that the virtuous heroine improve upon her own estate, forfeit charms for merit, epic beauty for domestic harmony.[30] But neither Belinda nor the *Rape* can rest content with such sensible advice; Pope's heroine, like Sarpedon, wants visible glory.

THE MIRROR OF INVENTION

When "awful Beauty puts on all its Arms" (I, 139), she does so in front of the mirror. For Pope in the *Rape,* the ephemeral is its own end. The poem's self-enclosed charm, like Belinda's, draws us with the tenuous fragility of a single hair, as if the lines on the page themselves were ornamental lures. Like the coquette, the *Rape* puts itself on display, offers itself up for appropriation and interpretation in the literary shop window. But neither the coquette nor the poem delivers. In the *Rape of the Lock* display—a word whose meanings link the art of the marketplace to the spoils of Belinda's dressing table and her "sacred Rites of Pride" to the sexual games of the drawing room—is definitely the thing.

If we approach this poem's unabashed artifice expecting to unveil literary depth or epic seriousness, we remain unsatisfied. The indiscriminate reduction of its zeugmas that equate Queen Anne's counsel to a cup of tea or Belinda's honor to her new brocade, and ultimately, albeit coyly, the depth of virtue to the superficial dazzle of face, the incessant fragmentation of its synecdoches that begins with the fetishization of the lock itself in the poem's title, deflect us to the continual dead-end of the double entendre. The *Rape* transforms heroism into an elegant oxymoron: in this flawless miniature world, war is only a card game, death is only a sexual pun, and the ultimate loss of Belinda's lock, severed "from the fair head forever and forever," has the power to move us as if it were a hero's tragic end. The power of the *Rape*'s miniaturization consists in its ability to make the reader long for a distant past—at once a heroicized present and a bourgeoisified paganism—which the poem redefines as an alluring, and ultimately lost object.[31]

Such sacrifice of understanding to the multidimensional pleasure of admiration makes this diminutive epic feel boundless. As curious as the perfectly carved mythological and Biblical scenes enclosed in walnut shells, displayed on gems, the *Rape* includes every epic convention within the relatively economical confines of a thousand lines. This mock-epic's machinery, in the form of the sylphs, performs and makes visible the theological, physical and allegorical functions of epic's larger gods; the poem is suitably adorned with similes, dream visions, battles and a journey to the underworld. Most importantly, epic since Aristotle's definition was expected to be didactic, and to tell the story of a nation. *The Rape of the Lock* displays England's growing empire on a lady's dressing table. All Arabia breathes from yonder box, and Achilles' shield seems as insubstantial as Belinda's petticoat.

Yet the shield Hephaistos created for the *Iliad*'s hero itself exemplifies art's metamorphic power; its surface displays an epic within an epic on which divinely mechanical art brings a timeless universe within and without the *Iliad* to life. The *Rape*'s meta-synecdoche equating all of epic history, and with it the history of empire, with the theft of a lock of hair, makes a continual dialectic of monument and ornament; the wide circumference of Belinda's hoop contains Achilles' shield:

> To Fifty chosen *Sylphs*, of special Note,
> We trust th'important Charge, the *Petticoat:*
> Oft have we known that sev'nfold Fence to fail,
> Tho' stiff with Hoops, and arm'd with Ribs of Whale.

Form a strong Line about the Silver Bound,
And guard the wide Circumference around.   (II, 117–122)

The *Rape* puts on display the process by which, in a world of mutually transformative analogy, feminine miniature parody transforms masculine "original."
The coquette's shield, designed to protect a very different, but equally material
sort of heroic honor, fails because of what escapes its purview, namely female
desire. And yet female desire, the refining force of epic masculinity, gives shape
to the world of the *Rape* precisely as curious object, and as the origin of epic.

If we look for Pope's imagination of origins in his translation of the *Iliad,*
we must first view his portrait in the Preface of a bard whose "great and peculiar
Characteristick" was "Invention":

> This strong and ruling Faculty was like a powerful Star, which, in the
> Violence of its Course, drew all things within its *Vortex*. It seem'd not
> enough to have taken in the whole Circle of Arts, and all the inward
> Passions and Affections of Mankind to furnish his Characters, and all the
> outward Forms and Images of Things for his Descriptions: but wanting
> yet an ampler Sphere to expatiate in, he open'd a new and boundless Walk
> for his Imagination, and created a World for himself in the Invention of
> *Fable.* That which *Aristotle* [*Poetics, vi* 19] calls the *Soul of Poetry,* was first
> breath'd into it by *Homer.*[32]

In both the *Iliad* and the *Rape,* as we have begun to see, Pope's process of
poetic composition is one of incessant visualization that results in a dialectic of
miniaturization and maximization of his original. Pope's vision of Homer's
distinguishing characteristic, his invention, is itself a grand simile which attempts
to imagine the violence of originality. Invention—containing both the sense of
original creation and the idea of literally coming upon, or finding something
already there—exemplifies the paradox of an originality seen as vision, and
therefore as representation. Whether serious or mock-epic, Pope's heroic couplets contain and frame what was originally ineffable, in motion, and play with
the relation between heroic spectacle and feminine display.

Pope envisions Homer's invention as an ever-expanding vortex which takes
in "the whole Circle of Arts, and the whole compass of Nature," and goes
beyond these in search of release from its own bounds—"an ampler Sphere," a
"new and boundless Walk for his Imagination." Homer's art becomes the eye
in motion, and what Pope describes, and sets in place, is the view. In his characterization of Homer's similes, the self-referential dimension of the epic genre
in which epic and mock-epic meet, in which great things are figured by small,

in which worlds within the narrative frame are connected to seemingly timeless worlds without, Pope's Homer becomes most pronouncedly a painter, and his text becomes a storehouse of images, a grand, comprehensive museum of vision from which all poets must borrow.[33] Even his poetic style, what Pope calls his expression, is framed in visual terms: "We see the bright Imagination of *Homer* shining out in the most enliven'd Forms of it . . . His Expression is like the colouring of some great Masters, which discovers itself to be laid on boldly, and executed with Rapidity. It is indeed the strongest and most glowing imaginable, and touch'd with the greatest Spirit."[34] Whether breathing, god-like, "the soul of Poetry" into the original or touching his expression with spirit, the ineffable in Pope's imagination of Homer is always the proof of what the poet's eye makes visible.

This emphasis on vision caused one critic to describe Pope's style, as it culminates in the *Iliad,* as that of a miniature painter. In this account, Pope reverses Lessing's formula for Homeric achievement, namely "turning the *co-existing* of his design into a *consecutive,* and thereby making of the tedious painting of a physical object the living picture of an action," by transforming living pictures into picturesque visions.[35] The most exemplary of Pope's landscapes, and the one which earns him the epithet of miniaturist, is displayed in that history-painting turned pastoral, *Windsor Forest,* a seriously "modern" heroic poem from the same period of Pope's career as the *Iliad* translation. Begun in 1704, it was completed and published in 1713, the year between the publication of the initial two-canto version and the issuing of the final five-canto revision of the *Rape.* Here the young poet, celebrating the Peace of Utrecht, which cleared the way for Britain's ascendancy in trade, envisions an English empire whose violence is transformed into tableau:

> The Groves of *Eden,* vanish'd now so long,
> Live in Description, and look green in Song:
> *These,* were my Breast inspir'd with equal Flame,
> Like them in Beauty, should be like in Fame.
> Here Hills and Vales, the Woodland and the Plain,
> Here Earth and Water seem to strive again,
> Not Chaos-like together crush'd and bruis'd,
> But as the World, harmoniously confus'd:
> Where Order in Variety we see,
> And where, tho' all things differ, all agree.
> Here waving Groves a checquer'd Scene display,
> And part admit and part exclude the Day;

As some coy Nymph her Lover's warm Address
Nor quite indulges, nor can quite repress.
There, interspers'd in Lawns and opening Glades,
Thin Trees arise that shun each others Shades.
Here in full Light the russet Plains extend;
There wrapt in Clouds the blueish Hills ascend:
Ev'n the wild Heath displays her Purple Dies,
And 'midst the Desart fruitful Fields arise,
That crown'd with tufted Trees and springing Corn,
Like verdant Isles the sable Waste adorn.
Let *India* boast her Plants, nor envy we
The weeping Amber or the balmy Tree,
While by our Oaks the precious Loads are born,
And Realms commanded which those Trees adorn.
Not proud *Olympus* yields a nobler Sight,
Tho' Gods assembled grace his tow'ring Height,
Than what more humble Mountains offer here,
Where, in their Blessings, all those Gods appear.
See *Pan* with Flocks, with Fruits *Pomona* crown'd,
Here blushing *Flora* paints th'enamel'd Ground,
Here Ceres' Gifts in waving Prospect stand,
And nodding tempt the joyful Reaper's Hand,
Rich Industry sits smiling on the Plains,
And Peace and Plenty tell, a STUART reigns.   (7–41)[36]

In its nostalgia for an invisible paradise and its use of words both concretely visual and abstractly conventional, this passage demonstrates how Pope's version of heroic diction both tuned the English tongue and framed an English perspective. Recreating a lost ideal original, a microcosm of the orderly variety of a world seen as art, Pope rhetorically points to scenes in this uniquely English and conventionally classical landscape as if to various parts of a canvas. Visual effects are personified both on a large scale, as in the simile of the coy nymph used to describe an effect of light, and in the small details of periphrases like "Purple Dies," and "sable Waste," which transform fruits and weeds into abstract qualities in a divine painting.

This painting exemplifies the power of hierarchy and concealed analogy between commanding and adorning encapsulated by the lines describing the English oak. By envisioning English ships (themselves a synecdoche for trade) as oaks, the national answer to (because container for) India's "weeping Amber," or "balmy Tree," relations of empire are painted as complementary landscapes, the movement of trade is both particularized and rendered static so that command could as easily refer to the view of Windsor the poem presents us with as to the distant India that trade controls. From such a perspective, monarchs are artists, and Queen Anne decreeing peace exists on the same order as Belinda at cards ("At length great ANNA said—Let Discord cease! / She said, the World obey'd, and all was *Peace!*" [*WF,* 327–328]: "*Let Spades be Trumps!* she said, and Trumps they were." [*Rape,* III, 46]). With the final comparison to Olympus, the passage escalates its level of abstract personification, and thereby its degree of aesthetic distance. England's plenty is envisioned as classical convention, the mythical gods returned, both visible and invisible, as various prospects painted on "th'enamel'd Ground" of a miniature painting. Both familiar and unrecognizable, closely observed and conventional, such a tableau, in its final characterization as "Peace and Plenty," indeed tells in its very absence of story of national power.

The same process which transforms a narrative of English ascendancy into a picturesque landscape and then reduces that landscape to the enamelled ground of a miniature also characterizes Pope's "maxim-ization" of Homer.[37] By viewing Homer as a repository not just of universal images but of universal wisdom, Pope both refines and magnifies certain moments in Homer as maxims, speaking pictures that bear the truth of a whole, and which elide the violence of time. Pope's propensity to visualize and thereby to distance himself from concrete particulars by enclosing that vision in heroic diction, leads to the sententious quality of his couplets. Story turns to spectacle, and the viewer is presented with a compelling illusion of universality from which a moral can be drawn.

To return, then, to Achilles' shield. Pope's version of ekphrasis, that miniature world compared with which the *Iliad* dwindles, best exemplifies such verbal vision.[38] His *Iliad* transforms the shield into "the Image of the Master Mind" (XVIII, 557), what he calls in his "Observations on the Shield of Achilles" a "universal Picture." Homer's purpose in Pope's account becomes "no less, than to draw the Picture of the whole World in the Compass of this Shield . . . In a word, all the Occupations, all the Ambitions, and all the Diversions of Mankind."[39] So clearly does Pope "see" the shield as artifact, "not only . . . as a Piece of Sculpture but of Painting," that he is able to describe it down to the last inch, and in fact did the first sketch himself for an engraving which would appear in the first edition of his *Iliad* (see Figure 5): a perfect set of circles, the inmost round depicting the universe, the next round the signs of the zodiac (not mentioned in Homer), the outermost round the ocean, with a center

Figure 5.

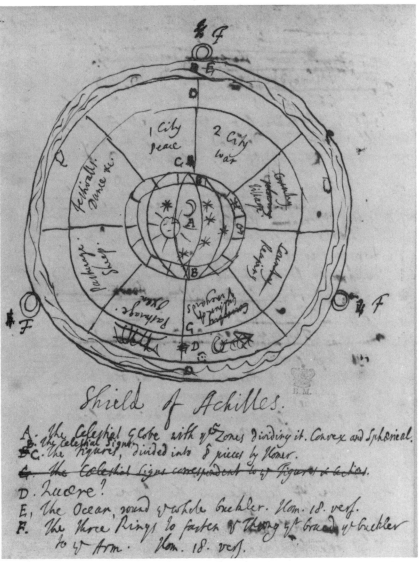

Pope's rough sketch and first description of the Shield of Achilles,
from the *Iliad* manuscript.

round neatly divided into four major sections—"town in peace," "town in war," "agriculture," and "pastoral life"; each major section subdivided into three smaller sections containing a different exemplary activity.[40]

Here nature is ordered along the lines of an art that is also social hierarchy. Homer's nameless characters are put in their proper places most importantly by gender (it is women who are distinguishable) and by visual signs, as part of Pope's reading of what he calls Homer's power of contrast and variety.[41] Pope envisions the shield in the form of his own couplets: multiplicitous distinctions positioned within regular patterns; each metaphor a picture, each picture with its own character, each character in strict adherence to the three unities. With such order the eternal nature of the shield turns a man into a "rustic Monarch," a simple supper of barley into "the Reaper's due Repast, the Women's Care," the "kind sweet fruit" into "the purple Product of the autumnal Year."

Pope's version abounds with cues, lacking in Homer, that the shield is a simulation; like his version of the *Iliad,* it constantly reminds us of the power and the limits of representation: "And the whole War came out, and met the Eye; / And each bold Figure seem'd to live, or die" (XVIII, 625–626). The final pattern of the dancers on Homer's shield, described in Homer as "when a potter, crouching, makes trial of his wheel" is transformed into Pope's characterization of his own poetic power in the *Iliad,* a power whose order, and whose artifice, is always visible:

> Now all at once they rise, at once descend,
> With well-taught Feet: Now shape, in oblique ways,
> Confus'dly regular, the moving Maze:
> Now forth at once, too swift for sight, they spring,
> And undistinguish'd blend the flying Ring:
> So whirls a Wheel, in giddy Circle tost,
> And rapid as it runs, the single Spokes are lost.   (XVIII, 690–696)

While Homer's shield was both two and three dimensional, visible and beyond vision, Pope insists on the regularity and most importantly the materiality of Achilles' shield. Like Sarpedon's heroism, the shield is a magnificently singular artifact, a spectacle, a heroic curiosity, sign of both the particulars of history and the genius of Pope's poetic imagination.

In his imitation and subsequent parody of one of the most shockingly artful of Homer's similes, Pope similarly makes the aesthetic a vehicle for ordering, and ultimately its own end.[42] Here is Homer describing Menelaos' flesh wound, inflicted when Pandaros breaks the fragile truce between Greeks and Trojans, which can be read as a repetition of the symbolic wound to Menelaos, the abduction of Helen, with which the Trojan war began:

> As when some Maionian woman or Karian with purple
> colours ivory, to make it a cheek piece for horses;
> it lies away in an inner room, and many a rider
> longs to have it, but it is laid up to be a king's treasure,
> two things, to be the beauty of the horse, the pride of the horseman:
> So, Menelaos, your shapely thighs were stained with the color
> of blood, and your legs also and the ankles beneath them.
>   (Lattimore, IV, 141–147)

> As when some stately Trappings are decreed,
> To grace a Monarch on his bounding Steed,
> A Nymph in *Caria* or *Maionia* bred,
> Stains the pure Iv'ry with a lively Red;
> With equal Lustre various Colours vie,
> The shining Whiteness and the *Tyrian* Dye.
> So great *Atrides!* show'd thy sacred Blood,
> As down thy snowie Thigh distill'd the streaming Flood.
>   (Pope, IV, 170–177)

Homer likens the hero's wound to an ornament which, like Helen herself, is "laid up to be a king's treasure," the object of envy and rivalry, the goal of Pope's version of Sarpedon's call to battle. Yet Pope chooses here to emphasize the purely visual elements of the simile, the contrast of colors, the alexandrine mimicking the slow flow of the blood down the length of the leg, the specific focus on the precise part of that leg, the "Tyrian Dye" (a brief nod to Carthage and the *Aeneid* where this simile shows up in truncated form describing Lavinia's blush) typifying the ways in which heroic diction displays its literary past, the simile itself the narrative of the power of adornment for a monarch whose blood is sacred. Pope's justification of the simile against charges of its superfluity is particularly revealing:

> We learn from hence that the *Lydians* and *Carians* were famous in the first
> Times for their staining in Purple, and the Women excell'd in Works of
> Ivory: As also that there were certain Ornaments which only Kings and
> Princes were privileged to wear. But without having recourse to Antiq-
> uities to justify this Particular, it may be alledg'd, that the Simile does not
> consist barely in the Colours; It was but little to tell us, that the Blood of
> Menelaus appearing on the Whiteness of his Skin, vyed with the purpled
> Ivory; but this implies that the honourable Wounds of a Heroe are the

beautiful Dress of War, and become him as much as the most gallant Ornaments in which he takes the Field.[43]

This method of interpretation transforms the passage from travelogue, to dictionary of antiquities, to a didactic maxim which revises heroic wounds into gallant ornaments, war into theater.

Taking the process of aesthetic transformation to its ultimate conclusion, the heroic realm of death on the battlefield which the Homeric simile evades by gesturing toward a timeless, often domestic world of art, becomes an aesthetic foil for the war of cards in Canto III of the *Rape:*

> Thus when dispers'd a routed Army runs,
> Of *Asia's* Troops, and *Africk's* Sable Sons,
> With like Confusion different Nations fly,
> Of various Habit and of various Dye,
> The pierc'd Battalions dis-united fall,
> In Heaps on Heaps; one Fate o'erwhelms them all.   (III, 81–86)

The "Dye" of the playing cards echoes the "Dye" which transforms Menelaos' wound into ornament. While Homer momentarily transforms blood on a warrior's flesh to the vision of an aesthetic object, so hermetically sealed against death is Pope's vision in the *Rape* that the various "dye" of the different suits of Belinda's playing cards aestheticizes national distinctions in order to avoid blood altogether. The world of serious epic in which fate is more than the loss of a game, is at this moment only a background, like the "level Green" of the card-table's baize, which the slightest shift of the reader's gaze might restore to focus.

UNIQUE CURIOSITIES

Curiosity is the place where timeless art and scientific origins, imitation and truth, ancient rules and modern progress, meet. Pope's own attempts at appropriating the classics make him both complicit with and opposed to the empirical and democratic attitude toward culture that curiosity signifies, an attitude that equates cultural value with market value, quality with quantity, an "aesthetic of selection . . . [with] that of abundance."[44] In her study of "The 'Curious Attitude' in Eighteenth-Century Britain," Barbara Benedict defines curiosity as "culture that can be bought."[45] The ambiguities in the field of meaning which curiosity delineates in the eighteenth century signal ambivalence about such a commodification of culture. If "curiosity manifests power by means of owning and of observation," its display of objects also makes such power newly and indiscriminately accessible, and the ownership and exercise of such power ambiguous. Curiosity poses questions of agency and ownership which confront Pope in his epic composition: "Who shall possess curiosity and who be possessed by means of it? Who shall be 'curious' and who a 'curiosity?' "[46]

If Homer is a kind of sublime museum of ancient vision for Pope, then *The Rape of the Lock* is his curiosity cabinet (also known as a "lady's cabinet"), his "museum of the present." Clarence Tracy's *The RAPE observ'd,* which annotates the poem with period images and elaborate descriptions of the objects it represents, makes explicit for twentieth-century antiquarians what the poem had put on display for its contemporary public.[47] Like the private collections of curiosities which abounded in the eighteenth century, *The Rape of the Lock* offers the spectator a continuous game of visual connections between great and small, domestic and exotic; the pleasure of such a game consists in finding similarities within differences, China's earth in a cup of tea.[48] A miniature of the totality of foreign cultures it claims to stand for, the poem operates, like the cabinet, by collapsing the differences created by time and alterity into contiguity; objects are both brought closer, and set apart in a closed world.[49]

From another perspective, the curiosity cabinet's display of material bases for scientific knowledge parallels the *Rape*'s disclosure of the origins of epic in objects. The *Rape* collects epic history in the form of the ornaments of empire and puts them on display. Pope gains a novel kind of cultural authority, an authority which his faithful adherence to neoclassical order would seem to belie, by creating such an ideal space within his texts, a luxury space which both exhibits his power to reorder and redefine cultural tradition, and grants a new and tenuous sort of power to the reader, particularly the female reader, who views, and by viewing defines, and by defining may devalue, such a display.

The *Rape,* in all its self-advertising triviality, in conjunction with its serious mirror-image, Pope's *Iliad,* particularly exemplifies the contentions of value to which curiosity gives rise and which lie at the heart of the commodity's mystery. Pope's appropriations of classical texts for English poetry mark him as both an example and active force in a nationalistic cultural "habit of curiosity," which "by the mid-century . . . had become a public activity, the show of collective cultural dominance."[50]

Such a show, the spoils of foreign and invisible conquests, is figured in the shape of, and displayed upon, the bodies of women. When Addison attends the Royal Exchange, he sees a theater of art which is a miniature of the universe, making "this Metropolis a kind of *Emporium* for the whole Earth." Walking the floor as a "Citizen of the World," he imagines a world landscape which trade transforms into the stuff of consumption, and ultimately, of female ornament:

> Nature seems to have taken a particular Care to disseminate her Blessings among the different Regions of the World, with an Eye to this mutual Intercourse and Traffic among Mankind, that the Natives of the several Parts of the Globe might have a kind of Dependance upon one another, and be united together by their common Interest. Almost every *Degree* produces something peculiar to it. The Food often grows in one Country, and the Sauce in another. The Fruits of *Portugal* are corrected by the Products of *Barbadoes:* The Infusion of a *China* Plant sweetned with the Pith of an *Indian* Can: The *Philipick* Islands give a Flavour to our *European* bowls. The single Dress of a Woman of Quality is often the Product of an hundred Climates. The Muff and the Fan come together from the different Ends of the Earth. The Scarf is sent from the Torrid Zone, and the Tippet from beneath the Pole. The Brocade Petticoat rises out of the Mines of *Peru,* and the Diamond Necklace out of the Bowels of *Indostan.*[51]

From the bird's-eye view of "Nature," the aesthetic view which makes order from variety in miniature form, all the world unites in the production of luxury. From such a perspective, objects, with uncanny charm, take on lives and motion of their own, and power and labour become invisible. Petticoats rise from mines fully made, diamonds emerge from mythically embodied bowels without effort, and women exist to display, and to consume, in full regalia, the triumph of such "common interest"; the universe in miniature.

But as an individual author and appropriator, Pope makes a different sort of curious show, the flip-side, the rhyming word if you will, of curiosity's couplet. While the curious collector composes a totality out of the juxtaposition of artificial and natural, of all of history and all of nature, the curiosity itself can also, by pointing to the unique unknown, delineate the limits of the natural, and the known.[52] A writer in the *Gazette* of 1758 illustrates this well: "What entitles a thing to the epithets of rare and curious?—Certainly it's being seldom to be seen; and when seen, it's being possessed of some powers or properties of an uncommon and extraordinary nature. Is there then a dromedary and camel, besides those shewn at the Talbot in the Strand, in the whole island of Great Britain!"[53] Whether local or imported, "uncommon and extraordinary nature" makes a curiosity. As the young Sir Joshua Reynolds observes when he sees Pope at the art auction where images of the author are on sale to virtuosi, "Pope was seldom seen in public, so it was a great sight to see him."[54] In just this way Warton's juxtaposition of two images of Pope are both curiosities and emblems of the collected works to follow. These images are curious for contradictory reasons, and as such help to illuminate how this particular poet's entry into the marketplace as a translator of epic puts the cultural oppositions inherent in the term curiosity into play.

Hoare's full-length sketch, curious because of its elusion of "official" authorial control, offers an "Unique of this celebrated Poet."[55] Just as Warton reproduces the handwritten note on the back of the original drawing as italicized print on the facing page, so by reproducing this image he publishes that which, like Pope himself appearing at the art auction, has been deliberately kept out of circulation, rarely seen in public and thus a sight to see.

Yet the official portrait which precedes the illicit image in Warton's edition is itself a curiosity precisely because of its fitness to circulate, its distance (as a line engraving of an oil portrait after a Roman type) from any original. As such it makes the perfect curio and its original takes its fit place, in the form from which an infinite number of copies generate, in the collection of "one of the most eminent virtuosi of his day," who had converted "his large and spacious house in Great Ormond Street . . . into a Temple of Nature, and a Repository of Time," amidst "the Busts of the great Masters, the antient Greeks and Romans."[56] The curiosity collection offers both the illusion of totality and the allure of uniqueness. At once the indecipherable mark of deformity and unmistakable sign of the coherence of literary tradition, Pope's image remains in both cases a collectable object; Pope himself both subject and object of curiosity.

Pope was well aware of the synecdochal relation between collectable images and ineffable quality when he furnished his own villa at Twickenham. He covered the walls of his house with portraits of his friends and adorned his library with busts of Homer, Newton, Spencer, Shakespeare, Milton and Dryden.[57] This forum of imaginary spectators creates a material incarnation of the benign Oedipal theater he imagines in the *Essay on Criticism:*

> *You* then whose Judgment the right Course wou'd steer
> Know well each ANCIENT'S proper *Character,*
> His *Fable, Subject, Scope* in ev'ry Page,
> *Religion, Country, Genius* of his *Age:*
> Without all these at once before your Eyes,
> *Cavil* you may, but never *Criticize.*   (118–123)

Here the critic, and as the poem goes on to demonstrate, any poet who follows Homer's poetry "Still with *It self compar'd*" (128), must collect and internalize the characters, both authorial image and text, of the ancient authorities as monitory examples. Both portrait of the author and product of his labor, such characters are to be gazed at while writing and in turn survey the writer.

All great art enters that hall of authorial portraits framed and surveyed by such a vision of limits. As Pope said in a letter about such halls of greatness, "A Man not only shews his Taste but his Virtue, in the Choice of such Ornaments . . . The History itself (if wellchosen) upon a Rich-mans Walls, is very often a better lesson than any he could teach by his Conversation."[58] In great halls and ladies' cabinets, temples of nature and repositories of time, the object, both poem and portrait, speaks for itself.

MASTERY AT FIRST SIGHT

For the eighteenth-century imitator of the classics, to put the ancients (and with them oneself) into such a museum was to cross the line not only between nature and art but also between the sexes. The imitator, who for the first time in this period was distinguished from the philologist and the scholar, civilized the classics by translating them into an elegant language accessible to proper feminine readers denied access to the originals by their lack of education in Latin and Greek.[59] Such a project thus mediates between the masculine sublime of the ancients and the beautiful refinement suitable for modern perusal and personal profit. Fidelity to the original was frowned upon not only as servile, but as impolite and ungentlemanly: the self-made classical philologist "slashing Bentley" (who in his professionalization of classical letters serves as a foil to Pope's project of making the classics widely accessible) in his uncivilized concern for textual detail, figures a kind of masculine violence not unlike that of an unrefined Homeric hero, a violence that affronts the polite reader and critic who dwell not in the study but in the drawing room of universal sentiment.

This feminization of the classics can also be played out in economic terms as feminine ornamentation of the rough, uncouth, impoverished English tongue. Empire's mirror is reversed, and the barbarousness of the ancients becomes the material of civilization. English poetry's ornamentation is the fruit of authorial plunder of classical riches: from this perspective the entrepreneurial imperialism that allows "all Arabia to breathe from yonder box" on Belinda's dressing table is also the source of both the sublime epic diction of Pope's *Iliad* and the refined and fragile neoclassical perfection of the *Rape of the Lock*'s mock epic. As Dryden argues in his "Preface to the *Aeneid*":

> If sounding Words are not of our growth and Manufacture, who shall
> hinder me to Import them from a Foreign Country? I carry not out the

Treasure of the Nation, which is never to return; but what I bring from
Italy, I spend in *England:* Here it remains, and here it circulates . . . I Trade
both with the Living and the Dead, for the enrichment of our Native
Language. We have enough in *England* to supply our necessity; but if we
will have things of Magnificence and Splendour, we must get them by
Commerce.[60]

Samuel Johnson, who said of Dryden that he saved English poetry from its
"former savageness," and that in so doing he "shewed us the true bounds of a
translator's liberty," makes the imperial analogy clear: "What was said of Rome,
adorned by Augustus, may be applied by an easy metaphor to English poetry
embellished by Dryden, 'lateritiam invenit, marmoream reliquit,' he found it
brick, and he left it marble."[61]

Bound to his classical original by a sense of republican liberty, Dryden the
cultured translator is both an imperial plunderer and the civilizer of both ancient
and modern tongues. If Dryden, Pope's most important predecessor as a classical
imitator, can be termed the Augustus of English poetry, what epithet would do
Pope justice, whose *Iliad* proved him the indisputable master and marketer of
literary imitation in the eighteenth century and, Johnson admits, "added much"
even to Dryden's achievements in heroic diction? "His version may be said to
have tuned the English tongue, for since its appearance no writer, however
deficient in other powers, has wanted melody. Such a series of lines so elabo-
rately corrected and so sweetly modulated took possession of the publick ear;
the vulgar was enamoured of the poem, and the learned wondered at the translation."[62] While Dryden's poetic achievement is described as imperial, Pope's
perfection of the heroic style is described as insinuating, a sweetness of music
which takes possession of the public ear like a siren's song. If Dryden's Virgil,
or the "nervous and manly" Homeric original which, Pope writes in his Preface
to the *Iliad,* seizes the reader with "rapture and fire," is an experience of the
masculine sublime, Pope's musicalization of epic diction, his perfect modulation
of a "language of refinement," seduces the reader with the feminine beautiful.

Yet Johnson's description of Pope's civilized imitation contains its own oppositions, both blurring and creating distinctions between the lettered and unlettered (masculine aristocratic and feminine middle class) sections of his audience: those ignorant of the original are enamoured by its beauty, those able
to appreciate the magnitude of Pope's act of translation are struck more sub-
limely with wonder. Penelope Wilson has noted the way in which the ability
to read Latin and Greek in the original becomes an increasingly nervously
defended aristocratic male province in the eighteenth century, a mark of mem-

bership in a secret male society threatened by bluestockings such as Pope's Homeric rival Madame Dacier and Johnson's friend Elizabeth Montagu.[63] In this sense, both Pope's *Iliad* and the *Rape* participate in a mass-marketing of culture that makes them curiosities; these texts are particularly threatening because of the way in which they make high culture accessible to women and other middle-class readers lacking in classical learning. The reader who capitalized most on the opportunity, or so Dennis and many other doubters of Pope's classical learning and gentlemanly status alleged, was Pope himself. With perhaps false modesty, Pope had written to Parnell in 1714 (the year of the publication of the expanded five-canto edition of the *Rape*), "You are a Generous Author, I a Hackney Scribler, You are a Grecian & bred at a University, I a poor Englishman of my own Educating."[64]

In the *Rape,* Pope both parodies and embraces the fantasy of quick visual appropriation of privileged and painstaking literary labor, a fantasy most elaborated and most sharply derided in the aptly feminine genre of the recipe, his "Receit to make an Epick Poem":

> Another Quality required is a compleat Skill in Languages. To this I answer, that it is notorious Persons of no Genius have been oftentimes great Linguists. To instance in the *Greek,* of which there are two Sorts; the Original *Greek,* and that from which our Modern Authors translate. I should be unwilling to promise Impossibilities, but modestly speaking, this may be learned in about an Hour's time with Ease. I have known one, who became a sudden Professor of *Greek,* immediately upon Application of the Left-hand Page of the *Cambridge Homer* to his Eye. It is, in these Days, with Authors as with other Men, the well bred are familiarly acquainted with them at first Sight; and as it is sufficient for a good General to have *survey'd* the Ground he is to conquer, so it is enough for a good Poet to have *seen* the Author he is to be Master of.[65]

Both the diligent Homeric translator's parody of well-bred indolence, and Johnson's description of the effects of Pope's *Iliad* on English readers, reveal the way in which this imitator's self-made and home-made authority, even when drawing on Homer's credit, guards the masculine original from, while presenting it to, a feminine audience. Such readers, as the *Rape of the Lock* makes clear, might otherwise treat Homer's rapture and fire as mere ornament, and Pope's labour, labour which curiosity transforms into display, as child's play.

Pope's *Iliad,* then, both preserves an epic tradition and improves upon it by embodying it as an object self-consciously for sale. "A sumptuous artifact of modern polite culture," Pope's translation demonstrates the way in which refinement is both a moral and a sensual quality, allowing Pope to redefine the printed image of a classic.[66] Pope's decision in the mid-1730s to print his poems in small octavo editions, including variant readings in the footnotes, Susan Staves argues, "had the effect of making his own work look like a classic text, one fit for the new national canon of English literature that was just being established."[67] The founding text of Pope's personal canon is his *Iliad,* adorned with illustrations, headpieces and tailpieces, in appropriate quarto and folio editions. When thinking of a "classic" this poet had a concrete vision of a particular form of commodity in mind (see Figure 6).

The Rape of the Lock brings Pope's relationship with the object-world of the feminine to precarious perfection. If Pope's *Iliad* translates the idea of a classic into material form, the *Rape* has been envisioned and described by critics throughout its history as an exquisite object worthy of Belinda's dressing table. "Pope distilled as much real poetry as could be got from the drawing-room world in which the art then lived—" writes Leigh Hunt, "from the flowers and luxuries of artificial life—into that exquisite little toilet-bottle of essence, *The Rape of the Lock*."[68] Addison speaks as a delighted consumer when he calls the poem "a delicious little thing."[69] Edmund Gosse, to whom Aubrey Beardsley dedicated his illustrated version of the *Rape,* exclaims that "the limited field of burlesque [was] never more picturesquely filled, than by this little masterpiece in Dresden china."[70] For Hazlitt the *Rape* goes beyond miniaturization to become a miracle of insubstantiality; the poem "is the most exquisite specimen of *fillagree* work ever invented. It is admirable in proportion as it is made of nothing . . . It is made of gauze and silver spangles."[71]

The *Rape*'s triviality is its best defense against any authority but its own beautiful surface. To attempt to speak at all seriously about this poem is to be somewhat embarrassed at making such an ado about nothing. From the perspective of this miniature epic, even the ancient poets seem overly serious. Such paragons of high literary achievement, Pope writes to Arabella Fermor, "are in one respect like many modern Ladies; Let an Action be never so trivial in it self, they always make it appear of the utmost Importance."[72] What links ancient poets to modern ladies, Pope explains, is a penchant for personification, a propensity for making persons out of things, out of almost nothing. *The Rape of the Lock* lays bare not only the machinery of epic but the insubstantiality of all creations of value.

When Pope, neither ancient poet nor modern lady but ambiguously positioned between the two, looks at heroic machinery, he sees worldly machination. The sylphs in all their diaphanous insubstantiality serve to gratify the

Figure 6.

Line engraving by George White (after Sir Godfrey Kneller), reproduced
here as a frontispiece to *Mr. Pope's Literary Correspondence for Thirty Years
. . . Volume the First* (London: E. Curll, 1735). Note that the Kneller
painting, ca. 1722, is also the source of Figure 1. Its emblematic character
is reinforced by the fact that it graces this volume of correspondence
supplied to Curll surreptitiously by Pope for unauthorized publication.
The original painting shows that the book Pope is leaning upon is
marked "HOMER."

most unmentionable of physical desires: "any Mortals may enjoy the most intimate Familiarities with these gentle Spirits, upon a Condition very easie to all true *Adepts,* an inviolate Preservation of Chastity," he archly tells Arabella.[73] Or as Ariel persuasively puts it in Belinda's dream in Canto I, "Whoever fair and chaste / Rejects Mankind, is by some Sylph embrac'd" (I, 67–68). Indeed, the sylphs gratify female desires with a process that parallels the poem's perpetually synecdochal procedures. By exchanging vulnerable flesh for airy substance, chaste maidens initiate an endless sylph-run round of exchange that puts desire unendingly on the market:

> Oft when the World imagine Women stray,
> The *Sylphs* thro' mystick Mazes guide their Way,
> Thro' all the giddy Circle they pursue,
> And old Impertinence expel by new.
> What tender Maid but must a Victim fall
> To one Man's Treat, but for another's Ball?
> When *Florio* speaks, what Virgin could withstand,
> If gentle *Damon* did not squeeze her Hand?
> With varying Vanities, from ev'ry Part,
> They shift the moving Toyshop of their Heart;
> Where Wigs with Wigs, with Sword-knots Sword-knots strive,
> Beaus banish Beaus, and Coaches Coaches drive.
> This erring Mortals Levity may call,
> Oh blind to Truth! the *Sylphs* contrive it all.   (I, 91–104)

The "truth" concealed from erring Mortals, the "mystick Maze" beneath the seemingly random strayings of ladies of fashion, is not an order or an end but rather an endless progression of substitutions that makes all objects of desire equally negligible.[74] Individual men have been reduced by the sylphs' and the poet's synecdochal strategies to identical wigs and swordknots, and the battle they fight within the heart's "moving Toyshop" prefigures the epic card game of Canto III and the heroic clash of actual beaus and nymphs in Canto V.[75] But the poem's own mystic maze makes it impossible to use the word "actual" seriously, or to distinguish between playing cards and persons, between the "moving Toyshop" within and that without. The human persons, as Pope observed to Arabella, are indeed as fictitious as the airy ones.

The power of the sylphs, then, is identical to that of the *Rape* itself: the power of levelling distinctions, of infinite exchange, envisioned as miniaturization. For adherents to epic's proper weight and scale, such as the irritable John Dennis, the miniaturization of Pope himself that inevitably results is dismissive:

The *Machines* that appear in this Poem are infinitely less considerable than the *human Persons,* which is without Precedent. Nothing can be so contemptible as the *Persons,* or so foolish as the *Understandings* of these *Hobgoblins* . . . these *diminutive Beings* of the intellectual World, may be said to be the *Measure* of Mr. *Pope's Capacity* and *Elevation* of Genius. They are, indeed, Beings so *diminutive,* that they bear the same Proportion to the rest of the intellectual, that Eels in Vinegar do to the rest of the material World. The latter are only to be seen thro' *Microscopes,* and the former only thro' the false Optics of a *Rosycrucian* Understanding.[76]

As is so often the case, Dennis gets the point by missing it; in the inverted value system of the *Rape,* machines are more divine the less considerable they become. By comparing the intellectual to the material world, Dennis shows himself to be inadvertently influenced, much as Hazlitt was when he looked at the wrong end of Pope's microscope, by the rhetorical force of figuring great things by small. Seduced by that force in the same way that Hazlitt was repelled, Leigh Hunt compares Pope favorably to the more "masculine" genius of Dryden:

Pope . . . had more delicacy and fancy . . . and was less confined to the region of matter of fact. Dryden never soared above earth, however nobly he walked it. The little fragile creature had wings; and he could expand them at will, and ascend, as if to no great imaginative height, yet to charming fairy circles just above those of the world about him, disclosing enchanting visions at the top of drawing rooms and enabling us to see the spirits that wait on coffee-cups and hoop-petticoats.[77]

And in an uncanny presaging of his transformation into airy substance, in a letter to Caryll, to whom the *Rape* is also dedicated, Pope announces himself a fit opponent for Homer:

I must confess the Greek fortification does not appear so formidable as it did, upon a nearer approach; and I am almost apt to flatter myself, that Homer secretly seems inclined to correspond with me, in letting me into a good part of his designs. There are, indeed, a sort of underli[n]ing auxiliars to the difficulty of the work, called commentators and criticks, who would frighten many people by their number and bulk. These lie entrenched in the ditches, and are secure only in the dirt they have heaped about 'em with great pains in the collecting it. But I think we have found a method of coming at the main works by a more speedy and gallant way than by mining under ground; that is, by using the poetical engines, wings, and flying thither over their heads.[78]

The original, like the reluctant heroine of a novel of seduction, is secretly inclined to correspond with a poet whose singular lack of substance charms, while pedantic critics "frighten . . . by their number and bulk." Whether figured as fun-house view at the wrong end of a telescope, the absurdity of eels in vinegar under a microscope, or the magic wand of a Pope-turned-sylph, the power of miniaturization set into motion by such "poetical engines" brings all persons, no matter how heroic their aspirations, and all personifications, no matter how divine their origin, down to size and into circulation.

EPIC ADORNMENTS

Such diminishment achieves its final apotheosis when the *Rape* becomes a book. While the *Iliad* looks like a proper "classic," the *Rape* shows an acute consciousness of itself as miniature object aspiring to, mimicking, and undermining such official entries into print. The published *Rape,* beautified and feminized by print, embodies Pope's entry into the marketplace as "original" mock-epic poet. *The Rape of the Lock* was one of only twelve out of 2,000 published poems to be illustrated between 1704 and 1724, and was itself adorned like Belinda, "the first octavo book of English verse to be decorated with engraved headpieces, a tailpiece, and an ornamental initial letter, decorations that had previously been reserved mainly for stately folios."[79] In 1897, its most famous illustrator, Aubrey Beardsley, designed "a tiny pocket edition, for which my pictures are being reduced to well-nigh postage stamps . . . 'Twill be a charmette."[80] Bearing the attribution "embroidered by Aubrey Beardsley," these 5.5-by-4-inch books Beardsley affectionately termed "Rapelets," and scholars call, perhaps with an unconscious echo of the *Rape*'s luxurious word-play, a bijou edition. Beardsley's sympathetic reading creates a cover which, in keeping with the poem's conflation of inside and outside, reveals as much as the book's contents. His "cloth-binding is striking for its . . . elegant, economical design. The single motif that is repeated and joined by an undulating line is richly ambiguous: a floral form or a grinning man's head or a nameless erotic configuration."[81] This visual design replicates the poem's verbal ambiguity, an indeterminacy of reference one critic calls "the perverted world inside the covers."[82]

Such slippage between verbal and visual excess signals the way in which much of the criticism of *The Rape of the Lock* either disavows or disapproves of the poem's luxury; a word which bears the double meaning of over-indulgence in material possessions and excessive desire for the flesh. As Geoffrey Tillotson suggestively puts it, "because of the very perfection of the surface of the poem, it is possible to read *The Rape* . . . without realizing that below the exquisite scintillation an ingenious obscenity is sometimes curling and uncurling itself."[83] This strange intermingling of surface and depth which Tillotson terms "the vertical variety of Pope's verse," makes it possible for a Swiss publisher in 1798 to praise *The Rape* as "free from coarseness, and ribaldry, which are too often mistaken for wit," and for it to have entirely escaped censorship in the Victorian era.[84] Taking Tillotson's spatial metaphor to dizzying heights, James Grantham Turner observes, "One source of the vertiginous pleasure of *The Rape of the Lock* is the way that a single word can serve as the pivot of the whole interpretation, the hinge between the most polite and the most scandalous meaning."[85] This sense of free-floating signification, which makes for prurient double meanings and the monstrous confusion of physical forms with figures of speech, is typical of the *Rape*'s poetics.[86] In effect, each moment of reading *The Rape,* each turn of its wit, offers the opportunity for either radical disorientation (the linking of "the most polite" with "the most scandalous") or for comfortable self-delusion.

To open this little book, such critical uneasiness implies, is to risk a look beneath Belinda's skirt. No matter how seemingly impermeable the poem's glittering surface, it is always forcing its reader to acknowledge the body below it. If serious epic is supposed to go beyond surface, if meaning is supposed to outlast the flesh, the paradoxes of the *Rape* serve only to reveal that there is nothing beneath, or outside, the hoop's "wide Circumference," that narrow and retired circle which so distorts standard proportion. Beardsley's bijou edition, writes Peter Conrad in terms and tone that are by this point familiar, "adapts the book to the fetishistic littleness of the poem, in which the adult responsibilities of existence, love, worship, executed wretches and regal councils, shrink into inconsequence, while trivia correspondingly dilate into threatening immensity."[87] For the male reader, this tiny jewel of a book, like the woman's part it plays upon (French slang bijou)—a fetishistic substitute for the chaos it represents—has frighteningly epic dimensions. To go beneath the exquisite world of the object is to confront the real world of the female body. Like Belinda choosing between short-lived beauty and marital obscurity, the reader of the *Rape* cannot escape the limits of the material.[88]

No poet knows the magnitude of such gendered inversions of scale better than Pope, whose deformity gives him an intimate acquaintance with little things. In a poem (after a rondeau by Voiture) enclosed in a letter to a male friend in 1710, the poet makes libertine capital out of sexual rejection on the basis of such feminine transformations:

> You know where you did despise
> (T'other day) my little eyes,
> Little legs, and little thighs,
> And some things of little size,
>   You know where.
>
> You, 'tis true, have fine black eyes,
> Taper legs, and tempting thighs,
> Yet what more than all we prize
> Is a thing of little size,
>   You know where.[89]

In his prurient pointing at unnameable places where size and value undergo radical transformation, in his aggressive alliance of his own impotence with the thing of little size that gives women value, Pope dismisses the woman he addresses by allying himself with her. As in his dedicatory epistle to Arabella Fermor in his revised edition of the *Rape,* the joke is at both the woman's and the poet's expenses, and to both their advantages, depending upon which end of the telescope one looks through. Regardless, the male poet, by controlling the telescope, allows himself the additional liberty of spectatorship. His vision grants the invisibility of the voyeur, hers only shame.

FRAIL CHINA

Both as a successful translator of the *Iliad* appealing to a female audience, and composer of *The Rape of the Lock,* Pope creates a fragile balance between heroic literary tradition and literary marketplace, a balance which demands prodigious feats of readerly vision. For Pope leaves his mark on epic—and in the process makes his fortune—by revising this monumental genre as collectable object. As a curiosity himself, the "ladies' plaything" guarantees himself authority as classical poet in print and on the market, an authority which, like an eighteenth-century lady's reputation, is as fragile as china.

If there is an object which can fairly substitute for the parade of ornaments that makes up the *Rape,* it must be made of china. China epitomizes the chain of substitutions with which the poem makes meaning: female virtue, defined by a cultural synecdoche as chastity, becomes synonymous with a fragile commodity, whose value rests in its frangibility. Both object of international trade and of excessive feminine desire, the figure of china combines the double meanings of woman's "curiosity" that make her both active agent, excessively desiring to know and to consume, and vulnerable object on the marriage market.[90]

73

Through the figure of china uneasiness about feminine forms of desire is rendered material: passive objects take on curious forms of uncanny agency in both the *Rape* itself and the prose written about it.[91] Thus china, in Aubrey Williams' classic account, not only exists in order to be, but in fact asks to be, broken. Pope's line, "Whether the Nymph should break Diana's Law / Or Some frail China Jar receive a flaw," comes to posit an "or" where readers assume an "and." The physicality of the verb "Break" is governed by an abstraction, while the possibility of real violence done to a real female body is relegated to the passivity of "receive" and the impersonality of a luxury object. The question of agency in Belinda's rape thus becomes disturbingly blurred. Williams continues, "There is a hint of mortality inherent in all the imagery which likens women to something so frangible as fine glass or China: existing in a state of tremulous instability and inconstancy, the vessels seem to lean themselves towards disaster. Made of the dust and clay of the earth, they seem destined for a shocking reversion to 'glittring Dust and painted Fragments.' "[92] The insubstantiality of this version of female desire deprives human beings (both men and women) of responsibility or agency and gives objects a life of their own. As Cleanth Brooks notes, the way in which Pope deals with Belinda's rape—and its origins in Arabella Fermor's loss—stands in all its ambivalence for the miniaturization process of the poem as a whole:

> the detachment, the amused patronage, the note of aloof and impartial judgment—all demand that the incident be viewed with a large measure of aesthetic distance. Whatever incidental fun Pope may have had with the epic conventions, his choice of the mock epic fits beautifully his general problem of scaling down the rape to its proper insignificance. The scene is reduced, and the characters become small and manageable figures whose actions can always be plotted against a larger background.[93]

The opacity of china, like the *Rape*'s smooth surface, enables the figuring of such miniature plots against the potentially threatening backgrounds of epic violence.

MOVING TOYSHOPS

If to read Pope is to confront the necessity of reading for the form, a form brought into sharp relief by the authorial deformity which exceeds and defines it, to read *The Rape of the Lock* in the mirror of Pope's serious heroic poetry is to read the commodity form—that vision of abstract and equivalent exchange by which discrepancies of power are both produced and concealed—as a phenomenon which "*is not* thought, but . . . has the *form* of thought."[94] Walter Benjamin's description of Baudelaire's brand of allegory is relevant to Pope's achievement in the *Rape*: "In the allegorical . . . the commodity attempts to look itself in the face . . . It was Baudelaire's endeavor to make the aura which is peculiar to the commodity appear. In a heroic way he sought to humanize *(humanisieren)* the commodity. His attempt had its equivalent in the simultaneous attempt of the bourgeoisie to personify the commodity *(vermenschlichen):* to give the commodity, like a person, housing."[95] To take pleasure in the *Rape* is to delight in looking the commodity in the face and seeing one's own reflection. To personify the commodity, to make it human and to give it a home, is to *own* it as the material fabric, the mechanical movement, from which meaning and beauty are made and which exceeds individual control. In the cultural context of the emergence of capitalism which the *Rape* celebrates and displays as miniature, Marx's initial remarks on commodity fetishism seem less whimsical and more descriptive:

> A commodity appears, at first sight, a very trivial thing, and easily understood. Its analysis shows that it is, in reality, a very queer thing, abounding in metaphysical subtleties and theological niceties . . . The form of wood, for instance, is altered, by making a table out of it. Yet, for all that, the table continues to be that common, every-day thing, wood. But, so soon as it steps forth as a commodity, it is changed into something transcendent. It not only stands with its feet on the ground, but, in relation to all other commodities, it stands on its head, and evolves out of its wooden brain grotesque ideas, far more wonderful than "table-turning" ever was.[96]

The Rape of the Lock could be said to illustrate what happens when commodities (among them coquettes) get ideas into their brains, ideas as "wonderful" as the immortality and the universality that the miniature embodies and which Clarissa's sensible but ineffective speech on the mortality of the body, however much it is the moral of the poem, futilely attempts to dispel from Belinda's pretty head. As Susan Stewart observes, and as the moving toyshop of female desire displayed in the *Rape* shows, the miniature "marks the pure body, the inorganic body of the machine and its *repetition* of a death that is thereby not a death."[97] Belinda's lock, severed "from the fair head, forever and forever," because it is cut off from the natural, has the power to move eternally.

In the mock-epic underworld of the Cave of Spleen, Pope brings some grotesque forms of such ideas to life. Umbriel's descent to the Cave of Spleen provides just such a curious vision:

Unnumber'd Throngs on ev'ry side are seen
Of Bodies chang'd to various forms by *Spleen.*
Here living *Teapots* stand, one Arm held out,
One bent; the Handle this, and that the Spout:
A Pipkin there like *Homer's Tripod* walks;
Here sighs a Jar, and there a Goose-pye talks;
Men prove with Child, as pow'rful Fancy works,
And Maids turn'd Bottels, call aloud for Corks.   (IV, 47–54)

These "hysteric hallucinations" take the poem's artifice to its natural conclusion. In a moving toyshop where beaus are reduced to swordknots, it makes sense that teapots should live or goosepyes talk. Perhaps more wonderful is that Pope drew not only from the Countess of Winchelsea's "Ode to Spleen" and Dryden's translation of Ovid's *Metamorphoses* ("Of Bodies chang'd to various Forms I sing"), but from actual medical histories of people of quality for this fashionable panoply of humanity objectified. In a note on the talking goosepye he mentions that "a Lady of real distinction imagined herself in this condition," and the Twickenham editors add that Sir Richard Blackmore, in his 1725 *Treatise on the Spleen and Vapours,* notes that one melancholic "has believed himself to be a Millet-Seed, another a Goose, or a Goose-Pye," in addition to giving a historical identity to the unfortunate pregnant man.[98] As one scholar elaborating the contemporary context of spleen observes, by making Belinda susceptible to the malady Pope provides her, aptly enough, "with a fashionable adornment to her personality."[99] What he neglects to mention is that her personality never consisted of anything but glorious adornment.

The Cave of Spleen, fittingly enough, poses problems of ambiguity for illustrators which Pope himself confronted heroically in his Homeric imitations: over the course of the poem's career (and from 1714 it appeared with illustrations), artists were consistently uncertain about whether pain and languor in the Cave of Spleen were to be visualized as simple afflictions or allegorical personifications.[100] The *Rape's* illustrations continue the chain of ambiguous agency which Pope's heroic diction in the *Iliad* began.

No illustrator was more sensitive to the particular importance of illustrations to the *Rape* than Aubrey Beardsley. In his depiction of the *Cave of Spleen,* Pope himself, turbanned as he is in his official *Iliad* portrait, peers forth wearily from the center (see Figure 7). An equally knowing comment on the poem's form is a turbanned African boy who appears in several of Beardsley's drawing-room scenes (see Figure 8), always looking straight at the viewer, apart from the characters caught up in the action. What he asks the viewer to recognize is his invisibility. Within the perfect form of the poem itself, objects can be personified, but the objectification of actual persons is a material fact which can only be acknowledged through omission. The boy's presence within and without the frame, like Pope's deformity, enables vision while itself disappearing from view.

It also makes sense in an epic which concerns the war between the sexes and the gendered glories of conquest and consumption that the ambiguous status of persons and things should translate into an ambiguity of gender and reproduction, i.e., "Men prove with Child." The "pow'rful female Fancy" let loose in the Cave of Spleen, in an anxiety-producing parody of the author's own imaginative devices, envisions male authorship as passive and feminine, and female desire, though inevitably hampered by anatomy and morality, as active: "Maids turn'd Bottels, call aloud for Corks." Turning ancient poets into modern ladies, shields into skirts, scepters to locks, Pope's transformational tricks in the Rape almost always revolve around and figure themselves through gender. Belinda's guardian sylph Ariel, "a youth more glittering than a Birth-night Beau," was once "inclos'd in Woman's beauteous Mold" (I, 48). And it is the Baron who, in a reversal of Ovid's story of Nisus and his transgressive daughter Scylla, castrates Belinda of her phallic lock (and he reinforces its phallic status when he swears by it as Achilles does by his scepter) with his curiously androgynous "two-edg'd Weapon" spread wide, just as in the card game his Queen of Swords invades Belinda's King of Clubs who is described as having "Giant Limbs in State unwieldy spread."[101]

How, then, does this epic allow the commodity to look itself in the face? For all of its satire on materialism, *The Rape of the Lock* ultimately upholds the moral that women and authors are the consumer's rightful property. Pope, unlike Belinda, both evades and embraces his own feminization by compromising heroic absolutes. He wields his own two-edged weapon in order to put the past on display. The imitator's traffic between the faithful translation of the *Iliad* and the *Rape*'s libertine rendition of epic creates a disconcerting zeugma that levels distinctions between ancient and modern, original and imitation. A good example, a kind of mini-allegory if you will, is the oath sworn by the Baron on Belinda's lock in Canto IV:

> But by this Lock, this sacred Lock I swear,
> (Which never more shall join its parted Hair,
> Which never more its Honours shall renew
> Clipt from the lovely Head where late it grew)
> That while my Nostrils draw the vital air,

Figure 7.

The Cave of Spleen. *The Rape of the Lock, an Heroi-comical Poem in Five Cantos,
Written by Alexander Pope, Embroidered by Aubrey Beardsley*
(London: L. Smithers, 1896).

Figure 8.

The African page. *The Rape of the Lock, an Heroi-comical Poem in Five Cantos, Written by Alexander Pope, Embroidered by Aubrey Beardsley* (London: L. Smithers, 1896).

> This Hand, which won it, shall for ever wear.
> He spoke, and speaking, in proud Triumph spread
> The long-contended Honours of her Head.   (IV, 133–140)

This oath parodies that of Achilles in Book I of the *Iliad* in which he abjures
Agamemnon's authority by depriving the symbol of that authority of its power.
The translation, of course, is Pope's:

> Now by this sacred sceptre, hear me swear,
> Which never more shall Leaves or Blossoms bear,
> Which sever'd from the Trunk (as I from thee)
> On the bare Mountains left its Parent Tree;
> This Sceptre, form'd by temper'd Steel to prove
> An Ensign of the Delegates of *Jove*,
> From whom the Pow'r of Laws and Justice springs.   (I, 309–315)

The nearest "original" of Pope's translation, and also of Pope's parody in the
Rape, is not Homer's Greek but Dryden's translation of the *Aeneid.* Virgil uses
the Homeric subtext of this oath to foreshadow disaster for the oath of peace,
soon to be broken, that King Latinus swears to Aeneas in Book XII:

> Ev'n as this Royal Scepter, (for he bore
> A Scepter in his Hand) shall never more
> Shoot out in Branches, or renew the Birth;
> (An Orphan now, cut from the Mother Earth
> By the keen Axe, dishonour'd of its Hair,
> And cas'd in Brass, for *Latian* Kings to bear.)   (XII, 310–316)

Dryden's translation (and the Latin original) make explicit the gender of the
birth imagery which Homer's Greek and Pope's revisions elide. Dryden emphasizes the sterility of this symbol of male authority by translating "caret ma-
tre" ("lacking its mother") as "shall never more renew the birth . . . an orphan
now, cut from the mother earth," as if the heroic translator is mourning the fate
of his own attempt at epic, cut off at once from the paternal tree of heroic
tradition and the mother earth of original composition.

Pope's debt to Dryden in the passage from the *Rape* becomes explicit when
we see how Dryden expands upon a hint of Virgil's ("coma" in Latin means
both hair and foliage) in a lofty epic periphrasis. Ironically, Dryden's diction
here enacts the process it describes and deplores; it encases its "original" in a
language which bespeaks the impossibility of originality. Such artificial diction
objectifies itself, displays its own disjuncture from what it describes. Homer's

simplicity (though Achilles' oath itself contains the seeds of self-reflexivity), and simple trees, are left far behind.

And it is precisely this self-enclosed artifice that Pope celebrates in both the Baron's oath and *The Rape of the Lock*. The royal scepter emptied of its authority by language is restored to a different kind of power when literalized as Belinda's lock. Pope triumphs over the epic tradition by outdoing epic diction at its own game: rather than lament what language has killed by objectification, Pope and the Baron boast of the conquest and creation of ornament. The Baron's repeated description of Belinda's hair as honors reminds us that she has indeed been dishonored of her hair, but the leap to the literal spreads like contagion to the metaphorical: the honors of her head stand synecdochally for an honor much more precious. In the *Rape of the Lock*'s terms, however, this moral honor is as easily stained as new brocade, as much a matter of surface as Belinda's curls; the honor of heroes and the honor of ladies are both reduced to the underside of a sexual pun. We move from Belinda's lock making its "Progress thro' the Skies" to "hairs less in sight, or any hairs but these."

"Who the Devil, besides this Bard, ever made a Wonder of it?" asked an aggravated John Dennis of *The Rape of the Lock*. "What! before *Troy* town, and triumphal Arches were built, was the cutting off a Lock of Hair a *miraculous* thing?"[102] The extraordinary thing about Pope's poetic answer is that, although both Callimachus and Catullus provide him with literary precedents for the apotheosis (and in their case the actual subjectivity) of a mere lock of hair, *The Rape of the Lock* makes a wonder uniquely suited to its cultural moment. In the *Rape* Pope achieves a trivial autonomy by celebrating display. Like the Baron suggestively spreading the long contended honors of Belinda's head in proud triumph and prurient provocation, Pope parades his poem before his readers, challenging them to compromise an authority which has already trivialized itself. The *Rape*'s allusions to serious epic constantly remind us of the author's own literary exchange between the authentic and the artificial. The *Iliad*'s scapegrace double, the *Rape* puts the integrity of the heroic poem—and of the heroic poet—into question by revealing and revelling in poetry's debt to the marketplace. In a world in which counsel and tea, honor and brocade, the scepters of kings and the locks of ladies are interchangeable, perhaps we can ultimately only be dazzled by the power of exchange itself to create and destroy value. "One is left," one smitten critic writes, "looking at the face of the poem as at Belinda's."[103] Confronted with such a mirror, Hazlitt observes with awe, "you hardly know whether to laugh or weep. It is the triumph of insignificance, the apotheosis of foppery and folly. It is the perfection of the mock-heroic!"[104] In exposing the complicity of epic and mock-epic, of heroic honor and female ornament, Pope's modern parody—like the triumphant Baron staking the permanence of his "Honour, Name, and Praise" on the small pillow, the coach and six, the popularity of Manley's *Atalantis* and the female reading public such a popularity implies—guarantees ancient authenticity an unassailably fragile survival.

3

Twickenham

and the

Landscape

of True Character

Words, when well chosen, have so great a Force in
them, that a Description often gives us more lively
Ideas than the Sight of Things themselves . . . In this
Case the Poet seems to get the better of Nature.

Joseph Addison, *Spectator* 416

SINGULARITY AND THE MOBILITY OF PROPERTY

The fragile artifice of the *Rape of the Lock* opposes what it excludes, in the form of disease, death, and grey hairs, as inexorable nature.[1] But when the poet who celebrates artifice in mock-epic form turns to nature itself in his garden, he abandons neither his love of the curious object nor his desire for immortality. Rather, he gives curiosity a natural landscape.

In the *Rape,* Pope had celebrated the playful art of the commodity: the pleasures and beauties of potential ownership and free-floating exchange that monumentalize the most trivial of feminine ornaments. Enacting and exposing the power of art to create and appropriate objects, the *Rape* thereby unmoored stable notions of nature, originality and identity. Pope's miniature epic distorted the trivial things on which his culture's loftiest notions of meaning and human agency were based. The poem thus enabled its poet to enter the literary marketplace with irony's double-edged protection: the *Rape*'s miniature world afforded both author and viewer a complicit, precarious and delighted distance from the objects which they own and are.[2]

In a parallel founding gesture, when Achilles opts out of the Trojan War, he swears an oath which dismantles the meaning of that symbol of royal authority, King Agamemnon's scepter. His words expose the scepter's metaphor, its meaning, as arbitrary metonymy, the conclusion to a particular narrative and the product of art's violence. The scepter is a dead thing, cut off from its natural origins, stripped of bark and leaves and covered with regal gold; but when compared to the sterile remnant it covers, gold is also exposed as the haphazard result of an equally violent disruption of nature's wholeness, namely mining. To assign Agamemnon's scepter value, then, is no more absurd than for Belinda to fetishize her lock, "clipt from the lovely head on which it grew." In both cases, the transparency of form, the illusion of timeless originality, is dependent on time-bound alienability and artifice; the "rape" of Belinda's lock displays the "mere" materiality of the most powerful of symbols of male authority. With such display comes the knowledge of an art—here reduced to the elemental "Steel" which transforms branch into scepter and Belinda's lock into trophy. Formed into weapons, it levels monuments and empires; formed into gardening shears, it makes topiary sculpture. Such art destroys as it creates. Troy falls, Belinda's lock ascends to heaven, gardens fade with the seasons and disappear with time: every eternity receives its date, every monument has its beginning and end in the particulars of art and ornament.

While *Windsor Forest* expands a garden to encompass an English empire, Pope's garden at Twickenham creates a counter-empire within the confines of individuality and with the seemingly stable material of land. The idea for such a garden existed in personal fantasy and classical precedent long before its realization at Twickenham as Pope's "personal mythopoeia"[3] in the 1720s, and Pope continually revised it, just as he did his literary work, throughout his life. Gardens and print offered the poet contested and complementary forums for self-expression and self-improvement; a perfect edition of his works and a finished garden were elusive goals that when attained left him nothing to do but die: "my Garden like my Life," he wrote in a letter, "seems to me every *Year* to want Correction & require alteration."[4] This chapter examines the relation of print to landscape: Pope's poetry (most particularly his *Moral Essays*, first published as a unit in the 1735 edition of Pope's *Works*),[5] provides the basis for my reading of the embodiment of his singular aesthetic, his idea of true character, in nature both human and ideal. The five rented acres at Twickenham (anti-Catholic legislation made it illegal for the poet to own land, a prohibition he turned to his own advantage)[6] allowed Pope to conceive of images of retirement (figured in both gardens and poems) that constructed both an invisible cultural authority and a transparent power over nature, a transparency the poet mars with the artful aberration of his grotto. By contrast the portraits of human nature in print in the *Moral Essays* (originally titled *Of the Use of Things*[7]), by framing character in relation to the objects that define it, render such clarity—

in the form of a coherent ruling passion—impossible; "truth" in print resides in artificial particulars, and in the poet's labor.

In both the *Moral Essays* and his landscaping endeavors, the ambiguities of art and nature, imitation and originality, ornament and monument raised by *The Rape of the Lock* are given new form in an ethics and an aesthetic of ownership. In his creation of a couplet of nature and art in his garden, the poet's techniques—miniaturization and *trompe l'oeil*—remain the same, but the field of their significance shifts from the *Rape's* trivialized world of feminine exchange to a fantasy of masculine self-sufficiency defined against feminine nature and mobile property. The process by which woman becomes the visible embodiment of the market's fantastic substitutions is thereby reversed.[8] In the garden and the grotto, femininity in all its natural aberration and social appropriability becomes the background against which masculine integrity makes itself visible.

Property in Pope's terms destabilizes identity and agency, reducing its owners to the status of women, having "no Characters at all" (*Epistle to a Lady*, 2). Possession is inherently unstable: to own objects is to be potentially owned. If in *The Rape of the Lock* femininity is celebrated as marketable, in the *Moral Essays* and the Horatian poems, femininity becomes "matter too soft a lasting mark to bear" (*Epistle to a Lady*, 3). The "mark" of character, like the inalienable sign of deformity, is defined against the background of the unpredictable cycle of exchange inaugurated by the possession of property, a cycle which reveals the characterlessness of both owner and owned. Twickenham defines true character by incorporating within its bounds that which, figured as femininity, challenges the possibility of such an ideal.

Self Cultivation

At age twelve Pope composed what his biographer Owen Ruffhead termed "the first fruit . . . of his poetical genius,"[9] the "Ode on Solitude": an "Horatian poem without an original" in which the poet "seems to pass directly from infancy to middle age or its literary equivalent."[10] The poem begins with a vision of an independence contained by securely possessed patrimony.

> Happy the man, whose wish and care
> A few paternal acres bound,
> Content to breathe his native air,
> In his own ground.

He concludes with a fantasy of retirement and anonymity:

Thus let me live, unseen, unknown;
Thus unlamented let me dye;
Steal from the world, and not a stone
Tell where I lye.[11]

On such fantasies of invisibility is Pope's fame based. Maynard Mack refers to this poem as "an Augustan landmark" in the "tradition of the *beatus vir* [blessed man]," a tradition which flowers in Pope's hands in the 1730s into "a composite of Roman outlines shaped to English seventeenth-century and Augustan circumstances, or . . . a collecting of traditional *topoi* into something like an identifiable physical presence by the voice of a speaker who is at once Pope of Twickenham and a universal type."[12] Raymond Williams sees the "Ode" as translating a classical utopian myth of Edenic nature into a contemporary social context (that of the independent freeholder), resulting in a "description and thence an idealization of actual English country life and its social and economic relations."[13] Both critics detect a variable blend of inheritance and originality. Even at age twelve Pope offers in this small poem paradoxes of ownership and independence. The "identifiable physical presence" formed by such acts of imitation in poetry and landscape figures both a self-sufficiency free of property, and a uniquely visible masculinity.

Gardening was the highest form of self-fashioning for Pope. When the poet tired of literary labors, and when profits from the Homer translation afforded him the luxury of renting five acres and a house at Twickenham in 1718, he worked on his small garden with such success that he became one of the most important figures in English landscaping history. Just as literary critics see Pope either as closing a Renaissance literary tradition or gesturing toward a Romantic one, so gardening historians debate whether Pope was one of the final inheritors of the Italian neoclassical gardening tradition or a founder of the national movement toward picturesque gardens: in either case the figure of Pope serves as a mark of transition.[14]

In both his poetry and his landscaping, Pope puts his signature to a long tradition of images of Paradise before the Fall. Such fantasies emphasize the mythic past over the present or future.[15] What Raymond Williams says of the Renaissance inheritance of the classical tradition of retirement is equally true of gardens as of poems: "the living tensions are excised, until there is nothing countervailing, and selected images stand as themselves: not in a living but in an enamelled world."[16]

"Enamelled," an adjective applied to the efforts of the miniature painter, and with which Pope describes the "ground" of *Windsor Forest,* describes a seamless surface which his own gardening efforts will both copy and crack. Just as the poet of retirement creates an illusion of past idyllic independence, so the English gardener envisions an ideal of Roman country life which is forever lost to his eye, and therefore all the easier to imagine. The neoclassical poetics of retirement that idealizes the garden as the site of moral integrity must vilify the city as the visible source of corruption. Such an opposition ignores the socio-economic links between the city and the country.[17] The disappearance of these links enables belief in a clear distinction between alienable and inalienable property, between the mobility of trade and the fixity of land.[18]

These distinctions are dissolved by Pope's singular imagination. Like the commodities that rise of their own free will from the corners of the world to clothe Addison's lady of fashion in *Spectator* 69, land in Pope's poetry has a mysterious life of its own. In Pope's poetry of retirement, land is magically animated by the invisibility of the systems which give it value. Precisely because the poet rents but neither owns, inherits, nor speculates, he is able to take true possession of an interior property in himself, a property he proudly marks with the sign of his literary labor.

In his remarks to Spence on gardening and his *Epistle to Burlington,* Pope calls landscape's animating force "the genius of the place." While he can be understood to mean particular character, genius can also signify guardian spirit, and thus a kind of eighteenth-century personification, animating the estate by natural and singular art.[19] This force

> Calls in the Country, catches opening glades,
> Joins willing woods, and varies shades from shade,
> Now breaks, or now directs, th' intending Lines;
> Paints as you plant, and, as you work, designs. (62–64)

Such genius reinforces the distinction between work, and design, aligning invisible ideas with the highest natural art. As Shaftesbury's enthusiast Theocles exclaims in the dialog *The Moralists* (1709): "Your *Genius,* the *Genius of the Place,* and the GREAT GENIUS have at last prevail'd. I shall no longer resist the Passion growing in me for Things of a *natural* kind; where neither *Art,* nor the *Conceit* or *Caprice* of Man has spoil'd their *genuine Order,* by breaking in upon that *primitive State.*"[20] Theocles exults at the sight of the genuine order that links man to nature and thus to God, which emerges in the transporting effects of genius unmediated by art. Projected onto an idealized and original past, "genius" gives a natural form to the mechanical energy which animates the commodity.

Pope boasted to Spence of having expressed all the rules of gardening "in two verses (after my manner, in a very little compass), which are in imitation of Horace's *Omne tulit punctum.*"[21] "He gains all points, who pleasingly confounds, / Surprizes, varies, and conceals the Bounds" (*Epistle to Burlington,* 55–56). The garden, imitating the method of the couplet, in very little compass provides the imagination with seemingly endless entertainment. The gardener, he who gains all points, plays an invisible game with the spectator, he who enjoys the variety which a walk through the landscape offers. This game takes place through the garden's "moving pictures"—its changing seasons—and takes on different meanings from different perspectives and in different moods. Both the gardener and the spectator have the power to transform the landscape.

Such a game, as the importance Pope placed on his "gardening poem" in his "Opus Magnum" indicates,[22] has both philosophical and psychological dimensions. Such orderly variety, artful chaos, *imitatio ruris,* is nature designed for human play, landscape as a medium for human nature. He gains all points who creates a garden as individual as a person, a person who possesses the landed stability necessary for true character. Whether the politics of such an emphasis on variety and freedom in design involve a Whiggish embrace of liberty, or, as is more likely in Pope's case, an Opposition allegiance to Augustan georgic and Royalist ideals, the garden is above all a crucible for masculine individuality.[23] As Pope's gardening and literary labors evolve over the course of his career, he figures himself as such a singular object in both landscape and text.

POPE IN MINIATURE

A Catholic forbidden by law from owning land, and a cultural entrepreneur instrumental in the legal definition of literary property,[24] Pope was deeply attracted to the Augustan ideological equation of the ownership of an estate with the moral stewardship of a nation. On the model of such near-divine power, the poet's invisible commands could bid, as in *Epistle to Burlington,* a great lord to build not only a Palladian mansion but also an English empire. Yet, as we will see, the power of ownership Pope celebrates in *To Burlington* takes on an unsettling variability in poems such as *To Bathurst* and *Satire II, ii,* a variability which that same power of invisible direction enables. When Pope champions the intellectual labor that entitles him to property in his texts themselves, such invisibility becomes problematic.

Pope's contemporary James Thomson, in the grand paean to British public works that concludes his poem *Liberty* (1735–36), alludes to the Twickenham estate as "Pope in miniature."[25] Twickenham owes its microcosmic quality not only to literary models of retirement but also to the Italian tradition of the garden as a "theatrum mundi," in which often-mechanized statues performed mini-dramas and the spatial relations between spectator and spectacle were in continual flux.[26]

The optimal ornamentation of a comparatively small amount of space was another tenet of the Italian gardening tradition that influenced Pope's work at Twickenham.[27] In a spatial equivalent of the *Rape*'s neat encompassing of the vast epic tradition, the neoclassical gardener could make a modest plot appear a world of "moving pictures," "a series of multiple oblique views that were meant to be experienced while one walked through it"[28] by ingenious implementation of curving paths and effects of perspective. As visitors to Twickenham testified, Pope was a master at such tricks of perspective, reminiscent of Palladian theater design.[29] "You may distance things by darkening them and by narrowing the plantation more and more toward the end," he advises Spence in a series of remarks on illusionistic manipulation of lights and shades. The best investment for such a garden was in what Pope avowed encompassed "all the beauties of gardening," namely variety.[30] This type of garden becomes an "album and commonplace book, philosophical *vademecum* and *memento mori*"[31] displaying landscape equivalents of history paintings,[32] a panorama of scenes for distanced contemplation. The viewer is given a perspective that takes in empires past and present, and makes him master of all he surveys. Pope invites Bishop Atterbury to such a prospect when he writes:

> I hope the advance of the fine season will set you upon your legs, enough to enable you to get into my garden, where I will carry you up a Mount, in a point of view to shew you the glory of my little kingdom. If you approve it, I shall be in danger to boast like Nebuchadnezzar of the things I have made, and to be turn'd to converse, not with the beasts of the field, but with the birds of the grove, which I shall take to be no great punishment. For indeed I heartily despise the ways of the world, and most of the great ones of it.[33]

Such a theatrical effect depends for its full realization on the spectator's consciousness of individual property and self-possession: "A man's house was the theatre of his self-fruition both because it was a stage for his self-knowledge and because 'to the possessors thereof [it was] an Epitome of the whole world.' "[34] This analogy worked equally well for the house's natural complement, the garden. John Barrell articulates the connection between spectatorship and suspension of disbelief that makes the world over into miniature property, and that allows Bishop Atterbury from the proper "point of view" to survey a "little kingdom":

> All nature was a garden, but only when seen from one particular 'station' or point of view . . . this practice shows how able the eighteenth-century connoisseur was to separate the impressions he received of a landscape from the reality he knew to exist. Perhaps in no other of the eighteenth-century landscape arts was the landscape kept so carefully remote from the observer, or did it depend so much on his willingness, his anxiety even, to see ideal structures in what he saw.[35]

In his expansion of Maynard Mack's work on the literary sources of Pope's villa, John Dixon Hunt compellingly characterizes Pope's landscaping efforts in relation to his poetic project not as a "straightforward translation," but rather as a process of "reduction and miniaturizing": "Pope knew at least by the 1730s that Augustan values could realistically be accommodated in contemporary England only in diminished or adjusted terms: this was as true of Horace's villa life as of Horace's poetry."[36] At Twickenham, as in the *Rape,* nostalgia for an irretrievable classical past is figured as spatial diminishment. If *The Rape of the Lock* can aptly be termed a miniature epic, Twickenham allows Pope to capture his own likeness in miniature and to mark it with his proper name.

Horace Walpole aptly called Pope's villa "that fragment of the Rock of Parnassus," and praised his "singular effort of art and taste" in making something out of almost nothing: ". . . it was a little bit of ground of five acres, enclosed with three lanes and seeing nothing. Pope had twisted and twirled and rhymed and harmonized this, till it appeared two or three sweet little lawns opening and opening beyond one another, and the whole surrounded by thick impenetrable woods." As Walpole describes it, Pope has managed to transform the limits of a modest plot into an infinite inwardness opening and opening within impenetrable bounds.[37] Pope himself proudly refers to his gardening labours in what he calls his "little Kingdom"[38] as those of a miniaturist: "I am as busy in three inches of Gardening, as any man can be in threescore acres. I fancy my self like the fellow that spent his life in cutting the twelve apostles in one cherry-stone. I have a Theatre, an Arcade, a Bowling green, a Grove, & what not? in a bitt of ground that would have been but a plate of Sallet to Nebuchadnezzar, the first day he was turn'd to graze."[39] From the perspective of Lord Bathurst, the recipient of Pope's epistle on the use of riches, whose holdings in land were massive, such diminutive proportions inspire dizzyingly Brobdignagian fantasies:

I'll cutt you off some little corner of my Park (500 or 1000 acres) which
you shall do what you will with, & I'll immediately assign over to you 3
or 4 millions of plants out of my Nursery to amuse your self with. if you
refuse coming I'll immediately send one of my wood-Carts & bring away
your whole house & Gardens, & stick it in the midst of Oakly-wood [this
was a part of Bathurst's estate] where it will never be heard off any more,
unless some of the Children find it out in Nutting-season & take possession of it thinking I have made it for them.[40]

What Bolingbroke called the "multiplied scenes of [this] little garden"[41] encompassed a panoply of neoclassical landscape features including "a grotto, three
mounts (one of these quite large), some quincunxes,[42] groves, a wilderness, an
orangery, a vineyard, a kitchen garden, a shell temple, and an obelisk [in memory of his mother]; [in addition to] his striking use of openings, walks, and
vistas, each terminating on a point of rest, supplied by urn or statue."[43] A visitor
to Twickenham in 1748 waxes poetic over the effects of "Hillocks . . . entirely
covered with Thickets of Lawrel, Bay, Holly, and many other Evergreens and
Shrubs, rising one above another in beautiful Slopes and Intermixtures, where
Nature freely lays forth the Branches, and disports uncontrol'd," the highest
mount "covered with bushes and Trees of a wilder Growth, and more confused
Order, rising as it were out of Clefts of Rocks, and Heaps of rugged and mossy
Stones; among which a narrow intricate Path leads in an irregular spiral to the
Top; where is placed a Forest Seat or Chair."[44] And Walpole describes a walk
through the garden in the melancholic mode of Pope's own description in *Eloisa
to Abelard*:

> Black Melancholy sits, and round her throws
> A death-like silence, and a dread repose:
> Her gloomy presence saddens all the scene,
> Shades ev'ry flow'r, and darkens ev'ry green,
> Deepens the murmur of the falling floods,
> And breathes a browner horror on the woods.   (165–170)

For Walpole, "the passing through the gloom from the grotto to the opening
day, the retiring and again assembling shades, the dusky groves, the larger lawn,
and the solemnity of the termination at the cypresses that lead up to his mother's
tomb," make the garden a thoroughly poetic experience.[45] Walpole reading
the garden through the heightened sensibility of its author bereaved of his
mother, Pope identifying with the love-distracted Eloisa, and Eloisa seeing
through the lens of the feminine personification of melancholy, each exemplify

the way in which the viewer's experience of the garden is mediated by a sympathetic identification coded as feminine that supplements the more distanced and abstract "meditation."

Juxtaposing artful quincunxes with unruly "wilderness," practical kitchen gardens with fantastic shell temples, Pope appropriates through diminishment the spatial grandeur of a nobleman's estate, the historical flavor of a classical Roman villa, and the picturesque effects of untamed "nature."[46] In its miniaturization of space and time, landscaping and literary traditions, Pope's garden at Twickenham epitomizes what Ronald Paulson calls that "transitional form" of "visual and verbal art," the emblem. Twickenham as emblem points away from a specific "imitated text to fidelity to 'nature' and ultimately to self-expression."[47] In this account, a walk through the garden becomes a page by page reading of nature's emblem book, a "poem manqué" or miniature epic journey.[48]

Both the couplet and the garden, as both Mack and Paulson have noted, function through principles of variety and economy given visual and verbal form as zeugma and pun.[49] When Pope praises Homer as "a skilful Improver, who places a beautiful Statue in a well-disposed Garden so as to answer several Vistas, and by that Artifice one single Figure seems multiply'd into as many Objects as there are Openings whence it may be viewed," he could be speaking of both his own improvements, in landscape and in print, of classical originals.[50]

MONSTROUS ART

When monstrosity enters the garden, it does so in the form of feminine art. Pope's essay "On Gardens" (1713), like the "Ode on Solitude" 's collection of retirement sentiments, offers a compendium of gardening truisms in line with its allegiance to the "Taste of the Ancients," commending the "amiable Simplicity of unadorned Nature" in opposition to the "nicer Scenes of Art," and applauding Virgil and Homer's choice of "the useful part of Horticulture" as the most beautiful.[51] In an example whose emblematic wholeness mimics the self-sufficiency it describes, Pope offers a translation of Homer's description of the Gardens of Alcinous from Book VII of the *Odyssey:*

> Four Acres was th' allotted Space of Ground,
> Fenc'd with a green Enclosure all around . . .
> The balmy Spirit of the Western Gale
> Eternal breathes on Fruits untaught to fail:
> Each dropping Pear a following Pear supplies,

> On Apples Apples, Figs on Figs arise:
> The same mild Season gives the Blooms to blow,
> The Buds to harden, and the Fruits to grow.

Homer's garden offers a literary ideal of untutored "Simplicity" which Pope's essay reads as reality. Just as the poet depicts Achilles' shield in his *Iliad* translation as a material artifact, so here he enlists Sir William Temple's aid in delineating garden poetry as actual landscape.[52] The title of Temple's influential 1692 *The Gardens of Epicurus: or, of Gardening, in the Year 1685* demonstrates the double perspective of historical particularity and classical idealism inherent in this impulse to author poetic origins in a concrete contemporary moment. In Pope's paraphrase of Temple's view, the garden of Alcinous offers a miniature model of perfection in design: "this Description contains all the justest Rules and Provisions which can go toward composing the best Gardens."[53]

Pope continues to draw on Temple when he notes that Homer's vineyard, which brings "all th' United Labours of the Year" into the scene with an account of the process of wine-making, "seems to have been a Plantation distinct from the *Garden;* as also the *Beds of Greens* mentioned afterwards at the Extremity of the Inclosure, in the Nature and usual Place of our *Kitchen Gardens.*"[54] Temple, whose gardening treatise contrasted the Edenic "State of Innocence and Pleasure" of gardens with "the Life of Husbandry and Cities . . . after the Fall, with Guilt and with Labour,"[55] has a great deal at stake in keeping even the innocent toil of Homer's vintners separate from the garden's charmed circle. In the garden labour is superfluous. Pope's translation credits Alcinous' fruit-trees with a self-perpetuating power of generation—"On Apples Apples, Figs on Figs arise"—which is uncannily reminiscent of the battles for predominance in the moving toyshop of Belinda's breast, "Where Wigs with Wigs, with Sword-knots Sword-knots strive, / Beaus banish Beaus, and Coaches Coaches drive" (I, 101–102). Nostalgic fantasies of well-governed natural ease and simplicity thereby come to merge with the most ironic and ornate celebrations of contemporary feminine artifice.

What Pope most objects to in his essay on gardens is the current fad for topiary, the obvious distortion of natural forms by an art which exceeds its natural bounds, "not only in the various Tonsure of Greens into the most regular and formal Shapes, but even in monstrous Attempts beyond the reach of the Art it self."[56] Such a love of monstrosity, what Pope terms "this curious taste," is indicative of a "common level of understanding," untutored by that which is most necessary for proper taste: a familiarity with "Nature," the basis for all good art, in the form of long-held property. "A Citizen is no sooner Proprietor of a couple of Yews, but he entertains Thoughts of erecting them into Giants, like those of *Guild-hall*. I know an eminent Cook, who beautified his Country Seat with a Coronation Dinner in Greens, where you see the Champion flourishing on Horseback at one end of the Table, and the Queen in perpetual Youth at the other."[57] The citizen who, unacquainted with the country, surrounds himself with the grotesquely gigantic forms of Guild-hall, the eminent Cook, who must transform his environs into the image of a dinner, exemplify the narrowness of those who use their unnaturally acquired (bought rather than inherited) estates to reflect their particular selves rather than the "genius" of nature. In thinking "that *finest* which is least Natural," they reveal their unsophisticated preoccupation with an aesthetic of trivia, the "little Niceties and Fantastical Operations," which blind them to the true beauties of the natural, the same trivia whose whimsical transformations constituted the charm of *The Rape of the Lock*.

The essay continues with Pope's invocation of a "Catalogue of Greens to be disposed of by an eminent Town-Gardiner," who characterizes himself as a "Virtuoso . . . capable of improving upon the Ancients of his Profession in the Imagery of Evergreens." In keeping with the narcissism of the nouveau riche, this gardener is first and foremost a portraitist, "arrived to such Perfection, that he cuts Family Pieces of Men, Women or Children. Any Ladies that please may have their own Effigies in Myrtle, or their Husbands in Hornbeam." Heading the list of available forms is "*Adam* and *Eve* in Yew; *Adam* a little shattr'd by the fall of the Tree of Knowledge in the great Storm; *Eve* and the Serpent very Flourishing."[58] Much as Pope enjoys the puns involved in describing such a creation, such obvious anthropomorphism invokes the fall as a descent into bad taste. Print, in Pope's view, is the proper place for such personal portraits; landscape offers him the possibility of a self-portrait so artful it appears natural.

The condemnation of topiary is standard in both contemporary gardening treatises and classical precedent; Pope enlists the aid of Martial and Horace in his playful diatribe, and Robert Castell, in *The Villas of the Ancients Illustrated* (1728) puzzles over the presence of such "unwarrantable forms" in Pliny's otherwise ideal villa at Tuscum:

> For it cannot be supposed that Nature ever did or will produce Trees in the Form of Beasts or Letters, or any Resemblance of Embroidery, which Imitations rather belong to the Statuary, and Workers with the Needle than the Architect; and tho' pleasing in those Arts, appear monstrous in this.[59]

In the form of an imagined "original" Roman landscape, Castell's text delineates a map of contemporary garden design. Dedicated to the Earl of Burlington (the central founder of Palladian architecture and gardening in England who was himself influenced by Castell's classicism), this translation contains multiple layers of description and fantasy. Pliny's original Latin epistle describing his villa is printed on facing pages with Castell's English translation, and is accompanied by the Englishman's elaborate topographical "illustrations" of the Latin text, along with his interpretative "remarks." Even more detailed than William Temple's guide to Alcinous' garden, such illustrations and their accompanying commentary provide maps of lost landscapes. Castell presents Pliny's villa as a microcosm of gardening style (much as Morris Brownell and others will come to praise Twickenham)[60] encompassing the extremes of unadorned nature, excessive art, and the happy medium of *imitatio ruris* [imitation of the country]. Castell attributes the invisible art designated by the latter phrase to the Chinese. Temple in his *Gardens of Epicurus* had made the Latin phrase synonymous with an English transcription of a Chinese word, "Sharawadgi":

> "The *Chineses* scorn [our symmetrical] Way of Planting, and say a Boy, that can tell an Hundred, may plant Walks of Trees in Straight Lines . . . But their greatest Reach of Imagination is employed in contriving Figures, where the Beauty shall be great, and strike the Eye, but without any Order or Disposition of Parts, that shall be commonly or easily observ'd. And though we have hardly any Notion of this Sort of Beauty, yet they have a particular Word to express it; and where they find it hit their Eye at first Sight, they say the *Sharawadgi* is fine or is admirable, or any such Expression of Esteem. And whoever observes the Work upon the best *Indian* gowns, or the painting that is upon their best Skreens and Purcellans, will find their Beauty is all of this Kind (that is) without Order."[61]

If in one view the ancients, like the bourgeois English villa-owners Pope and Temple condemned, also erred on the side of excessive art, they did so for the pleasure of the contrasts of such art with its absence, which "might appear more beautiful by being near those plain Imitations of Nature, as Lights in Painting are heightened by Shades."[62] For Castell and Pope, although the emphasis on contrast in landscaping as in painting is to be imitated, topiary exemplifies the "monstrous" limit to an art that should be contained by nature's bounds. Such artificial forms are the equivalent of fussy feminine "embroidery," better suited to "Workers with the Needle than the Architect." who stare so closely at their labour that they can only see and reproduce themselves distorted.

Castell's fantasy landscape unites the exotic with the familiar, the historically distant with the contemporary. Read in the light of Temple's Orientalist subtext, and thus with the self-reflective conventions of travel literature which make the reader strange to himself, the most "natural" effect of gardening is seen as the most strange, a foreign import, an untranslatable word. The paragon of masculine self-sufficiency, the artfully natural Roman estate, deformed by the "monstrosity" of female embroidery, is linked through Temple's reflection in an Eastern mirror to the delicate feminine "work upon the best *Indian* gowns," or the painting on china jars. Nature and art unite in the gendered inter-reflections of empire.

THE BEAUTIES OF USE

When discussing Pope's gardening enthusiasm with a friend, I was amused and intrigued by the question, "But was Pope physically able to work in a garden?" The image of Pope on his hands and knees with a trowel was indeed absurd: both his status (however temporary) as land-owner and his physical deformity made manual labor unimaginable. This simple question nevertheless raises key problems of agency as figured by individual labor, property ownership, and the scale, design and use of estates. Pope's physical and social marginality complicates his place in contemporary definitions of class and masculine self-hood, in much the same way that his exposure of the commodity in the *Rape* reveals his ambivalent complicity with the object-world he had imagined as feminine.

Early eighteenth-century England celebrated a fertile British empire enriched by international trade and advanced by independent and civically self-interested landowners. The aesthetic construction of such an ideal necessitated the invisibility of actual labor at home and abroad.[63] The human cost involved in the steadily increasing enclosure of common lands by large private estates cultivating the land for profit rather than sustenance (mostly for grazing and England's booming woolen export industry) remained largely hidden in both gardens and the texts that idealized them.[64]

Pope's fantasy of an unlabored and immediate relation between landowner and land is written large in his "gardening poem," the *Epistle to Burlington* (1731). In the construction of this fantasy, not labour but ownership, and with it the power of "direction," make for invisible and effective agency.[65] In an epic version of such a georgic vision, when Pope's Lord Burlington bids, at the poet's suggestion, "Harbors open, public Ways extend," in a grand amplification of the authority given concrete form by his estate, nature complies as if of its own accord.

> You too proceed! make falling Arts your care,
> Erect new wonders, and the old repair,
> Jones and Palladio to themselves restore,
> And be whate'er Vitruvius was before:
> Till Kings call forth th' Idea's of your mind
> Proud to accomplish what such hands design'd,
> Bid Harbors open, public Ways extend,
> Bid Temples, worthier of the God, ascend;
> Bid the broad Arch the dang'rous Flood contain,
> The Mole projected break the roaring Main;
> Back to his bounds their subject Sea command,
> And roll obedient Rivers thro' the Land;
> These Honours, Peace to happy Britain brings,
> These are Imperial Works, and worthy Kings.   (191–204)

At Pope's direction, Burlington "restores" his decayed English and Italian pre-decessors just as his gardening efforts restore nature to her lost perfection. He thereby becomes for his age, in an act of paradoxically original translation that parallels the imaginary reconstruction of Castell's dream maps, the paragon of classic architecture that Vitruvius was for his. To be such a paragon is to have the power of "Kings" at one's disposal: Burlington's "Ideas," in the perfection of their invisible form, supersede even the commands of the monarchs who "accomplish" them by ordering their construction.

As the Twickenham edition notes, the conscious Latinism "worthier of the God" signals Pope's pervasive debt in this passage to Dryden's translation of *Aeneid* VI. In this book, Aeneas descends to the underworld where his father Anchises presents him with a vision of Roman history accompanied by advice—"conquer the haughty and spare the suppliant"—which the hero, at the crucial moment of the epic's close, will forget. Resonant here is the sense of history reimagined as the origin of an ideal future in both Virgil and Pope's text; in both poems the reader is given the opportunity to fantasize the birth of a new and perfect empire from the perspective of its flawed and flourishing accomplishment. Pope's final line echoes Dryden's version of Anchises' words to his son: "These are Imperial Arts, and worthy thee." Burlington (and with him the poet who invisibly directs him) is thus equated with Aeneas and with the "Kings" who accomplish his design; from gardens and villas to empires. For Pope as both gardener and poet, then, natural origins are fantasized in the image of an ideal future that elides history.

If this aesthetic allowed the landowner of leisure to "appear . . . to be the creation of nature alone," so as the English landscape garden evolved, it discovered an untouched nature which concealed, through art, the social function and productivity of land.[66] Thus while England's landscape was increasingly compartmentalized by enclosure,

> as the real landscape began to look increasingly artificial, like a garden, the garden began to look increasingly natural, like the pre-enclosed landscape. Thus a natural landscape became the prerogative of the estate, allowing for a conveniently ambiguous signification, so that nature was the sign of property and property the sign of nature. It would only be a slight exaggeration to say that the ideological role of nature in the eighteenth century lay in this reversibility of signifier and signified.[67]

Pope's garden at Twickenham marks a social moment when such unmediated reversibility is not yet complete, when art and nature still exist in distinct interrelation.[68] Twickenham also exemplifies the ways in which English landscapers of the early eighteenth century, like the Roman villa-dwellers after whom they modelled themselves, attempted to combine the land's display value with use value.[69]

Such balances are best expressed by the implementation of the ha-ha, or sunk fence, at Twickenham. Originally designed to keep cattle within their owner's confines, this special trench eliminated visible boundaries between the formal garden and the wilder landscape without. The ha-ha, in other words, permitted the owners and renters of small gardens to aesthetically own what was beyond their means. Such a device sets up an invisible challenge to the division between nature and art and the division of property.[70] This landscape version of *trompe l'oeil*[71] contributes to a cultural recognition and appreciation of the origin-less, isolated object. Whether natural marvel depicted in a travel book, exotic commodity on show in a shop window, or artfully displayed natural scene, such objects put origins into permanent flux.[72]

The literary equivalent of Pope's georgic balance of aesthetic and productive gardening at Twickenham (he was particularly proud of his kitchen garden) is his proclamation of financial and moral self-sufficiency in imitation of Horace in *Satire II, ii* (1734), an independence in defiance of an embattled debt to the classical model from which he deviates and which he displays in Latin on the facing page:

> In *South-Sea* days not happier, when surmis'd
> The Lord of thousands, than if now *Excis'd;*
> In Forest planted by a Father's hand,

> Than in five acres now of rented land.
> Content with little, I can piddle here
> On Broccoli and mutton, round the year;
> But ancient friends, (tho' poor, or out of play)
> That touch my Bell, I cannot turn away.
> 'Tis true, no Turbots dignify my boards
> But gudgeons, flounders, what my Thames affords,
> To Hounslow-heath I point, and Bansted-down,
> Thence comes your mutton, and these chicks my own:
> From yon old wallnut-tree a show'r shall fall;
> And grapes, long-lingring on my only wall,
> And figs, from standard and Espalier join:
> The dev'l is in you if you cannot dine.   (*Satire II, ii,* 133–148)

This passage performs a further miniaturization and internalization of the English empire figured in *Windsor Forest* and *To Burlington,* an empire now diminished to the limits of a dining-room table furnished by bought mutton and the produce of a rented estate. Pope owns nothing, yet the sense of totality conveyed by his pointing toward the sources of his modest feast—"my Thames" providing fish, "my only wall" bearing grapes,[73] the witty joining of figs grown both on trees both left to nature and artfully bound to lattices—makes him the center of a self-constructed Eden. As property yields in this passage to the more fleeting pleasures of use, and as the exotic luxury of international trade shrinks to the modest bounty of local commerce, the possibility of a singular independence and stability begins to emerge.

Pope's version of unencumbered selfhood is inherently nostalgic, not only because of its debt to Horace's presence but because of its contrast to lost possessions, both speculative losses in the South Sea Bubble, and the loss of the family home in Windsor Forest, bought in 1700 before the law against Catholics owning property was passed, as *Satire II, ii* describes.

In the poem's new equation of use with stability, land is ultimately as unstable as the lethally invisible paper credit so ironically praised in *To Bathurst* (1733). In that epistle on "the use of riches," Pope waxes nostalgic for a world which predated the invention of "secret Gold," in which corruption and therefore character were visible: "Oh! that such bulky Bribes as all might see, / Still, as of old, incumber'd Villainy!" (35–36). Paper credit, more faceless and weightless than coins, epitomizes the unruliness of undetectable exchange:

> Blest paper credit! last and best supply!
> That lends Corruption lighter wings to fly!

> Gold imp'd by thee, can compass hardest things,
> Can pocket States, can fetch or carry Kings;
> A single leaf shall waft an Army o'er,
> Or ship off Senates to a distant Shore;
> A leaf, like Sibyl's, scatter to and fro
> Our fates and fortunes, as the winds shall blow:
> Pregnant with thousands flits the Scrap unseen,
> And silent sells a King, or buys a Queen.   (69–78)

Paper's ability to "imp," to mimic gold, is analogous to the poet's ability to direct Burlington in his building endeavors. Like the power of print, the power of miniaturization exemplified by Pope's couplet art, and the spirit of trade, personified as a woman's allure in *The Rape of the Lock,* paper can compass empires in its ephemeral bounds. Dangerously feminine, "pregnant with thousands," paper credit exemplifies the precariousness of a world of capital which is, to use Adam Smith's phrase, not "secured [in the] cultivation of land."[74]

The inverse of the miniature insubstantiality of paper credit is the gigantic onerousness of unnatural wealth and the "false taste of Magnificence" exemplified by Timon's villa in *To Burlington:*

> Greatness, with Timon, dwells in such a draught
> As brings all Brobdignag before your thought.
> To compass this, his building is a Town,
> His pond an Ocean, his parterre a Down:
> Who but must laugh, the Master when he sees,
> A puny insect, shiv'ring at a breeze!
> Lo, what huge heaps of littleness around!
> The whole, a labour'd Quarry above ground.   (103–110)

While paper credit can "compass hardest things," Timon's attempts to compass his own grandiosity put him in the precarious position of a puny insect in danger of being crushed by the weight of his own possessions, the trivia of the *Rape's* luxury writ large as huge heaps of littleness. Money in the *Moral Essays* sets in motion distortions of scale and disruptions of identity that abandon and threaten native ground.[75]

The poet excludes himself from such precariousness when he argues in *Satire II, ii* that only the renter, whether he lease an estate or a place across the page from a Roman original, can truly own. When Swift's voice (and with it the voice of contemporary worldliness) intervenes in Pope's soliloquy,

> "Pray heav'n it last! (cries Swift) as you go on;"
> "I wish to God this house had been your own:"
> "Pity! to build, without a son or wife:"
> "Why, you'll enjoy it only all your life."   (161–164)

Pope replies with a particularized elaboration of Horace's moral (which itself appropriates the words Horace had given to the character Ofellus in the original):

> Well, if the Use be mine, can it concern one
> Whether the Name belong to Pope or Vernon?
> What's *Property?* dear Swift! you see it alter
> From you to me, from me to Peter Walter,
> Or, in a mortgage, prove a Lawyer's share,
> Or, in a jointure, vanish from the Heir,
> Or in pure Equity (the Case not clear)
> The Chanc'ry takes your rents for twenty year:
> At best, it falls to some ungracious Son
> Who cries, my father's damn'd, and all's my own.
> Shades, that to Bacon could retreat afford,
> Become the portion of a booby Lord;
> And Helmsley once proud Buckingham's delight,
> Slides to a Scriv'ner or a City Knight.
> Let Lands and Houses have what Lords they will,
> Let Us be fix'd, and our own Masters still.   (165–180)

Using Swift's intervention (the English poet's intervention in the original), Pope characteristically personalizes Horace's text as he takes property in his own person. *"Property"* resonates in italics here, as if it were merely a proper name among the many that adorn his poems, a marker whose protean nature shifts with its owner and ultimately makes the very concept of ownership, and with it identity, impossible.

THE OBJECTS OF CHARACTER

In the estate he builds from print, Pope figures the invisible labor of writing as both personal and material. Reappropriating the objectification of lampooners who depicted him as deformed by excessive study, Pope transforms the bodily mark of difficult labor into his authorial trademark. What the young poet of the *Essay on Criticism* had celebrated as an "Ease in Writing" which "flows from Art, not Chance, / As those move easiest who have learn'd to dance" (362–363), is repudiated in *Epistle II, ii* (1737)[76] for a vehement assertion of visible and mechanical dis-ease:

> This subtle Thief of Life, this paltry Time,
> What will it leave me, if it snatch my Rhime?
> If ev'ry Wheel of that unweary'd Mill
> That turn'd ten thousand Verses, now stands still.   (76–79)

In his contemplation of character in the *Moral Essays* and Horatian poems, Pope attempts to reconcile these conflicting models of agency and ownership, natural spontaneity and mechanical artifice. In the process he transforms lack of financial capital into powerful symbolic capital, thereby appropriating obstructions to the transparent analogy between abstract and human nature that his gardening efforts had sought to reproduce.

Just as Pope appropriates Homer by depicting him, so he apprehends character by envisioning it. "Character" is a matter of framing objects to be identified, collected, owned and properly used. The early *Epistle to Mr. Jervas* (1716),[77] by rendering the "Sister-arts" (13), painting and poetry, as mirrors whose "images reflect from art to art" (20), defines character as visible and appropriable surface. Jervas was a London portrait painter from whom Pope took painting lessons. Pope reminisces about his travels with Jervas through imaginary classical landscapes; like Burlington restoring Vitruvius in his Palladian efforts, like Pope travelling to Greece by translating Homer, such ideal vision "builds imaginary *Rome* a-new" (32). In *To Jervas* such classically informed art produces not architectural monuments but the "small, well-polish'd gem[s]" (40) of Jervas' portraits of women:

> Oh lasting as those colours may they shine,
> Free as thy stroke, yet faultless as thy line!
> New graces yearly, like thy works, display;
> Soft without weakness, without glaring gay;
> Led by some rule, that guides, but not constrains;
> And finish'd more thro' happiness than pains!
> The kindred arts shall in their praise conspire,
> One dip the pencil, and one string the lyre.
> Yet should the Graces all thy figures place,
> And breathe an air divine on ev'ry face;
> Yet should the Muses bid my numbers roll,
> Strong as their charms, and gentle as their soul;
> With *Zeuxis' Helen* thy *Bridgewater* vie,
> And these be sung 'till *Granville's Myra* die;

> Alas! how little from the grave we claim?
> Thou but preserv'st a Face and I a Name.   (63–78)

The "they" with which Pope begins the poem's conclusion ambiguously conflates the female subjects of Jervas' portraits with the portraits themselves, and
judges them against a "faultless" standard of beauty set by the painter's skill, his
"stroke" and "line." Under Jervas' eye, women become perfect objects of representation; and in Pope's couplet art, such perfection is expressed through the
dynamic containment of opposites, as in "soft without weakness, without glar-
ing gay." The beauty these oppositions describe, the same litany of oxymorons
with which Pope will describe his ideal woman in *To a Lady,* consists as much
in what is missing as in what is visible, and what is most glaringly omitted are
the "pains" of detectable labor. Yet for all their flawlessness, these feminine
images fail to preserve anything but surface, leaving a definition of character
that refers only to visible impression and discernible label, faces and names. In
the *Moral Essays,* Pope attempts to go beyond particular images in order to
capture character's depth.

To Cobham (1734) attempts to imagine a reading of "the characters of men"
that accounts both for a plethora of surface particulars and an invisible constancy
beneath that surface:

> There's some Peculiar in each leaf and grain,
> Some unmark'd fibre, or some varying vein:
> Shall only Man be taken in the gross?
> Grant but as many sorts of Mind as Moss.
>   That each from other differs, first confess;
> Next, that he varies from himself no less:
> Add Nature's, Custom's, Reason's, Passion's strife,
> And all Opinion's colours cast on life.
>   Yet more; the diff'rence is as great between
> The optics seeing, as the objects seen.
> All Manners take a tincture from our own,
> Or come discolour'd thro' our Passions shown.
> Or Fancy's beam enlarges, multiplies,
> Contracts, inverts, and gives ten thousand dyes.   (15–28)

The problem of discerning male character becomes not simply a problem of
accurate vision, here phrased in the scientific terminology of optics and clouded
by external and internal variables, but also of encompassing external variety. In
To Cobham, character is to be read with a magnifying glass in order to be

collected, virtuoso-style, in all its diversity. To compass character this way is as impossible as it is to focus on a single life, an impossibility signalled by the visual terms in which it is phrased:

> But grant that Actions best discover man;
> Take the most strong, and sort them as you can.
> The few that glare each character must mark,
> You balance not the many in the dark.   (71–74)

As the poem progresses, nature (and with it human nature), emerges not as legible essence rather but as the rhetorical source of metaphors with which to make sense of the indeterminacy of social relations:

> Court-virtues bear, like Gems, the highest rate,
> Born where Heav'n's influence scarce can penetrate:
> In life's low vale, the soil the virtues like,
> They please as Beauties, here as Wonders strike.
> Tho' the same Sun with all-diffusive rays
> Blush in the Rose, and in the Diamond blaze,
> We prize the stronger effort of his pow'r,
> And justly set the Gem above the Flow'r.   (93–100)

This brilliant puzzle inverts social definitions of high and low as it interrogates the origins of material value, value which is substituted for the supposed immateriality of virtue. The social summit of the court is here figured as the depths of a mine; life's low vale is closer to the light and rich with imagined goodness. What earns the highest rate—court virtue—is most rare and requires the most labor. What is figured as the most solid and enduring of creations, the unbreakable diamond, is exposed as the most arbitrary of social fictions.

Pope's solution—"Search then the Ruling Passion: there alone, / The Wild are constant, and the Cunning known" (174–175)—is less convincing or compelling than the series of highly detailed satiric portraits that follow it. If *To Cobham* asserts the satirist's penetration to the invisible constancy of things— "Nature well known, no prodigies remain, / Comets are regular, and Wharton plain" (208–209)—such knowledge can ultimately be displayed only in the compressed miniature narratives of particular examples. The story of self-conscious Narcissa, "founded on fact," Pope tells us in the notes, is a fitting conclusion to the idealized feminine images of *Epistle to Jervas*. The poet projects his own fears about a penetrating gaze which may only see its own reflection:

> "Odious! in woollen! 'twould a Saint provoke,
> (Were the last words that poor Narcissa spoke)
> "No, let a charming Chintz, and Brussels lace
> "Wrap my cold limbs, and shade my lifeless face:
> "One would not, sure, be frightful when one's dead—
> "And—Betty—give this Cheek a little Red."   (242–247)

The vain woman's grisly inability to abandon her image is matched by the final negative example, the miser's refusal to let go of his estate:

> "I give and I devise, (old Euclio said,
> And sigh'd) "My lands and tenements to Ned."
> Your money, Sir; "My money, Sir, what all?
> Why,—if I must—(then wept) I give it Paul."
> The Manor, Sir?—"The Manor! hold," he cry'd,
> "Not that,—I cannot part with that"—and dy'd.   (256–261)

These death-bed vignettes attempt to miniaturize within the confines of a final moment the essence of their subjects' natures, natures constituted by their relation to the world of commodities, chintz and Brussels lace, money and manors, mundane natures which cling to precarious objects.

Pope's efforts to define character outside the cycle of property in *Satire II, ii* reenact by repudiation his complicity with the object world of the feminine in *The Rape of the Lock*. Such complicity resurfaces as the uncanny precariousness of the vision of character in *To Cobham* and the mobility of property in *To Bathurst*. If, as Catherine Ingrassia has observed, the commercial man and the man of letters are feminized and objectified by their dependence on imaginary value, in *To a Lady* (1735) Pope projects upon a portrait gallery of femininity his anxieties about the invisibility and indecipherability of value that haunt the epistles on men.[78] To consider the characters of women "only as contradistinguished from the other Sex," is to consider the impossibility of distinguishing character in material terms:

> Nothing so true as what you once let fall,
> "Most Women have no Characters at all".
> Matter too soft a lasting mark to bear,
> And best distinguish'd by black, brown or fair.   (1–4)

From the many marks of particularity in *To Cobham,* we arrive at an unmarkable mobility in *To a Lady* that results in an unclassifiable fluidity.[79]

As we shall see, Pope's own attempts to remove himself from the mobile world of property in order to gain a fixed and inalienable authority threaten to render him as potentially unreadable as women themselves. To claim an authorial independence based on social marginality and unexchangeable individuality, as Pope does in *Satire II, ii,* and as his work on the grotto embodies in a concrete structure, is to come dangerously close to the feminine position, excluded from and indecipherable to a world defined by public image and by property. Pope's women owe their charms to their changes: "Their happy Spots the nice admirer take, / Fine by defect and delicately weak" (43–44). His portrait of Calypso that follows forms a perverse echo to his balanced praise of Jervas' virtuous beauties:

> 'Twas thus Calypso once each heart alarm'd,
> Aw'd without Virtue, without Beauty charm'd;
> Her Tongue bewitch'd as odly as her Eyes,
> Less Wit than Mimic, more a Wit than wise:
> Strange graces still, and stranger flights she had,
> Was just not ugly, and was just not mad;
> Yet ne'er so sure our passion to create,
> As when she touch'd the brink of all we hate.   (45–52)

The "we" of the final line creates a tenuous defense against the panic of the baffled male eye this passage so convincingly evokes. Calypso charms by monstrosity, by undoing the bounds of virtue and beauty that separate the disembodied masculine viewer from the feminine object he surveys. She bewitches, like Pope's deformed body in the eyes of his lampooners, by coming too close to what ought to remain distant and distinct. Yet Pope celebrates his own moral integrity as "fine by defect," and bases the transparency of his virtue's medium on its spots: "In me what Spots (for Spots I have) appear, / Will prove at least the Medium must be clear."[80] In the inverted mirror of what *Satire II, i* termed "this impartial Glass," the women of *To a Lady* reflect Pope's Horatian dream of transparent self-sufficiency as opaque "true No-meaning" (114).

In *To a Lady* the impossibility of analogies between "Nature" and "Human Nature" is made most obvious. *To Burlington,* the first of the *Epistles* to be published and the last in Pope's final ordering, resolves the problem of character by limiting the field of inquiry to the material, by creating an oxymoronic conceptual couplet that defines the intractably idiosyncratic "use of riches" with the abstract happy medium of good taste. The poem begins by distinguishing Burlington from the extremes of the miser and the prodigal by pointing toward a proper definition of taste:

> Tis strange, the Miser should his Cares employ,
> To gain those Riches he can ne'er enjoy:
> Is it less strange, the Prodigal should wast
> His wealth, to purchase what he ne'er can taste?
> Not for himself he sees, or hears, or eats;
> Artists must choose his Pictures, Music, Meats . . .
> Think we all these are for himself? no more
> Than his fine Wife, alas! or finer Whore.   (1–12)

While *To Cobham* and *To a Lady* attempt, however futilely, to envision and to interpret the characters of men and women, and while *To Bathurst* reframes the question of character within a "natural" order of consumption and expenditure, *To Burlington* focuses the eye's attention not on the nature of the proprietors but exclusively on the disposition of objects themselves. The opening lines define true character as consuming for—and therefore as—oneself. Taste is initially defined as the physical enjoyment of material pleasure. The self-conscious "prodigal" consumer buys for others, accumulating objects that vie in their randomness with the jumble on Belinda's dressing table. This list culminates in his choice of "fine Wife . . . or finer Whore" that he "ne'er can taste," evidence of his lack of taste in more than one sense.

Burlington's status as paragon, by contrast, is documented by his allegiance to classical models, his ability to translate a lost ideal into present practice. He consumes not so much for himself but as a medium who keeps the correct past and present audiences in mind. "You show us, Rome was glorious, not profuse, / And pompous buildings once were things of Use" (22–23). *To Burlington*'s ideal of taste as unmediated self-fulfillment is paradoxically disembodied. While "Imitating Fools" take cold comfort in the knowledge that "if they starve, they starve by rules of art" (38), Burlington's enjoyment is of the eye alone. His taste is for no particular material object so much as a general Nature figured as feminine:

> To build, to plant, whatever you intend,
> To rear the Column, or the Arch to bend,
> To swell the Terras, or to sink the Grot;
> In all, let Nature never be forgot.
> But treat the Goddess like a modest fair,
> Nor over-dress, nor leave her wholly bare;
> Let not each beauty ev'ry where be spy'd,
> Where half the skill is decently to hide.   (47–54)

Taste forms the basis for a perfect identity by an abstract intimacy and a joining of productive forces with feminine Nature. Burlington the architect and Pope and Jervas the portrait painters are united in their abstract appreciation, their improvement, of a cooperative natural feminine beauty.[81] Unmediated enjoyment becomes the absolute power of direction celebrated at the poem's conclusion; the sign of perfect taste is one's own disappearance into a perfectly displayed feminine landscape.

The last aphoristic couplet of *Satire II, ii* miniaturizes such merging with an ideal nature as a personal invisibility, a freedom from property: "Let Lands and Houses have what Lords they will, / Let Us be fix'd, and our own Masters still" (179–80). Pope's elaboration on Horace's exhortation to "hold our hearts strong in adversity," inverts the subordination of property to owner. It credits property with the power of appropriating, like a wife choosing her husband, its owner. Will takes on the resonance of desire. In opposition to the chaotic movements and disturbed hierarchies of property falling and vanishing in an exchange society propelled by mortgages, jointures, taxes, and the levelling power of money, a society under the sway of feminine possessiveness, only the poet and his friends remain still. The final resonance of "still" is both spatial and temporal; the unencumbered self neither moves nor decays, in contrast to the collapse of space and time in the poem's portrayal of property's unruly mobility. The commodity's eternal motion, the stuff of the *Rape*'s precarious beauty, here becomes its insubstantiality against which the poet grants himself substance. This is as much a wish as a pronouncement.

THE WOMAN IN THE GARDEN

The object at the center of Pope's garden, and the "universal topos"[82] to which it was dedicated was the obelisk in memory of his mother, inscribed, "Ah Editha! Matrum Optima. Mulierum Amantissima. Vale." [Ah Edith! Best of Mothers. Most Beloved of Women. Farewell.][83] Describing a 1738 portrait of Pope by Jonathan Richardson (see Figure 9), William Kent comments on the strangely emblematic nature of the motherless poet in his garden: "Pope in a mourning gown with a strange view of the garden to shew the obelisk as in memory to his Mothers death, the alligory seem'd odde to me."[84]

The oddity of this allegory consists in the ambivalence of its reference, its exclusion of and allusion to Pope's mother and the femininity of nature as figures for origins in general. The obelisk in his mother's memory allows the poet in all his singularity to include what limits that singularity within the frame

Figure 9.

Jonathan Richardson, the Elder, *Alexander Pope,* 1738.

of his own creation, to accomplish, as Mack puts it, "his repossession of her . . . topographically . . . [and] psychologically."[85] This gesture is described by a female visitor to the garden in 1760 as transcending poetry's elite audience, "a Circumstance of more Credit to him than all his Works; for the Beauties of Poetry are tasted only by a few, but the Language of the Heart is understood by all."[86] Her "Language of the Heart" echoes Pope's tribute to his father at the close of the *Epistle to Arbuthnot:* "Unlearn'd, he knew no Schoolman's Subtle Art, / No Language, but the Language of the Heart" (398–399); a fantasy of unlettered simplicity in contrast to the poet's own achievement. While the maternal monument is a sincere act of filial piety, it also provides a visual parallel to Pope's deformed and origin-less brand of literary imitation. Both in gardening and in poetry, that which obscures the clear distinction between meaning and non-meaning, between form and deformity, whether particularized aberration or idealized femininity, is incorporated within the work of art itself.

The obelisk signifies the way in which, as in Castell's and Temple's dreamscapes, Pope's garden contains the feminine element that defines it. As *Eloisa's* mood-colored background demonstrates, Pope explicitly associated the romantic aspects of his garden with women, most particularly with his gardening companion Martha Blount, the addressee of *Epistle to a Lady.* Pope successfully encouraged Martha to read romances in order to cultivate a proper appreciation of landscape's psychological nuances, and wrote to her of his own experiences in viewing gardens as calling up her "shade."[87] This feminine side of Pope's gardening endeavors is thus inversely linked to his manly Horatian freedom from property's constraints; his mother's obelisk in the background foregrounds both the pathos and authority of his authorial image. Whether romantically picturesque or classically neo-georgic, the perfect landscape, like the perfect woman, transformed and appropriated by the individual masculine mind, is an immaterial image, the mark of an absence.

Martha, praised at the end of *To a Lady* as the ideal woman, staves off the chaos of the monstrous attractions of a figure such as Calypso. Woman at best is man's benign reflection, an orderly oxymoron, a "Contradiction still" (*To a Lady,* 270). Martha's perfection rests in her "exception to all general rules," her collapsing of a general definition of "Woman" into irreducible and to Pope irresistible particularity. Outside the circle of property and unencumbered by a dowry, "denied the Pelf / Which buys your sex a Tyrant o'er itself" (287–288), Martha replaces the corruption of gold with the irreplaceable currency of wit. In his construction of her disenfranchised singularity, she becomes Pope's reflection.

> The gen'rous God, who Wit and Gold refines,
> And ripens Spirits as he ripens Mines,
> Kept dross for Dutchesses, the world shall know it,
> To you gave Sense, Good-humour, and a Poet. (289–292)

Both the particularity of Martha's portrait in Pope's mirror, and the self-generating power marked by the maternal obelisk, are given distorted and inalienable form in that cave and theater of the mind, Pope's grotto.[88]

"ACCIDENTAL LANDSKIPS": THE CAMERA OBSCURA AND THE GROTTO WALL

The grotto at Twickenham disrupts the binary oppositions between male and female, disembodied viewer and objectified scene, which join the gardener to "nature." Pope's signature structure, the most personal part of his garden, prominently advertises the secret defects that Twickenham's diminished ideal seems to conceal. Reproducing the garden in disembodied form, images shimmered on the walls of his "shadowy Cave" turned camera obscura. What follows is Pope's own description of the grotto in a 1725 letter to Edward Blount:

> I have put the last Hand to my works of this kind, in happily finishing the subterraneous Way and Grotto; I there found a Spring of the clearest Water, which falls in a perpetual Rill, that echoes thro' the Cavern day and night. From the River *Thames,* you see thro' my Arch up a Walk of the Wilderness to a kind of open Temple, wholly compos'd of Shells in the Rustic Manner; and from that distance under the Temple you look down thro' a sloping Arcade of Trees, and see the Sails on the River passing suddenly and vanishing, as thro' a Perspective Glass. When you shut the Doors of this Grotto, it becomes on the instant, from a luminous Room, a *Camera obscura;* on the Walls of which all the objects of the River, Hills, Woods, and Boats, are forming a moving Picture in their visible Radiations: And when you have a mind to light it up, it affords you a very different Scene: it is finished with Shells interspersed with Pieces of Looking-glass in angular forms; and in the Cieling is a Star of the same Material, at which when a Lamp (of an orbicular figure of thin Alabaster) is hung in the Middle, a thousand pointed Rays glitter and are reflected over the Place . . . It wants nothing to compleat it but a good Statue with an Inscription, like the beautiful antique one which you know I am so fond of . . . You'll think I have been very poetical in this Description, but it is pretty near the Truth. I wish you were here to bear Testimony how little it owes to Art, either the Place itself, or the Image I give of it.[89]

The artless nature of the grotto unites image with object, turning a poetical scene suited for feminine "fairy steps,"[90] to pretty near the truth. The thing itself and its written image, like the camera's varying views, are interchangeable.

Gardening, which Pope termed "more Antique & nearer God's own Work, than Poetry,"[91] beckoned with the possibility of such complete correspondence. If this is so in part because the raw material of the gardener is a near pre-historic nature, such a statement nevertheless posits a divine work as the artist's unattainable goal whether his medium be landscapes or poems. For Pope, who claimed "of all his works [to be] most proud of his garden,"[92] cultivated nature excelled the printed page because it showed his art to the best advantage. In its rich dialogue with the arts of painting, theater, and poetry, the art of gardening gave the poet a concrete field in which to body forth his literary art. "All gardening is landscape-painting," he opined to Spence, "just like a landscape hung up"; while the editor of Pope's remarks on gardening refers to his school of landscaping as "ut pictura horticultura."[93] If the garden is a picture, what it depicts is as close to fantasy as to reality. Other classical topoi that came to Twickenham via Italy were the garden as "locus amoenus" [unwalled place], considered to be sacred and enchanted, and the garden as Ovid's fantastic compendium of "Monster after Monster," that plot of "enchanted Ground," the *Metamorphoses*.[94]

For Pope and his contemporaries, the garden afforded the pleasure of microcosm-making, of displaying nature and art in just proportions and with the optimal control of the pleasure involved in defining and blurring distinctions between them. In "The Pleasures of the Imagination," Joseph Addison insists on the interrelation of nature and art:

> "If we consider the Works of *Nature* and *Art*, as they are qualified to entertain the Imagination, we shall find the last very defective, in Comparison of the former; for though they may sometimes appear as Beautiful or Strange, they can have nothing in them of that Vastness and Immensity, which afford so great an Entertainment to the Mind of the Beholder. The one may be as Polite and Delicate as the other, but can never shew her self so August and Magnificent in the Design. There is something more bold and masterly in the rough careless Strokes of Nature, than in the nice Touches and Embellishments of Art. The Beauties of the most stately Garden or Palace lie in a narrow Compass, the Imagination immediately runs them over, and requires something else to gratifie her; but, in the wide Fields of Nature, the Sight wanders up and down without Confinement, and is fed with an infinite variety of Images, without any certain Stint or Number."[95]

The passage begins by linking nature and art in their common "works"; both are implicitly personified as artists, both possess agency.[96] Art is branded as defective because it lacks sublime vastness and immensity.

The lesser status of art is associated, as it was in Castell's analysis of Pliny's garden and Pope's condemnation of topiary, with feminine particulars and with apparent or careful labor: nature, Addison implies, happens almost by accident. Ultimately, art is associated with boundaries and limits, aestheticized versions of the fences enclosing private property, even those of a "stately Garden or Palace," that reign in an insatiably pleasure-seeking Imagination. The definition of the feminine then shifts to include both the consumable objects of art and the consuming faculty of Imagination herself. Addison's wording indicates that if art is proved lacking by an Imagination which always exceeds its bounds, nature is complemented by a gender-neutral sight, unconfined and limitless. The former posits an endless cycle of production, appropriation and consumption, the latter a passive and contented, almost pastoral interrelation.

Addison's equation of art, rather than nature, with defect and deformity is particularly intriguing, since it both echoes and inverts what will become the standard tenets of Augustan aesthetic theory. Sir Joshua Reynolds most influentially legislates this equation of the detail with natural defect: "If it has been proved, that the painter, by attending to the invariable and general ideas of nature, produces beauty, he must, by regarding minute particularities, and accidental discriminations, deviate from the universal rule, and pollute his canvas with deformity."[97] Reynolds' denouncement of particularity as mimetic pollution provides an illuminating frame for the development of Pope's aesthetic of deformity. The young poet's attempt to wittily reconcile the transparency of the heroic literary tradition with the feminine particulars of the *Rape*'s commodity aesthetic leads to his morally outraged championing of the details of history as a satirist-hero whose personal aberration is the sign of his integrity. Thus Pope, so often supposed to be at the center of conventional eighteenth-century aesthetic ideals, comes to champion at the end of his career a counter-aesthetic of singularity. Gardening for Pope involves not only the exclusion and occlusion of feminine aberration,[98] but also the riskiest of identifications with aberration's singularity in the construction of the grotto.

For while the polarities of nature and art seem clear in Reynolds, Addison's essay and Pope's grotto complicate the innocence of pleasure in looking: "We find the Works of Nature still more pleasant, the more they resemble those of Art: For in this case our Pleasure arises from a double Principle; from the Agreeableness of the Objects to the Eye, and from their Similitude to other Objects: We are pleased as well with comparing their Beauties, as with surveying them, and can represent them to our Minds, either as Copies or Originals."[99] The gaze described here, like the principle of pleasure that enables it, is double, affording both the delight of unmediated vision, "the Agreeableness of the Objects to the eye," and the enjoyment of comparison, "of Similitude to other Objects." The eye shifts from the appreciation of singularity and the object itself, to a pleasure in relativity and an apprehension of art. But for Addison these two sorts of looking are not opposed to each other; each augments the pleasure involved in the other, so that the ultimate pleasure rests in consciously comparing the different aspects of vision itself: "We are pleased as well with comparing their Beauties, as with surveying them, and can represent them to our Minds, either as Copies or Originals." The imagination gets most pleasure from an assumed innocence, a voluntary enjoyment of the deceit we will return to in the form of *trompe l'oeil*, like the owner of an estate who enjoys the beautiful nature of property, like the viewer who can turn the blur at the base of Holbein's *Ambassadors* into a skull by a shift of perspective. Such pleasure consists in the eye's apprehension of its own power to determine the form of accident, to identify "the Effect of Design, in what we call the Works of Chance." All viewing thus becomes a kind of collection of curiosity.[100]

Praising the "artificial Rudeness" of continental gardens in comparison with the "Neatness and Elegancy which we meet with in those of our own Country," Addison suggests that estates be revised as gardens, adding the practical consideration of profit to the aesthetic criterion of pleasure in nature: "If the natural Embroidery of the Meadows were helpt and improved by some small Additions of Art, and the several Rows of Hedges set off by Trees and Flowers, that the Soil was capable of receiving, a Man might make a pretty Landskip of his own Possessions."[101] The landscape that results is a reflection of the owner himself in the "nature" that is his property, a reflection he can pretend is an accident. Moving on to criticize topiary in British gardens, and recollecting the Chinese effect of accidental beauty, "sharawadgi," Addison suppresses another image from the East, included in an earlier draft of the essay, which characterizes art patterned on nature's perfection: "I believe, most readers are pleas'd with the Eastern King's device, yt made his Garden ye Map of his Empire . . . This natural draught of his Dominions was doubtless pleasanter yn a more accurate one of another kind made by ye strokes of a pen or pencil; because ye materials of ye Map had more of nature in 'em, and were liker ye things, they represented."[102] This omission illuminates the liberty of imagination and the absolute dominion of the proprietary eye that Addison's emphasis on accidental beauty obscures. As John Dixon Hunt comments in summation of these lines, "this 'draught of his Dominions' was, in short, but a portrait of the king."[103] The map captures the likeness of the landowner to his possessions, just as Pope reveals Sarpedon's heroism, and Belinda herself, in the window of her breast's moving toyshop. The transparent analogy genius makes between nature and human nature is here obscured by the objectification of nature, human and otherwise, as property.

The landscape Addison most appreciates, therefore, is the most ephemeral. The ideal garden is utterly transparent.

> The prettiest Landskip I ever saw, was one drawn on the Walls of a dark Room, which stood opposite on one side to a navigable River, and on the other to a Park. The Experiment is very common in Opticks . . . I must confess, the Novelty of such a sight may be one occasion of its Pleasantness to the Imagination, but certainly the chief Reason is its near Resemblance to Nature, as it does not only, like other Pictures, give the Colour and Figure, but the Motion of the Things it represents.[104]

The author of "Verses, Occasion'd by the Sight of a Chamera Obscura" (1747) exults more particularly in the power of the eye to create a universe in flawless miniature:

> How little is thy Cell? How dark the Room?
> Disclose thine Eye-lid, and dispel this Gloom!
> That radiant Orb reveal'd, smooth, pure, polite;
> In darts a sudden Blaze of beaming Light,
> And stains the clear white Sheet, with Colours strong and bright;
> Exterior Objects painting on the Scroll,
> True as the Eye presents 'em to the Soul;
> A New Creation! deckt with ev'ry Grace!
> Form'd by thy Pencil, in a Moment's Space!
> As in a Nutshell, curious to behold;
> Great *Homer's Iliad* was inscrib'd of old;
> So the wide World's vast Volume, here, we see
> To Miniature reduc'd, and just Epitome.[105]

The most important analogy here, one that the ambiguous "thine" of the passage emphasizes, is between the human and the mechanical eye. The transparency of the eye itself which informs this analogy extends to the analogy between active painting, figured here as a kind of deflowering or staining of the clear white sheet with color, and passive vision; the analogy thereby unites representation and presentation.[106] The viewers of the camera obscura both see and are shown; they appreciate the perfect mimesis of the natural—"true as the Eye presents 'em to the Soul"—and the theatrical display of art which creates a new world. The transparency of such natural art thus unites time and space, text and image, within the miniature's confines. The familiar image of Homer in a nut-shell, to which Bishop Atterbury likened Pope the Homeric translator in his coach,[107] collapses in "a moment's space" the content of the *Iliad* into the mir-acle of its tiny form, a "just Epitome" in its transparency and simultaneity of the miracle of reproduction witnessed as if it were original perfection. Such a flawless vision could be glimpsed on the walls of that exercise in aberration, that personal embodiment of the human mind, Pope's grotto at Twickenham.

THE DECEIVED EYE AND THE DISEMBODIED GAZE

As both Addison and the anonymous spectator testify, the ultimate pleasure of the camera obscura consists in the way in which it renders perception itself visible. By merging mimesis with creation, this device goes beyond verisimil-itude in a dazzling version of *trompe l'oeil,* an act of deceit in which the spectators are willing participants. The white sheet on which color and form are projected, like the blank page and *tabula rasa* of Locke's model of the mind, provides the space for an alternative universe; a space, like that of the veil painted by that master of mimesis, Pliny's Parrhasios, "in which figuration [is] destined to ap-pear."[108] The story of Zeuxis and Parrhasios, in its competitive pitting of mimesis against self-contained theatricality, bears repeating in the camera obscura's con-text:

> Parrhasios and Zeuxis entered into competition, Zeuxis exhibiting a pic-ture of some grapes, so true to nature that birds flew up to the wall of the stage. Parrhasios then displayed a picture of a linen curtain realistic to such a degree that Zeuxis, elated by the verdict of the birds, cried out that now at last his rival must draw the curtain and show his picture. On discovering his mistake he surrendered the prize to Parrhasios, admitting candidly that he, Zeuxis, had deceived only the birds, while Parrhasios had deceived himself, a painter.[109]

Lacan's summation of the moral of this story, the moral which makes Plato condemn painting, is that the story illustrates not the power of mimesis but rather the success of *trompe l'oeil.* He explains Plato's disapproval thus:

> What is it that attracts and satisfies us in *trompe l'oeil?* When is it that it captures our attention and delights us? At the moment when, by a mere shift of our gaze, we are able to realize that the representation does not move with the gaze and that it is merely a *trompe l'oeil* . . . The picture does not compete with appearance, it competes with what Plato designates

for us beyond appearance as being the Idea. It is because the picture is the appearance that says it is that which gives the appearance that Plato attacks painting, as if it were an activity competing with his own.[110]

Painting in *trompe l'oeil,* like poetry in *The Essay on Man,* competes with philosophy in substituting presentation for representation, in being what it says it is. For all its ephemerality, the *trompe l'oeil* of the camera obscura, which gives the eye the pleasure of shifting from the image to its source and back again, is the epitome of the art of gardening. In its unadulterated form, gardening is the study, and the (re)production, of the nature of things. "Gardening is near a-kin to Philosophy, for Tully says Agricultura proxima sapientae" [agriculture is near to wisdom], Pope opined, claiming to be "as much a better Gardiner, as I'm a worse Poet."[111] Poets were not allowed in Plato's *Republic,* but one could say that a gardener, usurping the philosopher's prerogative, designed it.

"The . . . example of Parrhasios," says Lacan, "makes it clear that if one wishes to deceive a man, what one presents to him is the painting of a veil, that is to say, something that incites him to ask what is behind it."[112] In the case of the camera obscura, the veil is never lifted, only projected upon. The miniature landscape of the camera obscura, projected upon the walls of Plato's cave, Pope's grotto, gives transparent form to a disembodied gaze, free from nature's particulars and excrescences, and therefore able to apprehend and produce things in the spotless reflection of their essence. What Parrhasios' veil and the camera's blank surface present us with is that which both frames and covers the real: the unraisable curtain of the theater of perception for the incorporeal male viewer.[113] As Jonathan Crary notes, "The camera obscura *a priori* prevents the observer from seeing his or her position as part of the representation. The body then is a problem the camera could never solve except by marginalizing it into a phantom in order to establish a space of reason."[114] Vision is thereby disembodied. Like Addison preferring the accidental landscape to the "true," the subject formed by the camera obscura rejects the details of his sensual experience for the self-reflective and objective distance the darkened room provides.[115] In his commentary on Pliny's famous anecdote in the related context of an essay on the Roman *xenia,* the illusionistic wall-painting found in ancient suburban villas, Norman Bryson emphasizes "its most remarkable [and little remarked] feature,"[116] the location of the episode in a theater. Thus, in the case of the marvels of the camera obscura (which we might think of as the enlightened Englishman's equivalent to the *xenia's* play with illusion), and the tricks of perspective of theaters and gardens, naive mimesis was never the point: "the pictures Pliny describes are in fact caught up in the most elaborate play of shifts between differing ontological levels."[117] For Bryson, this difference of levels is also social, signalling a move from "a pastoral world [of] pre-cultural harmonies between men and nature" to the "ironic, satirical world of vitiated appetite and social hierarchy."[118]

For an England whose anxieties about consumption, excess, and the enforcement of social hierarchies are reflected and projected in images, ideal and satirical, of ancient Rome, the miniature brilliance of the camera obscura offers an ideal method for regulating a cycle of exchange, both economic and aesthetic, which as depicted in the self-propelling infinite motion of *The Rape of the Lock* eludes individual control. What Bryson says about Trimalchio's feast in the *Satyricon* could equally apply to Belinda's life of luxury, or Timon's excessive display in *To Burlington:*

> [In the *xenia*] both representation and wealth are understood to have the Trimalchian capacity for exceeding the real and for creating a fictional expansion that transcends the limitations of appetite, the parameters of space, and the ontology of the actual world. Wealth and representation function here as cognate terms, so that to adorn the chamber with *xenia* and *trompe l'oeil* is to display not only one's wealth but the very principle of that wealth: the outstripping of necessity and limitation.[119]

Like the invisible boundary of the ha-ha which frames the unowned natural landscape, like the subtle transitions and gradations of tone in Pope's poems, the camera obscura on the grotto wall, by teaching its spectator to view a natural reality that is also property, provides just such an ontological exercise in "fictional expansion" and moderate return to limits.[120]

Carole Fabricant reads the early eighteenth-century's fondness for the camera obscura as indicative of the period's "simultaneous embrace and rejection of empirical reality . . . a process which discards nature in the raw for nature in a finer—which is to say, a more artificial and regulatable—tone."[121] She thus locates the familiar characterization of nature as feminine in a historically particularized ideology of gender that called for the amendment of woman and landscape in man's unfallen image of Paradise. Like the absolute Eastern monarch edited out of Addison's essay, and like Adam, indeed like God himself, in Eden, the landowner in his garden has absolute rule over a nature he improves, in fact redeems, so that she may better become herself in a process "whereby what Charles Cotton termed the 'warts and boils, the *Pudenda* of nature' were transformed into the purified and modestly concealed private parts of a restored Eden."[122]

The camera obscura is indeed perfectly suited to such a restoration process. Offering a control even more complete than that afforded by the fixed and ephemeral boundaries of the landscape garden, "the camera obscura allows the subject to guarantee and police the correspondence between exterior world and interior representation and to exclude anything disorderly or unruly."[123] While immersed in this paradigm, the self-objectification of Pope's grotto also disrupts it. A recognition of what is at stake in such gendered exclusions and oppositions should not obscure the ways in which the process, exemplified by the camera obscura on the grotto wall, of masculine "restoration" of nature's flaws also involved a fascinated desire to uncover her defects; defects which, as Addison's essay shows, can project themselves back upon a overly visible and therefore feminine art. In the grotto, the camera's projection of a transparent, representative and male nature can only be made visible against a defective feminine background.[124]

COINS WITHOUT CHARACTER

Pope continued to work on the grotto until his death, his design moving continually toward a reproduction of "nature" both objectively accurate and subjectively charged. Viewed from the poet's perspective in the 1740s, the grotto he described in 1725 might seem merely a "poet's plaything."[125] Fascinated by the geological marvels of his friend Ralph Allen's quarries in Bristol and Bath, in 1740 he "new-conceived his grotto as a cavernous place very much like an actual mine or an actual quarry,"[126] a place which "would resemble Nature in all her workings" and stand as "the best Imitation of Nature" he ever made.[127] As he labored toward this end, he wrote to Bolingbroke of his efforts to "patch up a Grotto (the same You have so often sate in the Sunny part of under my house), with all the varieties of Natures works under ground—Spars, Minerals & Marbles," in order to create "a Study for Virtuosi."[128] In all its natural detail, the grotto becomes in Pope's own view and in the eyes of readers and tourists to come, the most successfully realized metaphor for the poet's art, an art which simultaneously eschews and flaunts human intervention and personal appropriation.[129] In all its curiosity, the grot served as the perfect emblem of a self-constructed and self-publicizing poet.

In his "Verses on a Grotto by the River Thames, at Twickenham, composed of Marbles, Spars and Minerals," Pope describes a place adorned by the raw material of unconverted wealth, where "Unpolish'd Gemms no Ray on Pride bestow, / And latent Metals innocently glow." The visitor is commanded to

"Approach. Great NATURE studiously behold! / And eye the Mine without a Wish for Gold." The beauties of the grot remain unexchangeable, unpossessable, and thus invaluable, as does the marginal virtue of Pope and his politically excluded friends, Bolingbroke, Wyndham and Marchmont, whom the poem goes on to praise. The grot affords its beauty only to those who cannot use it, "who dare to love their Country, and be poor." Edited out of the poem was an obscure couplet that gets to the heart of the grot's nature: "Thou see'st that Island's Wealth, where only free, / Earth to her Entrails feels not Tyranny."[130] Only when glimpsed as the product of an inhuman revelation is wealth free of both human vice and arbitrary value; earth is opened to her entrails, but feels nothing. This idealization of mining as nature at its most primitive edits out the violence of human art needed to achieve such revelation. In this regard Milton's account of Satan's minions mining to create Pandaemonium in Book II of *Paradise Lost,* and Ovid's narrative of man's fall into art through the violation of nature by mining in Book I of the *Metamorphoses* haunt the grotto's natural revelations with the ghosts of human labor.

When Pope puzzles over the use of riches in *To Bathurst,* he begins by pondering the invention of money. Bathurst's opinion is summarized:

> That Man was made the standing jest of Heav'n;
> And Gold but sent to keep the fools in play,
> For some to heap, and some to throw away. (4–6)

But Pope contradicts this ironic and aesthetic view, a view held "from Jove to Momus," of a satiric universe with a narrative of the origins of wealth that reduces gold to its elemental status. To construct such an origin is inevitably to tell the story of a fall into labor; to call up memories of a long cultural equation of mining with the evils of human civilization, which equates human art and human curiosity with an uncanny bringing to light of what ought to have remained hidden.

> But I, who think more highly of our kind,
> (And surely, Heav'n and I are of a mind)
> Opine, that Nature, as in duty bound,
> Deep hid the shining mischief under ground:
> But when by Man's audacious labor won,
> Flam'd forth this rival to, its Sire, the Sun,
> Then careful Heav'n supply'd two sorts of Men,
> To squander these, and those to hide agen. (7–14)

With audacious labor comes visible revelation, and with visibility comes the true fall for Pope, the fall into exchange. "What Nature wants, commodious Gold bestows" (21), Pope goes on to suggest, immediately drawing back from the sentiment, for supplying Nature's wants leads to both usefulness and the catalog of corruption the poem goes on to outline. *To Bathurst* instead tries to imagine a nature that wants for nothing and whose provenance extends even to the most unnatural of human excess. Pope's trust of a natural order for the circulation of wealth in *To Bathurst* is an attempt to create a natural history of exchange, to reimagine the human vagaries and variety evidenced by extremes of consumption controlled by the fixity of a "ruling passion," to reconcile the discrepancies and injustices of his capitalist society in a grand conceptual couplet ordering of nature into "reconcil'd extremes of drought and rain" (168):

> Riches, like insects, when concealed they lie,
> Wait but for wings, and in their season, fly.
> Who sees pale Mammon pine amidst his store,
> Sees but a backward steward for the Poor;
> This year a Reservoir, to keep and spare,
> The next a Fountain, spouting thro' his Heir,
> In lavish streams to quench a Country's thirst,
> And Men and Dogs shall drink him 'till they burst. (171–179)

The brutality of the final couplet belies the uneasiness of the poet's trust in an invisible chaos of exchange which, as we have already seen in Part One, extends beyond any individual attempt to interpret or control it. Gold is secret both in its original location underground and in its ability to conceal what it stands for; paper credit, that simulation of gold's mystery, reveals even more disturbingly the precarious invisibility of value that "silent sells a King, or buys a Queen" (78). The vision of the grotto is all the more compelling in its insistence on visible nature, and on a host of invaluable elements, in some cases the stuff of which money is made, that stand for nothing but themselves.

What is invaluable in one perspective seems worthless in another. In 1729 Lady Mary Wortley Montagu satirizes the grotto as the home of the Goddess of Dulness, "Adorn'd within by Shells of small expence, / (Emblems of tinsel Rhime, and triffleing Sense)," the meaningless baubles which gave rise to the *Rape of the Lock*'s heroicomical worlds.[131] And though William Mason, in his elegy *Musaeus: A Monody on the Death of Pope in Imitation of Milton's "Lycidas"* (1747) sees the grotto as so powerfully emblematic that he sets Pope's deathbed scene within it, he evokes the shade of Milton to describe "this assemblage meet / of Coral, ore and shell" as emblematic of Pope's early poetry, and makes Pope's shade reject the grot as "toys of thoughtless youth."[132] Such toys are the stuff of coins without character, available for Pope's own imprint in the form of the personal narrative of the souvenir, inalienable in their singularity. For if nature comes alive in all its human variety ("Grant but as many sorts of Mind as Moss" (18), Pope observes in *To Cobham*) in gardens, she is more successfully immured, understood, and displayed as unique self-reflection in the grot, possessed more easily "in these [geological] sort of works . . . than in her Animal, much less in her Rational Productions,"[133] under ground.

To enter the grotto, then, is to see nature in its most primitive state, to witness the source of things. Shaftesbury's Philocles is converted to enthusiasm for nature's genius when he enters such a cavern (imaginary voyages through the universe in the eighteenth century almost always included a version of a "journey to the center of the earth"), and discovers "the principle of *irregularity* as an integral aspect of nature":

> Here, led by Curiosity, we find *Minerals* of different Natures which by their Simplicity discover no less of the Divine Art, than the most compounded of Nature's Works . . . So various are the Subjects of our Contemplation, that even the Study of these inglorious Parts of Nature, in the nether World, is able it-self alone to yield large Matter and Employment for the busiest Spirits of Men, who in the Labour of these Experiments can willingly consume their Lives.[134]

For Shaftesbury, geological phenomena reduce nature to her most basic components: variability and durability. The mine thus offers the greatest opportunity for the labor of virtuosi who consume their lives not with commodities but with active curiosity, with the desire for things in themselves, for form emerging "at the moment of visual genesis [when] things are charged with their full significance."[135] The quarry figures a moment of spatial and temporal origin; at the center of the earth, natural and human history begin in the discerning of the "character, [the] physiognomy" of stilled chaos. Noting that eighteenth-century geology "confirmed that change is everywhere: man could trust in nothing, not even the solid earth," and pointing to the Lisbon earthquake as concrete evidence, Barbara Stafford observes, "matter in its state of chaos was believed to possess a character, a physiognomy, qualifying it to have a bonafide history preserved in the records of geology. In fact, the study of human history was usurped by that of natural history, with all that the latter implied in terms of the action of irresistible titanic forces during the passage of aeons."[136] Pope remarkably miniaturizes such universal history in the grot as his own.

The landscape gardener's fantasy of an unmediated relation to nature, one free of the ideological and human labor that transform land into property, is best carried out not in the center but on the margins, in the earth's "inglorous parts." Thus Pope's "Inscription" can transform "A Grotto of Shells at Crux-Easton the Work of Nine Young Ladies" into a paradigm of transparency not unlike the camera obscura's merging of art and nature:

> Here shunning idleness at once and praise,
> This radiant pile nine rural sisters raise;
> The glitt'ring emblem of each spotless dame,
> Clear as her soul, and shining as her frame;
> Beauty which Nature only can impart,
> And such a polish as disgraces Art;
> But Fate dispos'd them in this humble sort,
> And hid in desarts what wou'd charm a court.[137]

Nature's most inglorious parts, those which mark her as feminine, are here transformed by the embroidery of women's hands, in humble and, or so this fantasy would have it, hidden circumstances like Pope's own, into identity's "glittr'ing emblem."

The evolution of Pope's grotto from the camera's transparency to the mine's obscurity is therefore one more of continuity than of contrast: the camera obscura's ideal landscape evolves into the wonder of a quarry created, or so the architect would have it seem, without human art or toil.[138] In both cases the spectator remains dazzled by the mind's singular capacity to confound art with nature. The ladies at Crux-Easton raise their "radiant pile" of shells themselves, but Pope's grotto simulates a natural subterranean obscurity. Thus a "fine and very uncommon Petrifaction from *Okey-Hole* in *Somersetshire, from Mr. Bruce,*"[139] was rumored to have been produced when "Pope employed soldiers to fire muskets to dislodge stalactites for his grotto in the famous cavern on the south-west slope of the Mendip Hills."[140] And though in 1742 the poet boasted to that great collector of natural curiosity, the virtuoso Sir Hans Sloane, that the grotto "consists wholly of Natural Productions, owning nothing to the Chissel, or Polish," his gardener lists "some very natural Rock-work, compiled of Flints and Cinders, from the Glass-houses, Furnaces, &c. with some Grains of Mundic artfully mixed with White Spar" as one of structure's most notable features.[141] A bitter epigram on the editor of the death-bed edition of Pope's *Works* (1751), William Warburton, illustrates the ways in which Pope's claims to singularity in both the grotto and in print can be undermined:

> Close to the grotto of the Twickenham bard—
> Too close adjoins a tanner's yard.
> So verse and prose are to each other tied,
> So Warburton and Pope allied.[142]

The singularity of Pope's grotto attempts both universality and individuality, evolving over the years into a collection of souvenirs generated from the minerals and rock samples brought from distant times and places by friends and fellow collectors, a social fantasy rich in private associations that only the owner could completely decipher. To say that Pope's grotto is a collection of souvenirs is to state a paradox. Both the collection and the souvenir remove the object from its natural context. But while the souvenir's context is replaced by a narrative of individual loss, an object infused with personal nostalgia, the collection transcends time in the service of a self-enclosed totality.[143] In the construction of his grotto Pope simultaneously insists on the particular significance of each fragment-souvenir, a meaning dependent on his individual memory and in need of his gardener's decoding, and on the timeless completion of the collection figured by the grot as a whole. He thus becomes *both* an antiquarian, devoted to objects made valuable by their loss, who attempts to "erase the actual past in order to create an imagined past which is available for consumption"; and a collector who erases history in a "total aestheticization of use value."[144] (One is reminded of Pope's emphasis on the uselessness of the grot's display.)[145] Pope attempts in the grot on the one hand to recreate a quarry as a kind of meta-souvenir, by using metonymy and fragmentation—the displacement of the meaning of an experience onto an object contiguous with it—to reinvent nature through art. On the other hand, conceived as a collection, the grot works through metaphor in order "to have the minimum and complete number of elements necessary for an autonomous world—a world which is both full and singular, which has banished repetition and achieved authority."[146] The mechanical universe of the *Rape of the Lock* is thereby made both personal and natural.

Just as Mack describes Pope's "collecting of traditional *topoi* into something like an identifiable physical presence,"[147] so the paradox of the grotto's personalized totality creates something like an individual natural history.[148] Stones incised with details from the *arma Christi* adorned the entrance and ceiling of the grot, thought to be remnants of older religious buildings and the gift of Catholic friends,[149] juxtaposed with specimens such as "a fine piece of Gold Ore from the *Peruvian* Mines; Silver Ore from the Mines of *Mexico;* several Pieces of Silver

Ore from *Old Spain;* some large Pieces of Gold Clift, from Mr. *Cambridge* in *Gloucestershire* . . . petrified Wood, *Brazil* Pebbles, Egyptian Pebbles and Blood-stones, from Mr. *Brinsden,"* along with one of the more evocative neoclassical examples, Joseph Spence's contribution of "several fine Pieces of the Eruptions from Mount *Vesuvius,* and a fine Piece of Marble from the Grotto of *Egeria* near *Rome*."[150] The grotto is thus both fragmented ruin and self-contained whole, depending, like the *trompe l'oeil,* on the viewer's perspective. It makes sense that Pope thought to adorn such a geological panoply with the classical insignia of "a good Statue with an Inscription."[151] Such a statue was never found, but its nostalgic classical associations inform Pope's brand of nature.

The statue Pope refers to in his letter, in an imaginative reconstruction of origins similar to that of Castell's illustrations, was thought to represent the nymph who adorned the grotto of Egeria near Rome, the source of Spence's gift of marble. The original grotto belonged, legend has it, to the virtuous Roman King Numa, "who was credited with receiving from the nymph Egeria the moral instruction that made his government memorable."[152] Plutarch tells a more provocative variation of Numa's story, giving the classical personification of "the genius of the place" erotic life:

> Numa spoke of a certain goddess or mountain-nymph that was in love with him, and met him in secret . . . and professed that he entertained familiar conversation with the Muses, to whose teaching he ascribed the greatest part of his revelations . . . His reign . . . [was] a living example and verification of that saying which Plato, long afterwards, ventured to pronounce, that the sole and only hope of respite or remedy for human evils was in some happy conjunction of events which should unite in a single person the power of a king and the wisdom of a philosopher, so as to elevate virtue to control and mastery over vice.[153]

Reminiscent of Bolingbroke's answer to Plato, *On the Idea of a Patriot King,* Numa's story also informs the Opposition's attempt in the late 1730s and early 1740s to construct Pope as philosophic adviser to the Prince of Wales.[154] In this myth, "the power of a king" joins with "the wisdom of a philosopher" in the figure of familiar conversation and private trysts with nature's feminine genii, personified as Egeria and the Muses. Arbitrary mastery is reserved for vice, while man's relation to nature is one of mutual desire and secret interrelation. The Oriental magnate's portrait of himself in his landscape is here transformed into a fantasy of reciprocity which makes power a private matter. A further classical source for the grotto locates it in the origins of Aeneas' Roman empire,

Evander's house in *Aeneid* VIII, ancient abode of Saturn and site of future Rome. Dryden translates,

> Mean as it is, this Palace, and this Door,
> Received *Alcides,* then a Conquerour.
> Dare to be poor: accept our homely Food
> Which feasted him; and emulate a God.   (VIII, 477–480)

Like Pope's and Burlington's miniaturization of the glory that was Rome in their respective estates, the "meanness" of Evander's house, and the grotto which imitates it, signifies a virtue that "dares to be poor" by gesturing toward past or invisible origins. When Juvenal's Umbricius, in his third Satire, leaves a corrupt Rome, he pauses to look at the remains of the Egerian grot: "Where *Numa* modell'd once the *Roman* State."[155] In the grot, Pope constructs the reflection of his own satiric disillusionment by superimposing Numa's ideal cave onto the image of Juvenal's "Adult'rate" ruined empire. He creates a polyvalent image, original nature inscribed with its own history, of nostalgia for an unwritten, personal version of the future.

James Ralph mocks the poet's pose of retired poverty in his lampoon *Sawney:*

> SAWNEY, a mimick Sage of huge Renown,
> To *Twickenham* Bow'rs retir'd, enjoys his Wealth,
> His Malice and his Muse: In Grottos cool,
> And cover'd Arbours dreams his Hours away.[156]

Pope's retirement thus becomes, in a masterly version of Williams' negative identification, a negation of "the world of stratagem and compromise and money-grubbing and self-interest" of London, "an imagined ideal community of patriarchal virtues and heroic friends."[157] If as Mack puts it, "all that happened there was translated by the poetic imagination (of which it was itself the handiwork and possibly the conscious symbol) out of history into dream,"[158] Pope insists on giving that history his particular mark.

The Twickenham grotto thus exemplifies the way in which "in the eighteenth century the Renaissance view of the grotto as possessing something static, outside of time, which removes man from the midst of appearances and inserts him into the more authentic core of reality, coexists with a more dynamic geological awareness of the process of mineral formation,"[159] a deathless motion inspired by the same magical power that animated the objects in *The Rape of the Lock,* here re-situated in the death-ridden world of nature. Shifting our gaze from the camera obscura's perfect art to the rock-studded wall itself, the grotto thus becomes a "muse-eum" in both senses of the word: the concrete self-reflection of a private devotion to a classical tradition, and a singular recreation of natural wonders as a collection of curiosities.

BLUNDERS INTO BEAUTIES

The Twickenham grotto came into being because of a defect in Pope's property; the garden was unreachable from the house without crossing the busy public road from London to Hampton Court. In addition to providing the necessary underground passage, the grotto afforded a plethora of naturally artful perspectives: the shell-temple perfectly framed by the view from the river, the Thames glimpsed through an arcade of trees, as if "thro' a Perspective glass."[160] Positioned, like Numa, between city and country in philosophical retirement, the grotto, once enclosed, becomes a model for the mind. From one view, the camera obscura transforms the cave into Locke's metaphor for the understanding, "a closet, wholly shut from light, with only some little openings left, to let in external visible resemblances, or ideas of things without."[161] From the perspective of "a mind to light it up," the grotto becomes the singular image of a self-illuminating chamber in a geological hall of mirrors.[162] Just as viewers of the grotto oscillate between nostalgia for its evocative fragments and appreciation of its scientific immanence, they perform what the camera obscura made impossible, moving in and out of the frame, both passive spectators and active sources of light and meaning.

By the use of water effects, Pope intensified the grotto's variety, and made it a plethora of particularity for the viewing eye.[163] The grotto becomes an essay on the variability of character; its displays of aquatic technology, a different one for each room, provide what Hunt calls a "psychological programme . . . a machinery of meditation"[164] which illustrates and recreates in the viewer an awareness of the protean nature of the human mind. As one eighteenth-century writer puts it: "So various are the characters which water can assume, that there is scarcely an idea in which it may not concur, or *an impression which it cannot enforce*."[165] In the grot's personalized rooms, "each with an anthology of reminiscence," the fluidity of character that was stigmatized in *To a Lady* becomes both personal and universal: as with water, so with nature male or female, character is never "fixed or still."

For a visitor to Twickenham in 1748, the dizzying nature of such a view, enabled by an awareness of art in which "Mr. *Pope's* poetick Genius has introduced a kind of Machinery, which performs the same Part in the Grotto that supernal Powers and incorporeal Beings act in the heroick Species of Poetry," provided "an undistinguishable Mixture of Realities and Imagery."[166] The mirrors in the grotto, like the machinery that animates Belinda's automated world, like the genius that invests an individual landscape with unique character, serve as Pope's most ironically self-conscious comment on the self-reflexive nature of an imagination in continual search for a diversity it creates for itself, whose inability to distinguish between realities and imagery is prominently advertised as the mechanism of its own fine taste, its production of the personal and the particular. For readers of Pope the grotto thus supplies a visual supplement to the printed text, an exhibition which, as Richard Altick has remarked in his history of other sorts of London shows, reified the word.[167]

In his "fantasy" drawing of Pope's garden (see Figure 10), William Kent captures this sense of a miniature world within which classical visions flourish, becoming visible signs of an original poetic sensibility. Pope and Kent stand beside the shell temple which precedes the entrance to the grotto, adjacent to a bust of Homer, which houses a smoking altar, Kent with his palette and brush, Pope holding his perspective glass to his eye. Before them, apotheosized in a beam of light, is a vision of Venus surrounded by sundry Olympian deities. In this image, poet and painter join in an epiphany of nature's genius, a genius made of trivial, mechanical things.

If the grotto at Twickenham, and Twickenham's miniaturization of a Roman villa, can be said to be souvenirs of the glory that was Rome, then it seems clear that Pope knew that such souvenirs are based on an ideologically imagined nature,[168] while personalized by a poet's sensibility in order to make the landscape legible. Pope's readers therefore read both the grot and the garden as he intended, as his signature text evidencing the singularity of that aesthetic of property, taste. The Newcastle visitor describes a place remarkable not for its luxury but for its evidence of "the Taste of the finest Genius that this or any other Age has produced."[169]

This superior taste is informed and deformed by the body, the body toward which the souvenir's narrative of presence gestures, the body whose visible defects, mirrored in the grot as excesses, leave its particular mark on nature's transparency. Susan Stewart might be speaking of the grotto when she links the nostalgia of the souvenir to Freud's construction of fetishism, delineating within the confines of the body the same dialectic of visibility and invisibility which Lacan links to the experience—exemplified by the camera obscura—of *trompe l'oeil*.

Figure 10.

The Shell Temple in Pope's Garden. Pen and sepia drawing by William Kent,
ca. 1725–30.

The souvenir generates a narrative which reaches only "behind," spiraling in a continually inward movement rather than outward toward the future. Here we find the structure of Freud's description of the genesis of the fetish: a part of the body is substituted for the whole, or an object is substituted for the part, until finally, and inversely, the whole body can become object, substituting for the whole. Thus we have the systematic transformation of the object into its own impossibility, its loss and the simultaneous experience of a difference which Freud characterizes as the fetishist's both knowing and not knowing the anatomical distinctions between the sexes.[170]

Thus while the commodity fetishism on phantasmagoric display in *The Rape of the Lock* transforms the metonymies of the social relations of actual production into the metaphors of self-enclosed exchange, the insatiable nostalgia which creates the souvenir removes the metaphor from an object rendered significant only by metonymy, by its proximity to the real thing for which it is a conscious substitute. The object thus becomes at once lost to and overcharged with meaning,[171] like Pope's deformity. In all its singularity and inalienability, Pope's body becomes the ultimate souvenir, fetish object of both an idea of nature and a classical past figured in its image.[172]

Landscape allows Pope to envision the body, and specifically in the case of the grot his own body, as nature, as a figure by which to shape the world. The grotto's display of nature's secrets attempts to restore the body to its origins. But because his body is itself an unnatural paradox, nature in Pope's grotto highlights its own artifice. Samuel Johnson objected to such self-transformation with a vision that cuts Pope down to size. His penetrating analysis of Pope's grotto in the *Life of Pope* makes Pope commonplace by reducing him to the spectacle of his unauthorized deformity:

> [At Twickenham] he planted the vines and quincunx which his verses mention; and being under the necessity to make a subterranean passage to a garden on the other side of the road, he adorned it with fossile bodies, and dignified it with the title of a grotto: a place of silence and retreat, from which he endeavoured to persuade his friends and himself that cares and passions could be excluded.
>
> A grotto is not often the wish or pleasure of an Englishman, who has more frequent need to solicit than exclude the sun; but Pope's excavation was requisite as an entrance to the garden, and, as some men try to be proud of their defects, he extracted an ornament from an inconvenience, and vanity produced a grotto where necessity enforced a passage.[173]

Johnson blinds himself to Pope's merging of geological verisimilitude with a literary tradition of grottos in which "simulaverat artem ingenio natura suo" [nature by her own talent imitated art].[174] Maynard Mack attributes the hostility of Johnson's remarks to "a characteristic lack of sympathy with the *furor rusticus,*" but credits him for having caught

> in passing at an ethical analogy that is highly characteristic of him and contains an important truth about Pope . . . This comfortable estate at Twickenham, famous for its gardens, its grotto, and its distinguished visitors, famous particularly for its occupant, the man who was, in every sense of the phrase he had himself applied to the indwelling powers of nature, "the Genius of the Place"—what was it all if not an exercise in extracting ornament from inconvenience?[175]

Pope's heir as man of letters refuses to do exactly what Mack does so well, namely read the form of Pope's grotto as the poet's own. What Mack fails to do, however, is reflect upon the disconcerting inter-reflections that result from identifying Pope's own particular genius with the idealized "indwelling powers of nature."

When Pope posted a phrase from Horace's Epistle 1.18, "Secretum iter et fallentis semita vitae" [secret passage and the path of an unnoticed life] above the entrance of his grotto, he may have appeared to be endorsing the Roman poet's recommendation of the pursuit of true happiness through private study and retirement rather than public glory. But "fallentis" [unnoticed] has a primary meaning of deceiving, and the grotto seen from this perspective is less a secret passage to a classically inherited privacy than a paradoxically public display of the deformity that barred Pope from public life and physical exertion, and made retirement less volitional than compulsory. A more sympathetic reader of such ambivalence, Swift wrote to Pope upon hearing of the grotto, "I have been long told . . . of your Subterranean Passage to your Garden whereby you turned a blunder into a beauty which is a piece of Ars Poetica."[176] And Pope agreed: "What we cannot *overcome* we must *undergo*."[177] This dynamic between aberrant nature and artful ornament, this submission to personal necessity which can also be seen as an act of monumental self-transformation, insists on the grotto as the polysemous origin of a host of metonymous metaphors for Pope himself. While Dustin Griffin writes that Pope is like what Maynard Mack says of his grotto, "an artful imitation of nature," it is important to keep in mind what both critics omit: Pope, like the grotto, is an artful imitation of a natural deformity.[178]

When tourists flocked to Twickenham, with "curious wish [Pope's] sacred Grott to see,"[179] they came to view the embodiment of the poet in such curiosity. In addition to a detailed map of the Twickenham estate, John Serle's 1745 "Plan of Mr. Pope's Garden, as it was left at his Death" (see Figure 11), published as a souvenir and guidebook for devoted fans, includes a "Plan and Perspective View of the Grotto . . . with An Account of all the Gems, Minerals, Spars and Ores of which it is composed, and from whom and whence they were sent," as well as an appendix of poems on the poet (one billed as "A Character of all his Writings") including Pope's own verses on his grotto translated into Latin and imitated in Latin and Greek sapphics, and R. Dodsley's own "The Cave of Pope: A Prophesy." The "Plan" thus continues Pope's own double trajectory in his design for the grotto by reproducing and cataloging the structure as comprehensive collection of external nature, while also reading and decoding the collection as a personal metaphor for the garden as a whole, and ultimately

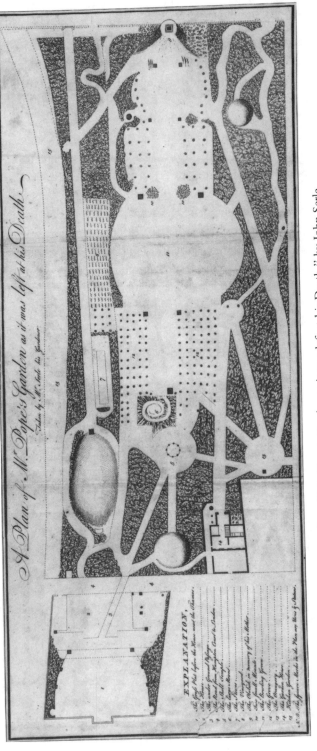

Figure 11.

"A Plan of Mr. Pope's Garden as it was left at his Death," by John Serle.

for the poet himself, who thus becomes collectable. In an act of devotion to the poet's aesthetic, visitors to Twickenham after his death reenact its nostalgically particular truth:

> Then, some small Gem, or Moss, or shining Ore,
>   Departing, each shall pilfer, in fond hope
> To please their Friends, on every distant Shore,
>   Boasting a Relick from the Cave of POPE.[180]

PRIVATE ETHICS

The aesthetic of singularity that the grotto at Twickenham exemplifies makes it unsurprising that Pope's plan for an all-encompassing *Opus Magnum*, his "system of ethics in the Horatian way," remained incomplete; but the grotto also allows us to envision such incompletion as a sort of *trompe l'oeil* in print.[181] The first book of this grand design, *An Essay on Man*, considered "Man in the abstract, his Nature and his State," and saw a transparent order in nature's apparent chaos: "And, spite of Pride, in erring Reason's spite, / One truth is clear, 'Whatever IS, is RIGHT.'" (I, 289–294) The fourth book, in which the *Moral Essays,* now known by their original title, *Epistles to Several Persons,* were to have played a part, was to have concerned "*Ethics* or practical Morality."[182] It is here that Pope's ethical system was abandoned, leaving what to some might seem a ruin, to others a productive transformation of an abstract, albeit grand, idea into particular form. Although the *Epistle to Burlington,* the "gardening poem" upon which Pope placed so much ideological importance, was composed and published first, when the poems were printed with a mind toward the *Opus Magnum,* it came last, in a group that began with *To Cobham* ("of the characters of men"), *To a Lady* ("of the characters of women considered as contradistinguished from the other sex") and *To Bathurst* ("of the use of riches"). Originally subtitled "of taste" (a subtitle revised first to "of false taste" and ultimately to "of the use of riches" in order to pair it as a positive model with the negative example of *Bathurst*), *To Burlington*'s insistence on the gardener's deference to "the genius of the place" takes on new resonance in the light of Pope's own implementation of genius in his garden. When we examine *To Burlington* with the grotto in mind, the poem's apparent formlessness can be traced to "the need for art to emanate from and so to satisfy the individual" in all his singularity.[183] The problem of reading human character by its expression through expenditure in the previous three epistles thus appears to be resolved by the judiciously displayed economy and the fantasy of unmediated power that end *To Burlington* and exemplify good taste. The poem that closes Pope's unfinished opus is from this perspective less about the nature of humanity in all its variety than it is about the power of individual ownership and authority expressed as aesthetic vision.

If Pope plays Adam in his garden and grot, creating tasteful miniature totalities above and below ground, the Paradise in which he dwells at Twickenham is decidedly a fallen one. His reflections on gardening, the culmination of his thoughts on practical morality, concern not the nature of things themselves but the relation of human beings to objects. For all of its idealism, *To Burlington's* celebration of taste must tacitly acknowledge the limits of a self defined by property, and by implication, the potential indecipherability of a self that opts out of such a definition. Unlike the deathless fragility of the *Rape of the Lock's* hermetic universe, Pope's gardens, in and out of print, are limited by time and mortality. The transparency of *To Burlington's* georgic ideal of man's harmony with willing nature is momentarily figured, in the fall of Timon's villa, as ruin. But as in the classical fantasy of Kent and Pope's vision in the garden, the sight of the disappearance of human pride is redeemed by the reanimation of the landscape:

> Another age shall see the golden Ear
> Imbrown the Slope, and nod on the Parterre,
> Deep Harvests bury all his Pride has plann'd,
> And laughing Ceres re-assume the land.   (173–176)

"Maybe," John Dixon Hunt surmises, Pope "came to realize more thoroughly than he did when he first wrote it in 1725 that 'no publick Professors of Gardening (any more than any publick Professors of Virtue) are equal to the Private Practisers of it.' "[184] Ultimately, virtue for Pope cannot exist in general; women, whose "virtues open fairest in the shade" (202) become, in all their excessive particularity, the rule rather than the exception. By making his deformed body visible, by giving it in the construction of the grotto a natural frame composed of singular fragments, Pope obliterates the possibility of transparent analogy, and of true or ideal character. Like Achilles dismantling Agamemnon's scepter above and below ground, exposing it as product of garden and mine, dead branch and worthless metal, Pope in his grotto reveals the arbitrary value of nature defined by and against the masculine abstract, nature invisible, nature without art. What remains is a couplet: a universality made of personal remnants, a whole formed and deformed by untranslatable particulars.

Pope wrote to Swift in 1736 about the slow progress of the *Opus Magnum*:

"But alas! the task is great, and *non sum qualis eram!* My understanding indeed, such as it is, is extended rather than diminish'd: I see things more in the whole, more consistent, and more clearly deduced from, and related to, each other. But what I gain on the side of philosophy, I lose on the side of poetry: the flowers are gone, when the fruits begin to ripen."[185] *"Non sum qualis eram"* [I am not what I was], alludes to the first ode of the fourth book of Horace, a reluctant love poem composed after the Roman poet had abandoned lyric poetry for the pursuit of philosophy in the *Epistles,* and the only complete imitation of a Horace ode in Pope's oeuvre. The series of tensions to which this passage gestures—between poetry and philosophy, between lyric and weightier genres, between personal passion and comprehensive vision, between imagination and understanding, between abstract vision and material execution—are figured in Horace's ode and Pope's imitation as if on matching sides of an ancient coin, as if the closer the English poet came to a vision of totality, the more diminished and particular the image.

4

Horace
and the
Art of
Self-Collection

[A] cabinet of Medals is a body of history.

Joseph Addison, *Dialogues upon the
Usefulness of Ancient Medals* (1721)

In its perpetually shifting shows of art and nature, its uniting of the variety of human character with the singularity of the poet's collection, its figuring of metaphoric inwardness as metonymic display of bodily deformity, Alexander Pope's grotto makes his unique mark. Both a museum of natural curiosities and an assemblage of literary topoi, the grotto is perhaps Pope's most representative and elusive self-portrait.

If the grotto allows the poet in his garden to figure his deformity with nature's material, the Horatian mode allows him to translate deformity into the mark of print. In both instances Pope offers his reader a disfigured emblem, uniting the visual and verbal by the pains of his own detailed labor and the reader's difficulty in interpretation.[1] Transparency and obstruction come to figure each other in a process of mutual distortion. Just as the indecipherability of the grotto's collection of fragments made it Pope's personal structure, so in the Horatian poems, the "spots" which mar his medium enable it to be read as transparent self-exposure.

While the previous chapter was organized around the topography of Twickenham, this chapter takes the form of an emblem, a tableau in which Alexander Pope views Horace. The imitation and heroically embattled emulation of Horace which consumed Pope's career after his translation of the *Iliad* find parallels in an image of the English poet poring over an indecipherable inscription beneath a familiar portrait on an ancient Roman coin. Pope's early epistle *To Mr. ADDISON Occasioned by his Dialogues on MEDALS* (drafted as early as 1713, published 1720)[2] had celebrated the exemplary power of the medal or coin to preserve what "all-devouring years" destroy. The poem begins with a panorama of Rome in ruins:

> See the wild Waste of all-devouring years!
> How Rome her own sad Sepulchre appears,
> With nodding arches, broken temples spread!
> The very Tombs now vanish'd like their dead!
> Imperial wonders rais'd on Nations spoil'd,
> Where mix'd with Slaves the groaning Martyr toil'd;
> Huge Theatres, that now unpeopled Woods,
> Now drained a distant country of her Floods;
> Fanes, which admiring Gods with pride survey,
> Statues of Men, scarce less alive than they;
> Some felt the silent stroke of mould'ring age,
> Some hostile fury, some religious rage;
> Barbarian blindness, Christian zeal conspire,
> And Papal piety, and Gothic fire.
> Perhaps, by its own ruins sav'd from flame,
> Some bury'd marble half preserves a name;
> That Name the learn'd with fierce disputes pursue,
> And give to Titus old Vespasian's due.   (1–18)

This view transforms the history of Rome's fall into a narrative of aesthetic failure. An empire whose excessive art flourished in "Imperial Wonders" that spoiled nations, whose spectacles emptied forests of wild beasts and whose mock-naval combats drained colonies of water, is faulted for a precariously grand scale of self-representation which, like Timon's villa, ultimately falls to the nature it plunders. Rome itself becomes a tomb without an inscription. The "admiring" reciprocity between human and divine characterized by Roman temples and living statuary falls to historical forces reduced to a series of abstractions. This process mimics the work of the medal the poem will go on to describe. Historical distinctions between pagan and Christian are effaced, leaving only a partially legible name, preserved "by its own ruins," and mistaken by its readers.

This monitory example of a Rome destroyed by its "vast design" is heeded by a personified Ambition, who takes the warning's aesthetic message:

> Ambition sigh'd; She found it vain to trust
> The faithless Column and the crumbling Bust;
> Huge moles, whose shadow stretch'd from shore to shore,
> Their ruins ruin'd, and their place no more!

> Convinc'd, she now contracts her vast design,
> And all her Triumphs shrink into a Coin: (19–24)

Like Pope shrinking the magnificence of classical epic into the *Rape of the Lock's* narrow confines and ultimately into the personal limits of his own brand of heroic Horatian satire, ambition learns that to preserve something intact one must diminish it into an object the eye and hand can grasp, into the body's scale:

> The Medal, faithful to its charge of fame,
> Thro' climes and ages bears each form and name:
> In one short view subjected to your eye
> Gods, Emp'rors, Heroes, Sages, Beauties, lie.   (31–34)

Horace is the miniature portrait, the medal if you will, within which Pope's grand and unfinished plan for an *Opus Magnum* is ultimately confined, and in relation to which Pope's "I"—both his lyric voice and his personal vision—defines and displays itself.

Like the minerals which adorn the grotto walls, such medals are coins without character; removed from social circulation and from historical context and assigned a value based on immaterial qualities. Philander, the proponent of the "usefulness of Medals" in Addison's *Dialogues* states: "you are not to look upon a cabinet of Medals as a treasure of mony, but of knowledge, nor must you fancy any charms in gold, but in the figures and inscriptions that adorn it. The intrinsic value of an old coin does not consist in its metal but its erudition . . . a piece of mony that was not worth a peny fifteen hundred years ago, may now be rated at fifty crowns, or perhaps a hundred guineas."[3] Medals are language embodied and envisioned, both "a collection of pictures in miniature" and "a kind of Printing, before the art was invented."[4] Old money turned worthless, medals outlast not only their value as coins but also the objects and persons whose likenesses adorn them. Diminished restorations of sublime ruins, they epitomize the power of representation to take on and to replace substance, to defeat decay by material means. In this regard, medals are not unlike Pope's satires, studded with "nameless names" which endure, thanks to the poet's art, beyond their time and beyond significance.[5]

But while print is limited by the confines of the page and the time and labor of reading, medals "tell their story much quicker, and sum up a whole volume in twenty or thirty reverses. They are the best epitomes in the world, and let you see with one cast of an eye the substance of above a hundred pages."[6] These artifacts thereby achieve both a visual immediacy and a historical particularity which exceeds that of print: "Every exploit has its date set to it . . . therefore it is much safer to quote a Medal than an Author, for in this case you do not appeal to a *Suetonius* or a *Lampridius,* but to the Emperor himself, or to the whole body of a *Roman* Senate."[7] If, as Sir Joshua Reynolds claims, "What is done by Painting, must be done at one blow; curiosity has received at once all the satisfaction it can ever have," medals augment the pleasure of instantaneousness by satisfying the antiquarian's need for narrative.[8] Metonymic substitutes for the authorities who minted them, medals are commodities that remember, histories that speak for themselves. As Richard Kroll argues in his discussion of one of Addison's most prominent literary-numismatic predecessors, John Evelyn, the medal is not so much a fragment as a "synecdoche, a concrete and objectified sign of a history whose movements and motives remain largely unreified and whose true process remains largely inaccessible . . . No single historical image more perfectly encapsulates, embodies and condenses historical significance than the medal, whose emblematic constitution fuses the pictorial and the linguistic."[9] It is this defense against entropy and chaos in the shape of a human body which Pope wants print to perform in Horace's likeness.

Distinguishing Addison from short-sighted collectors, the "pale Antiquaries" who "with sharpen'd sight . . . th'inscription value, but the rust adore" (35–36), who fail to see the medal's larger tableau, Pope asserts:

> Theirs is the Vanity, the Learning thine:
> Touch'd by thy hand, again Rome's glories shine,
> Her Gods, and god-like Heroes rise to view,
> And all her faded garlands bloom a-new.
> Nor blush, these studies thy regard engage;
> These pleas'd the Fathers of poetic rage;
> The verse and sculpture bore an equal part,
> And Art reflected images to Art. (45–52)

The same fantasy of perfect self-reflection that animated the landscape improved by Burlington's man-power and Pope's poetic command is invoked here as the perfectly transparent correspondence of verbal and visual modes of representation embodied by the medal. Such mutual illumination and reflection also characterize the happy co-dependence of painter and poet in the *Epistle to Jervas:* "How oft' our slowly-growing works impart, / While images reflect from art to art?" (19–20). Portrait, poem, landscape, and medal, all depend on an ideal of unobstructed transparency and concrete embodiment.

In his *Dialogues upon the Usefulness of Ancient Medals* Addison explicitly makes the comparison between medals and poems by using Horace's example. Restoring lost or ruined buildings to view, the structures depicted on medals

> are buildings which the *Goths* and *Vandals* could not demolish, that are infinitely more durable than stone or marble, and will perhaps last as long as the earth it self. They are in short so many real monuments of Brass.[10]

Horace's famous Ode 3.30, the "sphragis" or personal seal with which he closes and claims authority for his first three books of odes,[11] which begins "exegi monumentum aere perennius" [I have built a monument more lasting than brass], is here literalized as a "real monument of Brass" for which the poem serves as inscription. Achilles's condemnation of the scepter torn away from the earth for the sake of representing human authority is regrounded in an elemental representation that outlasts that which it figures. Medals return figuration to its essence, its element; as such they shape and preserve a kind of natural history, giving that which has been lost to sight a face and a form.

To define the Horatian, and thereby to discern what is unique about Pope's appropriation of the Horatian mode, is to puzzle over the literary version of an antique medal, a curious conjunction of visual and verbal registers which has endured past its context's complications. Petronius in the *Satyricon* refers to Horace's "curiosa felicitas," a quality which a contemporary of Pope's, Lewis Crusius in his *Lives of the Roman Poets* (1726–1732), defines with a nod to the *Ars Poetica* as "the art of doing what he looked upon to be so difficult, of speaking upon common subjects in an extraordinary manner."[12] The familiarity of Horace's subject matter, framed by the uniqueness of his manner of expression, determines "the two characteristicks of this Writer's Style, and these make him so very difficult to be translated above any other Writer;"[13] the character that makes Horace singular is thus both inimitable and so unmistakable as to verge on cliché.

Such curious felicity has over the centuries transformed the individual author Horace into an adjective. Modern and early modern readers of Horace are often certain about who he was, what he looked like, what sort of friend he would have made; biographies abound, much longer than Suetonius's brief "vita Horati." There is something about Horace in particular which makes readers prefer imagining the "real" Horace to reading his poems. Just as the neoclassical English garden discerns itself in a nostalgic vision of a Rome which never existed, so the Horatian mode originates in the creation of a self-reflective myth.

Horace has become a compelling mirror for poets and literary critics in part because, perhaps more than any other Augustan writer, he made the literary life, his own in particular, his main subject. "Art" and "life" in Horace are terms which his poetry constantly redefines and reconceives in new relationships. He begins the *Satires* in the guileless first person. In the first book, Horace plays the worldly poet who manages to live the simple life in town, commenting on daily life and human foibles; in the second, he retreats to the wings as the good-natured sufferer of voluble fools.[14]

New forms dictate a different self. In the *Odes* Horace is the public "vates," both priest and prophet writing odes in celebration (and sometimes castigation) of Roman power, or the lyric bystander opting for private pleasure over public obligation; he is the inspired poet singing the praises of Bacchus or the Bandusian fountain, or the Sabine farmer writing to prominent public figures as a private friend. The *Odes* explore the limits between public and private, the way in which private assertions are powerful public statements, the way in which life is art's material.

In a time of subtle censorship in which official propaganda rivalled literature for its craft and ingenuity,[15] Horace is one of many poets for whom a personal aesthetic becomes a public moral choice. Just as Rome's first emperor waived the public title to his power, calling himself "princeps" [first citizen] rather then "imperator,"[16] so a characteristic mode of Augustan poetry was the recusatio, the deceptively humble refusal of a private poet to comply with a patron's demand, usually for heroic literature in the state's service. To choose to write lyric rather than epic, and to address the opening poem of one's collection of odes (as Horace did) not to Augustus but to Rome's covert ruler Maecenas[17] is to make one's authorial career an implicit recusatio. Even Virgil, in taking on the task of creating a Roman heroic poem worthy of Homer, evades unequivocal support of public authority by producing what might be called a lyric epic.[18]

Perhaps the most representative of Horatian anecdotes concerns a recusatio that occurred late in the poet's career. Horace's singularity, the myth of his freedom both from political constraints and personal origins, is given biographical form by the way in which like the twelve-year old Pope writing the "Ode on Solitude," the Roman poet seems to have leapt already middle-aged from the brains of many of his critics. So appealing is this example that one critic starts his study of Horace with a chapter imagining the incident in minute detail, writing as if he were inside Horace's mind.[19] Its subject is, typically, not an action but a refusal to act: Horace's demurral to Augustus's request that he become the emperor's private secretary.[20] The emperor wanted a companion to help him with his correspondence—other secretarial duties were handled by a slave. Horace would have been a courtier with access to invaluable imperial information, and he would have been outfitted in a manner befitting such a lofty station. Maecenas's gift of the Sabine farm, scholars surmise, would have been dwarfed in comparison.

Horace refused Augustus's offer on the grounds of poor health. The emperor understood, or at least never gave up the friendship. Crusius, like many critics to follow, places this declaration of independence at the heart of the Horatian myth:

> [Augustus], being taken with his merit and address, admitted him to a great familiarity in his more private hours, and afterwards made him no small offers of preferment. The Poet had the greatness of mind to refuse them all; and the Prince was generous enough not to be offended at his freedom in doing so. A man indeed must perfectly be of that indifferent temper his Writings speak him to have been of, with respect to the pride and ostentation of life, and the vanities of a court, to refuse a place so honourable and advantageous, as that of his Secretary. The life he liked best and lived as much as he could, was the reverse of a Court life, in a retirement free from the hurry and trouble that attend the ambitious.[21]

Yet the myth of self-mastery which fixes this poet's image is jeopardized by a poetry which continually revises that image. The impulse to epitomize Horace in a gesture of tactful evasion of worldly authority is indeed appropriate, but it is also futile. Horace's ultimate independence is from himself.

When in his famous Ode 3.30, with which he closes and seals his first lyric collection, Horace claims to have built in his poetry a monument more lasting than brass ("exegi monumentum aeri perennius"),[22] he bestows on himself an authority which supersedes that of the monumental Augustus and appropriates even his title. Horace the poet declares himself a "princeps": "ex humili potens, / Princeps Aeolium carmen ad Italos / deduxisse modos" (13–14) [exalted from a low estate, the first to have translated Greek song into Italian measures]. While Augustus's assumption of the epithet of "princeps," rather than "imperator," was an act of false modesty which enabled him to accentuate his power by the freedom with which he waived its name, Horace's election of the title reveals and transforms the force behind its original. Like the emperor, he is a conqueror, but his conquest is the bloodless victory of successful imitation that is "original" Latin poetry. While Augustus first wanted it remembered, and later wanted it forgotten, that he was Caesar's nephew, Horace recalls his own lowly origins by reminding us that he is "ex humili potens." (Like Augustus, however, he does not recount the specifics of his debt to the past. Both emperor and poet present themselves as self-made men. Horace's fishmonger father has been edited out of this portrait of the "vates.") But in implicit contrast to the emperor's incontestable martial authority which governs the shape of the state, the poet's power, the spoil of his solitary, literary battles with his Greek models, can give shape to history. The poet Horace thus proclaims himself the true hero.

What is Horatian about this moment is the way in which biographical truth and literary artifact merge in Horace's "monumentum." Ode 3.30, both in its content, and as the crowning glory of a material artifact, the monument of Horace's three books, celebrates a progression from the real-life Horace to Horace the poet. Horace presupposes a past with which the reader is familiar, and remakes the familiar and private in the guise of the public and heroic.

In the *Epistles,* Horace reverses the poles of life and art.[23] A shift in genre in Horace signals not only a continuation of the Horatian myth, but also an awareness on the reader's part of who the persona of Horace has been. In the first lines of the *Epistles* Horace addresses Maecenas to whom, he reminds us, he also addressed the first of his *Odes.*[24]

> Subject of my first poetry, worthy to be the subject of my last, do you ask me, having been tested enough, and now having been given my discharge, to enter the old lists again? My age is not the same, nor is my mind. Veianius, his arms fixed to a post in the temple of Hercules, hides retired in the country, so that he won't have to once again beg the people for his release at the edge of the arena. There is someone who repeatedly makes my purified ear ring: "Be sensible, and release the aging horse at the right time, lest at last he go wrong, a laughing stock, and break his wind." Now therefore I put aside both verses and all other things of public show and I care for and seek out what is true and fitting, and I am wholly involved in this.

By addressing Maecenas, Horace links his project in the *Epistles* back to that of the *Odes,* while breaking the gesture's symmetry. Closure is only indicated; Horace's last poetry will have a new subject, and, worthy though Maecenas may be, this recusatio implies that the new type of poetry it exemplifies will not have a patron.

In Ode 1.1, Horace asks that Maecenas introduce him into the ranks of the lyric poet/priests, and promises that if he does so, he will "hit the stars with his lofty head" (35–36). He calls Maecenas his "guardian and sweet ornament," outlining a relationship of mutual admiration and affirmation. Horace requests that Maecenas validate his identity as "vates" by confirming that identity. Maecenas, by letting Horace into his private circle is also admitting Horace into a literary canon; as both discerning critic and generous patron, Maecenas will distinguish Horace from the "populus," from the ode's catalog of ambitions, and from the mass of aspiring poets whose heads do not reach the stars. Horace figures Maecenas's power here as critical discernment which is itself creative; Maecenas's greatest creation will be the odist Horace.

In this first epistle, however, Maecenas asks Horace for the favor. Horace shifts quickly from direct reference to poetry to the metaphor of the gladiator; this metaphor makes poetry spectacle, and transforms the poet from grateful subordinate and aesthetic equal into a slave who performs for his life. The original symbiosis between poet and patron has been recast as a relationship between audience and actor. In Ode 1.1, Horace asked Maecenas to support him as a poet, but in Epistle 1.1, Horace rejects this persona. Maecenas is no longer a discerning critic but a spectator who needs to be entertained (aptly enough, this is a synonym in Latin for critic); he only watches, and his function as judge is reduced to deciding when Horace has had enough. Horace describes himself as "spectatum satis" and "donatum rude", both terms applied to gladiators, the former to those who have fought with credit, the latter to those who have been discharged from service. Also called "rudarius," a gladiator who is "donatus rude" is given the "rudis," a wooden sword or rod, as an emblem of freedom. In this case Horace's "rudis" is his pen, which he is now claiming for his own.[25]

In Epistle 1.1 the "vates" of the *Odes* is exposed as a role for which the speaker has neither the "aetas non mens." "Mens" can mean, as in English, either "mental powers," or "inclination"; as in the recusatio, Horace defies Maecenas while humbling himself before him. To explain one's inadequacy by an inevitable falling off from a younger and more capable self implies a continuity with that earlier self; "my age is not the same, nor is my mind" could thereby be read as a natural progression, an awareness of what is proper and possible for an older man to do, which shows Horace as subordinate not only to Maecenas but also to a higher master, time. Readers, like Maecenas, can thereby feel they know the real Horace because they knew and read him in an earlier incarnation, and because they too live by the external rules to which Horace points.

But to read "mens" as "inclination" rather than "mental powers" causes an unexplained disruption. From this perspective, Horace keeps his reasons, and his rules, to himself. Meaning is reappropriated from the public realm and made private. As Horace announces in this letter, the poet is bound to swear upon the words of no master,[26] and Horace is free from words themselves. The poet declares himself to exist wholly in the process of such singular self-definition. Any story a reader will be tempted to tell about the real Horace based on this second reading of "mens" will be fiction.

If the Maecenas of Ode 1.1 was "decus meum" (my ornament), in the *Epistles* Horace's task is to redefine "decens," an emblematic word whose meanings blur the boundaries of the moral and aesthetic realms. In the poem's conclusion, by asking Maecenas to transform his sense of the proper from the visible to the invisible, Horace executes a delicate shift in the balance of power between poet and patron:

> If, my hair cut by an uneven barber, I come your way, you laugh; if perhaps I wear a worn shirt beneath a new tunic, or if my toga hangs askew unevenly, you laugh. What then, when my thought is at strife with itself, spurns what it sought, asks again for what it lately let go, rages and is out of sorts with the whole order of life, pulls down, builds up, changes square to round? You think it is usual for me to be insane, nor do you laugh at me nor believe that I need a doctor or a guardian assigned by the court, although you are the guardian of my affairs and get angry at the badly cut nail of one who hangs on you, and considers you as a friend.[27]

For Pope, who attempts to merge aesthetics and ethics in the figure of deformity, this passage's reversal (in which Maecenas is reimagined as Bolingbroke) is particularly fruitful ground for self-transformation through a reconceiving of his patron's (and his reader's) vision:

> You laugh, half Beau half Sloven if I stand,
> My Wig all powder, and all snuff my Band;
> You laugh, if Coat and Breeches strangely vary,
> White Gloves, and Linnen worthy Lady Mary!
> But when no Prelate's Lawn with Hair-shirt lin'd,
> Is half so incoherent as my Mind,
> When (each Opinion with the next at strife,
> One ebb and flow of follies all my Life)
> I plant, root up, I build, and then confound,
> Turn round to square, and square again to round;
> You never change one muscle of your face,
> You think this Madness but a common case,
> Nor once to Chanc'ry, nor to Hale apply;
> Yet hang your lip, to see a Seam awry!
> Careless how ill I with myself agree;

> Kind to my dress, my figure, not to Me.
> Is this my Guide, Philosopher, and Friend?
> This, He who loves me, and who ought to mend?   (161–178)[28]

Transforming Horace's conceptual "order of life" into Twickenham's literal landscape; hinting, with the phrase "common case," at the uncommon appearance of his own case or body, Pope all the more distinctly dissociates himself from his body. He similarly appropriates the Latin, and redirects Bolingbroke's gaze inward by elaborating on his patron's responsibility to serve as the poet's personal model and "maker," the "Guide, Philosopher, and Friend," for whom the *Essay on Man* (IV, 390) was written. From Pope's slovenly appearance, the epistle shifts to the ideal image of Bolingbroke that the poet has constructed and which must be maintained in the mind's eye:

> Who ought to make me (what he can, or none,)
> That Man divine whom Wisdom calls her own,
> Great without Title, without Fortune bless'd,
> Rich ev'n when plunder'd, honour'd while oppress'd,
> Lov'd without youth, and follow'd without power,
> At home tho' exil'd, free, tho' in the Tower.   (179–184)

Here as in *Satire II, ii*'s discussion of the freedom of use, and as in *To a Lady*'s characterization of Martha Blount, Horace and the Horatian mode provide Pope with a space within which to rehearse the paradoxes of his own version of authorial independence, and to assert the power of a marginality which evades public circulation. Although both the Latin and English versions end with an ironic twist that puts each poet at the mercy of his body—Horace concludes with, "except when he has a cold" (108), Pope, "except (what's mighty odd) / A Fit of Vapours clouds this Demi-God" (188), aptly feminizing the malady—both poets create an aesthetic that reifies the self by redefining it as static and disembodied.

Horace's criticism of Maecenas's superficial decorum reassesses the earlier aesthetic of the *Odes* in which poet and patron became each other's mutual ornament; such mutual admiration is rewritten as the poetics of the gladiator's arena in which a critic or patron is merely a "spectator," the poet only a performer providing amusement. To see only Horace's outer flaws is to force him to conform to the role of poet, which, like his toga, is no longer fitting. Maecenas has taken Horace for another by refusing to grant him an identity beyond appearances, beyond the poem. In Ode 1.1 the patron created the poet by his critical discernment. By redirecting Maecenas's vision in this Epistle to an aesthetics of the inner self, the poet makes of his patron an ideal reader of the art of life upon whose penetration, as the passage's final twist reveals, he depends. The patron must transform himself in order to read beyond the page, in order to properly reform, indeed remake, the poet himself.

The tradition of Horatian critics which such poems have created, and which Pope both participates in and resists, appeals to readers who prefer life to be governed by the rules of art; and who prefer art, particularly autobiographical art, to look real: "They that value Horace most are . . . Epicureans, Cyreniacs, as well as those governed by a love of ease who prefer literature to life, or, to speak perhaps more accurately, who prefer to look at humanity and human conduct through the medium of literature."[29] This benign narcissism unites poet and critic in their preference of literature to life, and in their stories of life created in literature. Such a preference is uneasily qualified in this passage by the conception of literature as a medium, and must never result in a confusion of literature and life. For the critic's Horace and the Horatian critics, the medium of literature keeps the reader and writer one comfortable step away from humanity and all its unruliness. The medium becomes a kind of mirror, in which "images reflect from art to art," which eliminates disconcerting discrepancies while preserving reassuring distinctions. It is this mirror which the spots of Pope's deformity so productively disfigure.

Paul de Man's question about autobiography directly addresses the mutability of such distinctions:

> We assume that life *produces* the autobiography as an act produces its consequences, but can we not suggest, with equal justice, that the autobiographical project may itself produce and determine the life and that whatever the writer *does* is in fact governed by the demands of self-portraiture and thus determined, in all its aspects, by the resources of his medium?[30]

What results from such an awareness, as de Man describes it, is a double perspective, a *trompe l'oeil* view, on any text, and particularly an autobiographical text, a perspective dependent on one's placement in relation to the text. From within the text, the arbitrary "real" detail, the real Horace who grows old, seems to have dictated the course of the narrative. From outside the text, such "real" detail is determined by aesthetic structure. Every autobiographical text can thus be read as both constantly affirming its roots in reality, and constantly undermining that claim. This double perspective most disconcerts the Horatian reader, who wants to keep art and life distinct.

While Horatian readers refer to literature as a medium which protects them from life, de Man refers to the autobiographical mode of reading as "specular." In his account, the medium of literature is constituted by a different kind of seeing–through process in which "the two subjects involved in the process of reading . . . determine each other by mutual reflexive substitution."[31] The "subject" of autobiography, then, is a joint creation of both readers and authors. Thus authors figuring themselves as characters, and critics figuring authors as living beings like themselves, are caught in a continuous "revolving door" between truth and fiction, between identity and distinction. Art and life never completely align, just as authors never completely align with their self-images, just as critics' readings never completely align with the poem.[32]

For de Man the mirror, the medium of literature, ultimately shows nobody's face; it can only reveal itself. If the trope of autobiography is "prosopopeia"— the putting on of a mask, the giving of human form and voice to dead language, "by which one's name [language] . . . is made as intelligible and memorable as a face"[33]—the danger is that to look upon such a face will reduce the viewer to a reflection, to silence. Prosopopeia's living speech evokes while it warns against "the latent threat . . . that by making the death speak . . . the living are struck dumb,"[34] turned to stone.

Horace can only define himself by locating such self-definition in the past. And "what we call time", as de Man writes of Proust, "is precisely truth's inability to coincide with itself."[35] So say the ruined statues and the eloquently rusted medals which shape Augustan England's fantasies of Rome. "Is the status of a text like the status of a statue?"[36]

Horace plays out the figure of himself through summoning up nostalgia, or in its more intense form desire, for a past self, and transforming that nostalgia or desire into a passionately moderate adherence to the order of the well-lived life. The Horatian critic responds by filling the void; he imagines a Horace who is immune to desire, a subject so perfectly self-enclosed that he becomes utterly knowable:

> The man Horace is more interesting than his writings, or, to speak more correctly, the main interest of his writings is in himself. We might call his works "Horace's Autobiography." To use his own expression about Lucilius, his whole life stands out before us as in a picture . . . We can see him, as he really was, both in body and soul. Everything about him is familiar to us.[37]

The "prosopopeia" of autobiography is here taken literally, both by the reader Horace and his critics: Horace's words and name become an actual face. The reference to "Horace's expression about Lucilius" is from Satire 2.1, a dialogue between Horace and a friend Trebatius. Horace draws an implicit contrast between himself and Lucilius, whom Trebatius holds up to Horace as a model of poetic excellence and political safety. "It pleases me to close up words in feet in the manner of Lucilius, a better man than either of us. He entrusted his innermost secrets to books as if they were faithful comrades, nor did he take off elsewhere if things turned out badly, or if they turned out well; so that it happens that the whole life of this old man lies open just as if copied out on a votive tablet" (28–34).[38] The meaning of "descripta" [copied out], hovers between the verbal and the visual in a way that turns this self-portrait in the style of Lucilius into an emblem. The verb's primary meaning is "to copy off, to transcribe from an original," then "to write down" or "to write out," "to sketch off" or "to describe in painting," and finally the conceptual "to represent, delineate, describe." So that just as Horace's poetry moves between public accessibility and private involution, so Lucilius's words shift from self-evident image to text. The image of the votive tablet upon which Lucilius' life lies open anchors the sense in the visual realm. The votive tablet, like the scenes of the Trojan war painted upon the walls of Dido's temple in the *Aeneid,* is a visualized narrative, upon which successive events are represented in a single picture. Like the Horatians' image of Horace, like the images that endure on medals, the votive tablet defeats time.

But the Lucilius of this passage is both mentor and foil to the speaker of the *Satires.*[39] Horace claims to follow this master, though he himself is of indeterminable origin: "I follow him, though I am in doubt whether I am a Lucanian or an Apulian" (34). The later poet complicates the visual metaphor of the votive tablet by describing himself as an indeterminate set of boundaries, unable to be described. Pope's version of this passage in the first of his Horatian imitations revises it as deformity's proof of print's medium and satire's morality:

> I love to pour out all myself, as plain
> As downright *Shippen,* or as old *Montagne.*
> In them, as certain to be lov'd as seen,
> The Soul stood forth, nor kept a Thought within;
> In me what Spots (for Spots I have) appear,
> Will prove at least the Medium must be clear.
> In this impartial Glass, my Muse intends
> Fair to expose myself, my Foes, my Friends. (51–58)

But Horace insists on an indeterminacy which is misread as transparency.

For Horace reading Lucilius, and more importantly for the Horatians who emulate such a mode of reading, poetry is no longer read or heard: it has become, like an image on a medal, a voice with a face, and is seen "as in a picture." The image of the author which results is static and complete, encompassing even the invisible: "we can see him, as he really was, both in body and soul." This portrait of Horace is familiar in the way that a reflection in the mirror is familiar before we identify it as a reflection. This Horace is indeed a "familiar," like the genius in Pope's garden a spirit under human power, a medium between literature and life.[40]

Another Horatian writes of Horace: "No poet establishes so easily and so completely the personal relation with the reader, no poet is remembered so much as if he were a friend in the flesh."[41] The complement to the familiarity—here meaning the embodied friendliness—of Horace the man seems to be the familiarity—here meaning the common, almost clichéd quality—of his wisdom: "the great factor in the character of Horace is his philosophy of life. To define it is to give the meaning of the word Horatian as far as content is concerned."[42] The unattainability of Horace's "curiosa felicitas" is thereby repressed. Just as Horace becomes Horatian, so in the hands of the Horatians literary conventions become conventional.

When critics confront Horace's love life, this familiar portrait becomes particularly powerful. The poet becomes loveable to many of his critics because they imagine him as incapable of passionate love. Horace for some Horatians is "essentially a man's man, a born celibate." The certainty on this point is remarkable: "[h]e never thought of marrying, he was never in love; he never deceived himself as to the nature of his emotions; his soul was never touched."[43] The Horatian Horace is an ideal dinner table companion; indeed one critic bases his "biography" of Horace on his reasons "for building a dinner party" around him.[44]

The Horatian story rejects flesh and blood desire in favor of the literary life which makes their Horace a "friend in the flesh." To write a poetry of composed convention, it seems, the poet himself must be composed. The portrait displays a roué with a heart of gold, whose

> great emotions were centered elsewhere, and even there they were kept under control. Control, restraint, balance, a delicate sense of the fitness of things; these were the motivating characteristics which made Horace the man and the poet he was.[45]

The reader's evidence for Horace's lack of susceptibility to women is the love poetry by which the reader is unmoved. From this pronouncement on the poetry the critic turns to biographical speculation for reassurance—the dispassionate control of the poetry characterizes and conflates the man and the poet.[46] The Horatians easily traverse the boundaries between poetry and poet, and between poet and man, by means of the governing metaphor of composition. When it comes to Horace's love poems, with their strange blend of personal feeling and technical control, even those critics who resolutely insist on battling naive biographical realism end up sounding like their opponents despite themselves. Crusius is one of the first of many to make a gendered distinction between the sublime enthusiasm of the *Odes* in general and the feminine delicacy of the amatory odes, thereby keeping Horace whole.

> To begin with his *Odes:* This kind of Poetry is that which of all other requires the greatest strength and elevation of Genius, and a sort of Enthusiasm that is to diffuse itself through the whole . . . There is another kind of Ode of a lower stamp, which delights in softer themes, where beauty, and the pains and joys of love are described, or the praises of *Bacchus* sung. The want of the sublime is here supplied by delicacy and elegance.[47]

What Steele Commager says of Horace's Ode 3.9 many are tempted to say of Horace himself: "the most significant love affair in Horace's poem . . . is between Horace and the Latin language."[48] For readers of the love poetry it is often crucial that such an affair be rewritten as a friendship.

The question Frank Stack asks of all Horace's odes is especially relevant to the amatory odes; speaking of the effect of Latin word placement which gives each Horatian ode a unique subtext, Stack wonders: "How genuinely autobiographical are these lyrics, and how much are they stylized explorations of Greek, Alexandrian, and elegiac conventions? How does one account for the strange 'veering' of the lines of thought in so many Horatian odes which often makes the isolation of a 'subject' difficult and, arguably, mistaken?"[49] How much, to paraphrase, are these *Odes* written and how much are they described, in the Latin sense of the word? How does Horace's "mosaic of words" enable us to see the face superimposed upon the text?[50]

Meaning in a Horace ode is by nature non-linear; the poet's art resides in his maximum use of a minimum number of symbols. Horace's economy of ambiguity produces a sense of order which paradoxically cannot be contained. And as Stack is right to notice, such an economy makes a location of one subject, be it of the poem or the author of the poem, almost impossible. Where then to locate the love in a love poem of Horace's? The discussion of two poems from Horace's fourth and final book of *Odes* that follows further complicates Horatian matters, and shows how such complications leave space, an empire within a lyric's narrow confines, for Pope to occupy.

In the first ode of the fourth book, Horace represents himself as lacking the conventions which give the poem its structure. As is so often the case in Horace, the poem constantly shifts between the confessional and the conventional, so that it becomes impossible to tell whether Horace is speaking under the compulsion of truth or by the rules of generic expectation and exploitation.

Book Four of the *Odes* was produced after a long silence which is itself the topic of the *Epistles,* and has been the subject of much critical debate. Most agree that Horace delayed in part because of the poor reception of the first three books of *Odes,* too complex and too fine to be generally popular.[51] Why does Horace finally speak? Suetonius claims the reason was imperial fiat: are you ashamed, Augustus asks the poet, to go down in history as my friend?[52] A fourth book of *Odes* is thereby commissioned. The emperor, it should be noted, plays not upon Horace's public obligation but upon his personal relationship to him; he plays ultimately upon Horace's consciousness of posterity's public judgment of a private friendship. Eduard Fraenkel counters this view with a claim that the fourth book arose from a new spurt in productivity, the result of Augustus having commissioned the Horatian hymn of the *Carmen Saeculare* and Horace's pleasure in having become a Roman "vates", a true Greek lyricist translated into Roman, and therefore public and spiritual, terms.[53]

But the ruling passion in either scenario of Book Four's origin, be it the emperor's passion or Horace's, is for fame: the public eye is upon Horace in an unprecedented way. In writing these *Odes* Horace is doubly conscious of his audience. Book Four of the *Odes,* written some time after the first book of the *Epistles* had abandoned lyric, must therefore be read as the poet's self-conscious return performance before contemporary and future audiences in a role he had rejected.

"The idea that lyric poetry can immortalize men's achievements is completely absent from the first three books of the *Odes,*" Fraenkel notes. But this claim is central to Book Four.[54] At the same time, as Commager makes clear, never has the split between public moral convention and private emotion in Horace seemed greater than in Book Four: "In the more private poems, we feel a change in the poet himself. His moral standards have not altered, but he persistently fails to reconcile his emotions with them. The split heretofore largely confined to the *Odes* on death becomes virtually endemic."[55]

Like its poet, Book Four is split between public panegyric and private self-castigation, between propriety and inappropriate outbursts, between poetry which can immortalize men and that within men which eludes the laws of poetry, decorum, and language itself. In this final book of *Odes,* Horace reads the Horatian version of himself and finds it wanting.[56] The confident abandonment of art for life in the *Epistles* cannot be so easily maintained, nor can the two poles be so easily defined or reconciled.

Book Four alternates between political praise (especially for Tiberius and Drusus, for whose benefit and at Augustus's behest, according to Suetonius, the book was written) and personal sorrow at the coming of age. The book's opening and emblem, Ode 4.1 juxtaposes these two modes, framing panegyric of a young and prominent Roman with the poet-speaker's middle-aged love lament. This juxtaposition gives the poem meaning by rendering meaning indeterminate. Jostling in the confines of the lyric form, public and private perspectives transform each other.

Various readings of 4.1 focus on the inappropriateness of Horace's insertion of political detail into the personal realm, a discrepancy which is then either ignored or explained as germane to the ode's representativeness.[57] This incongruity has also been dismissed as Horace's attempt to save his Roman subject from the moral impurities of Greek form.[58] The critic who takes the poem on its own terms attempts to see it, along with the book as a whole, as a serious abandonment of the lyric's self-enclosure and the life of the body in favor of civic transcendence.[59] But if one reads the poem's structure in the same way that one would read any line of a Horace ode, one is forced to reckon with an imbalance in the juxtaposition of the two modes, an indecorousness which is itself representative.

Though 4.1 is representative of Book Four as a whole, the poem's representativeness rests in its refusal to come to order. The personal outbreak which concludes 4.1 jeopardizes the control and civic-mindedness of what precedes, and thereby fails to resolve Horace's and Horatian notions of decorum.

An aberrant love poem, 4.1 is described by Fraenkel as an "apopompe" (a prayer not for a god's aid but for the god's absence), while Commager aptly terms it a "*recusatio* of the affections."[60] Each critic points to a paradox. Horace's plea to Venus doubly inverts Sappho's hymn to Aphrodite (a prayer to the goddess to come and aid her in love which is ultimately answered), first by sending the goddess away, second by directing her not, as was usual, to an enemy, but instead to Paulus, the object of the poem's central panegyric, a young Roman nobleman on his way to prominence through his courtship of Augustus's cousin.[61]

Sappho's hymn to Aphrodite was remarkable for the immediacy of the goddess's imagined presence, the familiarity with which she reassures Sappho of her support:

> Again whom must I persuade
> back into the harness of your love?
> Sappho, who wrongs you?
>
> For if she flees, soon she'll pursue,
> she doesn't accept gifts, but she'll give,
> if not now loving, soon she'll love
> even against her will.   (1, 18–24)[62]

Horace recalls the Greek hymn in the act of rejecting this intimacy. His Venus is above all a metaphor. Poetry should be, or so this poem seems to say, more conscious of itself as writing burdened by the weight of its inheritance. The powerful affect of 4.1's first stanzas comes from the resistance built into the literary references Horace makes to himself and to Sappho. The tension between the ode's present and the lyric past which shadows its reading engenders the writing of the poem itself. Immediacy in this poem, whether of the author or the goddess, defines itself in relation to its absence. In keeping with the poem's trope of indecency, if Sappho's Venus promises symmetrical reciprocity, Horace's will deny it.

Commager's phrase, "recusatio of the affections," describes the same inverted effect. The standard purpose of the recusatio was to reject the public mode for the private, to declare one's inability to write epic and thereby (not so) covertly champion a lyric aesthetic and with it the possibility of political independence.[63] The lyric genre became in Roman hands almost by definition a recusatio: the Roman lyric poet announces himself incapable of, and thereby superior to, both epic writing and political commitment. Whether the recusatio allows the lyricist to covertly demonstrate the heroic prowess he claims to lack,[64] or as in Horace's Ode 1.6 to Agrippa, to display his supposed incapability as tactless incompetence, its irony allows the lyricist to say the unspeakable.

A "recusatio of the affections," then, reverses the genre's standard moral touchstones. While the speaker of the first book of the *Epistles* had decorously rejected lyric for philosophy, in Ode 4.1 a discomposed Horace unsuccessfully declares himself unfit for that which he finds irresistible: love, love poetry or lyric. Fraenkel makes clear that "to say 'I am engaged in Love's warfare' was, according to a common literary convention, equivalent to saying 'I am writing erotic poems.' "[65] Thus in sending Venus away, Horace reasserts his previously announced unfitness for the youthful world of the *Odes,* the private realm of the symposium, and of love. But contradictorily, his choice of a meter common to love poetry for this ode calls into question his role as public odist. If the recusatio rejects the public for the private, then this involuntary love poem, written in response to an imperial order and inspired by a particularly indecorous love object, a boy named Ligurinus, attempts to reject poetry itself.[66]

Yet the very writing of this recusatio defeats its purpose. The speaker cannot remain single or singular: Venus's presence is a *fait accompli.*

> Intermissa, Venus, diu
>   rursus bella moves? Parce, precor, precor.
> Non sum qualis eram bonae
>   sub regno Cinarae. Desine dulcium
>
> mater saeva Cupidinum,
>   circa lustra decem flectere mollibus
> iam durum imperiis: abi,
>   quo blandae iuvenum te revocant preces.   (1–8)

Once again, Venus, are you setting in motion wars which have been neglected for a long time? Spare me, I pray, I pray. I am not as I was under the reign of good Cinara. Cease, fierce mother of sweet lusts, to bend one who is almost fifty, now hard to your soft commands; go hence where the flattering prayers of youth call you.

"Intermissa" [neglected], the first word of the poem, seems at first to describe Venus herself who has been neglected, like Horace's lyric poetry, for a long while. This ambiguity of agency resembles the indeterminacy of "mens" in Epistle 1.1; it is impossible to tell whether time or Horace is responsible for the silence. In either case, the choice of word returns us to lyric time and form at the same moment, and Horace's long absence from lyric can be subordinated to the overriding narrative of his poetic career.

Is this opening simply a witty device with which Horace resumes the lyric pen? "Intermissa" refers, as we read on, to "bella" and that brings us back to the world of sweet wars between girls and youths which is juxtaposed with imperial conquest in earlier odes (e.g. 1.6). But these "bella" are within the poet's heart. Ode 4.1 also echoes the opening line of Horace's Ode 1.19: "Mater saeva Cupidinum" [fierce mother of Cupids]. The younger Horace heralds the approach of a Venus who will not allow him to sing of Rome's wars against the Scythians or Parthians or anything which does not pertain to her affairs, and resolves to sacrifice wine and flowers to her so that she will relent. The ode is as much a hymn to decorum as it is to Venus herself. But in 4.1, Venus has already inappropriately arrived, and she is not to be placated or controlled. Decorum, despite Horace's best intentions, has been abandoned.

Similarly, the speaker's modest reference to his earlier days under the rule of good Cinara gains its ability to move by rejection of the standard elegiac vocabulary. Cinara is no longer playing the games which made her a conventional mistress in the *Epistles,* and thus she no longer seems generic. In Epistle 1.7 (25–28) Horace tells Maecenas that if he is to oblige his patron by returning to Rome, Maecenas must give Horace back his youth when he would lament the absence of forward Cinara with wine, a sadness which is part of the amatory game. In 1.14 (33) he speaks of lost youth by remembering how he would be received "immunem" [giftless] by the rapacious Cinara. And later in Ode 4.13, he speaks of Lyce, past her prime, as having come "post Cinaram" (21). Evoking the epistles' nostalgia for lyric, "Cinara" becomes a kind of code word for the way in which loss brings the past to a private life. In this lyric the world of the conventional becomes real once it becomes improper and therefore unattainable.

Venus, by contrast, is described in amorous antitheses, word order playing a large part in the modulation of our response. "Desine dulcium" [cease sweet] followed by a stanza break emphasizes the contrast of "saeva" [fierce]. "Flectere mollibus"[bending with soft] sets up a tension between adjectives which is reinforced by "durum imperiis" [resistant to commands]. "Durus" is usually used by a lover complaining of an obdurate mistress; now Horace is "durus" to the commands of a goddess, and with that word we realize that his resistance, like that of the mistress in a love poem, is a lost cause. As with Cinara, this superimposition of conventions allows us to remember their past configurations and to realize that past as lost.

The stanza is given regularity by the repetition of Horace's imperatives which are, unlike Venus's soft commands, quite firm: "parce, desine, abi" [spare, cease, go]. Horace's prayer, unlike those of the youths to whom he recommends Venus, is anything but "blanda." With "blanda," primarily defined as "flattering, smooth-tongued, caressing," the speaker hints at an aesthetic development couched as a falling away: he can no longer flatter, he is too old for such deceit, for an art which is light and appealing. Though not too old for love, he is too old for a certain kind of love poetry, too old to burn, as he claims to do in Ode 1.6, "lightly."

And to love in poetry anything but lightly is for this poet a breach of decorum. That such passion should come to Horace when he is "circa lustra decem" [about fifty] is what makes it figure as passion. Synonymous here with the indignity of old age, indecorum signifies disparity, an unsuitability of subject to expression which creates the illusion of desire. To be "indecens" is to be indecent and indecorative, to offend both morally and aesthetically. (Pope takes full advantage of this contrast between surface inelegance and inner harmony in his moral admonishments to Bolingbroke at the end of *Epistle I, i.*) "Decens" aptly enough means "regular, symmetrical," the visual complement to its moral use as "fitting, proper." The word is a miniature trope, both the medal's face and its inscription, and its disruption here figures as personal excess the gap between representation and the ruin it replaces. How can this indecent behavior be reconciled with Horace's decision in the *Epistles* to define himself by redefining what is "decens"?

> Tempestivius in domum
>   Pauli, purpureis ales oloribus
> comisabere Maximi,
>   si torrere iecur quaeris idoneum.
> Namque et nobilis et decens
>   et pro sollicitis non tacitus reis
> et centum puer artium
>   late signa feret militiae tuae;
> Et quandoque potentior
>   largi muneribus riserit aemuli,
> Albanos prope te lacus
>   ponet marmoream sub trabe citrea.
> Illic plurima naribus
>   duces tura lyraeque et Berecyntiae
> delectabere tibiae
>   mixtis carminibus non sine fistula;
> illic bis pueri die
>   numen cum teneris virginibus tuum
> laudantes pede candido
>   in morem Salium ter quatient humum. (9–28)

Winged, on purple swans, you will revel more seasonably at the house of Paulus Maximus, if you wish a more suitable liver to grill.

For he is of noble birth, and seemly, and not silent on the behalf of distressed defendants, and a youth of a hundred skills who will carry the standard of your service far and wide.

And whenever he will have laughed in triumph over an extravagant rival, he will place [an image of] you in marble by the lakes of Alba beneath a roof of citrus wood.

There you will inhale much incense, and you will be charmed by songs blending with the lyre and the Berecyntian pipes, not without the flute.

There twice a day the youths, along with the tender virgins, praising your divinity will three times shake the ground with shining foot in the Salian manner.

Paulus, Venus's more suitable target, is decorum personified. In a comically grisly metaphor, Venus would more "seasonably," more "appropriately," grill this young man's liver (believed by the Greeks and Romans to be the seat of emotion), which is described as "idoneum," once again, "fit" or "proper." "Tempestivius," with its double meaning of "timely" and "suitably" touches on the way that the aesthetic in 4.1 is bound up with the passing of time and a sense of proper timing. Paulus is also "decens" in the sense of decorative, his name alliterating admirably the purple of Venus's wings, his full name impressively flanking her approach with sound.

By praising Paulus, Horace prescribes propriety to a goddess upon whose impropriety the poem insists. As his letter of recommendation continues, the rhetoric becomes increasingly well ordered, the lines more and more neatly contained. Paulus is "nobilis," "decens," and can speak well. Paulus's speaking, however, takes place in the public professional arena, he is "pro sollicitis non tacitus reis" [not silent on behalf of distressed defendants]; and as readers of Ovid's *Ars Amatoria* know, even the most skilled of lawyers cannot produce a case against love. This uneasy slippage between public and private betrays the amorous metaphors. Paulus's skill at a hundred arts makes his status as a representative of the "ars amatoria" somewhat dubious; love, or so the speaker's opening distress would have us think, demands exclusivity. If the speaker is indecorously passionate, Paulus is decorous at the expense of passion.

Neither is Paulus a suffering lover. Like Venus herself, he is "ridens," happy whenever he defeats a more wealthy rival. (The "quandoque" [whenever] makes the action sound conditional and endlessly repeated: Paulus triumphs time after time, so that the shift to the unconditional future of "ponet" comes as a surprise, forcing us to turn back and read "quandoque" as "some day"). In order to commemorate his triumph, Paulus, like a poet, creates a work of art in the goddess's honor. But just as his speaking is public oration, and his amorous triumph suspiciously material (we gather now that perhaps he beats rivals by greater wealth, not like Horace who wins Cinara's favors "immunus"), so his tribute to Venus is a kind of imprisonment. Horace's circumlocution gets right to the point. Paulus is not described as erecting a statue of Venus, rather he "te . . . ponet marmoream" [will place you marble] by the Alban lake beneath a roof of citrus. In Paulus's decorous world, like the world of Addison's medal connoisseurs, art is taken so literally that it is removed from the realm of representation and becomes reality. Venus's location is appealing, but the delay of "marmoream" (at first we think "prope" governs "te") casts a kind of pallor over Paulus's promise. Venus, no longer "saeva" or "mollis" nor "ales" [fierce, soft, winged] has become non-threatening, static, merely ornamental, much like the Horatian Horace.

Paulus's relationship to the goddess of love is not a personal submission so much as it is a ritual conquest. Venus in the following two ornate and ordered stanzas becomes the focal point of ceremony, and that ceremony is itself a kind of poetry, "carmina" played on the lyric "fistula." She is fixed and externalized by the "illic" with which both stanzas begin. Like clockwork, twice a day, youths and virgins will praise Venus's "numen," and their dance, in the Salian manner, consists of exactly three steps. The poetry shifts from the inner space of Horace's heart to the visual, stylized, idealized spectacle of orchestrated ritual. And just as Paulus's prowess at a hundred arts confuses love's private slavery with public service, so the Salian ceremonial dance, performed annually by the Salian priests who guarded the sacred shields, ritually, and in the terms of Horatian lyric paradoxically, conflates the love battle with the martial battle.

This poem is haunted by an earlier ode written by Horace in celebration of the defeat of another powerful and potentially indecorous Queen: 1.37, the Cleopatra Ode, which begins "nunc est bibendum" [now is the time for drinking] and commands dances along with Salian feasts. Just as Horace's Cleopatra commits suicide rather than be displayed as an image in Augustus's triumphal procession, so Venus would be defeated by such a transformation into beautiful ornament. If 4.1, as Michael Putnam claims, is an ode about monumentalization, it is also about the loss that such monumentalization entails, a loss which unites decorous love and imperial war in static art.

The dances which Paulus orchestrates around the marmoreal Venus are a kind of ekphrasis or verbal vision, a figure for poetry within the poem. Like Achilles's shield, which suspends the *Iliad*'s action and moves the reader to an eternal and cyclical present, Paulus's shrine to Venus forgoes the immediacy of the lyric lover's outburst for the unmoved and immovable beauty of art. But Paulus's creation is framed by the speaker's irresolvably mortal conflict.

> Me nec femina nec puer
> iam nec spes animi credula mutui
> nec certare iuvat mero
> nec vincire novis tempora floribus.

Sed cur heu, Ligurine, cur
　　manat rara meas lacrima per genas?
Cur facunda parum decoro
　　inter verba cadit lingua silentio?
Nocturnis ego somniis
　　iam captum teneo, iam volucrem sequor
te per gramina Martii
　　Campi, te per aquas, dure, volubilis.　(29–40)

Neither woman nor youth pleases me now, nor the trusting hope of mutual minds, nor to battle in wine, nor to bind the temples with new
flowers.

But why, alas, Ligurinus, why, does a rare tear drip down my cheeks?
Why does my eloquent tongue in mid-speech fall into a less than becoming silence?

I hold you captive now in nightly dreams, now I follow you flying
through the fields of the Campus Martius, [I follow] you, cruel one,
through the rolling waters.

With the "me" of the next stanza we are brought back to our position as
spectators, excluded from Paulus's world and reunited with the speaker, who
lists the conditions of his exclusion with a series of "necs" complementing the
"et" clauses with which he listed Paulus's qualifications. Just as the "intermissa"
with which the poem began puts us into lyric time and brings with it a consciousness of an irretrievable personal past, so the "iam" delayed until the second
line of the stanza brings us back to a time-bound sense of loss. The speaker has
abandoned all hope of relationship, as well as the symposiastic world of wine
and flowers with which he ends the previous call to Aphrodite, the Glycera
ode. He marks himself most importantly as alone: the word order's juxtaposition
of "spes animi credula mutui" [trusting hope of a mutual mind] (one expects
"credula" to modify "animi" but instead it modifies "spes" as if such a state of
trust can only exist in the conditional) is poignant, cynical, and final.

Or so it seems until the "sed" of the following stanza. Here the rhetoric
and order of the previous stanzas break down: the "heu" comes between the
two "cur"s as if uncontrollably at the thought of Ligurinus's name, "decoro"
elides into the "inter" at the beginning of the next line in an indecorous sy-
nepha, the open vowels of "heu," "indecoro," "silentio," "cur" seem to sob.
The speaker has abandoned declarations for questions. Like Catullus imitating
Sappho in his fifty-first poem (another hall of mirrors), his language is at the
mercy of his body, which shows his passion more powerfully than words are

able. Unlike the confident Paulus, the speaker's "facunda lingua" is overcome by "parum decoro silentio"; he, neither eloquent, nor decorous, nor decorative, is at the mercy of his powerless tongue and an inappropriate passion.[67] But unlike the youthful Catullus and Sappho whose bodies are racked by desire, all the aging speaker can summon besides his silence is "rara lacrima."

Longinus uses the Sappho ode to which this moment of 4.1 alludes as an example of the circumstantial sublime, in which the poet orchestrates her own falling apart so that she can put herself back together again.[68]

> whenever I look quickly, for a moment—
> I say nothing, my tongue broken,
> a delicate fire runs under my skin,
> my eyes see nothing, my ears roar,
> cold sweat rushes down me,
> trembling seizes me,
> I am greener than grass,
> to myself I seem
> needing but little to die. (8, 7–15)

Horace locates himself in the absence of such death-defying dramatics. In his return to lyric, he is wearily aware of his lack of strength for the mode.

The final stanza shifts to a confessional and a differently visual mode, the world of the speaker's dreams: neither the temporal immediacy of the poem's beginning, nor the stylized show of Paulus's villa, nor the resignation to the barren present of the poem's apparent close two stanzas earlier. Time and space have shifted to a new indeterminacy; the "iam"'s with which the speaker grasps Ligurinus, and with which Ligurinus eludes him are fleetingly present, not so much recollected as recreated in the verse. Like winged Venus with her swans, Ligurinus is "volucris." Like the speaker in his initial disavowal of love he is "durus" like Venus's statue, and like that statue, temporarily "captus." And like the poem's initial paradoxes, Horace "durus" to her "mollibus imperiis," Ligurinus is "durus" amidst yielding "aquas." Combining the literal with the fantastic—Ligurinus exercises on the Campus Martius in the everyday life of Rome, and runs through the waves in a dream world—this scene links the first two halves of the poem in an indeterminate balance.

The final word of the poem—"volubilis"—echoes both the glib volubility of Paulus's eloquence, and signals the passing of time. The speaker's silence contrasts with the water's volubility; his frustrated attempt at youthful amorous eloquence is likened to the impossibility of stopping time's flood. The speaker falls silent, mute and drowning, pursuing his love and lost youth (which Ligurinus embodies and reflects and which the writing of lyric enacts), while sure of the impossibility of attaining either. He is drowned by love and by its language.

COLLECTED IN HIMSELF

In his only complete imitation of a Horace ode, Pope makes of 4.1 a monument to his own particular history.[69] What in Horace's poem figures as "real" and therefore irreparably lost to language, in Pope becomes the longed-for substitute for what in reality is impossible. In this and in other Horatian imitations, Pope inhabits the poems which Horace has so seductively vacated. Horace's self-dissolution becomes Pope's self-collection. For the purpose of discussion in this chapter, Pope's imitation of Ode 4.1 follows:

The First Ode of the Fourth Book of Horace

To Venus

Again? new Tumults in my Breast?
Ah spare me, Venus! let me, let me rest!
   I am not now, alas! the man
As in the gentle Reign of My Queen *Anne*.
   Ah sound no more thy soft alarms,
Nor circle sober fifty with thy Charms.
   Mother too fierce of dear Desires!
Turn, turn to willing Hearts your wanton fires.
   To *Number five* direct your Doves,
There spread round MURRAY all your blooming Loves;
   Noble and young, who strikes the heart
With every sprightly, every decent part;
   Equal, the injur'd to defend,
To charm the Mistress, or to fix the Friend.
   He, with a hundred Arts refin'd,
Shall stretch thy Conquests over half the kind:
   To him each Rival shall submit,
Make but his riches equal to his Wit.
   Then shall thy Form the Marble grace,
(Thy Graecian Form) and Chloe lend the Face:
   His House, embosom'd in the Grove,
Sacred to social Life and social Love,
   Shall glitter o'er the pendent green,

Where Thames reflects the visionary Scene.
  Thither, the silver-sounding Lyres
Shall call the smiling Loves, and young Desires;
  There, every Grace and Muse shall throng,
Exalt the Dance, or animate the Song;
  There, Youths and Nymphs, in consort gay,
Shall hail the rising, close the parting day.
  With me, alas! those joys are o'er;
For me, the vernal Garlands bloom no more.
  Adieu! fond hope of mutual fire,
The still-believing, still-renew'd desire;
  Adieu! the heart-expanding bowl,
And all the kind Deceivers of the soul!
  —But why? ah tell me, ah too dear!
Steals down my check th'involuntary Tear?
  Why words so flowing, thoughts so free,
Stop, or turn nonsense at one glance of Thee?
  Thee, drest in Fancy's airy beam,
Absent I follow thro' th'extended Dream,
  Now, now I seize, I clasp thy charms,
And now you burst, (ah cruel!) from my arms,
  And swiftly shoot along the Mall,
  Or softly glide by the Canal,
  Now shown by Cynthia's silver Ray,
And now, on rolling Waters snatch'd away.

Such literary abandon could be ordered by rhetorical precedent. Eighteenth-century readers of Longinus such as Pope might have recognized Horace's rhetorical abdication of self-control as alluding to what the theorist called "Sapphic sublimity," an explicitly feminine rhetoric of self-fragmentation and collection.[70] Here John Ozell translates Boileau's version of the passage of Longinus's eighth chapter, "Of the Sublimity which is drawn from Circumstances," which famously defines the Sapphic sublime:

Don't you admire how she collects all these things and blends 'em together; Soul, Body, Hearing, Language, Sight, Colour, as if they were so many different Persons, and all ready to Expire? See, with how many contrary Emotions she's agitated; she Freezes, she Burns, she's Mad, she's Wise; she's either entirely out of her Wits, or is Dying: In a Word, we can't say she's seized with one particular Passion, but that her Soul is the Rendezvous of all the Passions; which indeed is what happens to all that

are in Love. You find there, that as I have observ'd, all the grand Circumstances distinguish'd *a propos,* and collected with Judgment, are the chief
Beauty of her Poem.[71]

The phenomenon described here might also be aptly called the corporeal sublime. Sappho's language replaces and reassembles her body which, like a ruined
and restored statue, becomes an assemblage of compelling pieces animated as
"different Persons," collected within the poem's confines for greatest rhetorical
effect. The sublime thrill of the whole consists in the reader's awareness of its
unruly instability, an instability that is strictly rhetorical.

Such a feminine mode of sublimity is most reminiscent of Pope's assumption of the movement of a tormented woman's voice in a poem written twenty
years before his imitation of Horace's ode, *Eloisa to Abelard.* In a moment that
resonates with both Horace's emotion at the end of 4.1 and de Man's account
of language's Medusa-like qualities, Eloisa exclaims, "I have not yet forgot my
self to stone" (24). As Reuben Quintero argues, in *Eloisa,* Pope performs a
rhetoric of "ecstasis," a transportation or emotional displacement of the reader,
as Eloisa, like Sappho, is moved beyond herself, a rhetoric which "charms"
rather "than pleasing or persuading only."[72] This transportation or translation
of the self through the rhetoric of ecstasis is a formal alternative to ekphrasis,
the verbal vision which inspires Paulus's orderly art, Pope's re-vision of Achilles's
shield, and the emblematic constitution of Twickenham.[73]

When Pope turns to Horace's love poem, however, he rewrites Horace's
ecstasis as ekphrasis, reimagining the Roman poet's emotion as idealized vision.
Prefacing his reading of Pope's imitation of 4.1 with a biographical account of
the personal losses Pope was mourning at the time of the poem's composition
in 1737, Frank Stack argues that

> Pope's Imitation is an exploration of the ideal as it is present to the poetic
> imagination. Horace here is the poet of vision, and . . . [Pope] internalizes
> . . . the 'visionary Scene' of Horace's ritual for Venus and Horace's dream
> of Ligurinus, and develops the conjunction between the dream and the
> actual place in Horace's poem . . . The use of these contemporary names
> . . . helps to make this Imitation focus attention on the tension between
> the imaginary and the real . . . In Pope's poem this imaginative experience
> becomes either a substitute for love, or a higher form of love. Whereas
> Horace's ode seems to end on a painful note of unrequited love and per-
> haps self-betrayal . . ., Pope's conclusion stresses a creative involvement in
> the experience of loss.[74]

While Horace's imagination of Paulus's ritual for Venus, and his own final dream of pursuing Ligurinus, are contrasting and differently authored scenes within the poem, Stack is more interested in Pope's imaginative synthesis than in Horace's evasion of the imaginary. The material for this synthesis in Pope's case is both literary history and personal loss. Pope's mother and two of his closest friends, John Gay and John Arbuthnot, had died not long before the poem's publication in 1737. Pope had named Martha Blount as Patty in place of Ligurinus in the first printed version of the poem, only to omit her name in subsequent versions.[75] For Stack, this omission of Martha as particular object signals the way in which desire for Pope becomes increasingly ideal and imaginary, something to be viewed from a distance like an image on a medal.[76] In his account, as in Pope's imitation, discordant elements fuse into one emblematic "visionary Scene."

What Stack terms "Pope's creative involvement in the experience of loss," therefore, is the English poet's way of investing himself where Horace is absent. Horace's passive undermining of political panegyric is subsumed into Pope's confident assertion of an independent public voice; the Roman poet's absence is envisioned, his silence socialized and spoken. Both Horace and Pope use this poem to mark a return to lyric and love poetry after a long absence, but Horace's private nostalgic reference to his youth "sub regno bonae Cynarae," has become in Pope's translation "in the gentle Reign of My Queen Anne" (4), a marking of personal experience by public time.

The contrast between the abrupt disjunction of Horace's opening lines to Venus and the highly ordered rhetoric of the central passage which follows has been softened in Pope by rhyme and by the polishing of each line into a separate unit of coherence. Horace's irony in praising young Paulus as "pro sollicitis non tacitus reis" [not silent on behalf of distressed defendants] taints praise with banality by conjoining amorous convention with legal terminology. In Pope's version, Murray's political reputation as "an orator rivalled only by Pitt," taught oratory by Pope himself,[77] serves to suit him perfectly for the social world of Pope's imitation. Pope neutralizes the critical restraint of the Latin by elaborating upon it, using "equal" to govern and to level three balanced clauses in praise of Murray: "the injur'd to defend, / To charm the Mistress, or to fix the Friend" (13–14). Love's singularity in Horace's Latin becomes for Pope an idealized generality which omits Venus and woman: "He, with a hundred Arts refin'd, / Shall stretch thy Conquests over half the kind" (15–16).

The conventions which Horace tacitly rejects in the figure of Paulus, Pope rewrites as his own. Pope's Murray no longer "will place Venus marble"; instead Venus is lured with the promise, "Then shall thy Form the Marble grace, / (Thy

Graecian Form) and Chloe lend the Face" (19–20). Pope is more playful and less chilling than Horace; his Venus is not captured but is rather benignly willing, at once as worldly as an aristocratic lady posing for a painting in classical garb and as divine as Laughing Ceres when she reassumes the land at the end of the *Epistle to Burlington*. While Horace's Paulus immobilizes and thereby wards off the passion Venus brings, Pope, rather than his Paulus equivalent Murray, solves the problem of passion by domesticating the goddess. Paulus' Salian rituals with their martial overtones become for Pope a "visionary Scene" (24), "Sacred to social Life and social Love" (22).

In Pope's imitation, passion is refined into sentiment. Horace's lyric privacy has become public rhetoric, in much the same way that his uniquely indecorous desire has been personified and generalized as "smiling Loves, and young Desires" (26). The tableau presented here seems to unite the two halves of the landscaped couplet of Cobham's garden at Stowe of which Pope was so fond: one part "devoted to the pleasures and temptations of retirement," the other "devoted to public life, the life of action expressed in allegory"; "one to Venus, deity of the garden and of love, the other to Virtue; one to nature, the other to *civitas*."[78] The focal point of both Pope's poem and Cobham's garden is a statue of Venus, "both garden deity and goddess of love,"[79] a trope given concrete form as emblem, both allusion and monument to an appropriated past and a common social discourse.

While Horace is immersed and immerses his reader in his pursuit of Ligurinus, in Pope the potentially overwhelming forces of the dream are held at a distance, visualized in a series of brief scenes. Pope lingers over his rendition of Horace's dream, "extend[s]" (42) it with repetitive word ordering ("swiftly shoot," "softly glide" 45–46), familiarizes the sense of dislocation in Horace by pointing clearly to "the Mall" and "the Canal" (45–46), and conventionalizes it with the periphrasis of "Cynthia's silver Ray" (47), not in the Horace and recognizable to any reader of Pope's *Iliad*. The pun on "volubilis" (both "rolling" and "voluble") with which Horace closes is appropriately omitted. Paulus's "visionary scene" celebrates the monumentality of art, but Horace's dream reveals that art's foundations, and authors' names, are written in water. Pope does not drown in language so much as he refuses to leave it. While Horace creates a sense of authenticity by confessing to what poetry cannot control, for Pope poetry makes both control and feeling possible. With satire as his weapon, and Horace as both his model and adversary, Pope attempted to write a poetry disfigured by his own moral integrity, both personal and public, politically marginal and morally central. His sole effort at Horatian love lyric demonstrates how his Roman predecessor's rhetorical self-fragmentation challenged his own abilities to reassemble and thus to own the self in poetry.

ENDLESS REFLECTION

Before I go on to Pope's heroic satire, I want to return to Horace's mirrors of desire. Nine poems after 4.1, the poet is able once again to speak:

> O, cruel still, and powerful with the gifts of Venus, when an unexpected feather shall come upon your vanity, and those locks which now play upon your shoulders shall fall off, and that complexion which now takes precedence over the purple-red rose, changed, Ligurinus, will turn into a rough hairy face: you will say, "Alas," as often you will see yourself another in the mirror, "this inclination which is mine today, why was it not the same when I was young, or why don't my untouched cheeks return to my present feelings?"[80]

The "adhuc" ("still" or "till now") gives the temporal signal which links this ode back to 4.1, just as the introductory poem's opening word "intermissa" linked it to Horace's lyric past. The personal narrative created by these two odes replays and jeopardizes the questions of authority which the *Epistles* raise (and seem through their rejection of lyric to resolve) as questions of art and life.

In Epistle 1.1, the conflicting meanings of "mens" (both essential mind and arbitrary inclination) gave Horace a graceful way out of his patron's request for an encore. Here the poet plays out the meanings of the word in a narrative which continues Ode 4.1 and rewrites it as a first chapter in an infinitely symmetrical story. In Epistle 1.1 Horace's admission of lack of "mens," lack of ability for writing poetry, professed a helplessness which masked an act of will, his lack of inclination to continue. 4.10 translates such an assertion of invisible privacy into visual terms: Ligurinus is paradoxically imprisoned by his volition, by an "inclination" which must remain unfulfilled because he is no longer beautiful.

Ligurinus, a specular figure of the poet's imagination, is split between his present beauty and its inevitable future loss, between the realities of time and a subjectivity born of bad timing. Like the lyric writer of 4.1, this image of the youth doubly projected into the future and the speaker's own past, echoing the speaker's present sentiments in an imagined future repetition, plays out an endless scenario of unrequited desire which is figured as discrepancy between older man and youth; between the poet and his past lightly loving, lyric–writing self; between the future Ligurinus and his present beauty. In each case the self looks into the mirror and sees itself "alterum."

As the poet reveals in the figure of the callous Ligurinus, it is the nature of such awareness to come too late, just as it is the mirror's nature to refract. The sound seems to echo this sense: "mutatus, Ligurine, in faciem" breaks up the name over a metric foot, both lengthening it and truncating it with the elision. Name and face have become equally indeterminate. The reader is similarly suspended over the meaning of "mutatus": is it Ligurinus or simply his "color" which has changed? The question is unresolved since it is Ligurinus's very identity with such temporary ornaments which is being put into question as the poem moves through a continuing progression of tenses. Time shifts from future perfect to the future indicative of prediction to the present tense of Ligurinus's lament, directly echoing Horace's own "non sum qualis eram." But the symmetry which these two odes set in motion is based on asymmetry: Ligurinus must always be unattainable, especially at the moment when he becomes the speaker himself. The two can only be united in loss.

Thus Horace, through his art of mirrors, makes his name "as intelligible and as memorable as a face," and thereby makes Horatians of us all. But it takes the more pedestrian Horatians to remind us that such scenes of desire are, after all, only the most artful of simulations. If this reader of Horace never fails to be moved by such moments of transparent emotion as the discrepancies of Book 4 offer, she must also be careful not to fall into the trap of building a passionate Horace where the Horatians' phlegmatic icon once stood.

The Horatian who came closest to winning the impossible game of getting it right might have been Suetonius—who never had any qualms about admitting that he was a biographer. His Horace, round, short, a "pig from Epicurus's sty,"[81] enjoyed the pleasures of the flesh. In Horace's bedroom which, Suetonius informs us, was walled with mirrors,[82] perhaps the poet's greatest pleasure was to watch his images multiply.

5

Disfigured Truth and the Proper Name

In this office of collecting my pieces, I am altogether
uncertain, whether to look upon my self as a man
building a monument, or burying the dead?

Pope, Preface to the *Works* (1717)

MONUMENTS AND TOMBS

As early as the preface to his first collected edition of *Works* in 1717, Alexander
Pope puts himself on trial before posterity. Whether building a monument or
a tomb, the poet "collecting his pieces," like Sappho assembling the fragments
that become her body, is creating, commemorating, and ultimately legislating
the remnants of himself. The 1717 Preface from which my epigraph is drawn
continues:

> If time shall make it the former, may these Poems (as long as they last)
> remain as a testimony, that their Author never made his talents subservient
> to the mean and unworthy ends of Party or self-interest; the gratification
> of publick prejudices, or private passions; the flattery of the undeserving,
> or the insult of the unfortunate. If I have written well, let it be consider'd
> that no man can do without good sense, a quality that not only renders
> one capable of being a good writer, but a good man. And if I have made
> any acquisition in the opinion of any one under the notion of the former,
> let it be continued to me under no title than that of the latter.[1]

If what Pope has made in this collection is a monument, it is a transparent
monument to a good man rather than a good writer through which virtue is
seen rather than read. Such virtue is the product of a couplet logic that many
of Pope's Horatian self-portraits will repeat, and Martha Blount's self-sufficiency
at the end of *To a Lady* will reflect, a moral singularity that depends for its
existence on evoking the binary oppositions—of party allegiance and self-in-

terest, of public prejudices and private passions—it rejects without resolving. If this poet lives forever he will do so by himself and by negation.

"But if," the young Pope goes on, "this publication be only a more solemn funeral of my Remains, I desire it may be known that I die in charity, and in my senses; without any murmurs against the justice of this age, or any mad appeals to posterity."[2] Pleading his youth as cause for compassion, "as it never fails to be in Executions,"[3] Pope imagines the death of his literary fame, and of his authorial name, as a submission to public condemnation; he can only record his manly acquiescence. The death of Pope's name becomes the ultimate symbolic death of silence and invisibility.

To endure in print, as Pope defined it in the career in satire that followed, is to remain clearly visible against the opaque background of history that the medium records in detail. The poet thus enlists in the cause of impeccable transparency while refusing to be perfectly read. The printed copies of himself Pope transmits to posterity are less reliable versions of the valueless coins and medals in the Roman style that bore his profile (see Figure 12); neither classical nor contemporary, both monumental and ornamental, bearing both image and inscription, keeping his name and his face perpetually current. Print becomes the medium, the personal letter to posterity, with which Pope negotiates the tension between visual and virtuous immediacy and written and corrupt obscurity, living universality and dead particulars.[4] If medals give his face material substance, print for Pope bears an unmistakable corporeal and mortal mark.[5] Objectifying, owning and embodying the past through print, the poet attempts to stand out against that past as the man himself in order to legislate the future.

Pope's friend, critic, and fellow writer Aaron Hill becomes his ideal reader when upon reading Pope's first imitation of Horace, *Satire II, i,* he writes, "in your other writings, I am pleased by the *poet;* I am, here, in love with the *man.*"[6] A more recent critic can explain Hill's pronouncement by his own declaration that Pope's self in the Horatian imitations "is inseparable . . . from the poetry."[7] While the Horatian reader characterized in the previous chapter transforms the unsettling experience of reading poetry in the author's absence into a reassuring personification of the poet himself, Pope's compliant readers invert the process by making poetry itself, at the author's prompting, inseparable from the poet. In both cases, the reader transforms the experience of reading into a monument to an image of the poet at once synonymous with but beyond his text.

The image of Pope that his later satires generate confounds distinctions between author and text in a positive inversion of the monstrous conflation of body and book that characterized the adversarial images of Pope put forth in

Figure 12.

Copper medal of Alexander Pope (1743).

chapter 1. This chapter continues to explore how the first self-supporting professional poet to make the literary career itself a heroic genre deliberately blurs culturally contested differences between the authorial persona, the publisher, and the private person. In the process Pope's agency—whether as author, literary character, or actual human being—remains indeterminate. Pope challenges the same distinctions between public and private, satire and libel, author and individual, general example and particular instance, with which legal authorities of the period grappled as they adjudicated issues of copyright and libel law, in order to create his own particular version of moral law before the court of an imagined posterity.[8]

Whereas Horace claims to have made of his poetry "a monument more lasting than brass," Pope insists on advertising that his literary monument is built upon the sand that history is made of: particular names, local rivalries and his own tender frame. The particularity of print outlasts any other material monument for this author, even when such monuments are called for. In a gesture of genuine modesty (even Johnson could not doubt the sincerity of Pope's filial piety),[9] Pope was buried at his own direction in a vault in Twickenham church, near a monument he had erected to his parents bearing the inscription "Parentibus bene merentibus filius fecit" [their son made this for well deserving parents] adding only the words "et sibi" [and himself]. But a career designed to place the most private gestures in the public eye precluded this exit into filial anonymity. Next to the self-effacing memorial to the man, the clumsy but faithful William Warburton, Pope's literary defender and executor, commissioned another more suitable monument to the poet: a grey marble pyramid, some nineteen feet high, festooned with a marble plaque bearing a bust and inscriptions in Latin and English (see Figure 13). The conjunction, although not Pope's own, is certainly inspired by him. The Latin says that "Alexander Pope made the cause of friendship his care," and then gives Pope his own say, announcing him solemnly with "poeta loquitur" [the poet speaks].

> Heroes and Kings your distance keep
> In Peace let one poor Poet sleep:
> Who never flatter'd folks like you,
> Let Horace blush and Virgil too.[10]

Warburton ventriloquizes the poet by quoting his lines "For one who would not be buried in Westminister Abbey" in which the author takes the pose of the cynic Diogenes who when asked his wish by Alexander the Great, requested that the conqueror move his horse because it was blocking the light. In miniature, and in mock humility, this insulting epitaph embodies the power dynamics of Pope's satire by making moral virtue of necessity. Excluded by his Catholicism, Pope could not have been buried in Westminister Abbey with "heroes and kings"; he therefore becomes by default the truer hero. Horace and Virgil blush at the self-exposure which exposes them. The tension between the lofty monumental Latin and the English passage's bluff lack of ornament, between Warburton's adulation and Pope's eccentric dissociation of himself from flattery, creates an economy of self-effacement and self-advertisement constituted by author and reader which keeps the author's proper name in the balance.

Another such system of exchange, this one epistolary, went on between Pope and an American admirer, the Reverend Mather Byles, who was no enemy to flattery when it came to "such exalted Genius's as Mr. Pope." This devoted reader views Pope the author (whom he seems to confuse with all of the English literary pantheon in perplexing shifts from singular to plural)

> o'tother Side the inconceivable Breadth of Ocean, in the same Light, in which you behold the admired Classicks [sic]. We read you with Transport, and talk of you with Wonder. We look upon your Letter as you would upon the original parchment of *Homer*. We pay you a deference & veneration belonging to a Race of Superior Beings and you appear to our Imaginations, like so many Deities in Human Shape. But when we vote you all people of the Elyzium, we please our selves to fancy how much Mr. *Pope* appears the Musaeus of the shining Company Musaeum ante omnes: medium nam plurima turba Hunc habet, atque humeris exstantem suscipit altis. [Musaeus before all, for the vast throng makes him their

Figure 13.

Line engraving of the Twickenham Monument,
by S. F. Ravenet after a drawing by Samuel Wale.

center, and takes him in standing above them with shoulders high] (*Aeneid VI*, 667–668).[11]

Byles constructs a literary chain of being, an order of fame and successive reflection, which exceeds even the filial reverence of the *Essay on Criticism*. Separated from the authors he worships by a sublime stretch of water, Byles is to Pope as Pope is to the classics; the English poet's letter to his colonial readers becomes their ineffable "original parchment," and just as he idolizes the ancients, so he becomes a god to his acolytes. When the new world votes its own literary "Elyzium," it is Pope whom even the classics worship in a transumption Milton himself would have envied. Just as Warburton speaks for the absent Pope with the poet's own lines, Byles proclaims Pope's precedence over the ancients by putting these words from the *Aeneid* into Virgil's own mouth, reauthorizing the English author with a modern reading of an ancient text. Proving himself as observant as he is obsequious, this attentive reader of Pope chooses a passage that figures his idol's stature in terms of physical height. One can almost visualize a huge bust of Pope, like the one on Warburton's monument, looming above the other ancients "by the shoulders." Pope's balance between physical and poetic selves here gains legitimacy by taking on the shape of, while itself reshaping, a literary precedent. In this literary Elyzium, Pope's body has ceased to hamper him; rather it marks him as a true original whom even the great Virgil praises. As these exchanges of agency and authenticity indicate, if Pope's poetry constitutes his letter and legal brief to posterity, that letter is signed with his body's indelible signature.

Horace's text provides Pope with a persona in which to display his person. As Pope leaves his mark on the Horatian mode,[12] his increasingly satiric poetry, culminating with the *Epilogue to the Satires* (1738) and the *New Dunciad* (1742–43), forgoes analogy for antagonism, proper mediation for righteously indignant opposition; its author becomes less intent on making literary allies than on marking out literal enemies. The *Essay on Criticism*'s ideal of "unerring Nature" is refigured in the image of the poet's unnatural physique, and Nature's "clear, unchanged and universal" tenets are transformed into opaque, transient and particular aberration. Pope evolves from the faithful translator of Homer's heroic ideal to the heroic satirist rebel against that same Horatian propriety he had espoused, drawing the "last Pen for freedom" (*Dialogue II*, 248) in the name of a virtue which only he embodies and of which his unnatural deformity is the mark. Any external standard, any "nature" against which all can be measured and compared, has disappeared. Only the couplet's warring conjunctions remain.[13]

The *Epilogue to the Satires* ends characteristically with a rhetorical turn from living corruption to dead virtue and the power of names:

> Yes, the last Pen for Freedom let me draw,
> When Truth stands trembling on the edge of Law:
> Here, Last of *Britons!* let your Names be read;
> Are none, none living? let me praise the Dead,
> And for that Cause which made your Fathers shine,
> Fall, by the Votes of their degen'rate Line!   (II, 248–253)

This conclusion's absolutist fervor is doubly undercut. First, Pope's satiric adversary, the "friend" who provokes the dialogue, responds with the last word, "Alas! alas! pray end what you began, / And write next winter more *Essays on Man!*" (254–255) Pope himself adds a footnote:

> This was the last poem of the kind printed by our author, with a resolution to publish no more; but to enter thus, in the most plain and solemn manner he could, a sort of PROTEST against that insuperable corruption and depravity of manners, which he had been so unhappy as to live to see. Could he have hoped to have amended any, he had continued those attacks; but bad men were grown so shameless and powerful, that Ridicule was become as unsafe as it was ineffectual. The Poem raised him, as he knew it would, some enemies; but he had reason to be satisfied with the approbation of good men and the testimony of his own conscience.[14]

The 1717 preface's tentative moral resignation is here justified and documented by political circumstance. The poet of the Horatian poems rejects that showpiece of the 1717 *Works,* the peaceful hierarchy of authority and filial propriety of the *Essay on Criticism,* as servile and superficial; harmony between authors and their precursors, between nature and art, and between morality and good manners, has become for the satirist deceiving and corrupt. Pope justifies his aggressively improper self-advertisement as historically necessary: an aberration the complacent times demand. The *Essay on Criticism*'s perfect correspondences taught that no author writes alone. The later satires show that the only way for a poet to maintain self-possession is to root his isolated unequivocal self in the equivocal, while "Truth" trembles "on the edge of Law" in perpetual danger of being silenced.

The first appearance of the fourth book of the *Dunciad* in 1742 ends with a similar submission to the forces of the times, in a silence which documents its own necessity and which will in a later edition be expanded upon as the end of culture itself. Closing with a vision of Dulness bidding "Britannia sleep," and pouring "her Spirit o'er the Land and deep" (626), this version stops short of the grand apocalyptic vision of Universal Darkness burying all with which Pope closed the poem's earlier and final editions. Instead two rows of asterisks appear, along with the words, "De-est FINIS" [the end is lacking], and a note explains: "It is impossible to lament sufficiently the loss of the rest of this Poem, just at the opening of so fair a scene as the Invocation seems to promise. It is to be hop'd however that the Poet compleated it, and that it will not be lost to posterity, if we may trust to a Hint given in one of his satires (*Satire II, i, 59*). *Publish the present Age, but where the Text / Is Vice too high, reserve it for the next.*"[15] For the Pope of the late satires, as this note makes explicit, posterity is the ultimate judge of a series of aesthetic and moral distinctions that only the poet is capable of making. Such distinctions are matters of proportion and scale. As Geoffrey Tillotson characterizes Pope's evolution as mock-epic poet, if *The Rape of the Lock* is "an exquisitely diminished shadow cast by an entire epic" or, I would add, by an entire Western epic tradition, then *The Dunciad* is "the ludicrous, grotesque, lifesize shadow cast by a piece of an epic poem."[16] While the *Rape* preserves totality in miniature, that distorted fragment of Parnassus, the *Dunciad,* by its magnifying of contemporary detail into life-size scale, abandons coherent epic wholes for grotesque satiric remnants.

THE CURRENCY OF NAMES

The key to Pope's offensive integrity in his later satire is his use of the proper name to deform his poetry's perfect universality. The personal, social, and political dangers of naming names become the subject of increasingly heated, even vituperative dialogue between Pope and various friends. Most obviously, such dialogue revolves around the fact that pointing the finger at specific individuals enrages Pope's readers and jeopardizes his claims of morality and impartiality, while leaving him politically and legally vulnerable. More importantly, naming names compromises the poet's reception by a posterity unable to decipher the later poetry's proliferation of historical detail.

In a letter to Pope about the *Dunciad,* Swift characterizes the connection between specificity and indecipherability as a kind of contagion: "The notes I could wish to be very large, in what relates to the persons concern'd; for I have long observ'd that twenty miles from London no body understands hints, initial letters, or town-facts and passages; and in a few years not even those who live in London."[17] Swift points to the near-obsessive focus on particular names which propelled the poem's long publication history. Published anonymously, and accompanied by false advertisements for a non-existent work called "The Progress of Dulness, an Historical Poem. By an Eminent Hand," the first edition left the names of its victims blank, only to have them filled in by at least two unauthorized "Keys" to the *Dunciad,* and ultimately by Pope himself with the help of Richard Savage and several others in the *Dunciad Variorum* (1729). While James Ralph's *Sawney* (1728) criticized Pope in words from his own *Essay on Criticism* as one of those who "judge of Authors NAMES, not Works, and then / Nor praise nor blame the Writings, but the Men," Edward Ward's particularly vituperative *Apollo's Maggott in his Cups: Or, The Whimsical Creation of a Little Satyrical Poet* (1729) was one of many lampoons to explain Pope's teasing omissions of complete names by accusations of cowardice:

> No Sex or Quality escape
> The fury of his Lashes,
> And what he fears to say, the Ape
> Supplies with Stars and Dashes.[18]

Pope responded to such public clamour with bravado: "The Dunciad is going to be printed in all pomp," he wrote to Swift in 1728, "It will be attended with *Proeme, Prologomena, Testimonia Scriptorum, Index Authorum* and Notes *Variorum.*"[19] Ward described the finished result by conflating body and book: "I fancy'd the Author . . . had loaded his Satyr with a fresh Dose of Poyson, because it was so suddenly swell'd from a little thin-gutted *Duodecimo,* to a huge pot-belly'd *Quarto.*"[20]

Decked out as a material classic, this edition also afforded the author the pleasure not only of naming his victims but of elaborating on the particulars of his own provocation. He studded the poem with meticulous excerpts from four self-assembled volumes of libels against him, and "from such trivialities" built a mock-scholarly apparatus.[21] When a fourth book called the *New Dunciad* depicting types of dulness rather than historically specific examples appeared in 1742, the ever ambivalent critics complained that "the *Satire* is too *allegorical,* and the *Characters* he has drawn are too conceal'd: That *real Names* should have been inserted instead of *fictitious ones.*"[22] Pope countered that criticism with his last and grandest name change in 1743, the enthronement of Colley Cibber as Dulness's favorite in place of Lewis Theobald. Cibber makes his entrance in Pope's revision of Book I as "Bays," at once an emblem of the feminine impressionability and theatricality of the *Epistle to a Lady* and a symbol, surrounded by "much Embryo, much Abortion" (121) of his own composition, of monstrous productivity:

In each she [Dulness] marks her image full exprest,
But chief in BAYS's monster-breeding breast;
Bays, form'd by nature Stage and Town to bless,
And act, and be, a Coxcomb with success.   (I, 107–110)

A slur on Cibber's manhood in the poem's new fourth book—"soft on her lap her Laureat son reclines" (IV, 20)—provoked an epistolary print war between Pope and Cibber that produced one of the most vividly emasculated images of the poet on record: a "Tom Tit on the mound of love," rescued by Cibber, as he claimed in his open 1742 letter to Pope, from certain death in a prostitute's embrace (see Figure 14). For the author and his adversaries, indeed for the poem's contemporary public as a whole, the fascination, power and risk of the *Dunciad* lay in the scandal of its satire's particularity.

While the general evolution of content of the *Dunciad*'s satire can be characterized as a progression from individual to type, the poetics and publication history of this mock-epic move increasingly from the abstract to the material. Here for example is Dulness's exhortation to those the notes ironically refer to as the "restorers, of canonical or 'standard' authors":

—Thus revive the Wits!
But murder first, and mince them all to bits;
As erst Medea (cruel, so to save!)
A new Edition of old Aeson gave,
Let standard-Authors, thus, like trophies born,
Appear more glorious as more hack'd and torn,
And you, my Critics! in the chequer'd shade,
Admire new light thro' holes yourselves have made.
   Leave not a foot of verse, a foot of stone,
A Page, a Grave, that they can call their own;
But spread, my sons, your glory thin or thick,
On passive paper, or on solid brick.   (IV, 119–130)

If *The Rape of the Lock* playfully resolved the problem of the classical author's relationship to the marketplace by bringing commodities to life, the *Dunciad* commits a kind of murder by reducing intellectual value to mere material things. The *Rape*'s mechanically artificial substitutions are in the later mock-epic naturalized as a contagion of embodiment. As Emrys Jones observes, the dunces both threaten and attract Pope because they reveal poetry's affinity for an ugly material world as their poverty discloses their own dependence on the body's needs. The dunces reproduce the same "unsympathetic objects" they live among, not the beautiful classics that the *Rape* and the *Dunciad* embody but

Figure 14.

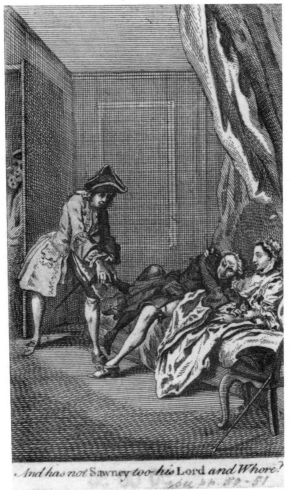

And has not Sawney too his Lord *and* Whore?

Frontispiece to the third edition of Colley Cibber's
*A Letter from Mr. Cibber, to Mr. Pope, inquiring into the
motives that might induce him in his satyrical works,
to be so frequently fond of Mr. Cibber's name.*

cheap bulky paper fit for lining birdcages and wrapping pasties.[23] Pope responds by making duncely poverty an aesthetic issue, but in doing so not even he can escape the corruption of the corporeal.

Warburton's editorial note to this passage paraphrases: "The Goddess applauds the practice of tacking the obscure names of Persons not eminent in any

branch of learning, to those of the most distinguished Writers; 'either by printing *Editions* of their works with impertinent alterations of their Text, as in the
former instances, or by setting up *Monuments* disgraced with their own vile
names and inscriptions in the latter.' "[24] Yet even this literal interpretation ends
with a metaphor which concretizes the literary in the shape of a monument.
Pope's poetry goes much further: indiscriminate editing is the equivalent of
murder, and in a condensed version of the *Rape's* disconcerting zeugmas, Medea's dismemberment of Jason's father is nothing more (or less) than a bad
edition. The difference is that here, as was not entirely the case in the *Rape,*
the fixed point of value and of irony is uncertain. "Standard-Authors" are visualized as literal "standards," flags or trophies "hack'd and torn" by intellectual
battle, and the "holes" of rampaging critics let in a light less intellectual than
blinding, especially when viewed in the context of the passage's reference to
Waller: "The Soul's dark cottage, batter'd and decay'd, / Lets in new light
through chinks that time has made."[25] The talent of the dunces as editors is to
transform the most inspiring of metaphors to the literal and banal, reducing
spiritual agency to their own destructive power. All that remains, as Pope himself acknowledges in his 1717 Preface, is the text's materiality and mortality: a
"Page" or a "Grave." As Warburton reflects in the notes: "For what less than a
Grave can be granted to a dead author? or what less than a Page can be allow'd
a living one?"[26] The *Dunciad,* like a ruined building in a classical garden, mes-
merizes like an "Ornament and Curiosity on dead bodies."[27]

MONSTROUS PARTICULARITY

Questioning the distinction between dead and living authors, along with dead
and living metaphors, the *Dunciad* transforms the unsavory physical environ-
ment of Grub Street into a metaphorical "Chaos dark and deep, / Where nameless Somethings in their causes sleep" (I, 55–56) while translating figures of
speech into shockingly material form.

> 'Till genial Jacob, or a warm Third Day
> Call forth each mass, a Poem, or a Play:
> How hints, like spawn, scare quick in embryo lie,
> How new-born nonsense first is taught to cry,
> Maggotts half-form'd in rhyme exactly meet,
> And learn to crawl upon poetic feet.   (I, 57–62)

The poem's fascinated portrayal of the formlessness which the mighty mother

Dulness personifies spreads to its characterization of dull writing as grotesquely unfinished births. What results is a spell-binding poetics of uncreation in which Pope is free to imagine a dazzlingly unnatural and theatrical universe:

> Here one poor word an hundred clenches makes,
> And ductile dulness new meanders takes;
> There motley Images her fancy strike,
> Figures ill-pair'd, and Similies unlike.
> She sees a Mob of Metaphors advance,
> Pleas'd with the madness of the mazy dance:
> How Tragedy and Comedy embrace;
> How Farce and Epic get a jumbled race;
> How Time himself stands still at her command,
> Realms shift their place, and Ocean turns to land.
> Here gay Description Aegypt glads with show'rs,
> Or gives to Zembla fruits, to Barca flow'rs;
> Glitt'ring with ice here hoary hills are seen,
> There painted vallies of eternal green,
> In cold December fragrant chaplets blow,
> And heavy harvests nod beneath the snow.   (I, 63–77)

From the overwrought excess of one poor word's punning, to the inappropriate use of rhetorical figures, to the mis-mating of genres, to the uncontained imagination of fantastic landscapes, Dulness's work is depicted as a force beyond Nature's bounds. In a parallel development (as Swift's letter had warned), the poem's readers' incomprehension spreads through first space and then time like a plague. As Fielding notes in the *Covent Garden Journal,* this plague taints both the satirist and his targets:

> He employed a whole Work for the Purpose of recovering such Writers as no one without his Pains, except he had lived at the same Time and in the same Street, would ever have heard of. He may indeed be said to have raked many out of the Kennels to Immortality, which, tho' in somewhat a stinking Condition, is to an ambitious Mind preferable to utter Obscurity and Oblivion; many, I presume, having, with the Wretch who burnt the Temple of Ephesus, such a Love for Fame, that they are willing even to creep into her common Shore.[28]

Pope and the inhabitants of immortality's stinking kennels are united in one "ambitious mind," preferring, like Achilles opting for power in hell over enslavement in the human world, immortality in a "common Shore" or sewer to "utter Obscurity and Oblivion." Both within and without the poem, there is no escaping the stench that rises from decayed meaning that was supposed to endure forever. As Swift's hack comments in *Tale of a Tub,* "nothing is so very tender as a *Modern* Piece of Wit, and which is apt to suffer so much in the Carriage."[29]

As the Dunces saw it, Pope himself suffered a great deal in the poem's carriage: the *Dunciad* disfigured the author's person with the decay of illicit imitation and unjust satire. As Chapter 1 demonstrates in great detail, Pope's satiric victims rewrote him in his book's deformed image, his satire both origin and reflection of a moral failing translated, in the most spectacular piece of duncely poetry, into a twisted frame. Such a bodily confounding of the textual with the personal in the service of a moral narrative of origins persists as late as *The Blatant Beast* (1742):

> If Beauty be the Subject of our Praise,
> A rude, mishapen Lump Contempt must raise.
>   When *Lucifer* with Angels first held Place,
> Seraphic Beauty sparkled in his Face.
> By Pride and Malice tempted to rebel,
> Vengeance pursu'd him to the lowest Hell:
> Not sulph'rous Lakes suffic'd, nor dreary Plains;
> Deformity was join'd t'improve his Pains.
>   Paint then the Person, and expose the Mind,
> Who rails at others, to his own Faults blind.[30]

However vehemently its prisoners protested against this grand "penal code"[31] fixing them in their proper confinement, the *Dunciad* in particular and Pope's later poetry in general is a process of continual carriage or translation which, like the construction of the grot, undergoes what cannot be overcome, and turns a submission to the necessity of living amidst moral and aesthetic chaos into an assertion of artistic authority. The put-upon satirist becomes the "King of Parnassus," whose power to name is also his power to judge.[32] An understandably angry victim of Pope's pen, Charles Johnson, coins this phrase in his Preface to *The Tragedy of Medea*:

> Many Years are not passed since a little Gentleman very well known and skill'd in Poetry, took it into his Head that he was really and truly the King of *Parnassus,* and that all People, who presumed to oppose this his Title to poetical Royalty or to make Verses without his Patent and Authority, were Rebels. Many of the Sons of the Muses did not like this Severity; Those, who woul'd have acknowledg'd a King, did not care to suffer a

Tyrant; upon which his versifying Majesty grew wrathful, and swore they should either stand in the Records of Fame as his Subjects, or as Dunces; and this Project we have seen him put in Execution, to the very Letter, in the most intrepid Manner. Since that Time, whoever, it seems, stands attainted by Name in this Proclamation of his, is never to recover Fame or Bread; such is his poetical Will.[33]

Johnson, who published this pamphlet in order to blame Pope for the failure of his play, shows himself to be anything but a dunce in his characterization of Pope's totalitarian mode of cultural power. Pope has blackened some extremely worthy names in the annals of literary history, Defoe and Bentley among them, by utilizing modern print technology in the service of an obsolete "classical" absolutist authority which he alone embodied. Byron noted of a later generation of poets that Pope's cultural authority maintained its effect despite the growing indecipherability of his work's historical detail: "The attempt of the poetical populace of the present day to obtain an ostracism against Pope is as easily accounted for as the Athenian's shell against Aristides; they are tired of hearing him called 'the Just.' They are also fighting for life; for, if he maintains his station, they will reach their own—by falling."[34]

So prevalent was this depiction of Pope as a literary tyrant inscribing the names of cultural offenders in his book of judgment that after his death, in 1752 Henry Fielding sardonically lamented that the Kingdom of Authorship had deteriorated to lawlessness. When Pope ruled, he "did indeed put a total Restraint on the Liberty of the Press: For no Person durst read any Thing which was writ without his License and Approbation; and this License he granted only to four during his Reign . . . After the demise of King Alexander, the Literary State relapsed into a Democracy, or rather indeed into downright Anarchy."[35]

Victims, critical commentators, and heirs alike describe Pope's literary authority in terms of his power to record a dunce's name in the records of fame, his undemocratic monopoly over the "patent and authority" and the "license" of language. For Pope, to name names is to corner and confine the literary market. The proper name is the "uncreating Word" which damns others to cultural ignominy while granting its author eternal life. Even in his attempt to reinscribe the monument such a monopoly creates, the author of *Pope Alexander's Supremacy Examined* (1729) in a curious presaging of Pope's own declaration "To VIRTUE ONLY and HER FRIENDS, A FRIEND," (*Satire II, i,* 121), only confirms its power by negation: "it [the *Dunciad*] will stand only as a Monument to his Infamy; and those that come after us will and must believe, the Persons who stood the Marks of his petulant Malice, to be Worthy and

Good Men; and the Enemies of the Author of the *Dunciad* will always be look'd upon as the Friends of Virtue; they will see a little invidious narrow Mind in every line he has written."[36]

Grub Street itself, as Pat Rogers documents, provided the satirist with a ready-made sub-urban landscape of marginality, deformity, poverty, insanity, and disease in which to imprison its inhabitants for eternity.[37] Yet the Grub Street phenomenon also made Pope's literary career economically possible, and Pope himself potentially indistinguishable from a host of other "scriblers." What better way to show their insignificance, and mark his own enduring value, than to confine the duces to the hell of historical particularity?

But as Rogers's own thwarted desire to remove Pope from the literal filth of this literary suburb demonstrates, when Pope records the realities of Grub Street, he effaces the distinction between the literal and the literary, and between himself and his targets, all the more dramatically. One cannot be sure whether Pope created the duces or they him, or to quote Pope's phrase, whether "the Poem was not made for these Authors, but these Authors for the Poem."[38] Rogers writes,

> Without assistance we can hardly make anything of Pope's satire. His interest in his literary opponents, *prior to* their transmutation into literary vehicles of his own manufacture, entails several obligations on us as readers . . . Indeed, there is a *malicious brand of specificity* which marks out all Pope's practice. It follows that we have to be alive to what may look at first to be the stray particulars, if we want to grasp the general implications of his attack.[39]

In the process of reading Rogers's impressive research, it becomes impossible to tell whether what he calls Pope's "malicious brand of specificity" is self-reflexive metaphor or descriptive truth. The critic's own confusion of art and life is as unconscious as Pope's is conscious, but the result is much the same: Pope's poetry is determined by as much as it determines the literal. Such confusion is exemplified by the way in which Rogers extends Pope's legalistic metaphors to a literal defense of their author in order to argue that to take Pope's account of Grub Street literally is "to attempt to use Hogarth's 'Distressed Poet' as a deposition in court."[40]

Just as Dustin Griffin neglects to include Pope's reference to his figure's "mean Original" in his analysis of the poet's epistolary self-exposure to Lady Mary,[41] Rogers neglects to acknowledge the way in which "stray particulars" challenge the coherence of Pope's literary creation and the integrity of his literary judgments. Quoting a contemporary definition of "Grub," for example, as "a dwarf or short fellow, the puny stature of a mediocre writer," Rogers, unlike Pope and his readers, averts his eyes from Pope's own "puny stature."[42] Infecting the literal with the literary, Pope's inclusion in the *Dunciad* of what the poem's editor calls "a nucleus of nobodies," and what Pope enumerated as "Each Songster, Riddler, ev'ry nameless name"[43] makes the meaninglessness of bad repute contagious; such contagion both jeopardizes and guarantees the legibility of his own good name against a chaotic background. As Pope opined to Spence in 1739: "Middling Poets are no poets at all. There is always a great number of such in each age that are almost totally forgotten in the next. A few curious inquirers may know that there were such men and that they wrote such and such things, but to the world they are as if they had never been."[44] Just as the characters of men are discerned against the background of women's characterlessness, Pope's reputation endures in sharply defined contrast to this deliberately preserved obscurity.

REJECTING HORACE'S SOBER ADVICE

An aggressively impolite satiric hero imprisoned in the historical particulars of his milieu, embracing his own authorial "dis-ease," protesting both Horatian informality and the form it tactfully conceals, Pope rebels against Horace's reticent art by insisting on his right to represent himself fully by literary imitation; he refuses to figure Horace in his own image or himself in Horace's. As Chapter 4 has shown in Ode 4.1's miniature form, the silence in Horace that many readers are compelled to supplement with their own imaginations is given in Pope the poet's particular name and inimitable form.

It is Pope's distinguishing characteristic that he will not allow the reader to draw the line between sincere self-colloquy and authorial self-consciousness. Into his art's seamless surface he incorporates the labor involved in Horatian artlessness. He never lets the reader forget that unlike Horace, he is free of patrons in an age of print, that he remains private by publishing, that the times call not for retirement but for the most dramatic self-display. Pope makes the contrast between Horace's relation to Augustus and his own political situation most vehemently in *The First Epistle of the Second Book of Horace, Imitated* (1737). The "Advertisement" states: "This Epistle will show the learned World to have fallen into [a] mistake . . . that *Augustus was a Patron of Poets in general;* whereas he not only prohibited all but the best Writers to name him, but recommended that Care even to the Civil Magistrate: *Admonebat Praetores, ne paterentur Nomen suum obsolefieri,&c"* [he warned his Praetors, that they ought not to allow his name to go out of style] (Suetonius, *Augustus,* sec. 89). While the Roman Augustus also bears the burden of some of Pope's more subtle irony, he is contrasted favorably with George Augustus by virtue of his awareness that his name is one that poets can make or destroy. All that can be said of potentates without such knowledge is, as Pope ends his truncated version of Horace's Ode 4.9, "They had no Poet and they dyd!"[45] Or as Lord Hervey wrote of Pope's *Epistle to Augustus* in his *Memoirs,* "Not that there was any similitude between the two princes who presided in the Roman and English Augustan Ages besides their names, for George Augustus neither loved learning nor encouraged men of letters, nor were there any Maecenases about him."[46] If the two Emperors share only a name, what most distinguishes them is their disparate awareness of the power Pope himself heroically figures. The *Epistle to Arbuthnot's* portrait of the poet as such a masculine ideal responsible to posterity alone follows Pope's demonization of Lord Hervey's horrifying ambiguity, a fascinated rejection of an androgynously "vile Antithesis" to which we will return:

> Not Fortune's Worshipper, nor Fashion's Fool,
> Not Lucre's Madman, nor Ambition's Tool.
> Not proud, nor servile, be one Poet's praise
> That if he pleas'd, he pleas'd by manly ways;
> That Flatt'ry, even to Kings, he held a shame,
> And thought a Lye in Verse or Prose the same.   (334–339)

The genesis of Pope's Horatian imitations locates the origins of such a power in the independent poet. Released at the same time as the anonymous *Essay on Man, Satire II, i,* or so Pope told Spence in the last year of his life, originated in a moment of characteristically proud self-effacement. According to Pope, the poem came into being almost by accident:

> When I had a fever one winter in town that confined me to my room for five or six days, Lord Bolingbroke came to see me, happened to take up a Horace that lay on the table, and in turning it over dipped on the First Satire of the Second Book. He observed how well that would hit my case, if I were to imitate it in English. After he was gone, I read it over, translated it in a morning or two, and sent it to the press in a week or fortnight after. And this was the occasion of my imitating some other of the Satires and Epistles afterwards.[47]

"To how casual a beginning," Spence remarks, "are we obliged for some of the most delightful things in our language."[48] Such a casual beginning is demanded by Pope's role of gentleman and gentleman's writer, unspotted by printer's ink or filthy lucre, confined to his room not by continual ill health but by a momentary fever, happening on the example of Horace by the chance notice of a bored nobleman, writing merely to oblige a patron and friend. Compulsion, writing as disease more contagious than any fever, does not figure in this scenario, and Pope's need to publish his offhand product is entirely unaccounted for. Writing merely happens to him.

Pope's official account of his decision to publish the Horatian poems two years after the first issue of *Satire II, i* is of a different kind of compulsion: "The Occasion of publishing these *Imitations* was the Clamour raised on some of my *Epistles*. An answer from *Horace* was both more full, and of more dignity, than any I cou'd have made in my own person."[49] Here the author denies the drive to write and to publish by assuming the guise of assaulted virtue. Whether incited by moral indignation or less lofty forces, Pope writes more by provocation than by choice. The "Advertisement" to the *Epistle to Arbuthnot* is a variation on the same theme. Pope refers to this poem as a

Paper . . . a Sort of Bill of Complaint, begun many years since, and drawn up by snatches, as the several Occasions offer'd. I had no thoughts of publishing it, till it pleas'd some Persons of Rank and Fortune [the Authors of *Verses to the Imitator of Horace,* and of an *Epistle to a Doctor of Divinity from a Nobleman at Hampton Court,*] to attack in a very extraordinary manner, not only my *Writings* (of which being publick the Publick judge) but my *Person, Morals,* and *Family,* whereof to those who know me not, a truer Information may be requisite.[50]

Pope fights dirty only in self-defense; he speaks of himself only to correct a false impression; he, unlike his attackers Lady Mary and Lord Hervey, will not name names. But in naming the publications of his attackers, he identifies them by pointing to their greatest defects. Such a move reveals how authorship makes a writer public property; Pope's satire's vicious circle of lampoon and response enacts this round repeatedly. By responding in Horace's person, Pope can reveal—without appearing to have done so—his own proper name and those of his enemies.

This vicious circle becomes all the more evident when we consider that the "clamour" about the *Epistles to Several Persons,* mentioned in the advertisement to *Satire II, i,* was generated by possible allusions to real contemporary figures in Pope's satire; the central target was Pope's erstwhile patron the Duke of Chandos, whom readers took for the *Epistle to Burlington*'s paragon of ostentatiously bad taste, Timon. "By Timon," Johnson writes in his *Life of Pope*, "he was universally supposed, and by the Earl of Burlington, to whom the poem is addressed, was privately said, to mean the Duke of Chandos; a man perhaps too much delighted with pomp and show, but of a temper kind and beneficent, and who had consequently the voice of the public in his favor."[51] This conjunction of universal supposition and private confirmation parallels Pope's own defense of his particular case in Horace's generally approved person. The armor of Horace's original protects the poet from his audience while making such protection its own necessity: more lampoons were written against (and in defense of) Pope in 1733, the year *Satire II, i* appeared, than in any other year.[52]

The greatest mistake for readers of Pope's satire, the advertisement to the *Dunciad* points out, is falsely to apply general examples to particular cases; to do so is to mistake the satirist himself: "And indeed there is not in the world a greater Error, than that which Fools are so apt to fall into, and Knaves with good reason to incourage, the mistaking a *Satyrist* for a *Libeller*; whereas to a *true Satyrist* nothing is so odious as a *Libeller*, for the same reason as to a man *truly Virtuous* nothing is so hateful as a *Hypocrite*."[53] Pope echoes here his own early epistolary injunction to Lady Mary to bare her soul lest she appear a prude and a hypocrite. Readers of such righteous indignation would be tempted to avoid playing the fool at all costs and to defend distinctions—between satire and libel, between virtue and hypocrisy—which are difficult to discern. How, in poetry so conscious of the artfulness of its own morality, to tell the difference between virtue and hypocrisy? How to mark resemblances without claiming identities? How to relish Pope's satire without caring about the particulars? The distinctions Pope asserts so firmly here may be as flimsy as those which separate deformity from the norm.

SATIRE I, II:

THE IMPROPRIETY OF THE PROPER NAME

Mademoiselle De L'Espinasse: I have just had a very silly idea.
Bordeu: What?
Mademoiselle De L'Espinasse: That perhaps man is merely a woman with freakish malformations, or woman a freakish man.[54]

Authored by no one in particular, both disconcertingly specific and conventionally typical, a particolored creation of Roman and English manners, a poetry misshapen in its formlessness yet more rigidly closed than its original,

Pope's Horatian poems engage in a constant dialogue with the reader not unlike the conversation Dr. Bordeu has with Mademoiselle De L'Espinasse, while behind the screen the mathematician D'Alembert, her unrequited lover, dreams and ejaculates in body and soul. (The resemblance to the Horatian poems is all the stronger when one notes that this fictional dialogue takes place among actual people who were alive at the time it was written.) A philosophical meditation brought into the drawing room, a solitary Cartesian raving overheard by polite society, a mighty maze of a text which is indeed without a plan, *D'Alembert's Dream* is like the *Essay on Man* gone wild at the moment of being domesticized. When such impolitely reasonable conversation entertains the notion of aberrant monstrosity, it jeopardizes the notion of a natural "norm." The great chain of being, and the great bundle of nerves which is the object of enlightened study, embraces all things; between a healthy human being and an inhuman monster there is no qualitative difference, only degrees of resemblance.

Just as this licentious dialogue ranges from a general questioning of the notion of monstrosity to a particularly disconcerting reconsideration of sexual identity,[55] so in representing the unusual case of Pope's deformity, contemporary readers figure distinctions between natural and unnatural in their most threatening guise as differences between male and female. Such depictions represent matching extremes of the poet's simian oversexed debauchery or unmanly impotence. In 1735, for example, Pope is accused of libelling Lady Mary "upon a Suspicion he had that she intended to ravish him."[56] Ward's *Apollo's Maggott* traces such ambiguity to the scene of the poet's creation by the Muses, who are rebuked by Apollo for a significant omission:

> Besides, my Dames, in this your Work,
> There's one Neglect that vexes,
> You've quite forgot the middle Mark
> That should distinguish Sexes.
> For what Anatomist can tell,
> By this poor thingless Body,
> Whether you mean it for a Male,
> Or for a Female Dowdy.
>
> . . .
>
> The Muses blush'd at this Reproof,
> B'ing modest, young and tender,
> So dab'd on just an Inch of Stuff,
> Enough to shew the Gender.[57]

The lampooned poet embodies Mademoiselle De L'Espinasse's image of sexual identity as a mirror of monstrosity which makes each sex a deformed version of the other. Like Martha Blount, described at the end of *To a Lady* as a "softer man" (a figure that destroys the very distinctions between the sexes which motivate the poem), Pope is neither entirely human nor entirely masculine. But while Pope celebrates Martha Blount for her composed transcendence of sexual distinctions, Pope's libellers use the same paradox to condemn rather than to praise. They respond to what they perceive as nature's failure to author her creature by depriving him of his own authority, driving him beyond the bounds which his expulsion defines.

In the natural order of Pope's poetry, monstrosity and scandal exist as freakish reflections of correctness and politeness. The monstrous and illicit aspect of Pope's art which I delineated in earlier chapters is the inverse of its refinement; the two exist by virtue of the constant impingement of one upon the other.[58] Pope masks this interdependence of the polite and the scandalous by refiguring them as opposed in the satirist's battle against the forces of aesthetic and moral disintegration. This sublimation of licentious ambiguity in the cause of clear moral distinctions becomes in Pope a question of the propriety of naming names. Prurient interest and righteous indignation are most clearly revealed as complicit in Pope's version of Satire 1, 2 on the financial, social, and corporeal dangers of adultery, *Sober Advice from Horace*.

The pseudo-anonymous translation of the racy *Sober Advice* offers a paradigm for the double reading the Horatian poems demand. The English forces upon the reader, and the editor of the Twickenham edition, a constant game of who's who, or "name that scandal." The real obscenities in this poem are not the Latin unmentionables which Pope, in his parody of Bentley, insists on mentioning in the notes, but rather the names of specific individuals, printed in the text as if they were obscenities (e.g., L——n, J——s). And just as in his later political satires, Pope seeks to recast the distinction between those who are socially "out" and "in" as the "strong antipathy of Good to Bad" exemplified by himself at battle with the world,[59] in *Sober Advice* the reader's pleasure in prurience is recast as the enjoyment of an alliance in sophistication with the poet. The poem's salacious energy resides not only in the way in which, as James Turner notes, a "refined and socialized form of libertine discourse . . . seeps through the partitions of decorum," nor just in the way that "chaste periphrases" and partial suppressions of obscenities "reinforce the display of transgression," but also, I would add, in the way that discourse points the reader beyond the text to historical agents and actual sins.[60] In a typical passage, the stereotype of the ravenously adulterous woman is named while the identity of the man mentioned is partially and provocatively omitted:

> *Con. Philips* cries, "A sneaking Dog I hate."
> That's all three Lovers have for their Estate!
> "Treat on, treat on," is her eternal Note,
> And Lands and Tenements go down her Throat.
> Some damn the Jade, and some the Cullies blame,
> But not Sir H—t, for he does the same.   (11–16)

In an equally characteristic note, the Twickenham editor is forced to join the male community of conjecture in determining the name: "Sir Horace Walpole and the anonymous annotators of Bodleian copies agree in supposing this to be Sir Herbert Parkington. I have not discovered to what the passage alludes."[61] The bond Pope creates in *Sober Advice* is a voyeuristic one between himself and the reader: between those "in the know" who point the finger at the expense of those who form the obscene tableau. Rewritten in less lascivious form this bond connects the virtuous author and the proper readers of satire who know how to avoid applying it to themselves and to distinguish it from libel.

The poem's moral, by which all women are reduced to flesh, gains particular resonance in Pope's translation. Horace's ironic celebration of the ability of the male imagination to create fictional (and therefore stable) distinctions between women becomes in Pope a kind of epistemological anxiety. Illusion becomes less important than the "thing" behind the veil, and the unmentionable is not a matter of body parts but of the particular beings who employ them. "And will you run to Perils, Sword, and Law, / All for a Thing you ne're so much as *saw?*" (135–136) For Horace, what constitutes the triumph of the poet's imagination over the perils of adultery is his ability to give "whatever name [he] pleases" [nomen quodlibet illi] (126) to the woman closest at hand. But Pope as lover amuses himself with arbitrary distinctions and fictional names, calling his beloved, in epithets mounting from general praise to particular satire, "Angel! Goddess! Montagu!" (166). Like the aspiring bards in *Epistle II, ii* who "take what names we please" (142) from the Augustan canon, Pope the successful satirist points his finger at the truth, makes names stick to their true owners and thereby earns himself a proper and historically documented place in posterity's esteem. If woman can be reduced to a general type, the poet insists upon his masculine right to remain specific and to maintain specifics. The strongest desire of both author and reader in *Sober Advice,* then, is to uncover the unmentionable particulars; to name the owner of the nameless thing is more important and more gratifying than to expose the "thing" itself.

While Pope's mock-Bentley, obsessed throughout the poem with the literal, demands that the poet call a spade a spade—"why *Thing?* the Poet has it *Cunnum;* which, therefore, boldly place here"—the editor of the Twickenham edition of the poem is frustrated at a different failure to speak plainly, namely Pope's needless elision of the name Sallust (line 63, assumed to refer to Bolingbroke but in the Horace referring to nobody in particular): "Why Pope should call Bolingbroke Sallust, except that Bolingbroke was interested in the writing of history, and why he should suppress a harmless name, which is printed in full on the opposite page, have not yet been explained."[62] The partial concealment of the pseudonym tempts the reader even more strongly to uncover the real name: the double veiling multiplies the prurient force of the reference. While the poem's readers expose the universal female "thing" behind the varied feminine facades,[63] they unearth the forbidden particulars behind the general example. The danger is that the moral might apply equally in both cases, and a name be as empty of meaning as any "thing." To point at particulars, however pruriently, is to combat this anxiety in order to preserve (while confounding) distinctions of greater weight, such as those between virtue and hypocrisy.

To call things by their names is a potentially shameful revelatory endeavor that Pope's Horatian poems struggle to justify and to provoke. Recast as moral mission, the compulsion to name extricates Pope from the potential compromises of the literary marketplace by transforming the writer from crowd-pleaser to defender of Virtue. But we have already begun to see how naming particular names serves to block rather than to transmit such general truth, how Pope's insistently specific satiric self-exposure skillfully distorts Horace's equally canny and self-protective evasiveness. Revelation itself thus becomes the most effective kind of self-protection.

The problems of distinction Pope flirted with in *Sober Advice* are laid out seriously in a "private" epistolary debate between Pope and his friend and medical doctor John Arbuthnot. Not long before his death, Arbuthnot writes to Pope that

> tho' I could not help valuing you for those Talents which the World prizes, yet they were not the foundation of my Friendship . . . and I make it my Last Request, that you continue that noble *Disdain* and *Abhorrence* of Vice, which you seem naturally endu'd with, but still with a due regard to your own Safety; and study more to reform than chastise, tho' the one often cannot be effected without the other.[64]

In 1717 Pope had written to the Blounts of "that Talent in me, which most

Ladies would not only Like better, but Understand better, than any other I have."[65] By 1734 the "Talents" Pope professes are personal endowments of a higher moral order. Arbuthnot sees the oppositional stance of Pope's satire, his "noble Disdain and Abhorrence of Vice," as part of his friend's nature. In an attempt to separate the man from the poet, Arbuthnot speaks privately: he values Pope for personal reasons, and entreats him to think first of his personal safety. Pope's artfully publicized response to Arbuthnot's death-bed sincerity makes clear that the private man and the public poet are inseparable. He replies to his friend in a letter he later revises and publishes as a public statement (termed by the editor of the correspondence "most probably a 'forgery,' but . . . certainly Pope's best defense in prose of his satire"), while further recasting their private dialogue into literary epistle.[66] Pope's "forgery" compromises the sincerity of his signature by making all of Arbuthnot's distinctions between privacy and publicity, between reform and chastisement, moot:

> To reform and not to chastise, I am afraid is impossible, and that the best Precepts, as well as the best Laws, would prove of small use, if there were no Examples to inforce them. To attack Vices in the abstract, without touching Persons, may be safe fighting indeed, but is fighting with Shadows. General propositions are obscure, misty, and uncertain, compar'd with plain, full, and home examples: Precepts only apply to our Reason, which in most men is but weak: Examples are pictures, and strike the Senses, nay raise the Passions, and call in those (the strongest and most general of all motives) to the aid of reformation. Every vicious man makes the case his own; and that is the only way by which such men can be affected, much less deterr'd. So that to chastise is to reform. The only sign by which I found my writings ever did any good, or had any weight, has been that they rais'd the anger of bad men. And my greatest comfort, and encouragement to proceed, has been to see, that those who have no shame, and no fear, of any thing else, have appear'd touch'd by my Satires.[67]

Pope argues that the general exists only by virtue of the particular. To read his satire therefore, is to be instructed to read literally. By equating "Precepts" with "Laws," Pope reveals that his task is neither to reform, nor to chastise, but rather to enforce: the concept serves as a middle term which allows the satirist to execute a logical couplet equating the two previous definitions—reform and chastise—between which Arbuthnot had distinguished. Enforcement is linked to the analogy of heroic battle, and thus to the physical. To remain in the general realm is to shadow box; the true satirist, oblivious of potential risk, must "touch . . . Persons." ("Touch" is a frequently used word in Pope's satire for libelling or lampooning, as in "Ev'n those you touch not, hate you" [*Satire II, i,* 41] or "touch me, and no Minister so sore" [*Satire II, i,* 76].)[68] He wounds by an appeal to man's baser nature, through pictures which, like the encapsulated histories depicted on medals, and like the poetic philosophy of the *Essay on Man,* "strike the Senses, nay raise the Passions." (One has the sense of Pope taking the plunge into the genuinely low with that "nay.")

Pope dignifies his defense of satire by alluding to a classic defense of poetry in general, Sir Philip Sidney's *Apology for Poetry* (1595). For Sidney, poetry "coupleth the general notion with the particular example . . . [the poet] yieldeth to the powers of the mind an image of that whereof the philosopher bestoweth but a wordish description, which doth neither strike, pierce, nor possess the sight of the soul so much as that other doth."[69] But just as Pope has equated Arbuthnot's oppositions of reform and chastisement, so in his equation of the subgenre of satire with poetry as a whole he identifies the persuasive power of historical detail with the "touching" power of poetry's fictions. While for Sidney, the historian is "captived to the truth of a foolish world" and thereby in danger of becoming "an encouragment to unbridled wickedness" by presenting immoral examples,[70] for Pope it is the power of verisimilitude which moves the corrupt reader to reform.

While Sidney's poet governs history in an effort to make it more pleasing to the reader, "beautifying it both for further teaching and more delighting, as it pleaseth him: having all . . . under the authority of his pen,"[71] Pope the satirist is governed by history, and obligated to reproduce it faithfully. In the process the authority of the satirist's pen is both diminished and bolstered. For while the poet cannot teach without delighting, and is therefore always at the mercy of his audience's pleasure, the satirist is free to judge and to punish his readers. Sidney's poet must appeal to his reader's baser natures by moving them to pleasure and a love of the good; Pope is free to touch his readers' viciousness and vanity by showing them their own particular reflections and causing them pain.

Pope's final equation of opposites, then, is his refusal to distinguish Sidney's "erected wit" from the "infected will"; for him the particular passions are not obstacles to be overcome but rather "the strongest and most general of all motives." Whereas for Sidney "our erected wit maketh us know what perfection is, and yet our infected will keepeth us from reaching unto it,"[72] for Pope passion, humanity's amoral lowest common denominator, can be bent to either good or evil.[73] The satirist, though committed to recording names, is free from the obligation to make the distinctions (to which Sidney's poet is bound) between low and high, between chastisement and reform, between the moral arbitrariness of truth and the perfection of literature.

Like the allusions to real names in *Sober Advice* which provoke the reader's prurient desires, like the deformity which both invites and evades interpretation, Pope's particular satiric examples achieve effects of which lofty reason, "erected wit," alone is incapable; the satirist, in the name of reason, achieves higher ends by manipulating baser means. The rhetorical appeal to particulars represents the high and low, the virtuous and vicious, as links in D'Alembert's chain of nature or Pope's great chain of being in the *Essay on Man;* diametrically opposed differences are revealed to be related by degrees. Yet those same particulars are the very grounds by which the distinction between Vice and Virtue can be made more than simply a "Shadow": the "anger of bad men" is "the only sign by which I found my writings ever did any good, or had any weight."[74] The text's actual impact on real individuals provides the author with the only possible proof of his text's worth and authenticity. The *Moral Essays* are worth writing, are more than just writing, because the shameless and the fearless "have appear'd touch'd" by them. Embarked on a sentimental journey turned satiric (both the sentimental and punitive dimensions of this endeavor are revealed in the double meaning of the verb "touch," i.e., to move and to strike), Pope reads the signs of his work on his readers in order to confirm himself. Completing the transformation of satire into heroic battle, he will rewrite the last line of this letter in the *Epilogue to the Satires* as "Yes, I am proud; I must be Proud to see / Men not afraid of God, afraid of me" (II, 208–209).

Such particular examples, however, are strangely general, and raise the passions by provoking identification; like partially filled-in proper names, specific examples create boundaries between individuals in order to incite their effacement: "Every vicious man makes the case his own." A kind of satirical sublime results, by which each man sees his own face depicted in the example's frightening mirror. Yet in the Advertisement to the *Epistle to Arbuthnot,* Pope states that

> Many will know their own Pictures in it, there being not a Circumstance but what is true; but I have, for the most part spar'd their *Names,* and they may escape being laugh'd at, if they please . . . However I shall have this advantage, and Honour, on my side, that whereas by their [Lady Mary's and Lord Hervey's] proceeding, any Abuse may be directed at any man, no Injury can possibly be done by mine, since a Nameless Character can never be found out, but by its *Truth* and *Likeness.*[75]

Libellers are guilty of abuse which is indiscriminate both in its method and its object; satire is distinguished here by its fidelity to particular targets, its "truth and likeness"; the satirist draws the line only (in deference, Pope claims, to Arbuthnot's request) at the free use of names. In this scenario satire creates through public and general exposure a private shame in its particular objects, who cannot help but recognize themselves in the mirror it holds up to foolish nature, and who are forced to be silent in order to "escape being laughed at." Pope's satire protects itself by its truth (and Pope indeed does respect his friend's request that he guard his own safety by his appeal to a legal system that his characterization of *Arbuthnot* as a "Bill of Complaint" constitutes); attention to particulars allows it to touch without public injury.

In the first private version of his reply to Arbuthnot, Pope wrote, "If a man writ all his Life against the Collective Body of the Banditti, or against Lawyers, would it do the least Good, or lessen the Body? But if some are hung up, or pilloryed, it may prevent others."[76] Only the spectacle of particular bodies can deter the "collective Body." The satirist becomes divine judge, lawgiver and executioner creating scenes with which to move the masses while at the same time subjecting himself to that same law before that same public as one with a "Bill of Complaint" who has been unjustly abused. In such a brazen world, divorced from Sidney's golden one, it is the satirist who becomes the final authority, and who, while bound to history's law, rules even the head of state. Pope ends his original letter to Arbuthnot with an ambiguous comment on ancient precedents:

> It is certain, much freer Satyrists than I have enjoy'd the encouragement and protection of the Princes under whom they lived. Augustus and Mecoenas [sic] made Horace their companion, tho' he had been in arms on the side of Brutus; and allow me to remark it was out of the suff'ring Party too, that they favour'd and distinguish'd Virgil. You will not suspect me of comparing my self with Virgil and Horace, nor even with another Court-favourite, Boileau: I have always been too modest to imagine my Panegyricks were Incense worthy of a Court; and that I hope will be thought the true reason why I have never offer'd any. I would only have observ'd, that it was under the greatest Princes and best Ministers, that moral Satyrists were most encouraged; and that then Poets exercised the same jurisdiction over the Follies, as Historians did over the Vices of men. It may also be worth considering, whether Augustus himself makes the greater figure, in the writings of the former, or of the latter? and whether Nero and Domitian do not appear as ridiculous for their false Taste and

Affectation, in Persius and Juvenal, as odious for their bad Government in Tacitus and Suetonius? In the first of these reigns it was, that Horace was protected and caress'd; and in the latter that Lucan was put to death, and Juvenal banish'd.[77]

The grounds for Pope's comparison of himself with Horace, Virgil, and Boileau seem as radically unstable as the power relations they involve. Pope seems to be commending Augustus and Maecenas for favoring Horace and Virgil despite their politics, but statements like the self-coined epitaph on "one who would not be buried in Westminister Abbey" throw into question Pope's reverence for any poet sheltered by political favor. Pope's apparently modest denial of comparison with his Roman predecessors rings of a certain arrogance—it is not that his Panegyricks are unworthy of a Court so much as that the Court is unworthy of his panegyric—and he tacitly admits to its duplicity when he adds that he hopes that such modesty "will be *thought* the true reason why I have never offered any" [my emphasis]. The conclusion of the passage makes all harmony between ruler and poet seem merely appearance, and all disjunction between the two simply lack of foresight on the ruler's part. All that remains is the author's representation; but Pope undermines the power of that representation by putting it into context. Pope's view of the ruler-poet dynamic makes morality uneasily level with aesthetic discernment, and aesthetics equivalent to individual relations with a particular poet. In both cases the dynamic has the effect of putting Pope, like the proper name, on the edge of the semantic field.

For Pope, to be on that edge is to be righteously opposed; this position of potential vulnerability enables the poet to attempt to control his audience and himself. Pope insists on remembering that he is not Horace and that London affords no Maecenas; rather, he is an author free from (and deprived of) patronage, fortunate to (and forced to) make his living by publishing. The satirist is an author who must authorize himself.

SELF-EXPOSURE AS HEROIC SATIRE
IN *SATIRE II, 1*

Pope's imitation of Horace's Satire 2, 1 makes poetry into its own law. One reader's response to a particular allusion can stand as an angry analogy to Pope's own relation to Horace. Pope begins an explication of human nature which accounts for his own weapon of satire amidst a host of others with the following couplet: "Slander or Poyson, dread from *Delia's* Rage, / Hard Words or Hanging, if your Judge be *Page*" (81–82). The poet's weapons are compared with the devices the real world uses in its defense; on the one hand, slander and hard words gain in force when put in the balance with poison or hanging; on the other, the poet's sole resource of language is revealed as essentially harmless when pitted against the grim actualities of human aggression. Pope, in a rage or at peace, is a fairer judge than Page; he can kill nobody, but he can keep the objects of his wrath in purgatory after their death by making them laughing stocks, "the sad Burthen of some merry Song," for time immemorial. In the case of Page, the object of the satire helps to dig his own grave. Upon reading the line originally read "if your J——ge be ———."

> Sir Francis Page, a judge well known in his time, conceiving that his name was meant to fill up the blank, sent his clerk to Mr. Pope, to complain of the insult. Pope told the young man that the blank might be supplied by many monosyllables, other than the judge's name:—"but, sir," said the clerk, "the judge says that no [other] word will make sense of the passage."—"So, then, it seems," says Pope, "your master is not only a judge, but a poet: as that is the case, the odds are against me. Give my respects to the judge, and tell him, I will not contend with one that has the advantage of me, and he may fill up the blank as he pleases."[78]

This is just the kind of audience participation that Pope, both poet and judge, most relishes; the only way the judge "can have the advantage" over the poet is to supply the particulars of his humiliation. The anecdote takes on even more resonance when we know that it was Page who sentenced the poet Savage (whom Pope befriended) for murder and treated him with what Johnson called "his usual insolence and severity," and that he once remarked, when a prisoner sentenced for horse-stealing was brought into court, "A very ill-looking fellow; I have no doubt of his guilt."[79] Such insistence on judging by appearances betrays a lack of appreciation for humanity in general and poets in particular, and is most justly revenged by the recognition of its own portrait. In the same way that Sir Joshua Reynolds, as discussed in chapter 1, reads Pope at first sight, describing his very face as language and identifying him as both deformed and an author, so Page reduces faces to the legibility of written names. Pope subverts such literalistic reading by turning the literal against his readers, employing it in his own defense. For while particularity pins down Pope's targets, it affords him the freedom to judge from a distance.

And what of Pope's own self-portrait in *Satire II, i*? In Horace's original, writing satire is presented as the poet's involuntary foible and particular pleasure, a flaw linking him with his fallible targets while giving him an identity. This first of natural catalogues in which the satirist places himself is prefaced by Horace's declining (yet another *recusatio*) to write in Augustus's praise. Better, says Trebatius, to do so than to attack others, "cum sibi quisque timet, quanquam est intactus, et odit!" (23) [since everyone is afraid for himself, although he is unharmed, and hates you]. Pope picks up on "intactus" with his frequent use of the verb "touch"; this addition emphasizes the physical violence the word implies:

> P. What should ail 'em?
> F. A hundred smart in *Timon* and in *Balaam:*
> The fewer still you name, you wound the more;
> *Bond* is but one, but *Harpax* is a Score. (41–44)

Two targets from the *Epistle to Bathurst,* Bond an actual swindler; Harpax a type whose name is Greek for "robber." By feigning naiveté, Pope provides himself with his own defense against the charges of being too particular, and opens the controversy over general example and particular identification around which the Horatian poems will revolve. Spoken by Pope, these words would sound like the proud boasts of the satirist David against the Goliath-like corruption of Walpole's England at the end of the *Epilogue to the Satires.*

On the facing page in *Satire II, i*'s Latin original, however, Horace proceeds in his own defense to identify himself with the rest of mankind: every man is distinguished by his pleasure, satire is simply Horace's own: "What shall I do? Milonius leaps, the moment his head grows warm and the lights multiply. Castor loves horses, he born from the same egg, wrestling; as many heads are living, so many thousands of pursuits. It delights me to close up words in feet, in the manner of Lucilius, a better man than either of us" (24–29).[80]

While Horace ranks his delight in closing up words in feet as no more important than any other trivial pursuit, Pope deflects the charge that satire is too sharp by describing satire as self-revelation. Pope's self-exposure in *Satire II, i* is contingent on his exposing others.

Chapter 4 discussed the way in which this Latin passage hovers between the verbal and the visual, how Horace's image of his poetic predecessor's life (a life, Horace adds, which "entrusted [its] innermost secrets to books" [30–31]) as a votive tablet visualizes satire's narrative, makes personal poetry a portrait of the poet himself which has been emptied of time. The tablet on which Lucilius's life lies open stands as a model for Horace's reading of his predecessor, but it does not account for Horace's compulsion to write. In opposition to the figure of Lucilius, Horace represents himself as a territory which cannot be delineated or described, an indeterminate set of boundaries: "I follow this man, although it is doubtful whether I am a Lucanian or an Apulian; for the Venusian farmer plows the boundary between both countries, sent (so the old legend has it), upon the expulsion of the Samnites, that the enemy might not invade the Romans through a vaccuum, or lest the Apulian people or the violent Lucanians, strike up a war" (34–38).[81] "Anceps" [doubtful] literally means "two-headed," and its connotations range from "double" to "dangerous." Although some editors see this initial qualification as "subordinate to the main line of reasoning," it is very much in keeping with the image of Lucilius as an open book, anchoring his follower Horace's identity in physical and historical space only to unsettle it. Horace's indeterminacy of birth allows him to trace his ancestry to a line of peacemakers called in to defend a boundary by defining it—"mediators" without borders of their own. If the satirist defines himself as a "medium," he can never be accused of aggression: one editor paraphrases the passage as follows: "I take Lucilius for my leader, for I too come of fighting stock. But I fight only in self-defense."[82] In this account Horatian satire becomes an endeavor to set the bounds for the excesses of others, while leaving the poet himself defined only in the view of those others. The main foolish impulse such a satirist must correct is too strong a desire to signify himself.[83]

In his version of the passage (lines 51–67), Pope fills in the blank where Horace should be, much as his readers are prompted to fill in the particular blanks of Pope's satire. Rather than following Horace's model of self-protective revision of Lucilius's candor, Pope becomes both Horace and Lucilius, transforming his mirror image into the written word. Eliding the contrast between poet and predecessor which is so strong in Horace, Pope makes of Horace's votive tablet a printed page.

Pope's own precursors are interchangeable, but he himself is a unique example of complete self-exposure all the more shining because of his flaws. In the same way that his deformity marks his work as authentic, so Pope's "spots" mark his "medium" as clear: in both cases the flaws in self-exposure, what cannot be authorized or seen through, guarantee authority and authenticity. Horace's image of himself as border-dweller has been transformed in Pope to one of the poet as a looking glass. Almost twenty years earlier he had written to Congreve, "Methinks when I write to you, I am making a confession, I have got (I can't tell how) such a custom of throwing my self out upon paper without reserve . . . The cleanness and purity of one's mind is never better prov'd, than in discovering its own faults at first view: as when a Stream shows the dirt at its bottom, it shows also the transparency of the water."[84] The transformation of the metaphor of the stream, in which the dirt on the bottom brings out the water's clarity, into a looking glass of sincerely spotted self-exposure parallels the way in which Pope uncovers himself to Lady Mary, recommending his letters to her as "the most impartial Representations of a free heart, and the truest Copies . . . of a very mean Original,"[85] in order to preempt her potentially derisive gaze. The shift in the metaphor is one of agency: in the figure of the stream, Pope is exposed; in his letter and his poem Pope exposes himself with proof. His spiritual self-revelation in this passage is designed to call attention to the particular deformity that stands in the way of the ideal transparency of Shippen and Montaigne in which the soul stands forth "as certain to be loved as seen."

In reminding the reader, as he does Lady Mary, of his refusal to make that "ugly thing a little less hideous,"[86] Pope forces her to countenance a nakedness which, without the benefit of his skillful rhetoric, would repel. He also reminds the reader that the proof of his sincerity is also the literal proof of the printed page, that the clarity of the printed "medium" is inherently compromised. (It is almost as if "this impartial Glass" points to the page itself.) Pope's oxymoronic blend of offensive physical self-exposure with selfless spiritual transparency makes an "impartial Glass" out of a "medium" as impervious as the failed work of his own deformity, and as the black spots of ink which form letters on the printed page. In both cases the reader must see through something which gets in the way.

The printed page, then, is both opaque and transparent. In the satirical glass of publication Pope's foes will see themselves plainly, identify themselves in prototypes, supply the blanks of particular names, and be silenced. His friends—the friends to virtue—excluded from the spectacle of the great world, are in the proper position to see through Pope's satiric medium. Pope can thus claim to be practicing Horace's brand of inoffensive satire while defending the moral border between the reader and his page which such proper reading defines. The medium's spots shield Pope from those who don't have the spiritual wherewithal to see through them. Horace's image of the votive tablet, forcing the reader to envision a Lucilius beyond the page only to abandon that image in search of an unimaginable Horace, has been rewritten as an image of Pope himself which touches readers, which the reader can touch, and which the author can own: the printed book.

The benign couplet oppositions comprising *Satire II, i*'s glory of moderation, Pope's oxymoronic versions of Horace's refusal to cut a figure, as in "Tories call me Whig, and Whigs a Tory" (66–67), expose Pope to the immoderate vagaries of misinterpretation. In the satirist's glass partisan viewers mark their opposition, thus affording the poet the pretext for defending himself and taking possession of his medium. "I find," Pope wrote to Caryll, "by dear experience, we live in an age where it is criminal to be moderate."[87]

With another mirroring gesture, the poem in both Latin and English goes on to invert itself, and satire, initially described as a harmless foible, is now included in a catalogue of weapons: Horace's pen is as natural as a wolf's teeth or a bull's horns, but he will use it only in defense ("ensis vagina tectum" [covered in a sheath]). The Roman poet's prayer to Jove that his weapon wear away with lack of use is rendered in Pope as an ironic critique of a threatening society:

> Satire's my Weapon, but I'm too discreet
> To run a Muck, and tilt at all I meet;
> I only wear it in a Land of Hectors,
> Thieves, Supercargoes, Sharpers, and Directors.
> Save but our *Army!* and let *Jove* incrust
> Swords, Pikes, and Guns, with everlasting Rust!   (69–74)

Walpole's maintenance of a standing army caps off a catalogue of potential menaces that would seem in this account to threaten the country's pockets as much as its moral rectitude.[88] "Hectors" are the least dangerous in a list that culminates with "Directors" in a direct allusion to the South Sea company investment scandal (in which Pope himself lost money), which took speculation to unprecedentedly damaging lengths. By translating Horace into his own contemporary milieu, Pope reconceives the issues of moral value in terms of an early capitalist economy; satire is his weapon because, in the same way that it renders his self-portrait absolute in its evasion of standard distinctions, it claims to render moral value in a time when the idea of value is fundamentally unstable.

Both Latin and English versions transform their defense of satire into an affirmation of identity amidst an inconsistent existence. Pope's imitation renders that identity all the more ominously unstable by a black and white translation of Horace's "Quisquis erit vitae, scribam, color" (whatever the color of my life shall be, I shall write): "Whether the darken'd Room to muse invite, / or whiten'd Wall provoke the Skew'r to write" (97–98). The author's natural habitat becomes either the madhouse or the prison; in the poem's depiction of a Grub Street world in which Bedlam and the Mint are inseparable (99), that prison is probably the debtor's prison. Pope fends off both the economic and existential dangers of authorship by making himself simultaneously satirist and proprietor. In a poem in which the self is identified with the printed page and circulation in a literary marketplace, moral integrity becomes identical with self-possession. Such composure is always a battle between surrender of control over one's texts and staking a claim.

As *Satire II, i* makes clear, Pope in the Horatian poems is intent upon defining the "unreal estate" of literature at the moment of his greatest investment in it. If, as Susan Staves argues, "Pope's revisions can also be considered as the linguistic equivalents of improvements made on commercial property,"[89] and his appropriation of classical originals can be seen as an enrichment of such property with foreign ornament, the Horatian poems can be read as attempts to set up a fence between owner and property, to continually ask *Satire II, ii*'s question, "What's property, dear Swift?," while at the same time revealing that the poet's only property is in the poems themselves.

When Aaron Hill warned Pope, in response to the poet's calculatedly modest devaluation of his poetry, that "your Honesty you possess in common with a *Million,* who will never be remembered: whereas your Poetry is a Peculiar, that will make it impossible, you should be forgotten," he hit a sensitive nerve. Pope's goal is to make exemplary virtue his distinguishing literary characteristic, to court publicity while claiming to disdain it; his poetry thereby becomes a conspicuously futile search for an honest man which leaves only himself intact. Though he claims in his answer to Hill that "I much more resent any Attempt against my moral Character (which I know to be unjust) than any to lessen my poetical one (which, for all I know, may be very just),"[90] poetic character and moral character are impossible to distinguish in the Horatian poems. Virtue signifies because Pope himself makes it mean something.

Thus while Horace responds to Trebatius's warnings of a possible fall from favor in *Satire II, i* by holding up the example of Lucilius, the first who dared to write satire and "detrahere et pellem, nitidus qua quisque per ora / Cederet, introrsum turpis" [to drag off the skin, by which each man walked among men shining, although ugly within], Pope's final example is himself. In utilizing Horace's metaphor ("detrahere pellem" could refer either to removing an actor's mask made of skin, or to Aesop's fable of the ass masquerading in a lion's skin), Pope renders it simultaneously more and less graphic, going beyond the figure's surface to point back toward his own self-revealing penetration of superficial ugliness to inner clarity.

> What? Arm'd for *Virtue* when I point the Pen,
> Brand the bold Front of shameless, guilty Men,

> Dash the proud Gamester in his gilded Car,
> Bare the mean Heart that lurks beneath a Star;   (105–108)
> . . .
> Could Laureate *Dryden* Pimp and Fry'r engage,
> Yet neither *Charles* nor *James* be in a Rage?
> And I not strip the Gilding off a Knave,
> Unplac'd, unpension'd, no Man's Heir, or Slave?
> I will, or perish in the gen'rous Cause.
> Hear this, and tremble! you, who 'scape the Laws.
> Yes, while I live, no rich or noble knave
> Shall walk the World, in credit, to his grave.
> TO VIRTUE ONLY AND HER FRIENDS, A FRIEND,
> The World beside may murmur, or commend.   (113–122)

The heroic absolutes that Pope generates from this final self-appropriation are based on a system of value of which Pope himself is the measure, like the shameless Scribler in *Arbuthnot* "thron'd in the Centre of his thin designs" (93), a spider in the heart of his own web spinning distinctions from the stuff of which fine print is made.[91] The general examples upon which he builds his satire, and himself, are constructed of particular historical fragments. No wonder Pope is drawn to the Horace of the *Epistles,* who vows to give up poetry in order to care for the self: the question Pope asks in response and increasingly in anger is whether there is a self apart from poetry, and more importantly, apart from the published poem.[92]

THE *EPISTLE TO DR. ARBUTHNOT*
AND THE FLIGHT FROM ABSOLUTES

If Horace makes of every genre a *recusatio* or ironic refusal, Pope transforms such refusals into his own appropriations. Whereas Horace claims to be unfit for heroic poetry, and finally for lyric (which for him is the highest form of poetry), Pope proclaims that it is the world that is unfit for heroic poetry and that only the poet himself embodies poetry's standard. For Pope, "arm'd for Virtue, while I point the Pen," all poetry is heroic. We could also say that for Pope all poetry becomes heroic by necessity: heroic poetry therefore is satiric by definition.

In the *Epistle to Dr. Arbuthnot,* Pope strikes an uneasy compromise between himself and Horace, a balance typified by the poem's status as "the most Horatian of Pope's original works."[93] (Warburton retitled, and accordingly repositioned, this poem as the *Prologue to the Satires* in his edition of Pope's oeuvre.) Pope distinguishes himself from Horace in *Arbuthnot* first by dramatizing the necessity of protecting his private identity: this poet is literally besieged by his readers. From the poem's initial command "Shut, shut the door, good *John!*," *Arbuthnot* attempts to set limits between Pope, his poetry, and the readers that poetry has created. They have been touched by his satire and have thereby become touched in the head; Pope's self-creation has given rise to a myriad of distorted doubles. The poem's opening, in which the experience of reading Pope's poetry has unleashed a literary Bedlam (equated with Parnassus in line 2) of aspiring poets intent on violating Pope's fortress of retirement at Twickenham—"They pierce my Thickets, thro' my Grot they glide"(7)—animates Pope's anxiety that he may be entirely public property, that his vision of Horatian retirement embodied in Twickenham is no more than a fiction. The scriblers who solicit Pope "to keep them mad or vain" (22) are caricatures of the proper readers of Pope's satire, who in their frenzy are all too aware (having learned their lesson from Pope's life in the literary fantasy of Twickenham) of the power Pope's art has over their lives—"Poor *Cornus* sees his frantic Wife elope, / And curses Wit, and Poetry, and *Pope*" (25–26)—and the deathly hold their attempts at art have over Pope himself—"if Foes, they write, if Friends, they read me dead"(32). The self-appointed "King of Parnassus" depicts himself in *Arbuthnot* as enslaved by his own critical faculty, "seiz'd and ty'd down to judge, how wretched I!"(33).[94] In *Arbuthnot,* the poet's crucial concern is neither criticism, nor poetry, but rather the possibility of an integral self, the ability to "sleep without a poem in my head," free of writing and an audience. Pope reveals just how flimsy the defenses of his public authority are and attempts to imagine, perhaps for the last time, an unwritten life, an unpublished identity.

The images of self-sufficiency and self-enclosure which Pope idealizes at Twickenham and in other Horatian poems are figured in *Arbuthnot* as forms of madness. Pope reflecting in his grotto seems little different from the heroically stoic indifference of a "Fool":

> Let Peals of Laughter, *Codrus!* round thee break,
> Thou unconcern'd canst hear the mighty Crack.
> Pit, Box and Gall'ry in convulsions hurl'd.
> Thou stand'st unshook amidst a bursting World. (85–88)

This allusion (almost an exact quotation of Addison's translation) to Horace's Ode 3.3, which Christopher Smart entitles "On Steadiness and Integrity," adds to the fool's paradoxically enviable aura; the bliss of oblivion looks curiously like Pope himself directing the theater of Chaos, drawing the final curtain over the Dunciad's "uncreating Word." But the fool is capable of indifference to ridicule, while Pope takes his position on the stage to tell the audience that they are in ruins. The image that follows is even more telling:

> Who shames a Scribler? break one cobweb thro',
> He spins the slight, self-pleasing thread anew;
> Destroy his Fib, or Sophistry; in vain,
> The Creature's at his dirty work again;
> Thron'd in the Centre of his thin designs;
> Proud of a vast Extent of flimzy lines.
> Whom have I hurt?   (89–94)

From stage to spider's web, Pope's image of the scribler is also an image of his own poetic self-production. Whether industriously creative or banefully destructive, Pope himself, like the aspiring poets secure in delusion, and like his description of the spider in *An Essay on Man,* "lives along the line."[95] Though he claims to have "lisp'd in Numbers, for the Numbers came" (128), and to have published at the flattering behest of a select male coterie (135–146), the key to Pope's writing compulsion lies in his distorted self-reflections. Pope rejects these nemeses most particularly when they try their hands at his own brand of self-creating fiction, flattering him in a caricature of his own attempts to ennoble his deformity:

> There are, who to my Person pay their court,
> I cough like *Horace,* and tho' lean, am short,
> *Ammon's* great Son one shoulder had too high,
> Such *Ovid's* nose, and "Sir! you have an *Eye*—"   (115–118)

By taking Pope literally in their praise of his person, his acolytes have not missed the point entirely; what they have failed to see, however, is the way in which Pope uses the literal, "the libel'd Person, and the pictur'd Shape" (353), in order to guarantee the authenticity of the figural. If Pope's goal in figuring his deformity is to reauthorize it by rendering it unmentionable, Pope's emulators expose his ploy by their inability to see through it. Just as fools rage at Pope although he has given them "but their due" (174), so Pope is at the mercy of his readers who cannot grasp what he calls

> each man's secret standard in his mind,
> That Casting-weight Pride adds to Emptiness,
> This, who can gratify? for who can *guess*?   (176–178)

By failing to read through the body, the scribblers render his standard of self-judgment secret and unintelligible.

The poem moves on to two scathing character sketches, first Atticus, then the ungenerous patron Bufo, then a lament for the death of Gay which turns into an exclamation of longing, the poet's prayer to protect himself from a world where writers signify something other than what they themselves determine:

> Oh let me live my own! and die so too!
> ("To live and die is all I have to do:")
> Maintain a Poet's Dignity and Ease,
> And see what friends, and read what books I please.
> Above a Patron, tho' I condescend
> Sometimes to call a Minister my Friend:
> I was not born for Courts or great Affairs,
> I pay my Debts, believe, and say my Pray'rs.
> Can sleep without a Poem in my head,
> Nor know, if *Dennis* be alive or dead.   (261–270)

It is difficult to tell whether "die so" refers to dying "my own" or dying in the relative obscurity of Gay (whom only the true friends and proper readers Pope and Queensberry are left to mourn). This confusion is telling, since for the published author to live or die in possession of himself is to do so in obscurity.[96] Pope at this point in the poem wants it all: to maintain "a Poet's dignity and Ease," an ease peculiar to the profession, to hobnob privately with ministers (as Lucilius does in Horace's version and Pope in his own of *Satire II, i*) while scorning the court, and to be free from financial or spiritual quandaries (paying debts is here equivalent to saying prayers, the duties of a gentleman). Most important, Pope wishes to be spared the literary insanity exemplified by the insomnia which made him call for coffee while writing at all hours of the night,[97] and the sensitivity to criticism which made satire his chosen genre, preserving Lord Hervey and many other "flies in amber" to this day. The final two lines of this passage reveal the rest as a fantasy of self-possession: it is not his freedom from want (which literature has earned him) nor his freedom from politics that Pope longs for, but his freedom from literature. "Heav'ns! was I born for nothing but to write?" (272) This question, along with the subsequent and even more telling "Why then publish?" remains unanswered.

Pope's subsequent rejection of Sporus repudiates and enacts both satire's indeterminate morality and the couplet's ambivalent form:

> Half Froth, half Venom, spits himself abroad,
> In Puns, or Politicks, or Tales, or Lyes,

Or Spite, or Smut, or Rhymes, or Blasphemies.
His Wit all see-saw between *that* and *this,*
Now high, now low, now Master up, now Miss,
And he himself one vile Antithesis.
Amphibious Thing! that acting either Part,
The trifling Head, or the corrupted Heart!
Fop at the Toilet, Flatt'rer at the Board,
Now trips a Lady, and now struts a Lord.
Eve's Tempter thus the Rabbins have exprest,
A Cherub's face, a Reptile all the rest;
Beauty that shocks you, Parts that none will trust,
Wit that can creep, and Pride that licks the dust.   (320–332)

In a state of continual Satanic metamorphosis reminiscent of the lampooners' constructions of Pope himself, Sporus's image is perhaps most shocking in its resemblance to Pope's grand assertion (by negation) of manly integrity which follows. Here we see most clearly the way in which Pope enlists moral absolutes to rescue himself from the implicating snares of public life and publication. The frenzied energy of the Sporus portrait's antithetical invective is reharnessed into the lofty rhythms of denial. This passage's moral indignation seems to mask a greater anxiety, audible in the vehemence of its hatred of Hervey, poet manqué and venomous libeller, namely, that poetry is restricted by circumstance, incapable of moral certainty or freedom from its public.

Pope "stoops to Truth" in order to protect himself from the implication of his own example: that neither his fame nor his virtue are absolute, that to achieve literary fame for one's virtue is to live a spurious paradox. But as if to acknowledge this, the poem does not end with the triumphant self-assertion of "Welcome for thee, fair Virtue!" (358). Rather, *Arbuthnot* ends with a portrait of Pope's father:

Stranger to Civil and Religious Rage,
The good Man walk'd innoxious thro' his Age.
No Courts he saw, no Suits would ever try,
Nor dar'd an Oath, nor hazarded a Lye:
Un-learn'd, he knew no Schoolman's subtle Art,
No Language, but the Language of the Heart.
By Nature honest, by Experience wise,
Healthy by Temp'rance and by Exercise:
His Life, tho' long, to sickness past unknown,
His Death was instant, and without a groan.   (394–403)

This passage offers an ideal image of effortless self-containment, free from self-consciousness, disease, and ultimately words themselves. Pope prays for such an ideal as hopelessly as he prays in closing for his friend and benign adversary Arbuthnot whom he knew to be on his deathbed, and who died a month after the poem's publication. The particular historical characters in *Arbuthnot*—Hervey and Addison on one side, Pope's father and Arbuthnot on the other—are refined into the Vices and Virtues of a morality masque, with Pope as Everyman, or perhaps I should say Every Writer. The poem's optative ending leaves the final conflict between particular compromises and general integrity unresolved.

DIS-EASE IN WRITING:
EPISTLE II, ii'S LABORED ART

With his imitation of Epistle 2, 2, Pope upsets *To Arbuthnot*'s balance; the "medium" of imitation is no longer clear. His attempt to define himself in Horace's name turns into a rejection of Horace and an advertisement for himself. Horace's Epistle 2.2 is perhaps his final recusatio. Of all of the *Epistles,* the date of 2.2 only is uncertain. It may have succeeded the fourth book of *Odes,* and therefore the success of Horace's resolution to give up lyric is also indeterminable. Like his Ode 4.1, this poem contemplates the loss of poetry, and the resolve to apply art to a lived, rather than a literary, moderation. But the Roman poet's epistle is just that, a letter to a friend, apologizing for not having written sooner. The genre of the epistle, a lyricization of the satiric hexameter, intimate and overheard, is itself a significant statement.

In the ironic dialogue of Horace's *Epistles* there are no fools to provide the particulars of the reader's image, only the absent correspondent, the reader himself. For the *Epistles* to have their full effect, as Pope's source Shaftesbury notes, they must be read as having been written to a particular historical person. (These late poems pick up on the line of particularity of Horace's *Satires,* poems like Satire 1.5 on the trip to Brindisium, which depend in part on the reader's awareness that the participants are real politicians and poets.) If we take them as fictions, Shaftesbury warns, "the elegant writer will disappear, as will the vast labour and art." Here, as in Pope's use of deformity, particularity guarantees sincerity and gives art the appearance of artlessness. The historical specificity of the epistle, for Shaftesbury, is part and parcel of its political freedom: in the epistles of Seneca, "that corrupter of Roman eloquence," no "measures of historical truth [are] preserved," since under a Nero, "there was no more possibility of making a stand for language than for liberty."[98]

Pope adheres to historical truth in his treatment of Epistle 2, 2 by advertising the fact of his labor. He does violence to Horace by ignoring genre, twisting the original into his own image. The poem which results, in its blend of epic, satiric and lyric modes, stand as Pope's monument to his inability to abide by the formal injunctions of poetry, propriety or philosophy. In *Epistle II, ii* the rules of decorum which determine when an older poet ought to give up writing poetry and attend to the study of the well-lived life, and which shape Horace's stoical resignation, become for Pope the stage upon which he declaims as the satirist-hero. Horace's public privacy is in Pope unabashed performance.

Taken from the Latin original (Horace is discussing the ideal poet), Pope's epigraph embodies in miniature the process of Pope's imitation: distorting in order to display. "Ludentis speciem dabit et torquebitur" [He will give the appearance of playing and be turned/distorted/tortured on the rack]. (Meanings are given in the order in which they are listed in the Oxford Latin Dictionary.) In context the line reads as follows: "Ludentis speciem dabit et *torquebitur* ut qui / nunc Satyrum, nunc agrestem Cyclopa movetur" (124–125) [as one who now dances the Satyr, now the boorish Cyclops], (emphasis Pope's). In Horace "torquebitur" takes on its neutral, objective meaning of "turn": the image of the author's duress becomes that of the effortlessness of a dancer able to simulate high art and artlessness with comparable ease. The pain behind the process, which Pope emphasizes by his truncation of the line, is in Horace elided, as if even the injunction of apparent effortlessness must avoid any mention of effort. Rather than sympathize with the pain of poetic production, Horace asks the reader to visualize such production as itself a finished work of art. The elegant informality of "ludentis speciem dabit" gives the epistles their air of authenticity, their calculated artlessness, and, for a reader such as Shaftesbury, their political integrity. For Pope, however, the emphasis is on "speciem," and the "appearance of play" is impossible. Writing's particular pain, its honest *dis*-ease, must not go without saying.

Horace's author is above all a polished performer who keeps his signature to himself. The perfect poem bears no mark of the author's labors, appears to be nothing but sprezzatura. This apparent authenticity is also the mark of artifice. Its signature is of no one in particular.

Pope's preempting of the passage responds to Horace's precept by violating its seamlessness, going behind the stage. By quoting less, he displays more. Pope represents both process and product, restoring to "torquebitur" its unrepresented and unrepresentable meanings, demanding sympathy from the reader for the suffering that goes into the production of the printed page. He will force the reader to acknowledge the "true" Alexander Pope. Paradoxically, while Pope edits out Horace's performance metaphor, it is Horace who is able to exit the stage of writing quietly. And it is Pope's rage for representation, for a written distinction between the poet and the poem, which makes him the supreme performer at the poem's end. This epigraph, insisting that the whole be represented, is Pope's signature.

In the body of the text Pope inserts another translation of these lines: " 'But ease in writing flows from Art, not Chance, / 'As those move easiest who have learn'd to dance" (178–179). Pope's quotation from his youthful virtuoso performance, the *Essay on Criticism,* is a faithful imitation of Horace's original; the fidelity of this imitation is undermined by the epigraph's subversive echo of the Latin itself. In the Latin text on the opposite page, Pope has put "torquebitur" in italics to remind the reader of the epigraph's emphasis. Imitation becomes opaque; the relation of "original" to "imitator" (who comes first?) is no longer clear. The quotation marks around the lines provide a further irony, framing an implicit response not only to the "you" of the previous line who is deceived by the poise of good poetry into thinking it only "Nature and a knack to please," but also to Horace and the earlier self of the *Essay on Criticism* who follows in his footsteps. This later version of Pope rejects ease and embraces dis–ease, just as he rejects a Horatian ideal of poetry for satire's power to judge his predecessors; the dance of filial piety which the *Essay* executed with respectful decorum is no longer proper.

Pope's signature is also evidenced by his rejection of Horace's epistolary fiction. His imitation begins with an additional couplet: "Dear Col'nel! *Cobham's* and your Country's Friend! / You love a Verse, take such as I can send" (1–2). While Horace's letter begins with an apology for laxity in correspondence, and proceeds to an explanation of his failure to produce "carmina" (odes), Pope defeats Horace's purpose by announcing his composition as "verse" sent voluntarily, so we believe until line 32. The distinction between epistle and poem, and with it any attempt to simulate artlessness or to renounce poetry, is abandoned at the outset.

Aubrey Williams has demonstrated that Pope's imitation gives a "new unity and focus" to Horace's original by highlighting and developing the metaphor of thievery.[99] This metaphor attracts Pope because he is most concerned in this imitation with property in his poetry and himself. To imagine the renunciation of writing allows him to contemplate the illusion of a self existing outside of writing, and in so doing to mark that self more completely in writing. *Epistle*

II, ii makes clear that Horace's dignified silence is an expense Pope cannot afford. This practitioner of "the better Art to know the good from bad" (55) insists on practicing morality in writing and before the world.

So that while Horace achieves his most moving effects in this poem by understatement, Pope's method is based on amplification. In *Epistle II, ii* the couplet itself becomes a mode of defiance. The effect resembles hearing an orchestrated version of an intricate piece for piano, and never more obviously than in Pope's imitation of this crucial passage: "Singula de nobis anni prae-dantur euntes; / Eripuere jocos, venerem, convivia, ludum; / Tendunt extor-quere poemata. quid faciam vis?" (55–57) [The advancing years plunder us of each thing; they have torn away mirth, love, feasting, play, they are trying to wrench away poems. What would you have me do?]

> Years foll'wing Years, steal something ev'ry day,
> At last they steal us from our selves away;
> In one our Frolicks, one Amusements end,
> In one a Mistress drops, in one a Friend:
> This subtle Thief of Life, this paltry Time,
> What will it leave me, if it snatch my Rhime?
> If ev'ry Wheel of that unweary'd Mill
> That turn'd ten thousand Verses, now stands still.   (72–79)

Horace laments both the trappings of youth and the conventions of lyric poetry, loved and looked back upon in this and other epistles as "ludicra." The power of the Latin here rests in its brevity and the escalation of the force of its verbs—"steal" turns to "tear away," finally to "wrench away"; the physical dimension of "torquebitur" here made painfully clear. These emphasize the poet's increasing passivity in the face of time's violence. His "what would you have me do?" is an admission of helplessness, the closest a letter can come to silence.

Pope's rendition is a literary *tour de force* that critics have traced back to Pope's own letters, a line from Broome's translation of his Odyssey, Dryden's *State of Innocence* and *All For Love*, Milton's sonnet "How soon hath Time . . ." and Montaigne. Like his fellow English reconstructors of lost Roman gardens, Pope defies time by allusion, standing his shadowy ground with the echoes of his past literature behind him. But the movement from the higher diction of "this subtle Thief of life, this paltry Time" back to the passage's monosyllabic norm, sounding particularly harshly on "snatch," renders both Time and time-lessness equally ruthless and undifferentiating. If Pope's poetry is an image of eternity, it is not the eternity of the *Essay on Criticism*'s dance with the ancients, but one of inhuman mechanization, "an unweary'd Mill" incapable of stopping.

But this moment is preface only. A certain kind of Horatian control over writing itself must be abandoned in order for Pope to control himself in writing. Pope's exit from the poem and from poetry marks a new acceptance of poetry as satire. "Tempus abire tibi est: ne potum largius aeque / Rideat, & pulset lasciva decentius aetas" (215–216) [It is time for you to go: lest, having drunk too much, a more properly playful/wanton age should laugh and push you out of their way].

> Walk sober off; before a sprightlier Age
> Comes titt'ring on, and shoves you from the stage:
> Leave such to trifle with more grace and ease,
> Whom Folly pleases, and whose Follies please.   (324–327)

While Horace is the butt of his own precepts, Pope makes the rest of the world the object of his dignified rejection. The world of the *Essay*'s "grace and ease," the "trifles" which in Horace are cherished as the figure for lyric, in Pope are charged with moral disapproval as "Folly." To please one's audience, to struggle to make oneself decipherable and delightful, is no longer sufficient.[100]

In order to earn this moment of self-assertion, Pope has rested upon, and rejected earlier in the poem, an older and more familiar stance of Horatian moderation.

> ego, utrum
> Nave ferar *magna* an *parva;* ferar *unus & idem.*
> Non agimur tumidis velis Aquilone secundo:
> Non tamen adversis aetatem ducimus Austris.
>   Viribus, ingenio, specie, virtute, loco, re,
> Extremi priorum, extremis usque priores.   (200–204)

[I, whether I am borne in a great or a small ship, let me be borne one and the same. I am not wafted with swelling sails before the North wind blowing fair, yet I do not bear my course of life with the South wind adverse to me: in force, genius, figure, virtue, station, estate, the last of the first, yet before the last.]

> What is't to me (a Passenger God wot)
> Whether my Vessel be first-rate or not?
> The Ship it self may make a better figure,
> But I that sail, am neither less nor bigger.
> I neither strut with ev'ry fav'ring breath,
> Nor strive with all the Tempest in my teeth.

> In Pow'r, Wit, Figure, Virtue, Fortune, plac'd
> Behind the foremost, and before the last.   (296–304)

Pope here rewrites Horace in a self-referential register which points beyond the page to his deformity. The turn on the body as vessel and the soul as mere passenger is absent from Horace's lines (in the Latin the "ship of life" is a common figure of speech, not limited to the body), as is the brave play on his own shape which he makes with the ship's figure, which allows him and the reader to pass without flinching the repetition of the word in the final composed lines. This movement from physical to spiritual metaphor, which includes the reader in the maneuver of acknowledging while overlooking the unmentionable, is a familiar one. What is unfamiliar here is that Pope seems not so much interested in moderation as its opposite: deformity guarantees the kind of fixed integrity which his emphasis in the Latin text highlights, and which so many of the exemplary anecdotes in *Epistle II, ii* treat—the scholar emerging from his study like a statue come to life, the mad Lord presiding over an empty House—a state of "unus et idem" which is easily mistaken for madness and incomprehensibility. "Unus et idem," the obstructing mark of the particular, has become in this poem identical to the transparency of moderation.

OBSTRUCTING FOR JUSTICE:
PARTICULARITY IN THE *EPILOGUE TO THE SATIRES*

In the *Epilogue to the Satires,* Pope celebrates such vulnerable integrity. Although these poems are subtitled "Dialogues," many critics have been tempted to see them as mad monologues, completely lacking in "objective correlative," just as they lack a Latin original, for the moral outrage with which each culminates.[101] These heroic diatribes, ostensibly provoked by a somewhat amoral and refined adversary who is no longer on Pope's side, as he was in *Satire II, i* or *Arbuthnot,* are marked by a particular moment (the original title of the first was *One Thousand Seven Hundred and Thirty Eight*) and a plethora of proper names approaching the level of innuendo of the prurient *Sober Advice.* (See for example the salaciously gossipy interchange between P. and F. in *Dialogue II,* 10–25, which begins with F's request that P. "Spare then the Person, and expose the Vice," and P's subsequent illustration that to "sowze on all the Kind" with general examples is to provoke even more effectively the response, "Scandal! name them, Who?") In the *Epilogue,* David Morris writes, Pope "speaks from inside history"; his "secrecy and innuendo are to meaning what interruption is to form."[102] In these embattled poems the satirist fully abandons "harmless *Characters* that no one hit" for vicious particulars ("yet none but you by Name the Guilty lash," remarks his polite adversary), rejects "that easy *Ciceronian* style, / So *Latin,* yet so *English* all the while, / . . . All Boys may read, and Girls may understand" (I, 73–76) for an exclusive opacity. In doing so he is staking a claim for control of the poem's interpretation against Horace and audiences past and future, not only, as Morris claims, in the name of Virtue, but more importantly in his own name. The only historical particulars which will remain immediately decipherable will be the letters of his signature. Though Pope's adieu to "Distinction, Satire, Warmth, and Truth" in *Dialogue I* is ironic, by embracing satire, warmth and the particular distinctions of historical truth, he takes genuine leave of the distinction that guarantees perfect correspondences between author and reader.

In *Dialogue I* the absence of a Latin original is coupled with an immediate rejection of Horace—or at least of a contemporary idea of Horace.[103]

> But *Horace,* Sir, was delicate, was nice;
> *Bubo* observes, he lash'd no sort of *Vice:*
> *Horace* would say, *Sir* Billy *serv'd the Crown,*
> Blunt *could do Bus'ness,* H——ggins *knew the Town,*
> In *Sappho* touch the *Failing of the Sex,*
> In rev'rend Bishops note some *small Neglects,*
> and own, the *Spaniard* did a *waggish thing,*
> Who cropt our Ears, and sent them to the King.
> His sly, polite, insinuating stile
> Could please at Court, and make AUGUSTUS smile:
> An artful Manager, that crept between
> His Friend and Shame, and was a kind of *Screen.*   (11–22)

The abundance of local references here, dizzying as it is, is not so dizzying as the shiftiness of the irony. Is F. damning Horace with faint praise, or is Pope damning F.'s insincerity? Is Horace being rejected out of hand or is this distorted image of Horace being presented as patently false? What is clear is that once Horace is named, he takes his place in the satiric portrait gallery that leaves none of its denizens untouched. His polite insinuations, although contrasted with P.'s righteous accusations, are still allowed to do their artful damage to Pope's chosen targets. There are, we are expected to believe, good and bad kinds of innuendo, just as there is a difference between Pope's "medium" of satire and Horace's "screen" ("a metaphor peculiarly appropriated," Pope informs us in a note, "to a certain person in power,"[104] namely Robert Walpole).

Yet Pope in the *Dialogues* is anything but transparent, and he uses the proper name as a screen against misinterpretation of those representatives of virtue whom he chooses to protect:

> I only call those Knaves who are so now.
> Is that too little? Come then, I'll comply—
> Spirit of *Arnall!* aid me while I lye.
> COBHAM's a Coward, POLWARTH is a Slave,
> and LYTTLETON a dark, designing Knave,
> ST. JOHN has ever been a wealthy Fool—
> But let me add, Sir ROBERT's mighty dull,
> Has never made a Friend in private life,
> And was, besides, a Tyrant to his Wife.   (II, 127–135)

Even moral distinctions become arbitrary here. Although accused of maligning Walpole unjustly and oversimplifying a morally complex figure, Pope boasts sincerely in a letter to Fortescue in 1738, of having made Sir Robert "a second compliment in print in my second Dialogue, and he ought to take it for no small one, since in it I couple him with Lord Bol——."[105] While the compliment is somewhat marred by an ironic reference to Walpole's tolerance of his wife's infidelity, the important thing to note is that Pope's faith in what he later refers to in this poem as his "provocation," the "strong Antipathy of Good to Bad" is so strong that he feels the highest compliment he can pay to Walpole is to "couple" him with Bolingbroke, a name which, like those that precede it, is immune to whatever can be said about it, a moral absolute standing outside the semantic system of the language, making the distinction between truth and lie moot.

Pope himself becomes just such an isolated moral absolute as he draws "the last pen for freedom" at the close of *Dialogue II* (248), or depicts the triumph of Vice at the end of *Dialogue I* (an allegory thinly veiling a reference to Walpole's marriage to Molly Skerritt, and which Pope has no fear of compromising by his subsequent "compliments" to Walpole) in illustration of his own lonely defense of Virtue. The snares of language, of history, of the printed word, no longer threaten Pope because he has disregarded external—and therefore corrupt—moral distinctions in order to create his own forms of absolute difference. F's diagnosis in *Dialogue II*—"I think your Friends are out, and would be in" (123)—is a perceptive one; perhaps such random distinction is what all the fuss is about. But to limit Pope in the *Dialogues* to the petty rivalries of contemporary politics would be to miss the magnitude of this poet's absolutism.

In the *Dialogues* all local differences are reduced to the simple black and white of "out" or "in," "good" or "bad," at Pope's sovereign will. Such dichotomies are arbitrary, but their arbitrariness is precisely the point. From Pope's perspective, contextual shades of meaning become irrelevant while the proper name and the poem itself, talismanic and untouched like the satirist himself, remain gloriously exempt. The integrity of this exemption is contingent upon the very particularity it defies: such historical particularity guarantees the poem's authenticity, and the poet's proper possession of the poem and himself, by marring the work's universality. The key to the final couplet of *Dialogue I*, Pope's grand response to the triumph of Vice over Virtue, in which all the world is reduced first to a morality play (and finally to an "it") and in which Pope alone stands "collected in himself and whole," is the parenthetical "if": "Yet may this Verse (if such a Verse remain) / Show there was one who held it in disdain." Swift warned Pope before he wrote the *Dunciad,* "Take care the bad poets do not outwit you, as they have served the good ones in every Age, whom they have provoked to transmit their Names to posterity . . . the difference between good and bad Fame is a perfect trifle."[106] On trifles as perfect as the particularized absolutes of his satire are Pope's propriety and self-possession founded.

It is fitting then that the poet who mastered a poetics of deformity should close his literary career with the fourth book of the *Dunciad*'s apocalyptic vision of the end of form:

> Thus at her felt approach, and secret might,
> *Art* after *Art* goes out, and all is Night . . .
> *Religion* blushing veils her sacred fires,
> And unawares *Morality* expires.
> Nor *public* Flame, nor *private,* dares to shine;
> Nor *human* Spark is left, nor Glimpse *divine!*
> Lo! thy dread Empire, CHAOS! is restor'd;
> Light dies before thy uncreating word:
> Thy hand, great Anarch! lets the curtain fall;
> And Universal Darkness buries All.   (IV, 640–656)

What remains after such a spectacle of disappearance, after the eclipse of Nature's *"clear, unchang'd,* and *Universal* Light,"[107] is not darkness but the bare remnants of form itself. The curtain dropped to conceal and frame a chaos that it transforms, like Zeuxis's painting of a veil, into a space in and against which disfiguration is destined to appear.[108] By incorporating deformity, and ultimately the loss of form, into the frame of his representations, Pope has transformed representation into an inimitable matter of both resemblance and disgrace.

ABBREVIATIONS

NOTES

INDEX

Abbreviations

Correspondence: The Correspondence of Alexander Pope. Ed. George Sherburn. 5 vols. Oxford: Clarendon Press, 1956.

Prose Works: The Prose Works of Alexander Pope. Ed. Norman Ault. Oxford: Basil Blackwell (for Shakespeare Head Press), 1936.

Spence, *Anecdotes:* Joseph Spence, *Observations, Anecdotes, and Characters of Books and Men* (1820). Ed. James M. Osborn. 2 vols. Oxford: Clarendon Press, 1966.

TE: *The Poems of Alexander Pope.* Ed. John Butt et al. 11 vols. London: Methuen, 1939–1969.

Notes

INTRODUCTION

1. Alexander Pope, "Preface to *The Works* (1717)," in *The Prose Works of Alexander Pope,* ed. Norman Ault (Oxford: Oxford University Press, 1936), vol. 1, p. 292. Pope used the phrase again in his portrait of Atossa in *Epistle to a Lady,* line 118, who "Shines, in exposing Knaves, and painting Fools, / Yet is, whate'er she hates and ridicules" (119–120) in a dialectic of negation which Pope himself has reason to fear.

2. Pope to Steele, 15 July 1712, *Correspondence,* vol. 1, p. 148.

3. Voltaire, *Oeuvres,* 42 (Paris, 1819–1825), p. 157, quoted by William K. Wimsatt in *The Portraits of Alexander Pope* (New Haven: Yale University Press, 1965), p. xxiv. Pope, *The Guardian* No. 92, June 26, 1713, in *Prose Works,* vol. 1, p. 125.

4. Jonathan Swift, *A Full and True Account of the Battel Fought Last Friday, Between the Antient and the Modern Books in St. James's Library,* in *A Tale of a Tub,* ed. D. Nichol Smith, 2d. ed. (Oxford: Clarendon Press, 1958), pp. 231–232.

5. While I am duly warned by David B. Morris's caution that the heroic couplet is only "the smallest fragment of [Pope's] genius," I am reading the couplet as a vehicle of multiplicity, a method for linking particular fragments together in a mosaic; I'm thus in sympathy with Morris's emphasis on a "Protean" Pope of constant refinement and revision. *Alexander Pope: The Genius of Sense* (Cambridge, Mass.: Harvard University Press, 1984), pp. 2–3.

6. See, for example, Margaret Anne Doody, *The Daring Muse: Augustan Poetry Reconsidered* (Cambridge: Cambridge University Press, 1985), chapter 1, "Appetite, imperialism and the fair variety of things." Spence notes that Pope's *Moral Essays* were originally titled *Of the Use of Things* in *Anecdotes,* p. 131. See Morris, *Alexander Pope,* pp. 188–189, for an illuminating catalog of Popean objects.

7. Paulson here describes Hogarth, whose densely textured visual narratives have been compared to Pope's poetry. *Emblem and Expression: Meaning in English Art of the Eighteenth Century* (Cambridge, Mass.: Harvard University Press, 1975), p. 53.

8. In this regard see Morris, *Alexander Pope,* chapters 8, 9, 10.

9. For accounts of the cultural shift to "feminine" values and its relation to burgeoning consumerism in eighteenth-century England, see J. G. A. Pocock, *Virtue, Commerce, and History* (Cambridge: Cambridge University Press, 1985), particularly chapters 3 and 6; Colin Campbell, *The Romantic Ethic and the Spirit of Modern Consumerism* (London: Basil Blackwell, 1985); G. J. Barker-Benfield, *The Culture of Sensibility* (Chicago: University of Chicago Press, 1992). For related arguments about the representative function of the feminine in the fiction of this period, see Nancy Armstrong, *Desire and Domestic Fiction* (Oxford: Oxford University Press, 1987); Catherine Gallagher, *Nobody's Story: The Vanishing Acts of Women Writers in the Marketplace, 1670–1820* (Berkeley: University of California Press, 1994).

10. "In the absence of any guarantee of higher authority Pope's obsessive negation drew attention inevitably to the arch-negator himself, who was no more able than those whom he attacked to climb outside or above the marketplace." Peter Stalleybrass and Allon White, *The Politics and Poetics of Transgression* (Ithaca: Cornell University Press, 1986), pp. 117–118.

11. See Stalleybrass and White, *Politics and Poetics of Transgression,* pp. 80–124, for eighteenth-century authorship in the context of the carnivalesque; Laura Brown, *Alexander Pope* (London: Basil Blackwell, 1985), and *Ends of Empire: Women and Ideology in Early Eighteenth-Century English Literature* (Ithaca: Cornell University Press, 1993) for Marxist readings of Pope's oeuvre as ongoing response to "the interconnected developments of capitalism and mercantile imperialism"; Ellen Pollak, *The Poetics of Sexual Myth: Gender and Ideology in the Verse of Swift and Pope* (Chicago: University of Chicago Press, 1985) for a feminist attack on Pope; Catherine Ingrassia, "Women Writing/Writing Women: Pope, Dulness, and 'Feminization' in the *Dunciad,*" *Eighteenth-Century Life,* 14, 3 (November 1990): 40–58, for an account of Pope's later stigmatization of cultural feminization as embodied by female writers.

12. Pope, *Dialogue II,* 198. See Carole Fabricant, "Pope's Moral, Political, and Cultural Combat," *The Eighteenth Century: Theory and Interpretation,* 29, 2 (1988): 165–187.

13. See Reuben Brower, *Alexander Pope: The Poetry of Allusion* (Oxford: Oxford University Press, 1959); Maynard Mack, *The Garden and the City* (Toronto: University of Toronto Press, 1969) and *Alexander Pope: A Life* (New York: Norton, 1986).

14. William Dowling, *The Epistolary Moment: The Poetics of the Eighteenth-Century Verse Epistle* (Princeton: Princeton University Press, 1991), pp. 12–15.

15. Dowling's Pocockian reading of Augustan poetry's historical importance might perhaps overstate the economic and social powerlessness of the landed aristocracy in eighteenth-century England. Two recent readings of Pope's relation to classical sources, both of which focus on literary history and the history of ideas rather than the history of ideology, are Frank Stack, *Pope and Horace: Studies in Imitation* (Cambridge: Cambridge University Press, 1985), and Harry M. Solomon, *The Rape of*

the Text: Reading and Misreading Pope's Essay on Man (Tuscaloosa: University of Alabama Press, 1993).

16. In the most pronounced example of this phenomenon, Stalleybrass and White accuse Dryden and Pope among others of disowning the "grotesque body" of popular culture, claiming that for an author to bridge the gap between high and low culture is "a monstrosity," while curiously failing to acknowledge how Pope calls attention within the frame of his orderly couplets to his own deformity. See *Politics and Poetics of Transgression,* p. 116.

17. Barbara Stafford, *Body Criticism: Imaging the Unseen in Enlightenment Art and Medicine* (Cambridge, Mass.: MIT Press, 1991), p. 3.

18. Monstrosity, of which deformity is a kind of subset, developed into the science of teratogeny by the end of the century. Stafford notes that the English tended to gawk at monsters on display, while the French took the lead in scientifically analyzing them. Stafford, *Body Criticism,* p. 264. See Stafford's chapter, "Conceiving," particularly p. 254, and Marie-Hélène Huet, *Monstrous Imagination* (Cambridge, Mass: Harvard University Press, 1993), pp. 101–102, for a description of the coexisting senses of monstrosity at the end of the eighteenth century.

19. See *Monstrous Imagination,* part 1, for a detailed account of this evolution. For Aristotle, "anyone who does not take after his parents is really in a way a monstrosity, since in these cases Nature has in a way strayed from the generic type. The first beginning of this deviation is when a female is formed instead of a male." *Generation of Animals,* vol. xiii, trans. A. L. Peck, Loeb Classical Library (1963), p. 401; quoted in Huet, *Monstrous Imagination,* p. 3.

20. Georges Canguilhem, *La connaissance de la vie* (Paris: Vrin, 1965), p. 177; translated and quoted in Huet, *Monstrous Imagination,* p. 102.

21. Stafford, *Body Criticism,* p. 254. Stafford's catalog of literary monsters supports Huet's maxim on the eighteenth-century view of monsters: "If Art must imitate Nature, in cases of monstrous procreation Nature imitates Art." *Monstrous Imagination,* p. 7.

22. In Huet's account, that truth is always linked to the feminine, and specifically to the woman's ability to create life. She continues, "In earlier times it disclosed the secret longings of pregnant women; and in Romanticism it reveals . . . the desire to do away with the mother herself. This desire, however, never leads to a simple repudiation. Rather, it yields an incestuous anguish mingled with the suspicion that the artist himself was born from a woman who considered images with a fateful admiration. Thus is art conceived." *Monstrous Imagination,* p. 128.

23. See Stafford, *Body Criticism,* pp. 178–199, who discusses the eighteenth-century effort to establish "permissible parameters for the representation of pain and [to identify] what medium might rightfully show it." The neoclassical premium "on the maintenance of heroic decorum even in monumental suffering" left the remnants and fragments of deformity and disease to be represented by the lower popular media of caricature and the grotesque. *Body Criticism,* p. 179.

24. Ibid., pp. 192–193. Stafford links this characteristic of the genre of caricature to Hume's founding of identity not on coherent thought but rather on a "counter-physiology of the passions," p. 192. In his *Essay on Man* and his *Moral Essays,* with

their simultaneously uniform and particularized theory of the "ruling passion," Pope elaborated a similar view of a human nature based on the body. For an assessment of what Hume and Pope had in common (Hume admired the *Essay on Man* enough to give Pope an autographed copy of his *Treatise of Human Nature*), see Solomon, *The Rape of the Text,* pp. 132–135.

25. Christian Ludwig von Hagedorn, *Reflexions sur la Peinture,* trans. M. Huber (Leipzig: Chez Gaspar Fritsch, 1775), vol. 1, pp. 105–108, quoted in Stafford, *Body Criticism,* p. 184.

26. Stafford, *Body Criticism,* p. 195.

27. Ibid. While Stafford draws most of her examples from the late eighteenth century in this particular passage, her book delineates a century-long development. Pope serves as a liminal figure in this history much as his contemporary Hogarth does for Paulson's account in *Emblem and Expression.*

28. See Michel Foucault, *The Order of Things: An Archaeology of the Human Sciences* (New York: Random House, 1970, reprinted 1973), for an analysis of the forms of knowledge in the classical age which sees language as divided from literature in the way that form is divided from deformity. See also Paulson, *Emblem and Expression,* p. 49.

29. For a discussion of Augustan poetry's fascination with grotesque transformations, see Doody, *Daring Muse,* chapters 5 and 6.

30. Huet, *Monstrous Imagination,* p. 95.

31. Thomas Laqueur, *Making Sex: Body and Gender from the Greeks to Freud* (Cambridge, Mass.: Harvard University Press, 1990), chapter 1, p. 35. See also Stafford, "Brain-Born Images," in *Body Criticism,* pp. 233–254.

32. David Saunders and Ian Hunter, "Lessons from the 'Literary': How to Historicize Authorship," *Critical Inquiry,* 17 (Spring 1991): 485. For the history of the legal definition of authorship as it concerned issues of literary property, see Mark Rose, *Authors and Owners: The Invention of Copyright* (Cambridge, Mass.: Harvard University Press, 1993), particularly chapter 4 for Pope's legal interventions. For a discussion that relates definitions of high and low culture to such questions, see Martha Woodmansee, *The Author, Art, and the Market: Rereading the History of Aesthetics* (New York: Columbia University Press, 1994).

33. For a few of many accounts of the ways in which the English Augustans found a mirror in the first Augustan Age's indebtedness to an imagined and elusive past, see Dowling, *The Epistolary Moment;* Joseph M. Levine, *The Battle of the Books: History and Literature in the Augustan Age* (Ithaca: Cornell University Press, 1991).

34. Frances Burney recorded in her diary in 1782 Samuel Johnson's vehement objection to these lines. Johnson called Pope's definition of wit "both false and foolish," "confounding words with things." Johnson's characterization of the difference between thought and expression as one between words and things, in the defense of a differently modern possibility of originality, demonstrates the direction in which eighteenth-century aesthetics moved after Pope. *Dr. Johnson and Fanny Burney, Being the Johnsonian Passages from the Works of Mme. D'Arblay,* ed. Chauncy Brewster Tinker (New York: Moffat, Yard & Co., 1911), pp. 150–152.

35. Pope, *An Essay on Man,* TE, vol. 3, p. 7. The *Essay* could be read in terms of Foucault's *Order of Things* as yoking the disparate epistemes of the Renaissance and Classical ages, the former based on similarity and resemblance (analogy based on the human body, for example), the latter on the coherent difference of classification.

36. Ibid.

37. William A. Warburton, *A Critical and Philosophical Commentary on Mr. Pope's Essay on Man* (London: John and Paul Knapton, 1742), p. 137, quoted in Solomon, *Rape of the Text,* p. 165; Mack, "Introduction, *An Essay on Man,*" TE, vol. 3, p. lxxx. See also Morris, *Alexander Pope,* chapter 6.

38. Solomon's phrase characterizes a history of philosophy's distrust of poetry that begins with "the antique antagonism of Plato to Homer." *Rape of the Text,* p. 17.

39. Ibid., p. 131.

40. Robert Dodsley, *An Epistle to Mr. Pope, Occasion'd by his Essay on Man* (London: L. Gilliver, 1734), p. 4, quoted in Solomon, *Rape of the Text,* p. 36; Morris, *Alexander Pope,* p. 177.

41. Samuel Johnson, *Life of Pope,* in *Lives of the English Poets,* ed. George Birkbeck Hill (Oxford: Clarendon Press, 1905, reprinted 1967), vol. 3, pp. 243–244.

42. For a history of the hostile critical reception of the *Essay on Man* which often enlists a rhetoric of seductive femininity against the poem, see Solomon, *Rape of the Text,* chapter 1. On the gendered rhetoric of display, see Patricia Parker, *Literary Fat Ladies: Rhetoric, Gender, Property* (London: Methuen, 1987); Felicity Nussbaum, *The Brink of All We Hate: English Satires on Women, 1660–1750* (Lexington: University of Kentucky Press, 1984).

43. For "disrobed of its ornaments," Johnson, *Life of Pope,* vol. 3, p. 243; Johnson quoted in Tinker, *Dr. Johnson and Fanny Burney,* pp. 150–152. Johnson's ambivalence can be described as a response to what Sigmund Freud has described in his essay "The 'Uncanny,' " as "that class of the terrifying which leads back to something long known before to us, once very familiar," and which is ultimately linked to the mother's body. Chapters 2 and 3 will enlist this notion of the uncanny in readings of Pope's relation to the sterile repetitiveness of the feminine world of the commodity, and the hidden secrets of feminine nature. Sigmund Freud, *Collected Papers,* vol. 4, ed. Ernest Jones, trans. Joan Riviere (London: Hogarth Press, 1948), pp. 369–370.

44. Montaigne, *The Complete Essays of Montaigne,* trans. Donald M. Frame (Stanford: Stanford University Press, 1958), p. 539. Quoted in Julia Epstein, "Either/Or—Neither/Both: Sexual Ambiguity and the Ideology of Gender," *Genders,* 7 (Spring 1990): 108.

45. *Verses Address'd to the Imitator of the First Satire of the Second Book of Horace. By a Lady.* (London: A. Dodd, 1733), p. 2. This pamphlet was jointly authored by Lord Hervey. In *Lady Mary Wortley Montagu: Essays and Poems,* eds. Robert Halsband and Isobel Grundy (Oxford: Clarendon Press, 1977), p. 266, l. 15.

1. THE "TRUEST COPIES" OF A "MEAN ORIGINAL"

1. David Saunders and Ian Hunter, "Lessons from the 'Literatory': How to Historicize Authorship," *Critical Inquiry,* 17 (Spring 1991): 485.

2. Ibid., p. 757.

3. Marcia Pointon, *Hanging the Head: Portraiture and Social Formation in Eighteenth-Century England,* (New Haven: Yale University Press, 1993), p. 6.

4. "Pope was probably the most frequently portrayed English person of his generation, perhaps of the whole eighteenth century." William K. Wimsatt, *The Portraits of Alexander Pope* (New Haven: Yale University Press, 1965), p. xv. Pointon calculates 66 primary types of portraits of Pope (reproduced in various forms, including engravings, lithographs, mezzotints, medals, and miniatures) in circulation in eighteenth-century England. See *Hanging the Head,* p. 2.

5. Pointon, *Hanging the Head,* pp. 62–63.

6. Deidre Lynch, "Overloaded Portraits: The Excesses of Character and Countenance," in Veronica Kelly and Dorothea E. Van Mücke, eds., *Body and Text in the Eighteenth Century* (Stanford: Stanford University Press, 1994), pp. 116–117. Lynch's account of the evolution of the depiction of character in eighteenth-century portraiture points to the "overloaded face as a deterrent example: a warning signal . . . marking the point at which the seemliness of the body, the propriety of meaning, and the artistic hierarchy came into jeopardy," a point which Pope's deformed body signals more flagrantly.

7. "The analysis focused on the 'ideological meaning' of monsters overlooks the fact that previous to signifying something, previous even to serving as an empty vessel of meaning, monsters embody enjoyment *qua* the limit of interpretation, that is to say, *nonmeaning as such.*" Slavoj Žižek, *Enjoy Your Symptom!: Jacques Lacan in Hollywood and out* (New York: Routledge, 1992), p. 134. See also Fredric Jameson, on the "polysemous function" of the shark in *Jaws,* in *Signatures of the Visible* (New York: Routledge, 1990), pp. 26–27; cited in Žižek, p. 134.

8. Mark Rose, "The Author as Proprietor: *Donaldson v. Becket* and the Genealogy of Modern Authorship," *Representations,* 23 (Summer 1988): 75. See also Martha Woodmansee, "The Genius and the Copyright: Economic and Legal Conditions of the Emergence of the Author," *Eighteenth Century Studies,* 17, 4 (Summer 1984): 425–448; Ian Watt, "Publishers and Sinners: The Augustan View," *Papers of the Bibliographic Society of the University of Virginia,* 12 (1959): 3–20; Harry Ransom, "The Rewards of Authorship in the Eighteenth Century," *University of Texas Studies in English,* 18 (1938): 47–66. For Pope's particular part in the proceedings see Pat Rogers, "Pope and His Subscribers," *Publishing History,* 3 (1978): 7–36, and James A. Winn, "On Pope, Printers and Publishers," *Eighteenth Century Life,* 6 (1981): 93–102. The definitive work on Pope and the literary market is D. F. Foxon, *Pope and the Eighteenth-Century Book Trade,* ed. James McLaverty (Oxford: Oxford University Press, 1992).

9. Herman Lewis Asarnow, "Pope's Early Public Character, 1709–1729: His Creation and Promotion of a Public Image in the Early Career," abstract in *Dissertation Ab-*

stracts International 42, 11 (1982): p. 4829A. Asarnow argues that the phrase "true character" was first used in this sense in English in Dennis' text.

10. John Dennis, *The Critical Works of John Dennis,* ed. Edward Niles Hooker (Baltimore: Johns Hopkins University Press, 1939–1943), vol. 2, p. 103.

11. See the *First Satire of the Second Book* (1733), line 68; *Epilogue to the Satires, Dialogue I* (1738), lines 7–8: " 'Tis all from *Horace: Horace* long before ye / Said, 'Tories call'd him Whig, and Whigs a Tory.' " In typical Popean fashion, the initial (and imitative) claim to unique originality is later self-consciously and critically cited (in the words of an imagined adversary) as derivative of a classical original.

12. Dennis, *Critical Works,* vol. 2, pp. 103–104. See John Dryden, "Essay on Satire" in *John Dryden: Selected Criticism,* eds. James Kinsley and George Parfitt (Oxford: Clarendon Press, 1970), pp. 229–267, for a discussion of satire's possible etymologies, which include "satura" or mixture, and "satyr." Edward Tyson's collapsing of the great chain of being in *Orang-Outang sive Homo Sylvestris or, the Anatomy of a Pygmie compared with that of a Monkey, an Ape, and a Man. To which is added, A Philological Essay concerning the Pygmies, the Cynocephali, the Satyrs, and Sphinges of the Ancients. Wherein it will appear that they are all either Apes or Monkeys, and not Men, as formerly Pretended* (London, 1699), could serve as a kind of catalog from which abusive names for Pope were chosen. In its collapsing of distinctions between monkeys and men (despite its title's attempt to assure the reader otherwise), Tyson's speculation gives a cultural context for the anxieties that Pope's figure inspires in his attackers. The ape, man's distorted mirror image, is known and feared for its skill at mimicry, and in Tyson's hands conflates art with nature. Tyson claims to be looking for the "Real Foundation for [Ancient] Mythology," and to have found the orang-outang to be synonymous with what the ancients called "wild men," "little men," "Pygmaean men," "black men," "wild Beasts," "satyrs," "fauni," "Pan," "Sylvanus," "Silenus," and even "Nymphae." *Orang-Outang,* p. 1.

13. Dennis, *Critical Works,* vol. 2, p. 104.

14. Ibid., p. 105.

15. Ibid., p. 105. Dennis refers here to Pope's prisoning of the pirate bookseller Curll, as published earlier in 1716 by Pope as "A Full and True Account of a Horrid and Barbarous Revenge by Poison, On the Body of Mr. Edmund Curll, Bookseller; With a faithful Copy of his Last Will and Testament." The "True Character" is written to a large extent in response to Pope's bodily/textual attack on Curll, and Dennis' editor assures us that he was patiently silent in the face of other assaults for five years. In this highly scatological narrative, Curll repents of his many misdeeds against authors while first "perpetually interrupted by vomitings," and then "from his close-stool." His most important sin is appropriating authorial agency: "Gentlemen, in the first Place, I do sincerely pray Forgiveness for those indirect Methods I have pursued in inventing new Titles to old Books, putting Authors Names to Things they never saw, publishing private Quarrels for publick Entertainment; all which, I hope will be pardoned, as being done to get an honest livelihood." In *Prose Works,* vol. 1, p. 262. While Pope too publishes private quarrels, he does so with the most direct of methods; he reduces Curll to the gripings of his own body. It is

also worth noting that Pope recollected and reappropriated this particular passage of Dennis' attack in the notes to the *Dunciad Variorum,* II, 134; TE vol. 5, p. 119.

16. Dennis, *Critical Works,* vol. 2, p. 106. For the mournful affect of such textual self-consciousness, see chapter 4, on Pope, Horace and prosopopeia, the trope by which, as Paul de Man puts it, "one's name . . . is made as intelligible and memorable as a face," a face which always eludes our memory of its original. "Autobiography as De-Facement," in *The Rhetoric of Romanticism* (New York: Columbia University Press, 1984), p. 76.

17. John Milton, *Paradise Lost* I, 84–85, with references from *The Poems of John Milton,* eds. John Carey and Alastair Fowler (London: Longmans, 1968). This is the first speech in the poem, termed "rhetorically the *ianua narrandi* or the opening of narrative proper."

18. James Ralph, *Sawney. An Essay on the Dunciad an Heroick Poem* (London: Whitehall Evening Post, June 27, 1728); Pope, *To Bathurst,* line 305.

19. For more on Pope's exploitation of the ambiguities of agency inherent in both contemporary ideas of satire and of authorship, see chapter 5. For this image, see William K. Winsatt, *Portraits,* no. 7. 11, pp. 70–72.

20. For a historical analysis of the various ideological valences of Catholicism as a cultural sign in Stuart England, see Peter Lake, "Anti-popery: the Structure of a Prejudice," in Richard Cust and Ann Hughes, eds., *Conflict in Early Stuart England* (London: Longman, 1989), pp. 72–106.

21. *Pope Alexander's Supremacy and Infallibility Examined* (London: *Monthly Chronicle,* 1729), p. v.

22. Ibid., p. 1.

23. Roland Barthes, *S/Z* (New York: Hill and Wang, 1974), trans. Richard Miller, p. 54.

24. Ibid., p. 61.

25. Voltaire, Letter XXIII of *Letters Concerning the English Nation. By Mr. De Voltaire,* 2d. ed. (London: C. Davis, 1741), p. 178; quoted in Wimsatt, *Portraits,* p. xvii. Written c. 1728–1731, these letters were first published in English at London in 1732.

26. From James Boswell's notes for a biography of Sir Joshua Reynolds in Frederick W. Hilles, ed., *Portraits by Sir Joshua Reynolds* (New York: McGraw Hill, 1952), pp. 24–25. For the bracketed material, see James Prior, *Life of Edmund Malone* (London: Smith, Elder & Co., 1860), p. 429.

27. Rose, "Author as Proprietor," p. 54.

28. Francis Hargrave, *An Argument in Defense of Literary Property,* 2d. ed. (London, 1774), pp. 6–7; quoted in Rose, "Author as Proprietor," p. 72.

29. *Verses Address'd to the Imitator of the First Satire of the Second Book of Horace. By a Lady* (London: A. Dodd, March 9, 1733), p. 2. This text was jointly and anonymously authored by Lord Hervey. In *Lady Mary Wortley Montagu: Essays and Poems* (Oxford: Clarendon Press, 1977), p. 266.

30. Samuel Johnson, *Life of Pope,* in *Lives of the English Poets,* ed. George Birkbeck Hill (Oxford: Clarendon Press, 1905), vol. 3, p. 247.

31. The same weapons are used, ironically enough, by those who come to the moralist's defense, such as the "Gentlewoman" authoress of "Advice to Sappho occasioned

by her Verses on the IMITATOR of the First Satire of the Second book of Horace." This fair anonymous supporter, who declares that the "Nymph" who conquers Pope's "mighty Soul" is due more "Honour . . . than if she reigned o'er all the fopling Crew," also resorts to a reading of the poet's body:

> Nature, surpris'd to see a Mind so great,
> Forgot to form the supple Limbs with Care,
> 'Twas immaterial to a Soul so fair.

So that if Pope's crooked mind marks his body in Lady Mary's account, the immaterial greatness of his soul for this devoted mythographer makes his body's weakness "immaterial." In either case, the poet himself, and not his book, is to be read. *Advice to Sappho occasioned by her Verses on the IMITATOR of the First Satire of the Second Book of Horace. By a Gentlewoman* (London, 1733).

32. "For this last half year I have been troubled with the disease (as I may call it) of translation; the cold prose fits of it (which are always the most tedious with me) were spent in the *History of the League;* the hot (which succeeded them) in this volume of Verse Miscellanies." John Dryden, "Preface to *Sylvae,* or *The Second Part of Poetical Miscellanies*" (1685), in *Selected Criticism,* p. 194.

33. Pope to Swift, 19 December 1734, *Correspondence,* vol. 3, p. 444.

34. Edward Young, *Conjectures on Original Composition,* ed. Edith J. Marley (London: Longmans, 1918), p. 7.

35. These lines first appear in *An Essay on Criticism* 362–363, and are ironically cited and rejected (quoted in the epigraph, revised in the body) in Pope's imitation of Horace's Epistle 2, 2 (1737). See chapter 5.

36. David B. Morris, *Alexander Pope: The Genius of Sense* (Cambridge, Mass.: Harvard University Press, 1984), p. 3.

37. Spence, *Anecdotes,* vol. 1, pp. 7, 9–10, 13, 15; Johnson, *Life of Pope,* vol. 3, pp. 474, 475; Morris, *Alexander Pope,* p. 249. For an account of Pope's glimpse of Dryden, see Spence, *Anecdotes,* vol. 2, p. 611. Pope said of Dryden, in words reminiscent of Reynolds' attempt to read Pope's own face, "I remember his face, for I looked upon him with the greatest veneration even then, and observed him very particularly." Spence, *Anecdotes,* vol. 1, p. 25. Johnson notes that Pope is keeping poetic models in mind in his inability to remember "the time when he began to make verses. In the style of fiction it might have been said of him as of Pindar, that when he lay in his cradle, 'the bees swarmed about his mouth.' " *Life of Pope,* vol. 3, p. 474. For Pope's account of learning by imitation, see Spence, vol. 1, pp. 17–21.

38. John Dryden, "Preface to *Ovid's Epistles*" (1680) in *Selected Criticism,* pp. 186, 184. For an excellent introduction to eighteenth-century poetic imitation, see Arthur Sherbo's introduction to his edition of *Christopher Smart's Verse Translation of Horace's Odes, English Literary Studies Monograph Series* (University of Victoria Press, 1979), pp. 5–42. Sherbo usefully distinguishes between Pope's "formal" Horatian Imitations, which remain more or less connected to a specific text of Horace, and Pope's poems in the "spirit and tone" of Horace, such as the *Ode to Solitude* and *Epistle to*

Arbuthnot. Reuben A. Brower terms Pope's life and literary career an *imitatio Horati,* and asserts that "nearly everything" Pope wrote after his translation of the *Iliad* "shows more or less distinctly the influence of Horatian poetic modes and themes." *Alexander Pope: The Poetry of Allusion* (Oxford: Clarendon Press, 1959), p. 165.

39. Johnson, *Life of Dryden,* in *Lives of the English Poets,* ed. George Birkbeck Hill (Oxford: Clarendon Press, 1905), vol. 1, p. 423; quoted by Sherbo, p. 31.

40. Johnson as quoted in James Boswell, *Boswell's Life of Johnson,* ed. George Birkbeck Hill (Oxford: Clarendon Press, 1934), vol. 3, p. 256. For Johnson's implementation of similar metaphors intent on distinguishing surface ornament from substantial essence with regard to Pope's *Essay on Man,* see my introduction.

41. Morris, *Alexander Pope,* p. 260.

42. Dryden, "Preface to *Sylvae,*" in *Selected Criticism,* p. 195.

43. Ibid., pp. 195, 196.

44. Dryden, "Preface to *Ovid's Epistles,*" in *Selected Criticism,* p. 186.

45. Henry St. John, Lord Viscount Bolingbroke, *Letters on the Study and Use of History* (London: A. Millar, 1752), vol. 1, p. 62.

46. Pope prefaces his first Horatian Imitation, *The First Satire of the Second Book,* by explaining, "The Occasion of publishing these *Imitations* was the Clamour raised on some of my *Epistles.* An Answer from *Horace* was both more full, and of more Dignity, than any I cou'd have made in my own person." TE, vol. 4, p. 3.

47. TE, vol. 4, p. 74. See Frank Stack, *Pope and Horace: Studies in Imitation* (Cambridge: Cambridge University Press, 1985), p. 78. For Pope's ambivalent relationship to antiquarianism, and in particular to the modern philological classical scholarship that Bentley represented, as exemplified in his *Iliad* translation, see Joseph Levine, *The Battle of the Books: History and Literature in the Augustan Age* (Ithaca: Cornell University Press, 1991), chapter 6.

48. For a rich essay on Pope's ambivalence toward self-representation, see S. L. Goldberg, "Integrity and Life in Pope's Poetry," in R. F. Brissenden and J. C. Eade, eds., *Studies in Eighteenth-Century Culture* (Toronto: University of Toronto Press, 1976).

49. Leopold Damrosch, *The Imaginative World of Alexander Pope* (Berkeley: University of California Press, 1987), p. 29.

50. Ibid., p. 28.

51. Spence, *Anecdotes,* vol. 1, p. 258, Spence's emphasis. Dustin Griffin writes that Pope "was in effect composing the features of the self-image he planned to leave for posterity. Indeed, his remark suggests that his life's goal was nothing more or less than to leave a 'perfect edition.'" *Alexander Pope: The Poet in the Poems* (Princeton: Princeton University Press, 1978), p. 35.

52. Carol Jacobs, "The Monstrosity of Translation," *Modern Language Notes,* 90 (1975): 758.

53. Walter Benjamin, "The Task of the Translator," quoted in Jacobs, p. 757. See also pp. 758–759 for an illuminating description of the independence of the genre of translation which "is always on the verge of eluding understanding," much as the visual sign of Pope's deformity eludes coherent categories.

54. Pope to Martha Blount, 30 October [1719?], *Correspondence,* vol. 2, p. 17.

55. Deformity, through both Pope's and his attackers' efforts, made him exemplary. Pope led Curll on in part by feeding the publisher the story of his having been whipped as a boy for writing a lampoon on his teacher. Curll's response was to advertise the anecdote in the *Daily Journal* as "a Proof of that Natural Spleen which constitutes Mr. Pope's Temperament, (as my Lord Bacon observes of Deformed Persons) and from which he has never yet deviated." See James A. Winn, *A Window in the Bosom: The Letters of Alexander Pope* (Hamden: Archon Books, 1977), p. 31.

56. Pope to Cromwell, 24 June 1710, *Correspondence,* vol. 1, p. 89.

57. Pope's body thereby blocks the portraitist's access to his "true character." If portraiture is, as Pointon puts it, a "mechanism to bridge the chasm between material existence and the interiority of the individual," then to portray Pope's body is to portray instead the chasm itself. *Hanging the Head,* pp. 62–63.

58. For a related discussion, see Cynthia Wall, "Editing Desire: Pope's Correspondence with (and without) Lady Mary," *Philological Quarterly,* 71, 2 (Spring 1992): 221–237.

59. Pope to Lady Mary, 18 August [1716], *Correspondence,* vol. 1, pp. 352–353.

60. Ibid., p. 353.

61. Ibid., [October 1716], vol. 1, p. 364.

62. Griffin, *Alexander Pope,* pp. 5, 32.

63. Pope, *Satire II, i,* 55–56.

64. Pope, 18 February 1734/5, *Correspondence,* vol. 3, p. 451. See also Pope's earlier letter to Jervas, 16 August 1714: "to follow Poetry as one ought, one must forget father and mother, and cleave to it alone." *Correspondence,* vol. 1, p. 243.

65. Ibid., [June 1717], vol. 1, p. 407.

66. Ibid., [September 1717], vol. 1, p. 430.

67. The title of a painting by W. P. Frith, c. 1854, depicting a laughing Lady Mary and an enraged Pope, described in Wimsatt, *Portraits,* as perhaps the finest of the nineteenth-century visual fictions about Pope, p. 362.

68. For a parallel account of Pope's transformation of the soul-body relationship over the course of his correspondence, see Wall, "Editing Desire."

69. Pope, 18 December [1730?], *Correspondence,* vol. 3, p. 156.

70. Johnson recounts how Pope "once slumbered at his own table while the Prince of Wales was talking of poetry." Johnson, *Life of Pope,* p. 198. Pope remarked on his inability to speak well in public, and Pope's sister Mrs. Rackett observes of her brother that "I never saw him laugh heartily in all my life." Spence, *Anecdotes,* vol. 1, pp. 6, 102.

71. Pope to Broome, 29 June [1725], *Correspondence,* vol. 2, p. 302.

72. See, for example (and there are many others) this fantasy of retirement from poetry itself in *Epistle II, ii:*

> To Rules of Poetry no more confin'd,
> I learn to smooth and harmonize my Mind,
> Teach ev'ry Thought within its bounds to roll,
> And keep the equal Measure of the Soul.

> Soon as I enter at my Country door,
> My mind resumes the thread it dropt before;
> Thoughts, which at Hyde-Park-Corner I forgot,
> Meet and rejoin me, in the pensive Grott. (202–209)

73. Pope, 27 September 1732, *Correspondence,* vol. 3, p. 316.

74. Johnson, *Life of Pope,* vol. 3, pp. 196–197.

75. On Pope's cultural feminization, see Kristina Straub, "Men from Boys: Cibber, Pope, and the Schoolboy," *The Eighteenth Century: Theory and Interpretation,* 32, 3 (Autumn 1991): 219–239. Pope exploits this image of himself as child in his *Guardian* 91, on "The Club of Little Men" (1713): "At our first Resort hither an old Woman brought her Son to the Club Room, desiring he might be Educated in this School, because she saw here were finer Boys than ordinary." *Prose Works,* vol. 1, pp. 121–122. In the sequel to this essay, *Guardian* 92, Pope ironically situates himself in a tradition of diminutive authors that includes Horace, Voiture, Scarron, and Aesop. On the debate alluded to here over Aesop's deformity interpreted as a figure for the contested forum of print, see Jayne Elizabeth Lewis, *The English Fable* (Cambridge: Cambridge University Press, 1996), chapter 3.

76. Spence, *Anecdotes,* vol. 1, p. 6.

77. Johnson, *Life of Pope,* p. 198.

78. William Empson, *Seven Types of Ambiguity* (New York: New Directions, 1947), p. 128.

79. Norman Ault, *New Light on Pope* (London: Methuen, 1949), p. 6.

80. For eighteenth-century portraiture's ordering of the body's parts in accordance with social hierarchies rather than mimetic accuracy, for its codes of representation that put "the head—and above all the face—with its cognitive and physiognomical particularities . . . in metonymic relation to the body as a whole," see Pointon, *Hanging the Head,* p. 56. Pointon also points out that eighteenth-century portraits of Homer differed according to whether the author of the *Iliad* or the *Odyssey* was portrayed; the ideal of Homer, and not Homer himself, was what mattered. *Hanging the Head,* p. 63.

81. Wimsatt, *Portraits,* No. 65, p. 311.

82. Ibid., No. 52.1, pp. 205–207. Figure 3 is Warton's frontispiece, No. 52.2, p. 210. In this regard Mead is not unlike Pope himself, whose library was adorned with busts of Homer, Newton, Spencer, Shakespeare, Milton, and Dryden. The multiple attributions listed beneath this frontispiece, concluding with the designation of its rightful possessor, also demonstrate how ownership legitimates the ambiguous originality of images of the poet.

83. Ibid., No. 64.1, pp. 298–299.

84. Ibid., pp. 300, 304.

85. Ibid., p. 304.

86. An early example of Pope's equation with the materiality of a writing reimagined as print with the possibility of transparency is his essay "On the *Origin* of *Letters*": "By this means we materialize our Ideas, and make them as lasting as the Ink and

Paper, their Vehicles . . . The Philosopher who wish'd he had a Window to his Breast, to lay open his Heart to all the World, might as easily have reveal'd the Secrets of it this way, and as easily left them to the World, as wish'd it." *The Guardian* 172, 28 September 1713, in *Prose Works,* vol. 1, pp. 142–143.

2 . THE RAPE OF THE LOCK *AS MINIATURE EPIC*

1. Aaron Hill, "The Progress of Wit: A Caveat" (1730), reprinted in Geoffrey Tillotson, ed., *Eighteenth-Century English Literature* (San Diego: Harcourt Brace, Jovanovich, 1969), p. 813. I am indebted to Claudia Thomas, "Pope's *Iliad* and the Contemporary Context of his 'Appeals to the Ladies,' " *Eighteenth-Century Life,* 14 (May 1990): 1–17, for my choice and explication of this phrase.

2. Hill, "Progress of Wit," p. 813.

3. Samuel Johnson, *Life of Pope,* in *Lives of the English Poets,* ed. George Birkbeck Hill (Oxford: Clarendon Press, 1905), vol. 3, p. 240.

4. Thomas, "Pope's *Iliad,*" p. 2.

5. In this regard, both poems enter into a contemporary debate, both aesthetic and political, about the value of "greatness" imagined in terms of largeness, also evident in texts such as Swift's *Gulliver's Travels* (1726), Fielding's "midget-play" *Tom Thumb; or, the Tragedy of Tragedies* (1730), or Pope's own portrait of Timon dwarfed by his own architectural "greatness" in *Epistle to Burlington* (1731).

6. The contest for the apple between Aphrodite, Hera, and Athena results in the Judgment of Paris. Paris is asked to choose the fairest of the three goddesses. Each offers him an emblem of herself as prize or bribe should he choose her. In a repetition of the apple's inscription, Paris chooses Aphrodite by choosing Helen, fairest of mortal women, whose ambiguous "rape" (since her desire for Paris is irrelevant) stirs the homosocial workings of the *Iliad* into motion.

7. William Hay, *Deformity: An Essay* (London: printed for R. and J. Dodsley, sold by M. Cooper, 1754, 2d. ed.), p. 3. Hay's text pays self-conscious tribute to Pope and even hypothesizes, in an attempt to stabilize the reproduction of deformity, that Pope's father was deformed: see p. 21.

8. Spence quotes Pope's sister Mrs. Rackett on the subject of the pistols. *Anecdotes,* vol. 1, p. 116; Hay, *Deformity,* pp. 27–28.

9. Owen Ruffhead, *Life of Pope* (London: C. Bathurst, 1769), pp. 15–16.

10. Hay, *Deformity,* p. 22.

11. Ibid., p. 75 and postscript.

12. Ruffhead, *Life of Pope,* p. 16.

13. Laura Brown, *Alexander Pope* (London: Basil Blackwell, 1985), pp. 25–27. John Dennis in his commentary on the *Rape* also links this "idolatry" to Pope's Catholicism. *The Critical Works of John Dennis,* ed. Edward Niles Hooker (Baltimore: Johns Hopkins University Press, 1943), vol. 1, p. 130.

14. William Hazlitt, "Pope, Lord Byron, and Mr. Bowles," in *The Complete Works of William Hazlitt,* ed. P. P. Howe (London: J. M. Dent & Sons, 1933), vol. 19, p. 84.

15. Ibid., pp. 82–83.

16. Such a construction of Pope comes from a long tradition of nature-art oppositions in authorial biography, beginning perhaps as early as Dryden on Shakespeare and Jonson in his *Essay on Dramatic Poesy,* running through Pope on Homer and Virgil in his *Preface to the Iliad,* and culminating for my purposes in Johnson on Dryden and Pope in his *Life of Pope.* My use of the terms "sublime" and "beautiful" is grounded in Edmund Burke's *A Philosophical Enquiry into the Origin of our Ideas of the Sublime and Beautiful* (1757), ed. James T. Boulton (South Bend, Ind.: Notre Dame University Press, 1968). For a reading of Burke's conception of these categories in gendered terms and his complicated attempts in the process to distinguish between visual and aural realms, see W. J. T. Mitchell, *Iconology: Image, Text, Ideology* (Chicago: University of Chicago Press, 1986), pp. 116–149.

17. Pope, "Dedication to *The Rape of the Lock,*" TE vol. 2, pp. 142–143.

18. See frontispiece, TE, vol. 2. Perhaps Arabella waived the poetic dedication because of the explicit analogy made between her "rape" and Helen's:

> Pleas'd in these lines, *Belinda,* you may view
> How things are priz'd, which once belong'd to you:
> If on some meaner head this Lock had grown,
> The nymph despis'd, the Rape had been unknown.
> But what concerns the valiant and the fair,
> The Muse asserts as her peculiar care.
> Thus *Helens* Rape and *Menelaus'* wrong
> Became the Subject of great *Homer's* song.   (1–8)

From "To BELINDA on the RAPE OF THE LOCK," in Pope, *Minor Poems,* TE vol. 6, p. 107.

19. Susan Stewart, *On Longing: Narratives of the Miniature, the Gigantic, the Souvenir, the Collection* (Baltimore: Johns Hopkins University Press, 1984), pp. 53–54.

20. Laura Brown, *Alexander Pope,* p. 20. The sentence continues, "this is the primary formal configuration of the poem."

21. Ellen Pollak, *The Poetics of Sexual Myth: Gender and Ideology in the Verse of Swift and Pope* (Chicago: University of Chicago Press, 1985), pp. 77–107.

22. Deborah C. Payne, "Pope and the War Against Coquettes; or, Feminism and *The Rape of the Lock* Reconsidered—Yet Again," *The Eighteenth Century: Theory and Interpretation,* 32, 1 (Spring 1991): 4. Payne does an admirable job of taking feminist critique of the poem one step further in order to account for the poem's appeal to women readers. While Payne is right to insist on the potential unity of ideological critique and aesthetic appreciation for a reader of the *Rape,* she too suggests the necessity of an ideologically enlightened poststructuralist critic for the creation of such a unity.

23. Howard D. Weinbrot, "*The Rape of the Lock* and the contexts of warfare," in G. S. Rousseau and Pat Rogers, eds., *The Enduring Legacy: Alexander Pope tercentary essays* (Cambridge: Cambridge University Press, 1988), p. 30. Weinbrot's essay is partic-

ularly useful for the way in which it restores both traditional and marxist-feminist critiques of the *Rape* to a broader literary-traditional context which include the burlesquing of Homer and the deploring of Amazons.

24. Samuel Johnson, *Life of Pope,* vol. 3, p. 239.
25. Pope, *Episode of Sarpedon* (1709), TE vol. 1, pp. 450–451.
26. This focus on the detail serves to align Pope's discourse with eighteenth-century aesthetic ideas of the feminine. See, for example, Naomi Schor, *Reading in Detail: Aesthetics and the Feminine* (London: Methuen, 1987; reprinted by Routledge, 1989), chapter 1. Both Shaftesbury's *Second Characters; or, the Language of Forms,* ed. Benjamin Rand (Cambridge: Cambridge University Press, 1914), and Edmund Burke's *A Philosophical Enquiry into the Origin of Our Ideas of the Sublime and Beautiful* link attention to the detail with a vision of the feminine.
27. Homer, *The Iliad,* trans. Richmond Lattimore (Chicago: University of Chicago Press, 1951), XII, 310–328. In the Lattimore translation the speech reads:

> "Glaukos, why is it you and I are honored before others
> With pride of place, the choice meats and the filled wine cups
> in Lykia, and all men look on us as if we were immortals,
> and we are appointed a great piece of land by the banks of Xanthos,
> good land, orchard and vineyard, and ploughland for the planting of wheat?
> Therefore it is our duty in the forefront of the Lykians
> to take our stand, and bear our part of the blazing of battle,
> so that a man of the close-armoured Lykians may say of us:
> 'Indeed, these are no ignoble men who are lords of Lykia,
> these kings of ours, who feed upon the fat sheep appointed
> and drink the exquisite sweet wine, since indeed there is strength
> of valour in them, since they fight in the forefront of the Lykians.'
> Man, supposing you and I, escaping this battle,
> would be able to live on forever, ageless, immortal,
> so neither would I myself go on fighting in the foremost
> nor would I urge you into the fighting where men win glory.
> But now, seeing that the spirits of death stand close about us
> in their thousands, no man can turn aside nor escape them,
> let us go on and win glory for ourselves, or yield it to others."

28. Pope, *The Rape of the Lock,* TE vol. 2, p. 199, note to line 7.
29. See Pollak, *Poetics of Sexual Myth,* pp. 77–107, for the most cogent reading in this vein.
30. Here I am indebted to Weinbrot's reading. Clarissa in his view "meets the challenge of respecting and transcending her source, of avoiding duplicity and sensuality while insisting upon the obligations . . . of turning noble death into useful life." The key word here is "useful": just as Pope refines Homer, so Belinda (fruitlessly) is called upon to put potentially destructive beauty to productive use. "*The Rape of the Lock* and the contexts of warfare," pp. 43–44.

31. "The transcendence presented by the miniature is a spatial transcendence, a transcendence which erases the productive possibilities of understanding through time. Its locus is thereby the nostalgic. The miniature here erases not only labor but causality and effect. Understanding is sacrificed to being in context." Stewart, *On Longing,* p. 60.

32. Pope, "Preface to the *Iliad,*" TE, vol. 7, p. 5.

33. "It is certain there is not near that Number of Images and Descriptions in any Epic Poet; tho' every one has assisted himself with a great Quantity out of him: And it is evident of *Virgil* especially, that he has scarce any Comparisons which are not drawn from his Master." Ibid., p. 9. Joseph Levine sees Pope's view of Homer as painter as part of his larger attempt in the *Iliad* translation to imagine a middle ground between ancients and moderns, combining an antiquarian fascination with recapturing the material with an ambitious poet's imagination. See *The Battle of the Books* (Ithaca: Cornell University Press, 1991), pp. 205, 212.

34. Pope, "Preface to the *Iliad,*" p. 9.

35. Gotthold Ephraim Lessing, *Laocoon* (London: Everyman's Library, 1930), p. 68; quoted in David Ridgley Clark, "Landscape Painting Effects in Pope's Homer," *The Journal of Aesthetics and Art Criticism,* 22, 1 (Fall 1963): 26. Clark comments, "Pope, of course, recognizes Homer's wisdom in this technique, but he is also fascinated by the possibility of actual pictures in Homer—and here must be meant not simply vivid description, but pictures of a static composed kind, views obtaining aesthetic distance through a suggestion of painting perspective. Where the original does not provide these, Pope freezes the action in order to paint them."

36. Pope, *Windsor Forest,* TE vol. 1, pp. 148–152.

37. On Pope's pictorialism and sententiousness see Maynard Mack's introduction to TE, vol. 7, section VI, pp. liii–lviii.

38. For a definition of ekphrasis as the "verbal representation of a visual representation," see James Heffernan, "Ekphrasis and Representation," *New Literary History,* 22, 2 (Spring 1991): 297–316.

39. Pope, "Observations on the Shield of *Achilles,*" TE, vol. 8, p. 358.

40. Ibid., p. 363. Pope drew on an antiquarian tradition in his design for the shield, but his flighty imagination triumphed over more disciplined antiquarian labors. When Troy was excavated, and shields like that of Achilles were discovered, Pope's drawing was revealed to be accurate. I contend that both Homer's and Pope's shields are neither entirely imaginary nor entirely man-made. See Levine, *Battle of the Books,* pp. 146, 216–217.

41. For a typical note distinguishing women of various character and rank on the shield, see Pope's "Observations," p. 365.

42. For a slightly different argument that in his translation of Homer's similes "Pope annihilates Nature in one sense in order to resuscitate it in another," see H. A. Mason, *To Homer through Pope: An Introduction to Homer's* Iliad *and Pope's Translation* (London: Chatto & Windus, 1972), p. 77.

43. Pope's note to *Iliad* IV, 170; TE vol. 7, p. 229.

44. Barbara Benedict, "The 'Curious Attitude' in Eighteenth-Century Britain: Observing and Owning," *Eighteenth-Century Life,* 14, 3 (November 1990): 75.

45. Ibid., p. 77.

46. Ibid., p. 59.

47. Clarence Tracy, *The RAPE observ'd: an edition of Alexander Pope's poem The rape of the lock, illustrated by means of numerous pictures, from contemporary sources, of the people, places, and things mentioned, with an introduction and notes by / Clarence Tracy* (Toronto: University of Toronto Press, 1974). Tracy's style in the title makes explicit his own antiquarian impulse.

48. "Eighteenth-century curio cabinets and collections promote an aesthetic that relies on the eye forming connections between separate objects, finding similarities within differences. No longer does one object represent its class; rather, the spectator defines a class by comparing several—as many as possible—objects. Collecting thus functions as an exercise of definition by distance over culture and history, both one's own culture and the culture of others." Benedict, "The 'Curious Attitude,' " pp. 77–78.

49. Ibid., p. 75.

50. Ibid., p. 82.

51. Joseph Addison, *Spectator* 69, in *The Spectator,* ed. Donald F. Bond (Oxford: Clarendon Press, 1965), vol. 1, pp. 292–295. For two early and important essays locating Pope's construction of Belinda "as a consumer, the embodiment of luxury" in a cultural context of great ambivalence, see Louis A. Landa, "Pope's Belinda, The General Emporie of the World, and the Wondrous Worm," *South Atlantic Quarterly,* 70 (Spring 1971): 215–235; and "Of Silkworms, Farthingales and the Will of God," in R. F. Brissenden, ed., *Studies in the Eighteenth Century,* vol. 2 (Toronto: University of Toronto Press, 1973), pp. 259–277. The critic to draw most heavily and most recently on Landa's work in her characterization of Pope's mercantile poetics is Laura Brown in *Alexander Pope,* a reading which this chapter attempts to complicate in the direction of the aesthetic. See also her reading of this passage in *Ends of Empire: Women and Ideology in Eighteenth-Century English Literature* (Ithaca: Cornell University Press, 1993), particularly chapter 2.

52. Benedict, "The 'Curious Attitude,' " p. 84.

53. *Gazette,* 26 January 1758, quoted in Benedict, "The 'Curious Attitude,' " p. 83.

54. James Boswell, in Frederick W. Hilles, ed., *Portraits by Sir Joshua Reynolds* (New York: McGraw Hill, 1952), pp. 24–25.

55. See Figure 4.

56. *Authentic Memoirs of the Life of Richard Mead, M.D.* (London, 1755), p. 51; quoted in Wimsatt, *Portraits,* pp. 205–207.

57. Maynard Mack, *The Garden and the City* (Toronto: University of Toronto Press, 1969), pp. 31–32, 251.

58. Pope, 30 April 1736, *Correspondence,* vol. 4, p. 13.

59. See Thomas, "Pope's *Iliad,*" pp. 1–2.

60. John Dryden, *The Dedication of the Aeneis,* in *The Poems of John Dryden,* ed. James Kinsley (Oxford: Clarendon Press, 1958), vol. 3, p. 1059.

61. Johnson, *Life of Dryden,* in Hill, *Lives of the English Poets,* vol. 1, p. 469.
62. Johnson, *Life of Pope,* vol. 3, p. 238.
63. See Penelope Wilson, "Classical Poetry and the Eighteenth-Century Reader" in Isabel Rivers, ed., *Books and Their Readers in Eighteenth-Century England* (New York: St. Martin's Press, 1982), pp. 69–96.
64. Pope, 25 May or 1 June 1714, *Correspondence,* vol. 1, p. 226.
65. Pope, *The Guardian* 78, 10 June 1713, in *Prose Works,* vol. 1, pp. 116–117. This essay, later included in Pope's mock-Longinian treatise *Peri Bathous* (1728), was published while Pope was working on the first six books of the *Iliad* translation and revising the two-canto version (published in 1712) of *The Rape of the Lock.*
66. Susan Staves names as one of Pope's contributions to neoclassical epic the extensive critical apparatus with which the civilized English poet called visible attention to the ancient's barbarism. "Pope's Refinement," *The Eighteenth Century: Theory and Interpretation,* 29 (1988): 154. See also Mack's introduction to the Twickenham edition of Pope's *Iliad,* and Weinbrot, "*The Rape of the Lock* and the contexts of warfare."
67. Staves, "Pope's Refinement," p. 149. See also James McLaverty, "The Mode of Existence of Literary Works of Art: The Case of the *Dunciad Variorum,*" *Studies in Bibliography,* 37 (1984): 82–105, who argues that "the pomp of the [*Dunciad's*] presentation is genuinely appropriate to the poem's importance." Pope himself spoke of the *Dunciad Variorum* quite seriously as an "English classik with huge Commentaries."
68. Leigh Hunt (anonymous), *Examiner,* 1 June 1817.
69. Joseph Addison, quoted in Johnson, *Life of Pope,* vol. 3, p. 103. Pope took umbrage at the compliment since part of its intent was to discourage him from revising and expanding the poem.
70. Edmund Gosse to A. E. Gallatin, 19 June 1902, Princeton University Library ms.; quoted in Robert Halsband, *The Rape of the Lock and Its Illustrations* (Oxford: Clarendon Press, 1980), p. 87.
71. Hazlitt, *Complete Works,* vol. 5, p. 72.
72. Pope, "Dedication," TE vol. 2, p. 142.
73. Ibid., p. 143.
74. Pope's description of the endless exchange within a woman's breast is remarkable for the ways in which it parallels marxist accounts of the deceptiveness of commodity production. Just as the commodity conceals the source of its production in an appearance of randomness decked out in alluring metaphor, so coquettes appear arbitrary and appealing while concealing the contrivance of the sylphs. For the dynamic of substitution in which commodity-exchange masks the causal metonymy of its production with random and totalizing metaphor, see Terry Eagleton, *Walter Benjamin, or, Towards a Revolutionary Criticism* (London: Verso, 1981), p. 30.
75. For a reading of such substitutions as part of the poem's process of refining and sublimating epic violence into display, see Weinbrot, "*The Rape of the Lock* and the contexts of warfare," p. 31. For Pope's vision of himself in such a "moving Toyshop," see his *Guardian* 106, 13 July 1713, in *Prose Works,* vol. 1, pp. 131–132. Pope's alter-

ego, Peter Puzzle, sees himself succeed a "Lap-dog . . . a *Guiney* Pig, a Squirril and a Monky," only to witness "my Place taken up by an ill-bred awkward Puppy with a Money-bag under each Arm." Both here and in the *Rape,* for the speaker to gaze at himself from his mistress' eyes is to see himself as an object of amusement with nothing but market value.

76. Dennis, *Critical Works,* vol. 2, pp. 338–339.

77. Leigh Hunt, *Wit and Humour, Selected from the English Poets* (1846), quoted in F. W. Bateson and N. A. Joukovsky, eds., *Alexander Pope: A Critical Anthology* (Harmondsworth: Penguin, 1975), p. 220.

78. Pope, 1 May 1714, *Correspondence,* vol. 1, pp. 219–220.

79. Halsband, *The Rape and Its Illustrations,* p. 4.

80. Aubrey Beardsley, *Letters,* eds. H. Maas, J. L. Duncan, and W. G. Good (London: Cassell, 1970), p. 297; quoted in Halsband, *The Rape and Its Illustrations,* p. 114.

81. Halsband, *The Rape and Its Illustrations,* p. 115.

82. Ibid., p. 114.

83. Geoffrey Tillotson, *On the Poetry of Pope* (Oxford: Clarendon Press, 1950; 2d. ed.), p. 157.

84. Ibid., p. 158. The most famous of such couplets itself enacts a displacement of high and low typical of the poem's emphasis on surface. After her "rape," Belinda exclaims to the Baron, "Oh hadst thou, Cruel! been content to seize/Hairs less in sight, or any Hairs but these!" (IV, 175–176). William Ayre writes in defense of these lines: "It is said, that to some very nice Ears of the Fair Sex they have given Offense, by Reason of the *Double-Entendre* they admit of: but as there is a Possibility to take them in a Sense, wholly innocent and Chaste, it is hoped they will construe them so." *Memoirs of the Life and Writings of Alexander Pope* (London, 1745), vol. 1, p. 46. The pun on "hairs" was made famous in this century by Cleanth Brooks, in "The Case of Miss Arabella Fermor," reprinted in Maynard Mack, ed., *Essential Articles for the Study of Alexander Pope* (Hamden: Archon Press, 1964), pp. 237–255.

85. James Grantham Turner, "Pope's Libertine Self-Fashioning," *The Eighteenth Century: Theory and Interpretation,* 29 (1988): 133.

86. Barbara Stafford notes that such puns and confusions of material with immaterial meanings were the verbal equivalent of monsters in the eighteenth century. See *Body Criticism: Imaging the Unseen in Enlightenment Art and Medicine* (Cambridge, Mass.: MIT Press, 1991) p. 254.

87. Peter Conrad, *Times Literary Supplement,* 25 March 1977, p. 336, quoted in Halsband, *The Rape and Its Illustrations,* p. 115.

88. Beardsley's affectionate "embroidering" of the poem is reminiscent of Susan Stewart's description of the book collector's nostalgia for the coincidence of text and object, labor and production, a union in which, like the curiosity, "the book as pure object abandons the realm of use value and enters an ornamental realm of exchange value." Her description of the early nineteenth-century fashion phenomenon of miniature books is particularly striking in its evocation of the *Rape's* aesthetic:

The social space of the miniature book might be seen as the social space, in miniature, of all books: the book as talisman to the body and emblem of the self; the book as microcosm and macrocosm; the book as commodity and knowledge, fact and fiction . . . The fact that the miniature book could be easily held and worn attaches a specific function to it. Its gemlike properties were often reflected in its adornment by real gems . . . This book/jewel, carried by the body, multiplies significance by virtue of the tension it creates between inside and outside, container and contained, surface and depth.

This multiplication of significance is a unique result of the miniature book's adornment of the *female* body, a body whose uncanny conjunction of inside and outside, familiar and strange, make it a jewel of dazzling proportions. *On Longing,* pp. 35, 41.

89. This poem was inspired, according to Pope, by a situation reminiscent of the poet's mythical battle with Lady Mary over the control of his image. See Pope's letter to Cromwell of 24 June 1710: "I was the other day in company with a Lady, who rally'd my Person so much, as to cause a total Subversion of my Countenance: some days after, to be reveng'd on her, I presented her amongst other Company the following Rondeau." *Correspondence,* vol. 1, pp. 89–90. Reprinted in Pope, *Minor Poems,* TE vol. 6, p. 61.

90. Conjuring up Oriental associations by its very name, originally brought to Europe by the Portuguese—who named it porcelain—in the sixteenth century, china was not manufactured in Europe until early in the eighteenth century. "China-mania" becomes a word in English in 1875, and the gendering of such enthusiasm has become so standard by 1823 that Charles Lamb can write "I have an almost feminine partiality for old china." *Elia, Old China,* cited under the third definition of "china" in the *Oxford English Dictionary.* Curiosity was often synonymous with luxury in this period, and both words, as we have seen, were also in close proximity with excessive sexual desire figured as feminine. Indeed, as Benedict shows, when curiosity is figured as feminine, it inevitably takes the form of pornographic narcissism. See "The 'Curious Attitude,' " p. 92. For the male curiosity figured in Pope's satires on women, in particular by the trope of "obsessive and ambiguous dressing and undressing of women," as "a serious reflection on the mystery of commodity fetishism by a culture in the early stages of commodification," see Laura Brown, *Ends of Empire,* pp. 103–134.

91. Pope's use of china as a metaphor for female honor takes its place in a long rhetorical history that itself follows the economic law of supply and demand. "Perhaps," Aubrey Williams surmises, "it was a heightened and growing passion for fine China among women themselves that led writers, in the course of the 17th century, to a substitution of China vases for crystal glasses in their imagery." "The 'Fall' of China and *The Rape of the Lock,*" in Mack, ed., *Essential Articles for the Study of Alexander Pope,* p. 278. For more on the links between consumption, desire and the feminine in the eighteenth century, see Neil McKendrick, John Brewer, and J. H. Plumb, *The Birth of a Consumer Society: The Commercialization of Eighteenth-Century England* (Bloomington: Indiana University Press, 1982); J. G. A. Pocock, *Virtue, Commerce,*

and History (Cambridge: Cambridge University Press, 1985), pp. 103–124. For femininity and the literary market, see Catherine Gallagher, *Nobody's Story: The Vanishing Acts of Women Writers in the Marketplace, 1670–1820* (Berkeley: University of California Press, 1994); Catherine Ingrassia, "Women Writing/Writing Women: Pope, Dulness, and 'Feminization' in the *Dunciad*," *Eighteenth-Century Life,* 14, 3 (November 1990): 40–58.

92. Williams, " 'Fall' of China," p. 281.

93. Brooks, "Case of Miss Arabella Fermor," p. 254.

94. Alfred Sohn-Rethel, *Intellectual and Manual Labor* (London, 1978), p. 59; quoted in Slavoj Žižek, *The Sublime Object of Ideology* (London: Verso, 1989), p. 19.

95. Walter Benjamin, "Central Park," trans. Lloyd Spencer, *New German Critique,* 34 (Winter 1985): 42.

96. Karl Marx, "The Fetishism of Commodities and the Secret Thereof," *Capital, Vol. I: A Critical Analysis of Capitalist Production,* ed. Frederick Engels, trans. from the third German edition by Samuel Moore and Edward Aveling (New York: International Publishers, 1967), p. 71. For Žižek, who is elaborating on an insight of Lacan's, the "symptom" (and with it the modern subject) is discovered by Marx in his account of "the *passage* from feudalism to capitalism," an account grounded in the notion of commodity fetishism. Pope writes at the tail-end of such a transition in England, when a consumer society has begun to flourish and the ground for an industrial society is laid. Žižek, *Sublime Object,* p. 23.

97. Stewart, *On Longing,* p. 69. This "inorganic body," I would argue, has much in common with what Žižek calls the sublime body, which, like money that retains its value despite material wear-and-tear, endures by nature of its externality to any individual subject, by nature of its form. Žižek, *Sublime Object,* pp. 18–19. When viewed from this perspective, the distinction David B. Morris makes between the "sterile" repetition of Belinda's beau monde and the "fruitful" repetition of Pope's revisions of the *Rape* is a tenuous one. *Alexander Pope: The Genius of Sense* (Cambridge, Mass.: Harvard University Press, 1984), pp. 96–97.

98. *Rape,* TE, vol. 2, p. 188.

99. For more examples of this prevalent upper middle-class phenomenon in this period, see John F. Sena, "Belinda's Hysteria: The Medical Context of *The Rape of the Lock*," *Eighteenth-Century Life,* 5, 4 (Summer 1979): 29–42.

100. Halsband, *The Rape and Its Illustrations,* p. 14.

101. See Pollak, *Poetics of Sexual Myth,* pp. 77–107; Ralph Cohen, "The Reversal of Gender in 'The Rape of the Lock,'" *South Atlantic Bulletin,* 37, 4 (1972): 54–60.

102. Dennis, *Critical Works,* vol. 2, p. 343.

103. Geoffrey Tillotson, TE vol. 2, p. 120.

104. Hazlitt, *Complete Works,* vol. 5, p. 72.

3. TWICKENHAM AND THE LANDSCAPE OF TRUE CHARACTER

1. My use of the word singularity in the context of Pope's landscaping efforts is indebted to Barbara Maria Stafford's "Toward Romantic Landscape Perception: Illus-

trated Travels and the Rise of 'Singularity' as an Aesthetic Category," in Harry C. Payne, ed., *Studies in Eighteenth-Century Culture,* vol. 10 (Madison: University of Wisconsin Press, 1981), pp. 17–75. Similarly, my use of the concept of mobility of property owes much to J. G. A. Pocock's discussion of eighteenth-century ideas of the relation of property to personality and good citizenship which contrasts "a conception of property which stresses possession and civic virtue with one that stresses exchange and the civilization of the passions," traditional landed with modern commercial forms of identity. See "The mobility of property and the rise of eighteenth-century sociology," in *Virtue, Commerce, and History* (Cambridge: Cambridge University Press, 1985), pp. 103–123.

2. "Precariousness" is singled out by James H. Bunn in a compelling essay as a key metaphor for describing the "polyglot effect" of the booming early eighteenth-century British import market. This aesthetic, like Pope's vision of objects gone mad in the Cave of Spleen, "seemed to have a life of its own, as if Pygmalion's beloved grew grotesque." Bunn's defense of his brand of cultural semiotics is in complete accord with my reading of Pope's deformity as cultural sign: "Because the metaphor of precariousness combines two dissimilar categories—the physical weight of imports plus their ethical effect of collapsing English social structures—semiology is useful for clarifying the connection assumed by the contemporary observer between 'imports' as commodities and 'import' as signification." "The Aesthetics of British Mercantilism," *New Literary History,* 11, 2 (Winter 1980): pp. 303–304.

3. Ronald Paulson, *Emblem and Expression: Meaning in English Art of the Eighteenth Century* (Cambridge, Mass.: Harvard University Press, 1975), p. 32.

4. Pope to Allen, 6 November 1736, *Correspondence,* vol. 4, p. 40.

5. I choose this name, actually coined by Warburton in his edition of Pope's works, for the *Epistles to Several Persons* because of its connection to the *Essay on Man* and Pope's uncompleted design for an *Opus Magnum,* a "system of ethics in the Horatian way," for which his gardening efforts provided both the impetus and the form.

6. For a concise summary of anti-Catholic legislation in Pope's lifetime as alluded to in *Satire II, ii,* line 60, see TE vol. 4, pp. 168–169.

7. Spence records Pope's plan for his opus in November of 1730: "The first four or five epistles will be on the general principles, or of 'The Nature of Man', and the rest will be on moderation, or of 'The Use of Things.' " The *Moral Essays* were thus aligned from the beginning with particularity. *Anecdotes,* vol. 1, p. 131.

8. On woman as the ultimate commodity fetish, see Laura Brown, *Ends of Empire: Women and Ideology in Eighteenth-Century English Literature* (Ithaca: Cornell University Press, 1993), pp. 103–134.

9. Owen Ruffhead, *The Life of Alexander Pope, Esq.* (London: C. Bathurst, 1769), p. 17.

10. David B. Morris, *Alexander Pope: The Genius of Sense* (Cambridge, Mass.: Harvard University Press, 1984), p. 249.

11. TE, vol. 6, pp. 3–5. The editors hear echoes of Cowley's translations of Horace, Martial and Seneca, all of which continue to inform Pope's poetics of retirement throughout his career.

12. Maynard Mack, *The Garden and the City* (Toronto: University of Toronto Press, 1969), pp. 100, 104. Mack studies Pope's garden in the context of a poetic tradition of retirement that begins with Horace's Odes and Virgil's Georgics and is strongly inflected by seventeenth-century English country house poetry (e.g., Ben Jonson's *To Penshurst*) and Christian humanism. I read Pope's relation to this tradition as one of *both* fantasy and resistance, and push harder than Mack does for the interdependence (rather than simple opposition) of garden and city in both Pope's work and in the structure of the society in which he lived.

13. Raymond Williams, *The Country and the City* (London: Chatto & Windus, 1973), p. 26.

14. For the key players in that debate see, on the neoclassical side, John Dixon Hunt, "Pope's Twickenham Revisited," in Robert P. Macubbin and Peter Martin, eds., *British and American Gardens in the Eighteenth Century* (Williamsburg: Colonial Williamsburg Foundation, 1984), pp. 26–35, and *Garden and Grove* (London: J.M. Dent & Sons, Ltd., 1986); on the picturesque side, Morris Brownell, *Alexander Pope and the Arts of Georgian England* (Oxford: Oxford University Press, 1984). For the most comprehensive account of Pope's role in gardening history see Peter Martin, *Pursuing Innocent Pleasures: The Gardening World of Alexander Pope* (Hamden, Conn.: Archon Books, 1984).

15. One of the classic topoi for the "beatus ille" tradition, Horace's Second Epode, is thereby conveniently truncated: "the celebration of herds and honey and fruit and clear streams, far from war and the city and the cold practice of usury, had been in Horace the sentimental reflection of a usurer, thinking of turning farmer, calling in his money and then, at the climax of the poem, lending it out again." Williams, *Country and the City*, p. 18.

16. Ibid.

17. Ibid., p. 46.

18. Of particular interest to me here is Pope's stance on the debate over whether pastoral referred to an eternally perfect Golden Age (the neoclassical view) or an actual country life. The pastoral, for Pope, must draw on an art that recreates history to make up for the degeneracy of the present. Here, as Williams points out, Pope mistakes aristocratic art for the pastoral's historical origins, recommending description "not . . . as shepherds at this day really are, but as they may be conceiv'd to have been; when the best of men follow'd the employment." TE vol. 1, p. 25; quoted in *Country and the City*, p. 20. In his projection of ideal form back onto a lost historical Golden Age in the service of a narrative of decline, Pope begins a proleptic pattern that will evolve into the angry particularity of his late satires.

19. For a genealogy of Pope's lingering "intuition of a mysterious life in things" indicated by his use of "genius," see Mack, *Garden and the City*, pp. 23–24.

20. Anthony Ashley Cooper, Third Earl of Shaftesbury, *The Moralists*, Part III, Section III. In *Standard Edition: Complete Works, Selected Letters and Posthumous Writings*, ed. Wolfram Benda, Gerd Hemmerich, and Ulrich Schlodlbauer (Fromman-Holzboog, 1987), vol. 2, pt. 1, p. 316; quoted in John Dixon Hunt and Peter Willis, eds., *The Genius of the Place: The English Landscape Garden 1620–1820* (Cambridge, Mass.: MIT Press, 1988), p. 124.

21. *Ars Poetica*, 343–344, in Spence, *Anecdotes*, vol. 1, p. 254. Both James Turner, "Stephen Switzer and the Political Fallacy in Landscape Gardening History," *Eighteenth-Century Studies*, 11, 4 (Summer 1978): 489–496; and John Dixon Hunt, *The Figure in the Landscape: Poetry, Painting, and Gardening during the Eighteenth Century* (Baltimore: Johns Hopkins University Press, 1976), link Pope's debt in gardening theory in general and in this couplet from Horace in particular to Stephen Switzer's *Iconographia Rustica* (1718) (originally published as *The Nobleman, Gentleman, and Gardener's Recreation* in 1715 and reprinted with two extra essays influenced in part by Pope, in 1742). As in the "Ode on Solitude," Pope's achievement in *To Burlington* is not so much an original venture into gardening theory as it is an exceptionally cogent and skillful restatement of old precepts in the guise of originality.

22. Pope outlined his "system of ethics" in a conversation transcribed by Spence in which "ye gardening poem" is mentioned. Spence, *Anecdotes*, vol. 1, pp. 132–133; Pope, *Epistles to Several Persons*, TE vol. 3, pt. 2, p. xxi.

23. See Hunt, *Figure in the Landscape*, and Turner, "Switzer and the Political Fallacy," for the poles of such a debate, which also involves the possible moral valences of an "Augustan" ethos for post–1688 England. As Howard Weinbrot's *Augustus Caesar in Augustan England* (Princeton: Princeton University Press, 1978) argues, Augustus was just as (if not more) likely to be vilified for his tyranny by both Whigs and Tories than celebrated by either in the name of liberty. Still, for a prosperous England recently liberated from civil strife, it was convenient to praise Augustus, as did Switzer (and as did, however ambivalently, Virgil and Horace), as an example of a monarch who could co-exist with liberty. Whatever the political ramifications of liberty in gardening design, gardens offered not only models for individual selves but images of empire.

24. In "The Author in Court: *Pope v. Curll* (1741)," *Cultural Critique*, 21 (Spring 1992): 197–217, Mark Rose argues that Judge Hardwicke's decision granting Pope intellectual but not material property in his correspondence with Swift was instrumental in creating the concept of intellectual property. On femininity as a ground for figuring the legal and epistemological paradoxes involved in founding concepts of identity and authorship on the idea of property, see Ann Louise Kibbie, *The Woman in the Bargain: Property and Female Character in the Eighteenth-Century Novel* (Ph.D. diss., University of California at Berkeley, 1990), and "Sentimental Properties: *Pamela* and *Memoirs of a Woman of Pleasure*," *ELH*, 58, 3 (Fall 1991): 561–577. See also Irene Tucker, "Writing Home: *Evelina*, the Epistolary Novel and the Paradox of Property," *ELH*, 60, 2 (Summer 1993): 419–439, and Catherine Gallagher, *Nobody's Story: The Vanishing Acts of Women Writers in the Marketplace, 1670–1820* (Berkeley: University of California Press, 1994).

25. James Thomson, *Liberty*, in *The Poetical Works of James Thomson*, ed. J. Logie Robertson (London: Oxford University Press, 1908), p. 412, l. 698. The passage follows praise of Burlington's architectural feats that begins: "Lo! numerous domes a Burlington confess—." In Thomson as in Pope, the objects speak for themselves by "confessing" their author. But Thomson's gendered contrast of Burlington's masculine Taste in public buildings and elegant private dwellings with the feminine

display of art's dress of nature in miniature at Twickenham, restored to its proper masculine size by Bathurst, is one Pope might have resisted.

26. Hunt, *Garden and Grove*, p. 67.

27. Ibid., see especially chapter 11 on " 'Palladian' Gardening," for early eighteenth-century English gardens, including Twickenham. For a concise verbal and visual introduction to Twickenham, see Morris Brownell, *Alexander Pope's Villa. Views of Pope's Villa, Grotto, and Garden: A Microcosm of English Landscape*, Marble Hill House exhibition catalog (London: Greater London Council, 1980), revised and reprinted as "The iconography of Pope's villa: images of poetic fame," in G. S. Rousseau and Pat Rogers, eds., *The Enduring Legacy: Alexander Pope tercentary essays* (Cambridge: Cambridge University Press, 1988), pp. 133–150. John Summerson, in a series of lectures on "The Classical Country House in Eighteenth-Century England," encapsulates the tradition of the villa in what sounds like a condensed version of the *Epistle to Burlington*'s narrative: "the idea of the villa is the essential innovation of the century, and . . . the development of the country house can be elucidated as a struggle between the greater house and the villa in which the villa first achieves the disintegration of the greater house and then supersedes it." *Journal of the Royal Society of Arts,* 107 (July 1959): 552; quoted in Brownell, *Pope's Villa,* pp. 16–17.

28. Ann Bermingham, *Landscape and Ideology: The English Rustic Tradition, 1740–1860* (Berkeley: University of California Press, 1986), p. 12.

29. See Hunt, *Garden and Grove*, pp. 59–72. For an essay which argues that Italian theater design is the most important influence on English landscape gardens, see S. Lang, "The Genesis of the English Landscape Garden," in Nikolaus Peusner, ed., *The Picturesque Garden and Its Influence Outside the British Isles* (Washington, D.C.: Dumbarton Oaks, 1974), pp. 1–30.

30. Spence, *Anecdotes,* vol. 1, pp. 251 and 253. In his influential treatise *Iconographia rustica* (1718), Stephen Switzer frugally recommends that the gardener: "buy as many twinings and windings as the villa will allow . . . diversify his views, always striving that they may be so intermixed, as not to be all discovered at once, but that there should be as much as possible something appearing new and diverting, while the whole should correspond together by the natural error of its natural avenues and meanders." Quoted in Bermingham, *Landscape and Ideology,* p. 12.

31. Mack, *Garden and the City,* p. 22.

32. Mack, *Garden and the City,* pp. 22–23; Hunt and Willis, *Genius of the Place,* p. 15. The latter equate the garden's debt to history painting with Pope's creation of "Homeric pictures" in the *Iliad* translation. The phrase "history painting" aptly captures the spatial-temporal conflation that gardening makes possible for Pope.

33. Pope, 19 March 1721/2, *Correspondence,* vol. 2, p. 109.

34. Sir Henry Wotton, *Elements of Architecture* (1624), pp. 65 and 82; quoted in Hunt, *Garden and Grove*, p. 67.

35. John Barrell, *The Idea of Landscape and the Sense of Place* (Cambridge: Cambridge University Press, 1972), p. 48; quoted in Bermingham, *Landscape and Ideology,* p. 199.

36. Hunt, "Pope's Twickenham Revisited," p. 32. Bermingham points out that during the period of the English landscape garden at the peak of its form in the latter half

of the century, "such elaborate effects, seen as silly attempts to make up for want of size, were nowhere to be found in the expansive gardens of Capability Brown and Humphrey Repton. The indispensable condition for the true landscape garden was *land,* not simply as the raw material to be worked but as its own ornament and aesthetic effect as well." Such vast expanses were cheaper to maintain, but required a great deal more capital to create. *Landscape and Ideology,* pp. 11, 13. The transitional semi-formal garden Pope creates at Twickenham was both an aesthetic choice and fitted to his means as self-supporting author.

For an account of Burlington's villa at Chiswick as "undoubtedly the most magnificent and accomplished of . . . translations" into "English conditions [of] the highlights of classical and Renaissance villa gardens," a translation which is explicitly a process of miniaturization, see Hunt, *Garden and Grove,* pp. 197–200; quotation from p. 200. Pope takes this process one step further by working on the smallest of plots, translating lack of actual capital into a surplus of symbolic capital.

37. Horace Walpole, 20 June 1760, in *The Correspondence of Horace Walpole,* ed. Wilmarth S. Lewis (New Haven: Yale University Press, 1937), vol. 21, p. 417; quoted in Mack, *Garden and the City,* pp. 26, 40.

38. Pope to Atterbury, 19 March 1721/22, *Correspondence,* vol. 2, p. 109.

39. Ibid., 5 October 1725, vol. 2, p. 328.

40. Ibid., 19 September 1730, vol. 3, p. 134.

41. Bolingbroke, *Works,* (1754), vol. 3, p. 318; quoted in Mack, *Garden and the City,* p. 27.

42. A quincunx has been conventionally defined as "an arrangement of trees whereby four are placed in the corners of a square with a fifth in the middle," according to Morris R. Brownell, "Quincunx or Groves in Pope's Garden?" *Notes and Queries,* 24 (May–June 1977): 243. Brownell goes on to answer the title's question by redefining quincunx in the terms of Pope's gardening contemporaries as simply "rows of evenly spaced trees." His efforts are here reminiscent of those of Pope and others to reconstruct the lost landscapes of their classical forebears in complete detail.

43. Mack, *Garden and the City,* p. 28.

44. *Newcastle General Magazine,* January 1748; quoted in John Dixon Hunt, *The Figure in the Landscape: Poetry, Painting, and Gardening during the Eighteenth Century* (Cambridge, Mass.: Harvard University Press), p. 81; reprinted in Mack, *Garden and the City,* pp. 240–241.

45. Horace Walpole, *A History of the Modern Taste in Gardening,* ed. Isabel W. U. Chase (Princeton: Princeton University Press, 1943), pp. 28–29; quoted in Mack, *Garden and the City,* p. 26.

46. On the double meanings of picturesque, one referring simply to an external picture-like effect of landscape, the other to an emotionally colored transformation of the scene, and for a summary of the unresolved debate over the picturesque nature of Twickenham, see Martin, *Pursuing Innocent Pleasures,* chapter 1, n. 14, p. 241.

47. Paulson, *Emblem and Expression,* p. 14.

48. For the garden as a poem manqué which opens closed forms through the variety of allusion, see Paulson, *Emblem and Expression,* p. 21.

49. See Mack, *Garden and the City,* p. 28; Paulson, *Emblem and Expression,* p. 22.

50. Pope, "Essay on Homer's Battles," TE vol. 7, p. 255; quoted in Paulson, *Emblem and Expression,* p. 24. Paulson goes on to characterize this emphasis on the multifacetedness of the object as a uniquely transitional moment in the history of English art which leads to a "loosening of the . . . zeugma," an abandonment of the possibility of totality for "the various response of different observers." *Emblem and Expression,* p. 27.

51. Pope, *Guardian* No. 173, *Prose Works,* vol. 1, pp. 145–146.

52. We have already seen how *The Rape of the Lock* and the literary topoi it plays upon link the spoils of imperial trade with the English literary imitator's imperial conquest of the ancients. John Gay plays on the trope of imitation as exploration, as travel through space rather than time, in an imitation of canto XLVI of Ariosto's *Orlando Furioso,* "Mr. Pope's Welcome from Greece a copy of Verses wrote by Mr. Gay upon Mr. Pope's having finisht his Translation of Homers Ilias," which begins:

> Long hast thou, Friend, been absent from thy Soil,
> Like patient *Ithacus* at Siege of Troy: . . .
> Lost to thy Native Land with great turmoil
> On the wide Sea, oft threatning to destroy;
> Methinks with thee I've trod Sigaean ground
> And heard the Shores of Hellespont resound.

First published in *Additions to the Works of Alexander Pope,* 1776, in John Gay, *Poetry and Prose,* ed. Vinton A. Dearing with the assistance of Charles E. Beckwith (Oxford: Clarendon Press, 1974), p. 254.

53. Pope, *Prose Works,* vol. 1, p. 147.

54. Ibid., p. 148.

55. Sir William Temple, *Upon the Gardens of Epicurus: or, Of Gardening, in the Year 1685* (1692), quoted in Hunt and Willis, *Genius of the Place,* p. 96.

56. Pope, *Prose Works,* vol. 1, p. 148.

57. Ibid., p. 149.

58. Ibid.

59. Robert Castell, *Villas of the Ancients Illustrated* (London: printed for the author, 1728), pp. 116–118.

60. In addition to Brownell's comprehensive study *Alexander Pope and the Arts of Georgian England,* see his *Alexander Pope's Villa.*

61. William Temple, *Gardens of Epicurus,* quoted in Hunt and Willis, *Genius of the Place,* p. 99. Temple's condemnation of regularity of landscape is echoed in Pope's *To Burlington* by the negative example of Timon's Villa, in which "Grove nods at Grove, each Alley has a Brother" (117). Like the makers of topiary in the *Guardian* essay's tirade, Timon's hyper-symmetry reveals the rigid structure of his own narcissism.

62. Castell, *Villas,* p. 117.

63. The knowing figure of the African boy which breaks the frame of Beardsley's illus-

trations of *The Rape of the Lock* gestures at the elision of slavery in English celebrations of the glories of trade. On the interrelations of slavery and femininity in Aphra Behn's *Oroonoko*, see Brown, *Ends of Empire*, pp. 23–63.

64. On the importance of the wool trade, see Williams, *Country and the City*, p. 44. On the transfigurative power of enclosure which "suppress[es] the agricultural meaning of ground by displacing attention toward the semiological value of wool as a sign of exchange," see Bunn, "Aesthetics of British Mercantilism," p. 305.

   For a discussion of British travel writing which links the advance of the enclosure movement through the latter half of the eighteenth century to an increasing emphasis on individuality and particularity rather than exchangeability, see Frances Ferguson, *Solitude and the Sublime: Romanticism and the Aesthetics of Individuation* (New York: Routledge, 1992), pp. 129–145, especially p. 134.

65. "The effective distinction is between the owner 'farming' and 'grazing' and the labourers only labouring . . . the whole of the process . . . has been appropriated by the owner and the employer and . . . not being in the labourers' direction, is in a real sense not truly theirs." Williams, *Country and The City*, p. 90. It should be noted that Williams here refers to Crabbe's anti-pastoral poetry which, late in the century, signals a break with the celebratory neopastoral and emergent georgic tradition I discuss, and which Williams considers in the chapter titled "The Morality of Improvement," pp. 60–67.

66. Bermingham, *Landscape and Ideology*, p. 13.

67. Ibid., pp. 13–14.

68. Ibid., p. 14.

69. Of particular interest here is the fashion for ornamental farms or "ferme ornées" which attempted to sustain both modes of perceiving land. Stephen Switzer, Pope's contemporary and supporter, whose recommendations for constructing a garden "may well have formed a model for Pope's *Epistle to Burlington*," and whose practical treatises on gardening were "clearly guided by the poetry of Virgil, Milton, Cowley, and Pope," credited himself with having invented the ferme ornée. For a shrewd characterization of the shared nostalgic georgic tradition of gardener and poet in terms of contemporary opposition politics, see Turner, "Switzer and the Political Fallacy," quotation from p. 495.

70. See Bermingham, *Landscape and Ideology*, pp. 12–13. In *Pursuing Innocent Pleasures,* Martin locates Pope's importance as a transitional figure in the history of English landscape by pointing to the poet's use of natural frames in general and his transformation of space with the ha-ha in particular.

   Carole Fabricant observes that enclosure is a key word for eighteenth-century aesthetics, "functioning on economic, architectural, psychological, and verbal levels at once." The ha-ha, in her account, meets the desires of "men who wanted to be gratified by the full sensual and boisterous reality [in her terms, woman] existing beyond the fence while yet keeping this reality within clearly defined boundaries so that it could be controlled and possessed." See "Binding and Dressing Nature's Loose Tresses: The Ideology of Augustan Landscape Design," in Roseann Runte, ed., *Studies in Eighteenth-Century Culture* (Madison: University of Wisconsin Press, 1979), vol. 8, pp. 131–132.

71. Bermingham, *Landscape and Ideology,* p. 14.

72. Both Barbara Stafford, in her study of illustrations in scientific travel narratives, "Toward Romantic Landscape," and James Bunn, in his semiotic analysis of Britain's emergent consumer culture, "Aesthetics of British Mercantilism," document how eighteenth-century England constructed meaning, what Bunn calls "import," from objects seemingly independent of context and connection.

73. Pope, 1 February 1728/29, *Correspondence,* vol. 4, p. 66. Pope, who offered the meal described to Lord Oxford in 1729, asked him, "If you would drink good wine, pray bring just two bottles with you for I have but two in the house."

74. Adam Smith, *An Inquiry into the Nature and Causes of the Wealth of Nations,* ed. R. H. Campbell, A. S. Skinner, and W. B. Todd (Oxford: Clarendon Press, 1976), vol. 1, p. 426; quoted in Bunn, "Aesthetics of British Mercantilism," p. 317.

75. See Bunn, "Aesthetics of British Mercantilism," pp. 317–318.

76. See chapter five.

77. TE vol. 6, pp. 156–160.

78. See Catherine Ingrassia, "Women Writing/Writing Women: Pope, Dulness, and 'Feminization' in the *Dunciad,*" *Eighteenth-Century Life,* 14, 3 (November 1990): 40–58. My reading of *To a Lady* is indebted to Laura Brown, *Alexander Pope* (London: Basil Blackwell, 1985), pp. 101–108. Ellen Pollak's *The Poetics of Sexual Myth: Gender and Ideology in the Verse of Swift and Pope* (Chicago: University of Chicago Press, 1985), shrewdly analyzes Pope's omission of genuine difference in his construction of woman in *To a Lady* as the "other" to a definition of man; a definition which in the economic context of the *Moral Essays* figures woman as "unfruitful decadent wealth (domestic treasure) and useless art (merely ornamental)," p. 125.

79. Marcia Pointon notes in this regard that in eighteenth-century classifications of portraiture, both women and nature were regarded as "mixed subjects." *Hanging the Head: Portraiture and Social Formation in Eighteenth-Century England* (New Haven: Yale University Press, 1993), p. 89.

80. *Satire II, i,* 55–56.

81. In her examination of a gendered hierarchy of improvement exemplified by Pope in *To Burlington* and the Horatian poems, and especially convenient for Pope's situation as "gentleman tenant farmer," Carole Fabricant draws the connection between the imperative that nature "yield" and women marry, so that men may gain possession by "proper usage." "Binding and Dressing," pp. 124–125. While in essential agreement with Fabricant's argument about the gendered hierarchy of such orderly disorder, I obscure her terms by examining how Pope incorporates deformity and femininity within the fence of his garden.

82. Paulson, *Emblem and Expression,* p. 32.

83. Mack describes it as "the principal point of rest in a garden of memory and meditation." *Garden and the City,* p. 29. For a reproduction of a 1797 engraving of the obelisk see p. 30; for a clear transcription of the inscription, p. 241.

84. William Kent to the Earl of Burlington, 28 November 1738, in Pope, *Correspondence*, vol. IV, p. 150.

85. Mack, *Garden and the City*, p. 29.

86. Henrietta Pye, *A Short Account of the Principal Gardens in and about Richmond and Kew* (1760), p. 11; quoted in Mack, *Garden and the City*, p. 29.

87. For Pope's sharing of Martha's "Romantic taste" in landscaping, see Martin, *Pursuing Innocent Pleasures*, pp. 12–13; see also Addison's imagination on such an ideally innocent female reader of gardens, Leonora, in *Spectator* 37. Pope and Addison idealized women as closer to nature and therefore better audiences for it. Martin speaks of Pope's perception of Martha's childlike innocence and her consequent responsiveness to evocative and natural landscapes. Perhaps she did read romances all her life because for all of Pope's life she remained the perfect "Idaea of a gardening companion," an Eve to Pope's Adam.

88. For the double meaning of grotto in latin as both "cava" [cave] and "cavea" [theater], see Hunt, *Garden and Grove*, p. 63. Its connection with "grotteschi" or the grotesque is perhaps the most important for my purposes.

89. Pope, 2 June 1725, *Correspondence*, vol. 2, pp. 296–297.

90. Ibid., p. 296.

91. Pope to Earl of Oxford, 8 October 1724, *Correspondence*, vol. 2, p. 264.

92. Joseph Warton, *An Essay on the Genius and Writings of Pope* (London, 1782), 4th. ed., vol. 2, p. 180; quoted in Spence, *Anecdotes*, vol. 1, p. 251.

93. Spence, *Anecdotes*, vol. 1, p. 252 .

94. Joseph Addison, *Spectator* 417, in *The Spectator*, ed. Donald F. Bond (Oxford: Clarendon Press, 1965), vol. 3, pp. 564, 566. Addison rehearses a familiar trope when he compares the authors of epic to varieties of landscape. On the interrelatedness of these two arts see Hunt, *Figure in the Landscape*, p. 67: "the literary history of the eighteenth century could partly be written in terms of the development of precisely those genres which were identified with the landscape garden." See also Hunt, "Ovid in the garden," *Garden and Grove*, pp. 42–58.

95. Addison, *Spectator* 414, pp. 548–549.

96. Stafford comments on the "exchange of identity and function that occurs between natural object and artifact," a habit of mind that Addison "inaugurates," as indicative of the evolution of singularity as an aesthetic category. "By the second half of the eighteenth century," she argues, "the natural object becomes the true work of art." "Toward Romantic Landscape," pp. 18–19.

97. Sir Joshua Reynolds, in *The Idler and Adventurer*, in *The Yale Edition of the Works of Samuel Johnson*, eds. W. J. Bate, J. M. Bullitt, and L. F. Powell (New Haven: Yale University Press, 1963), vol. 2, p. 258; cited by Naomi Schor, *Reading in Detail: Aesthetics and the Feminine* (New York: Methuen, 1987; reprinted Routledge, 1989), p. 16. Schor comments that this passage demonstrates that the "logic of the detail [in eighteenth-century aesthetics] is the logic of the supplement." Schor does not note, however, that the last six words of the passage were added by Johnson, thereby "polluting," in a parallel gesture, the univocality of Reynolds's authority.

98. Fabricant registers the "paradoxical impression . . . that, despite the pervasive and explicit femininity of the century's gardens, they were nevertheless very much of a man's world . . . Female shapes and structures were, it is true, allowed to occupy a place in the Augustan elysiums, but generally speaking they constituted stage props and ornaments in a great symbolic drama specifically, essentially male in character." "Binding and Dressing," p. 130. As we have seen, Pope places Bolingbroke (and therefore himself) at the center of such a drama at the end of the *Epistle to Burlington* in a fantasy of unmediated power that edits out the figure of woman almost entirely.

99. Addison, *Spectator* 414, pp. 549–550.

100. In *Garden and Grove,* pp. 73–82, Hunt describes the Italian Renaissance practice of turning the garden itself into a cabinet of curiosity, confounding notions of inside and outside by, for example, displaying one's curios in state on the "walls" of hedges and loggia.

101. Addison, *Spectator* 414, p. 552.

102. Ibid., included in editor's note, p. 550.

103. Hunt, *Figure in the Landscape,* p. 77.

104. Addison, *Spectator* 414, p. 550.

105. British Museum ms., quoted in Marjorie Nicolson and G. S. Rousseau, *"This Long Disease, My Life": Alexander Pope and the Sciences* (Princeton: Princeton University Press, 1968), n. 88, pp. 284–285. Printed in London for a noted optical instrument maker, John Cuff, the poem traces the evolution of the popular perception of the camera obscura from magical object to scientific device.

106. Norman Bryson implements this distinction between presentation and representation in a discussion of a Caravaggio still life that could apply equally well to the technical virtuosity of the camera obscura:

"the [painting's] interest lies exactly in the power of art—and of this artist— to raise an intrinsically humble branch of painting to the level of the heroic . . . It is of no consequence if, in the process, the reality of the still life as part of an actual world is sacrificed, and indeed that sacrifice is necessary if painting is to move from representation to presentation, from a stage of transcribing reality to a stage where the image seems more radiant, more engaging, and in every way superior to the original—which the painting can dispense with."

Looking at the Overlooked: Four Essays on Still Life Painting (Cambridge, Mass.: Harvard University Press, 1990), p. 81. Thus Addison prefers the illuminated landscape on the walls of a dark room cut off from nature to nature itself. Bryson credits his use of the terms presentation and representation to Stephen Bann, *The True Vine: Visual Representation and Western Tradition* (Cambridge: Cambridge University Press, 1989), pp. 68–101, who argues for a painterly mode of " 'representation as presentation,' where the viewer does not 'see' but 'is shown.' " *Looking at the Overlooked,* chapter 2, n. 11, pp. 183–184.

107. "I have another chariot, besides that little one you laugh'd at when you compar'd me to Homer in a nut-shell." Pope, 19 March 1721½, *Correspondence*, vol. 2, p. 110.

108. Bann, *The True Vine*, p. 35; quoted in Bryson, *Looking at the Overlooked*, chapter 2, n. 17, p. 184.

109. Pliny, *Natural History* 35, p. 65; quoted in Bryson, *Looking at the Overlooked*, p. 30.

110. Jacques Lacan, *The Four Fundamental Concepts of Psychoanalysis*, ed. Jacques-Alain Miller, trans. Alan Sheridan (New York: Norton, 1978; reprinted 1981), p. 112.

111. Pope to Swift, 25 March, 1736, *Correspondence*, vol. 4, p. 6.

112. Lacan, *Four Fundamental Concepts*, p. 112.

113. That something which the *trompe l'oeil* turns out to be "is on the order of the object small a, which is to say the fetish." See Schor's commentary on this passage in *Reading in Detail*, pp. 150–151. The love of the (masculine) eye for transparent deceit in the form of the fetish provides an interesting contrast to the fixed gaze at the uncannily feminine particulars of the still life. See Bryson, *Looking at the Overlooked*, pp. 136–178.

114. Jonathan Crary, *Techniques of the Observer: On Vision and Modernity in the Nineteenth Century* (Cambridge, Mass.: MIT Press, 1990), p. 41. Crary's chapter "The Camera Obscura and its Subject" describes the apparatus as a "dominant paradigm through which was described the status and possibilities of the observer": at once a discursive metaphor for vision, a model in the science of optics, and a technical apparatus. *Techniques of the Observer*, p. 27. What is sacrificed to the frame of the camera obscura—as in the deathless world of *The Rape of the Lock*—is the flux and mortality of nature. What is gained from the subsequent separation of "knower and known" is "the appearance of a new model of subjectivity . . . a figure for both the observer who is nominally a free sovereign individual and a privatized subject confined in a quasi-domestic space, cut off from a public exterior world." *Techniques of the Observer*, pp. 38–39.

115. The camera obscura thus becomes "a model simultaneously for the observation of empirical phenomena *and* for reflective introspection and self-observation." Ibid., p. 40.

116. Bryson, *Looking at the Overlooked*, p. 30.

117. Ibid., p. 31.

118. Ibid., p. 32.

119. Ibid., pp. 51–52. See also Crary's use of Baudrillard's description of the capacity in capitalist societies "of newly empowered social classes and groups to overcome the [aristocratic] 'exclusiveness of signs' and to initiate 'a proliferation of signs on demand'. . . The problem of mimesis here is not one of aesthetics but of social power, a power founded on the capacity to produce equivalences." *Techniques of the Observer*, p. 12.

120. For the camera obscura, as for the *xenia*, Bryson's qualification of Trimalchio's excess is important: "the movement is not one of headlong flight away from the real, as with Trimalchio, but of carefully graduated transitions and liaisons between reality and representation." *Looking at the Overlooked*, p. 52.

121. Fabricant, "Binding and Dressing," pp. 126–127.

122. Willis and Hunt paraphrasing Charles Cotton, *The Wonders of the Peake* (1681), *Genius of the Place*, p. 93; quoted in Fabricant, "Binding and Dressing," p. 132. While Fabricant quotes Pope's description of the camera obscura, she fails to acknowledge the way in which the grotto that constitutes it displays rather than conceals nature's secret parts.

123. Crary, *Techniques of the Observer*, pp. 42–43.

124. See Brown, *Ends of Empire*, pp. 103–134.

125. Benjamin Boyce, "Mr. Pope, in Bath, Improves the Design of his Grotto," in Caroll Camden, ed., *Restoration and Eighteenth-Century Literature: Essays in Honor of A. D. McKillop* (Chicago: University of Chicago Press, 1963), p. 146.

126. Ibid.

127. Pope, 9 and 10 March, 1739/40, *Correspondence*, vol. 4, pp. 228, 229.

128. Ibid., 3 September 1740, vol. 4, pp. 261–262.

129. Brownell in *Alexander Pope's Villa* lists examples of a "cult of verse" and a habit of tourism in regard to Pope's villa which "flourished into the nineteenth century" and notes that "Pope's grotto did more to establish the fame of Pope's villa than the house or garden." Quotation from p. 11. See also Paulson, *Emblem and Expression*, p. 32, who refers to the grotto as the "really significant element" of Twickenham's landscape.

130. For alternate versions of this poem see TE, vol. 6, pp. 382–385.

131. *Lady Mary Wortley Montagu: Essays and Poems*, eds. Robert Halsband and Isobel Grundy (Oxford: Clarendon Press, 1977), p. 247, lines 4–9.

132. Quoted in Brownell, *Pope's Villa*, p. 12.

133. Pope to Dr. Oliver, 10 March 1739/40, *Correspondence*, vol. 4, p. 229.

134. Shaftesbury, *The Moralists*, vol. 2, pt. 1, p. 290.

135. Stafford, "Toward Romantic Landscape," p. 25.

136. Ibid., p. 53.

137. TE, vol. 6, p. 353.

138. For a history of the evolution of eighteenth-century travellers' interest in mines which moves from an emphasis on "the deeds of men" to "those of timeless nature," see Stafford, "Toward Romantic Landscape," p. 22.

139. John Serle, *A Plan of Mr. Pope's Garden* (1745), *Augustan Reprint Society* 211, introd. Morris R. Brownell (Los Angeles: William Andrews Clark Memorial Library, 1982), p. 10.

140. Ibid., Brownell's introduction, p. vi.

141. Pope, 22 May 1742, *Correspondence*, vol. 4, p. 397; Serle, *Plan*, p. 10.

142. Quoted in Brownell, *Pope's Villa*, p. 11.

143. My use of the terms collection and souvenir is informed by Susan Stewart's discussion in the fifth chapter of *On Longing: Narratives of the Miniature, the Gigantic, the Souvenir, the Collection* (Baltimore: Johns Hopkins University Press, 1984).

144. Ibid., pp. 143, 151.

145. As Stewart puts it, "the spatial whole of the collection supersedes the individual narratives that 'lie behind it,'" and in that sense the aesthetic of antiquarianism, with its emphasis on origins, "is thus in an important way the antithesis" of the

aesthetics of mercantilism which James Bunn describes and which informs the collector's placement of the object "within the play of signifiers that characterize an exchange economy." Ibid., p. 153.

146. Ibid., p. 152.

147. Mack, *Garden and the City,* p. 100.

148. "While the point of the souvenir may be remembering, or at least the invention of memory, the point of the collection is forgetting—starting again in such a way that a finite number of elements create, by virtue of their combination, an infinite reverie." Stewart, *On Longing,* p. 152.

149. Mack, *Garden and the City,* pp. 64–65.

150. Serle, *Plan,* pp. 7, 8.

151. Pope, 2 June 1725, *Correspondence,* vol. 2, p. 297.

152. Mack, *Garden and the City,* p. 70.

153. Plutarch, *Lives,* trans. Dryden-Clough (New York: Modern Library, 1932), p. 80; quoted in Mack, *Garden and the City,* pp. 70–71.

154. See Mack, *Garden and City,* p. 71.

155. Dryden translation, 17–36; Juvenal 10–20; quoted in Mack, *Garden and the City,* pp. 73–74.

156. James Ralph, *Sawney. An Essay on the Dunciad an Heroick Poem* (London: Whitehall Evening Post, June 27, 1728), ll. 1–4.

157. Mack, *Garden and the City,* p. 66.

158. Ibid., p. 69.

159. Stafford, "Toward Romantic Landscape," p. 22.

160. See Pope to Blount, 2 June 1725, *Correspondence,* vol. 2, p. 296.

161. For an allegorical reading of the position of the grotto, see Mack, pp. 47–51; John Locke, *Essay Concerning Human Understanding,* II.xi, p. 17, quoted in Mack, *Garden and the City,* p. 47.

162. For this alternative model of the mind based not on the camera obscura's objectivity but on self-enclosed reflection, see Mack, *Garden and the City,* p. 47; Crary, *Techniques,* p. 27.

163. Hunt, *Figure in the Landscape,* p. 82.

164. Ibid., p. 85.

165. Whately, *Observations on Modern Gardening,* 5th ed. (London, 1793), pp. 63–64; quoted by Hunt, *Figure in the Landscape,* p. 84.

166. *Newcastle General Magazine,* reprinted in Mack, *Garden and the City,* p. 239.

167. "They were, in fact, an alternative medium to print, reifying the word; through them, the vicarious became the immediate, the theoretical and general became the concrete and specific." Richard D. Altick, *The Shows of London* (Cambridge, Mass.: Belknap Press, 1978), p. 1. Particularly of interest in this regard is Altick's discussion of eighteenth-century mechanical shows or moving pictures, often called, like the gardens and museums they mimicked, "theatrum mundi." See pp. 60–62.

168. "All souvenirs are souvenirs of a nature which has been invented by ideology." Stewart, *On Longing,* p. 150.

169. *Newcastle General Magazine,* quoted in Mack, *Garden and the City,* p. 56.

170. Stewart, *On Longing,* p. 135.

171. Ibid.

172. For a reading of Marx's use of the metaphor of camera obscura in describing the strange allure of commodity fetishism which has interesting implications for Pope's use of the device in the grotto, see W. J. T. Mitchell, *Iconology: Image, Text, Ideology* (Chicago: University of Chicago Press, 1986), pp. 160–208.

173. Johnson, *Life of Pope,* vol. 3, pp. 134–135.

174. Ovid, *Metamorphoses,* III, 157–161. Mack in *Garden and the City* also cites at length Sidney's description in the *Arcadia* of "A cave, made as it should seen by Nature in despite of Arte," pp. 58–59.

175. Mack, *Garden and the City,* p. 61.

176. Swift, 29 September 1725, in Pope, *Correspondence,* vol. 2, pp. 325–326.

177. *Autobiography, Letters, and Literary Remains of Mrs. Piozzi,* ed. A. Hayward (London, 1861), vol. 2, p. 154; quoted in Mack, *Garden and the City,* p. 63.

178. Dustin Griffin, *Alexander Pope: The Poet in the Poems* (Princeton: Princeton University Press, 1978), p. 36, citing Mack, *Garden and the City,* p. 60.

179. Robert Dodsley, "The Cave of Pope," in Serle, *Plan,* p. 19, line 7.

180. Ibid., p. 20. Such curiosity largely destroyed Twickenham and the grotto in the end. In 1807, Baroness Sophia Charlotte Howe, also known to lovers of Twickenham as "Queen of the Goths," frustrated by the influx of tourists and Pope-worshippers, had Pope's villa torn down and much of his planting uprooted. Alexander the Great, her detractors observed, who had spared Pindar's house when sacking Thebes, was more merciful. Mack notes that she was also reputed to have "stripped the grotto of many of its minerals so as to destroy its attraction to visitors," a process which the tourists and souvenir hunters would have completed without her. For an account of Howe's destruction, see *Garden and the City,* p. 283; for the state of the grotto today, see figure 28 and its description on p. 289.

181. Miriam Leranbaum in *Alexander Pope's 'OPUS MAGNUM', 1729–1744* (Oxford: Oxford University Press, 1977), p. 6, pinpoints the period of Pope's deepest engagement with this "ethic scheme" as 1729–1735.

182. See TE vol. 3, pt. 2, pp. xvii–xx, for a reproduction of Pope's outline and notes for this project. For precise dating of the project, see Leranbaum, *Pope's Opus Magnum.*

183. Hunt, *Figure in the Landscape,* p. 91. My thinking on *To Burlington* is influenced by Hunt's reading in this book of the poem in particular and Twickenham in general.

184. Hunt, quoting Pope to the Earl of Stratford, 6 July [1725], *Correspondence,* vol. 2, p. 309, in *Figure in the Landscape,* p. 101.

185. Pope, 25 March 1736, *Correspondence,* vol. 4, p. 5.

4. HORACE AND THE ART OF SELF-COLLECTION

1. For "difficulty" as an aesthetic value associated with the emblem, and in particular with the indivisibility of language and vision characteristic of Hogarth and Pope, see Ronald Paulson, *Emblem and Expression: Meaning in English Art in the Eighteenth Century* (Cambridge, Mass.: Harvard University Press, 1975), pp. 51–56.

2. TE vol. 6, pp. 202–207.

3. Addison, *Dialogues Upon the Usefulness of Ancient Medals,* in *Miscellaneous Works,* ed. A. C. Guthkelch (London: G. Bell & Sons, 1914), vol. 2, pp. 283–284.

4. Ibid., pp. 284, 289.

5. "Nameless names" refers to *Dunciad* III, 150 (version A): "Lo Bond and Foxton, ev'ry nameless name, / All crowd, who foremost shall be damn'd to Fame." TE vol. 5, p. 164. See chapter five for further discussion of the role of the proper name in Pope's late satire.

6. Addison, *Dialogues,* p. 289.

7. Ibid., p. 289.

8. Quoted in Paulson, *Emblem and Expression,* p. 82.

9. Richard Kroll, *The Material Word: Literate Culture in Restoration and Early Eighteenth-Century England* (Baltimore: Johns Hopkins University Press, 1991), p. 178. Kroll's fine book meditates on the neo-Epicurean "analogy between physical atoms and linguistic letters," an analogy which allows for a post-Puritan variability of inter-pretation, an imagination of the grounds of language "in terms of spatial or somatic metaphors, whose visualism seeks to reinforce the primacy of written or printed over aural media," and which allies print with the body. *Material Word,* pp. 184–185. Of particular relevance to my meditation on medals and statues as concrete visual embodiments of the power of print is chapter 5, "Living and Speaking Statues; Domesticating Epicurus," pp. 140–179.

10. Addison, *Dialogues,* p. 291.

11. For a discussion of the convention of the "sphragis" as an establishment of the Hellenistic author's "copyright," which Horace turns to his own devices, see Eduard Fraenkel, *Horace* (Oxford: Clarendon Press, 1957), pp. 362–363.

12. Lewis Crusius, *Lives of the Roman Poets* (London, 1726–1732), vol. 1, p. 145.

13. Ibid., p. 148. Crusius continues by remarking that "none has had less justice done him that way than he, nor been oftener attempted."

14. See W. S. Anderson, "The Roman Socrates: Horace and His Satires," for a discussion of Horace's evolution from a Socratic exposer of folly to a Platonic recorder of foolishness. In *Essays on Roman Satire* (Princeton: Princeton University Press, 1981), pp. 13–49.

15. On propaganda in the first Augustan Age, see Ronald Syme, *The Roman Revolution* (Oxford: Oxford University Press, 1939), especially chapters 1, 11, and 17. Syme depicts Augustus as an expert manipulator of the language of power.

16. For a discussion of Augustus's sense of his power not as "potestas," but as "auctoritas," which analyzes the emperor's authority as a self-effacing style of authorship much like Horace's own, see Leo Braudy, *The Frenzy of Renown: Fame and Its History* (New York: Oxford University Press, 1986), especially pp. 90–115, and 129–133.

17. Although Syme admits Maecenas's de facto status as the one "in charge of Rome" in Octavian's frequent absence, his description of what he tellingly brands Maecenas's "character and vices," serves to undermine any orthodox representation of this min-ister's public authority. But whereas Syme reads Maecenas's aristocratic excess as a sign of his inability to stand as a public figure of authority, the poets in his circle

(and Horace's complicated relationship to his patron and to the New State supports this latter point) might have read and covertly sympathized with such dramatics as a calculated rejection of "model" public status. Poetic authority (and I am thinking particularly of the elegists) flaunted convention too, and upheld its own stance covertly. See Propertius 2.1, a recusatio made all the more ironic by its description of Maecenas as a warrior.

For a discussion of Horace's Odes as postmodern and revisionist in relation both to contemporary politics and Greek literary tradition, see Matthew Santirocco, *Unity and Design in Horace's Odes* (Chapel Hill: University of North Carolina Press, 1986), pp. 22–34.

18. For a reading of the *Aeneid* which elaborates upon this sense of ambivalence, see W. R. Johnson, *Darkness Visible* (Berkeley: University of California Press, 1976).

19. See Alfred Noyes, *Horace: A Portrait* (New York: Sheed and Ward, 1947), chapter 1.

20. Suetonius, *De Poetis,* trans. J. C. Rolfe (New York: MacMillan Co., 1914), vol. 2, p. 487. Suetonius quotes a letter in which Augustus asks Maecenas to release Horace from his "parasitica mensa" to the custody of the emperor's "regia" (royal) board.

21. Crusius, *Life of Horace,* p. 116.

22. All citations from Horace's Odes are taken from *Horace: Epodes and Odes,* ed. Daniel H. Garrison (Norman: University of Oklahoma Press, 1991). All translations are my own.

23. William S. Anderson's provocative statement could have served as an epigraph to this chapter: "When he was writing the Odes, art became autobiography because poetry was Horace's life. In this final stage of development, we must reverse the equation." For a helpful discussion of Horace's career-long use and reuse of biographical material, in particular his relation to his father, see his "Autobiography and Art in Horace," in *Essays on Roman Satire,* p. 73.

24.   Prima dicte mihi, summa dicende Camena
      spectatum satis et donatum iam rude quaeris,
      Maecenas, iterum antiquo me includere ludo.
      Non eadem est aetas, non mens. Veainius, armis
      Herculis ad postem fixis, latet abditus agro,
      ne populum extrema totiens exoret arena.
      Est mihi purgatam crebro qui personet aurem:
      'Solve senescentem mature sanus equum, ne
      peccet ad extremum ridendus et ilia ducat.'
      Nunc itaque et versus et cetera ludicra pono;
      quid verum atque decens curo et rogo et omnis in hoc sum;   (1–11)

All citations from Horace's Satires and Epistles are taken from Edward P. Morris's edition (Norman: University of Oklahoma Press, 1939, reprinted 1967). All translations are my own.

25. The pen as weapon and token of self-possession is emblematic of Pope's increasingly embattled Horatian stance. In *Satire II, i* (1733) he describes himself as "arm'd for *Virtue* when I point the Pen" (105), and even more dramatically resolves in *Dialogue*

II (1738), "the last Pen for Freedom let me draw" (248). See chapter 5 for more on Pope's satiric heroism.

26. Samuel Johnson chose this line as the epigraph to his *Rambler* essays, and Kant similarly used it to begin his essay, "What is Enlightenment?" In both cases, in a phenomenon which Pope's appropriation of Horace's assertion of originality also demonstrates, originality is paradoxically based on a cited model.

27.   Si curatus inaequali tonsore capillos
        occuri, rides; si forte subucula pexae
        trita subest tunicae vel si toga dissidet impar,
        rides: quid, mea cum pugnat sententia secum,
        quod petiit spernit, repetit quod nuper omisit,
        aestuat et vitae disconvenit ordine toto,
        diruit, aedificat, mutat quadrata rotundis?
        Insanire putas sollemnia me neque rides,
        nec medici credis nec curatoris egere
        a praetore dati, rerum tutela mearum
        cum sis et prave sectum stomacheris ob unguem
        de te pendentis, te respicientis amici.   (94–105)

28. TE vol. 4, pp. 275–293.
29. Henry Dwight Sedgewick, *Horace. A Biography* (Cambridge, Mass.: Harvard University Press, 1947), pp. viii–ix.
30. Paul de Man, *The Rhetoric of Romanticism* (New York: Columbia University Press, 1984), p. 69.
31. Ibid., p. 70.
32. Autobiography, then, exemplifies most vividly this paradox: "But just as we seem to assert that all texts are autobiographical, we should say that, by the same token, none of them is or can be." Ibid., pp. 70–71.
33. Ibid., p. 76.
34. Ibid., p. 78. De Man alludes here to Wordsworth's *Essay on Epitaphs* and that text's allusion to Milton's *On Shakespeare* (1630), whose poetry "dost make us Marble with too much conceiving" (14).
35. de Man, *Allegories of Reading: Figural Language in Rousseau, Nietzsche, Rilke, and Proust* (New Haven: Yale University Press, 1979), p. 78.
36. de Man, *The Rhetoric of Romanticism*, p. 95.
37. J. Lonsdale and S. Lee, eds., *The Works of Horace* (London, 1887); quoted in Steele Commager, *The Odes of Horace* (New Haven: Yale University Press, 1962), p. 99.

38.   . . . me pedibus delectat claudere verba
        Lucili ritu, nostrum melioris utroque.
        Ille velut fidis arcana sodalibus olim
        credebat libris, neque si male cesserat, usquam
        decurrens alio, neque si bene; quo fit ut omnis
        votiva pateat veluti descripta tabella
        vita senis.   (28–34)

39. For a discussion of Horace's covert critique of Lucilius's "inartistry" in this poem, see Anderson, "The Roman Socrates," in *Essays on Roman Satire*, pp. 31–32.

40. The Horatians I have chosen may seem like straw men, but they are only the more extreme examples. A critic as unimpeachable as Reuben Brower, in his introduction to *Alexander Pope: The Poetry of Allusion* (Oxford: Oxford University Press, 1959), speaks of Horace as the critic's personal friend. Steele Commager, who remains one of the most sophisticated of Horace's critics, imagines a Horace who in his love poems envies the state of total absorption in the irrational that he can only depict as empty convention. Commager is quick to deny the easy conclusion that Horace is incapable of real feeling. But in contradicting one simplistic judgment to make a more sophisticated one, Commager falls into the same inescapable pathetic fallacy. *Odes of Horace*, pp. 141–159.

41. Grant Showerman, *Horace and His Influence* (Boston: Marshall Jones, 1922), p. 4. Part of a series aptly titled *Our Debt to Greece and Rome.*

42. Ibid., p. 44.

43. Sedgewick, *Horace*, p. 65.

44. Ibid., p. ix.

45. Helen Rowe Henze, *The Odes of Horace Newly Translated from the Latin and Rendered into the Original Metres* (Norman: University of Oklahoma Press, 1961), p. 9. For further examples, see Commager, *Odes of Horace*, pp. 141–159.

46. Henze, *Odes*, p. 9. "Yet the various women who flit through Horace's *Odes* doubtless had, at least in some instances, human prototypes . . . Cinara was probably real; as for the rest, whether real or not, we cannot identify them . . . Nor does it matter; it is not always necessary for a poet to be in love with his originals. The quality of his affection was for friendship rather than for love, and he set as high a value on it as any Epicurean."

47. Crusius, *Life of Horace*, p. 135.

48. Commager, *Odes of Horace*, p. 58.

49. Frank Stack, *Pope and Horace: Studies in Imitation* (Cambridge: Cambridge University Press, 1985), p. 102.

50. Nietzsche traces "this veering of the lines of thought" as "this mosaic of words, in which every word, by sound, by placing, and by meaning, spreads its influence to the right, to the left, and over the whole; this minimum in extent and number of symbols, this maximum thereby achieved in the effectiveness of the symbols, all this is Roman, and believe me, elegant par excellence." *Werke, Taschenausgabe* (Leipzig, 1906), vol. 10, p. 343; quoted in Commager, *Odes of Horace*, p. 50.

51. For a contrary argument about the consonance of poet, politics and audience in Horace's fourth book of odes, see Gordon Williams, "Phases in Political Patronage in Ancient Rome," in Barbara K. Gold, ed., *Literary and Artistic Patronage in Ancient Rome* (Austin: University of Texas Press, 1982), pp. 3–27.

52. Suetonius, *Vita Horati*, p. 489.

53. Fraenkel, *Horace*, p. 410.

54. Ibid., p. 423.

55. Commager, *Odes of Horace*, p. 291.

56. And so, it seems, do the Horatians. Book Four was viewed as an inferior effort until very recently. One of the main goals of Michael Putnam's important study of this text is to prove it first-class Horatian art. See Michael Putnam, *Artifices of Eternity. The Fourth Book of Horace's Odes* (Ithaca: Cornell University Press, 1986).

57. "Like the overture of many a classical opera it [4.1] introduces the main themes of the subsequent work and merges them into an organic whole . . . But these themes, important in themselves, have in the introductory poem still another function: they surround as a kind of frame the eulogy of a Roman nobleman. By this arrangement Horace has made it clear that he proposes to treat, along with familiar subjects of lyric poetry, something novel, the praise of select contemporaries, not in occasional remarks, but as the predominant theme of entire poems." Fraenkel, *Horace,* p. 413. The "portrait gallery" of Book Four as Fraenkel describes it thus constitutes a project which Pope would have found particularly congenial.

58. See Gordon Williams, "Poetry in the Moral Climate of Augustan Rome," *Journal of Roman Studies,* 54 (1964): 186–196.

59. See Putnam, *Artifices of Eternity,* p. 29.

60. Fraenkel, *Horace,* p. 410; Commager, *Odes of Horace,* p. 292.

61. For a discussion of the figure of Paulus as an anomalous—because eminently marriageable—hero of a love poem, see Thomas N. Habinek, "The Marriageability of Maximus: Horace, Ode 4.1.13–20," *American Journal of Philology,* 107 (1986): 407–416.

62. All translations of Sappho are from *Sappho's Lyre. Archaic Lyric and Women Poets of Ancient Greece,* trans. Diane Rayor (Berkeley: University of California Press, 1991).

63. For examples, see Propertius 2.1 to Maecenas, Horace Ode 2.1 to Pollio, and Horace Ode 1.6 on the poet's inability to sing Agrippa's praises.

64. It is interesting to note in this context that Horace 4.1 is followed by a real recusatio, in which Horace declares himself unable to write like Pindar by doing so.

65. Fraenkel, *Horace,* p. 413.

66. The critical debate about whether or not Ligurinus really existed continues some of the biographical realism inspired by Horace's poetry already examined in this chapter. See Williams, "Poetry in the Moral Climate of Augustan Rome," pp. 186–196, for the claim that for Horace to pose as a lover of boys in his poetry was only to emulate Greek literary convention and not actual behavior. D. R. Shackleton-Bailey in *A Profile of Horace* (London: Duckworth, 1982) disagrees, citing the example of Maecenas's relatively open homosexuality and Horace's own professed bisexuality in the *Satires.* For Grigson Davis in *Polyhymnia: The Rhetoric of Horatian Lyric Discourse* (Berkeley: University of California Press, 1991), pp. 69–70, p. 255, n. 64, the choice of the name "Ligurinus" ("liguritio" signifies "fondness for dainties" while "Cinara" is synonymous with "artichoke") is more playfully rhetorical in its signalling of the gastronomic pleasures of the convivium than particular or emotional. For the social inappropriateness of an older man's love for a boy, and for the unthreatening but certainly noticeable presence of legislation against such relationships in Augustan Rome, ruled by an emperor intent on morally reforming and physically reproducing an independent aristocracy, see *A History of Private Life,* vol.

Notes to Pages 155–170

1, *From Pagan Rome to Byzantium,* ed. Paul Veyne, trans. Arthur Goldhammer (Cambridge, Mass.: Belknap Press, 1987), especially pp. 183–206.

67. Horace's choice of love object in this ode, in both its unfittingness and its same-sex mirroring of his lost youth, rehearses the poem's interrogation of self-representation.

68. "Do you not marvel how she seeks to make her mind, body, ears, tongue, eyes, and complexion, as if they were scattered elements strange to her, join together in the same moment of experience?" Longinus, *On Great Writing (On the Sublime),* trans. G. M. A. Grube (Indianapolis: Bobbs Merrill, 1957), p. 18.

69. *The First Ode of the Fourth Book of Horace,* TE, vol. 4, pp. 147–153.

70. On the Sapphic sublime and eighteenth-century interpreters' rejection of it, see Reuben Quintero, *Literate Culture: Pope's Rhetorical Art* (Newark: University of Delaware Press, 1992), p. 89.

71. Longinus, *A Treatise of the Sublime, or, The Marvellous in Discourse* in *The Works of Monsr. Boileau Despreaux,* trans. John Ozell (London: E. Sanger and E. Curll, 1711–1712), vol. 2, pp. 31–32; quoted in Appendix D of Quintero, *Literate Culture,* pp. 145–146.

72. Ozell, *Treatise of the Sublime,* pp. 12–13; quoted in Quintero, *Literate Culture,* p. 91.

73. For a reading of ekphrasis that analyzes the genre's relation to a visual "other" it represents by silencing, see W. J. T. Mitchell, *Picture Theory* (Chicago: University of Chicago Press, 1994), pp. 151–181.

74. Stack, *Pope and Horace,* pp. 110–111.

75. Ibid., p. 109.

76. Stack uses this fact to emphasize Pope's separation, in the service of an ideal image, of the "te/ego" juxtaposition in the last stanza of Horace's Latin. Ibid., p. 110.

77. TE, vol. 4, p. 372.

78. Paulson, *Emblem and Expression,* p. 23.

79. Ibid., p. 22.

80.
> O crudelis adhuc et Veneris muneribus potens,
> insperata tuae cum veniet pluma superbiae
> et quae nunc umeris involitant deciderint comae,
> nunc et qui color est puniceae flore prior rosae
> mutatus, Ligurine, in faciem verterit hispidam:
> dices "Heu" quotiens te speculo videris alterum,
> "quae mens est hodie, cur eadem non puero fuit,
> vel cur his animis incolumes non redeunt genae?"

81. Horace's phrase for himself, Epistle 1.4, line 16.

82. Suetonius, *Vita Horati,* p. 488.

5. DISFIGURED TRUTH AND THE PROPER NAME

1. Pope, *Prose Works,* vol. 1, p. 295.

2. Ibid.

3. Ibid.

261

4. Horace closes his *Epistle to Augustus* (2.1) with a plea to stay out of the public eye, specifically alluding to the Roman custom of having one's wax portrait offered for sale: "Nil moror officium quod me gravat, ac neque ficto / in peius voltu proponi cereus usquam" [I will not be delayed by attentions which burden me, and neither will I ever be displayed in wax with my face made worse] (264–265). Pope transforms this literal injunction against representation and marketing of the author's person into a self-consciously unoriginal and unauthored couplet homily that skirts the issue of his own considerable investment in such self-exposure.

> A vile Encomium doubly ridicules;
> There's nothing blackens like the ink of fools;
> If true, a woful likeness, and if lyes,
> "Praise undeserv'd is scandal in disguise:"   (410–413)

5. Richard Kroll's characterization of the couplet in his postscript to *The Material Word* (Baltimore: Johns Hopkins University Press, 1991), pp. 323–324, is particularly apt: "The couplet serves most obviously as the foundational atom of poetic utterance . . . Especially in Pope's hands, the couplet also becomes intensely organized at the level of the individual line, which itself emphasizes the printed materiality that directs attention to such minutiae of punctuation as commas . . . Pope can assume an aesthetic in which words are first endowed with discrete atomic weight before they become objects of authorial arrangement and readerly judgment." In the late satires of Pope, names take on exceptional weight.

6. Hill to Pope, 16 May 1733, *Correspondence*, vol. 3, p. 370.

7. Frank Stack, *Pope and Horace: Studies in Imitation* (Cambridge: Cambridge University Press, 1985), p. 57.

8. For a discussion of the co-emergence of legal definitions of libel and of professional authorship, see Catherine Gallagher, "Political Crimes and Fictional Alibis: The Case of Delarivier Manley," *Eighteenth-Century Studies*, 23 (Summer 1990): 502–521, reprinted in *Nobody's Story: The Vanishing Acts of Women Writers in the Marketplace, 1670–1820* (Berkeley: University of California Press, 1994), pp. 88–144. See Mark Rose, "The Author as Proprietor," *Representations*, 23 (Summer 1988): 51–85, and "The Author in Court," *Cultural Critique* (Spring 1992): 197–217, both reprinted in *Authors and Owners* (Cambridge, Mass.: Harvard University Press, 1994), for crucial accounts of Pope's instrumental role in defining the author as owner of a uniquely immaterial literary property.

9. "Whatever was his pride, to them he was obedient; and whatever was his irritability, to them he was gentle. Life has, among its soothing and quiet comforts, few things better to give than such a son." Johnson, *Life of Pope*, vol. 3, p. 154.

10. A reproduction of Pope's monument is the frontispiece to the first edition of Owen Ruffhead's *Life of Pope* (London: C. Bathurst, 1769).

11. 18 May 1728, *Correspondence*, vol. 2, pp. 495–496.

12. For a discussion of Pope's place in a tradition of neoclassical imitation that didactically elaborated upon the obliquities and implications of the Latin original, see Leonard

Moskovit, "Pope and the Tradition of the Neoclassical Imitation," *Studies in English Literature*, 8, 3 (1968): 445–462.

13. Laura Brown describes well the conflict in Pope's later work between the contextual and the absolute: "the very failure of this poetry to move beyond its time is also its enabling 'advantage,' the constraint that assures its significance. The futility of Pope's struggle to assert a non-contingent and absolute standard of judgement generates that famous adversary stance of his late poetry, the stance of the virtuous satirist, the privileged arbiter whose vehement defiance takes on history itself . . . Pope's own 'True Wit' . . . derives its 'advantage' from the contradictions and contingencies of its context." *Alexander Pope* (London: Basil Blackwell, 1985), pp. 126–127.

14. TE vol. 4, p. 327. For a detailed account of the historical events which provoked Pope's moral outrage in the *Epilogue to the Satires*, events which led to a brief resurgence and ultimate disappointment of both Opposition optimism and Pope's personal investment in his role as moral adviser to the Prince of Wales, see Paul Gabriner, "Pope's 'Virtue' and the Events of 1738," *Scripta Hierosolymitana*, 25 (1973): 96–119. In "Pope's Moral, Political, and Cultural Combat," *The Eighteenth Century: Theory and Interpretation*, 29, 2 (1988): 165–187, Carole Fabricant convincingly argues that there is no true "objective correlative" for Pope's rage in the late satires, a rage which depends on binary opposition between good and evil so absolute as to lose all credibility. For a version of eighteenth-century English history which often finds Pope and his fellow Tory satirists both convincing and accurate, see E. P. Thompson, *Whigs and Hunters: The Origin of the Black Act* (New York: Pantheon Books, 1975). Commenting on Pope's allusion to the government's persecution of Catholics in the *Epistle to Arbuthnot*, Thompson writes, "We should read some satires not as extravaganzas but in a more literal way—expertly flighted and with a shaft of solid information." Quotation taken from p. 294.

15. TE, vol. 5, pp. 406–407.

16. Geoffrey Tillotson, *On the Poetry of Pope* (Oxford: Clarendon Press, 1950, 2d. ed.), p. 55.

17. Swift to Pope, 16 July 1728, *Correspondence*, vol. 2, p. 504.

18. James Ralph, *Sawney. An Essay on the Dunciad an Heroick Poem* (London: *Whitehall Evening Post*, June 27, 1728). Edward Ward, *Apollo's Maggott in his Cups: Or, The Whimsical Creation of a Little Satyrical Poet* (London: *Monthly Chronicle*, August 7, 1729), Stanza CVIII, p. 28.

19. Pope, 28 June 1728, *Correspondence*, vol. 2, p. 503.

20. Ward, *Apollo's Maggott*, p. 42.

21. James Sutherland, TE vol. 5, p. xxvii. Pope's inscription to this collection is quoted in the preface.

22. *The Universal Spectator*, April 3, 1742; quoted in TE, vol. 5, p. xxxi. It is interesting to note in this regard that Pope's final attempt at explicit satire, *One Thousand Seven Hundred and Forty*, was left unfinished. Carole Fabricant speculates that Pope's relentless negation made him incapable of completing a poem with a hero other than himself in "Pope's Cultural Combat." John Butt, in TE vol. 4, p. 331, surmises that the poem is " 'ruined' rather than incomplete, for the blanks indicate that Pope

feared for what he had written, rather than that he was undecided what to write." In either case, it seems that by 1740, Pope deemed particularity in satire politically or psychologically impossible.

23. For Jones, the dunces "force into violent antithesis the notions of body and mind by showing the ethereally spirited poet of tradition yoked to a clumsy machine of a body" and by "insisting on the primacy of matter, mere things, mere bodies." Emrys Jones, "Pope and Dulness," in Maynard Mack and James A. Winn, eds., *Pope: Recent Essays by Several Hands* (Hamden, Conn: Archon Books, 1980), p. 632. For more on the materiality of the *Dunciad,* see also William Kinsley, "The *Dunciad* as Mock-Book," in Mack and Winn, pp. 707–730. For the minutely detailed topography of the poem, see Aubrey Williams, *Pope's Dunciad: A Study of Its Meaning* (London: Methuen, 1955).

24. William Warburton's note to the *Dunciad,* TE, vol. 5, p. 323.

25. TE, vol. 5, p. 354.

26. Ibid.

27. Pope to Martha Blount, 22 June 1724, *Correspondence,* vol. 2, p. 239.

28. Henry Fielding, *Covent Garden Journal* No. 59, in *The Criticism of Henry Fielding,* ed. Ioan Williams (London: Routledge, 1970), p. 116.

29. Jonathan Swift, *A Tale of a Tub,* eds. A. C. Guthkelch and D. Nichol Smith (Oxford: Clarendon Press, 1958, 2d ed.), p. 43.

30. *The Blatant Beast. A Poem.* (London: J. Robinson, 1742), pp. 3–41; summarized in J. V. Guerinot, *Pamphlet Attacks on Alexander Pope, 1711–1744. A Descriptive Bibliography* (New York: New York University Press, 1969), pp. 305–308; reprinted by Augustan Reprint Society, no. 114 (Los Angeles: William Andrews Clark Memorial Library, 1965). See also chapter 1 for a discussion of James Ralph's twin epigraphs to *Sawney* (1728), which also evoke Lucifer, and which conflate the monstrosity of the *Dunciad* with the deformity of its author in a similar fall from grace.

31. The phrase is coined by Pat Rogers, who in his essay "Pope and the Social Scene," puts as great an emphasis on the legal disability of Pope's Catholicism as I do on Pope's physical deformity. Rogers argues quite persuasively for the "medieval implacability" of the anti-Catholic laws (which were no less psychologically effective for their lack of strong enforcement in daily life), and for the strong legalistic overtones of Pope's satire. In Peter Dixon, ed., *Writers and Their Background: Alexander Pope* (Columbus: Ohio University Press, 1972), p. 105.

32. Charles Johnson, *The Tragedy of Medea. As it is Acted at the Theatre-Royal in Drury Lane. With a Preface containing Some Reflections on the New Way of Criticism, Monthly Chronicle,* December, 1730 (London: R. Francklin, 1731). Quoted in Guerinot, *Pamphlet Attacks,* pp. 197–198.

33. Johnson continues with practical advice, namely to submit "before the Curtain draws up. Upon these Terms perhaps he may restore them their understandings, take off the Blot he has put upon their Names, and suffer them to eat and be praised; but if they neglect This I do assure them they will feel the Force of his Bulls as I have done." Ibid. Unfortunately, the curtain of the *Dunciad* dropped forever as the last authorial act of Pope's career.

34. George Gordon, Lord Byron, Letter to [John Murray] Esquire, on the Rev. W. L. Bowles' Strictures on the Life and Writings of Pope (March 1821), *Selected Prose,* ed. Peter Gunn (Harmondsworth: Penguin, 1972), p. 406.

35. Particularly of interest is Fielding's account of Pope's punishment of the dunces as a bodily marking suitable to both his tyranny and his poetics: "He is said to have . . . employed various Spies, by whom if he was informed of the least Suggestion against his Title, he never failed of branding the accused Person with the Word DUNCE on his Forehead in broad Letters; after which the unhappy Culprit was obliged to lay by his Pen forever; for no Bookseller would venture to print a Word that he wrote." *Covent Garden Journal* No. 23, in *Criticism,* p. 109.

36. *Pope Alexander's Supremacy and Infallibility Examined* (London: *Monthly Chronicle,* 1729), pp. 2–3.

37. Pat Rogers, *Grub Street: Studies in a Subculture* (London: Methuen, 1972).

38. Pope quoted in TE vol. 5, p. xliv.

39. Rogers, *Grub Street,* p. 76; first emphasis his, second emphasis mine.

40. Ibid., p. 376.

41. Dustin Griffin, *Alexander Pope: The Poet in the Poems* (Princeton: Princeton University Press, 1978), p. 5, quoting Pope, 18 August 1716, *Correspondence,* vol. 1, pp. 352–353.

42. Rogers, *Grub Street,* p. 24.

43. James Sutherland, TE, vol. 5, p. xlv. *Dunciad* III, 157, version B. The first version of the phrase in the Twickenham Version A., III, 150, insists on particulars: "Lo Bond and Foxton, ev'ry nameless name, / All crowd, who foremost shall be damn'd to Fame"; while the line quoted in the body of my text elides details in keeping with the later version's tendency to generalize.

44. Spence, *Anecdotes,* vol. 1, pp. 177–178.

45. First published in Warburton's edition of the *Works,* 1751, line 13. Reprinted in TE, vol. 4, p. 159.

46. Hervey, *Memoirs,* p. 261, cited in TE, vol. 4, p. 191.

47. Spence, *Anecdotes,* vol. 1, p. 143.

48. Ibid.

49. TE, vol. 4, p. 3.

50. TE, vol. 4, p. 95.

51. Johnson, *Life of Pope,* vol. 3, p. 152. Recent scholarship has rejected the identification of Timon with Chandos, but the tendency, mistaken or not, of contemporary readers to identify the two is what interests me.

52. Guerinot, *Pamphlet Attacks,* p. xxiv.

53. TE, vol. 5, p. 3.

54. Denis Diderot, *Rameau's Nephew and D'Alembert's Dream,* trans. Leonard Tancock (Harmondsworth: Penguin, 1966), p. 192.

55. D'Alembert had earlier stated: "Man is merely a frequent effect, a monstrosity is a rare one, but both are equally natural, equally inevitable, equally part of the universal and general order." Ibid., p. 181. For a reading of Diderot's theories of monstrosity

and their relation to conceptions of gender, see Marie Hélène Huet, *Monstrous Imagination* (Cambridge, Mass.: Harvard University Press, 1993), pp. 82–95.

56. *The Poet Finish'd in Prose. Being A Dialogue Concerning Mr. Pope And His Writings* (*General Evening Post,* June 26, 1735), in Guerinot, *Pamphlet Attacks,* p. 256.

57. Ward, *Apollot's Maggott,* Stanza LXXI, pp. 18–19.

58. James Turner convincingly situates Pope "on the edge of masculinity, poised uneasily between the old libertinism and the new refinement," linking the indeterminacy and fluidity of Pope's sexual identity with the poet's ability to "pass easily between the intellectual milieu and the world of pleasure," the former "masculine," the latter, "feminine." "Pope's Libertine Self-Fashioning," *The Eighteenth Century: Theory and Interpretation,* 29, 2 (1988): 124, 143.

59. What Carole Fabricant terms the "vicious cyclicality" of Pope's definition of virtue in the *Epilogue to the Satires* also provides grounds for the dunces' complaints of unfair tautological judgment: "He reproaches his Enemies as poor and dull; and to prove them *poor,* he asserts they are *dull;* and to prove them *dull* he asserts they are *poor.*" "Pope's Cultural Combat," p. 172; Letter signed "W. A.," *Mist's Journal,* June 8, 1728, quoted in TE, vol. 5, p. xlviii.

60. Turner, "Pope's Libertine Self-Fashioning," pp. 124–127.

61. TE, vol. 4, p. 75.

62. TE, vol. 4, p. 81.

63. Despite Bentley's cavils to the contrary: "Here the Imitator grievously errs, *Cunnus albus* by no means signifying a *white* or *grey* Thing, but a Thing under a *white* or *grey Garment,* which thing may be either black, brown, red, or particoloured." The Mock-Bentley's note on Pope's suggestive translation of the phrase "Cunnus albus" as "hoary shrine," TE, vol. 4, p. 78.

64. Arbuthnot to Pope, 17 July 1734, *Correspondence,* vol. 3, p. 416.

65. Pope, [late 1717?], *Correspondence,* vol. 1, p. 456.

66. Perhaps Johnson had this epistolary exchange in mind when he opined that "Pope may be said to write always with his reputation in his head . . . but Arbuthnot [writes] like one who lets thoughts drop from his pen as they rise into his mind." *Life of Pope,* vol. 3, p. 160. Editorial note, Pope, *Correspondence,* vol. 3, p. 419.

67. Pope, *Correspondence,* vol. 3, p. 419, July 26, 1734 (revision of a letter dated August 2 in the same volume).

68. For the very literal sense in which Pope means this metaphor, see Spence, *Anecdotes,* vol. 1, p. 149, in which Pope predicts with relish the effect the fourth book of the *Dunciad* will have on Cibber. "He will be stuck, like the man in the almanac, not deep but all over." Osborn notes of this passage that "the 'man in the almanac' refers to the standard drawing of a man's body, pricked with sword points to indicate the anatomical parts associated with the signs of the zodiac." For an illustration, and a reading of the physical nature of Pope's satire, see Morris, *Alexander Pope,* pp. 214–240.

69. Sir Philip Sidney, *An Apology for Poetry,* ed. Forrest G. Robinson (Indianapolis: Bobbs Merrill, 1970), p. 27.

70. Ibid., p. 35.

71. Ibid., p. 34.

72. Ibid., p. 17.

73. See Pope's theory of the ruling passion in the *Essay on Man,* in particular Epistle II
for meditations on its particular results:

> Reason the byass turns to good from ill,
> And Nero reigns a Titus, if he will.
> The fiery soul abhor'd in Catiline,
> In Decius charms, in Curtius is divine.
> The same ambition can destroy or save,
> And make a patriot as it makes a knave.   (II, 197–202)

See chapter 3, for a reading of the *Moral Essays* that highlights the ways in which
Pope's abstract theories of human nature take visible form in particular portraits.

74. Pope to Arbuthnot, 26 July 1734, *Correspondence,* vol. 3, p. 419.

75. TE vol. 4, p. 95.

76. Pope, 2 August [1734], *Correspondence,* vol. 3, p. 423.

77. Pope to Arbuthnot, 16 July 1734, *Correspondence,* vol. 3, p. 420.

78. Johnson, *Works* (1824) vol. 11, p. 194n; quoted in TE, vol. 4, p. 13.

79. Johnson, *Life of Savage,* quoted in TE, vol. 4, p. 376.

80.
> Quid faciam? Saltat Milonius, ut semel icto
> Accessit fervor capiti numerusque lucernis.
> Castor gaudet equis; ovo prognatus eodem
> Pugnis: quot capitum vivunt, totidem studiorum
> Millia: me pedibus delectat claudere verba,
> Lucili ritu, nostrum melioris utroque.   (24–29)

81.
> Sequor hunc, Lucanus an Appulus anceps:
> [Nam Venusinus arat finem sub utrumque colonus,
> Missus ad hoc pulsis (vetus est ut fama) Sabellis;
> Quo ne per vaccuum Romano incurreret hostis,
> Sive quod Appula gens, seu quod Lucania Bellum
> Incuteret violenta].   (34–38)

82. Edward P. Morris, ed., *Horace: Satires and Epistles* (Norman: University of Oklahoma
Press, 1939, reprinted 1967), p. 149.

83. William S. Anderson, *Essays on Roman Satire* (Princeton: Princeton University Press,
1982), pp. 30–32. He notes that this passage in praise of Horace's predecessor is
implicitly critical of Lucilius's crudely excessive self-exposure.

84. Pope, 16 January 1714/15, *Correspondence,* vol. 1, p. 275. The image recurs in almost
exactly the same words in Pope's *Thoughts on Various Subjects,* cited in TE vol. 4,
p. 9: "The best way to prove the clearness of our mind, is by shewing its faults; as
when a stream discovers the dirt at the bottom, it convinces us of the transparency
and purity of the water."

85. Pope, 18 August 1716, *Correspondence,* vol. 1, p. 353.

86. Ibid.

87. 25 July 1714, *Correspondence,* vol. 1, p. 238. Something of the same pattern of ostensible abandonment of a text in order to defensively claim possession of it is evident in Pope's anonymous dissemination of an unauthorized version of his correspondence to pave the way for his own self-righteous publication of the "definitive" version.

88. For a context for Pope's rhetoric here, specifically for an understanding of the tactic of declaiming against a standing army, see J. G. A. Pocock, "Machiavelli, Harrington and English Political Ideologies," in *Politics, Language and Time* (Chicago: University of Chicago Press reissue, 1989), pp. 104–147, particularly pp. 122–123.

89. Susan Staves, "Pope's Refinement," *Eighteenth-Century Theory and Interpretation,* 29, 2 (1988): 145–163.

90. Hill to Pope, 28 January 1730–31, Pope to Hill, 5 February 1730–31, *Correspondence,* vol. 3, pp. 168, 172.

91. The comparison of Pope as moral arbiter to the scribler/spider is not, of course, Pope's, but my own. But years before, in an early self-mocking moment, Pope described himself anonymously to the public as "a lively little Creature, with long Arms and Legs: A spider is no ill Emblem of him." *Prose Works,* vol. 1, p. 125. See the introduction for further reflections on this metaphor.

92. As Leo Braudy puts it, "Pope's manipulations seem an effort to divide himself into famous and anonymous parts, the outward assertion justified by the inward solitude—held together by the simultaneous public and private gesture of writing one's story in a book." For Pope, "to be singular, to seek literary and philosophical fame, is in some basic way to be private." *The Frenzy of Renown: Fame and Its History* (New York: Oxford University Press, 1986), pp. 364, 365. At the same time Pope must constantly defend himself against the encroachment on the private realm by his public audience.

93. John Butt, TE, vol. 4, p. 94.

94. Braudy hints at the grotesque proportions of this writing furor when he remarks somewhat sentimentally that the shameless "Scriblers" who pestered Pope were not interested in becoming poets. Rather "they were interested in learning how to become their true selves, whatever that might be, and soaking in the famous man's aura of completeness was the first step." *Frenzy of Renown,* p. 382. This "aura of completeness" is jointly authored by Pope and his readers.

95. *Essay on Man,* I, 218.

96. This passage helps to illuminate how Pope's attraction to the dunces he excoriates is in part due to their unabashedly public particularity, the ease with which they can name themselves and be named by others. Rogers observes: "Part of the seductive appeal of Dulness lies in the fact that its avatars are so unselfconsciously, so solipsistically, so splendidly *themselves* . . . A Dunce is a Dunce, largely because he is a specified and identifiable figure in the first place." *Grub Street,* p. 200. Emrys Jones similarly notes that when Pope pillories the dunces, "the poet of consciousness and wit can be said to be contemplating a form of the mindless." "Pope and Dulness," p. 634.

97. Johnson, *Life of Pope,* vol. 3, p. 199.

98. Shaftesbury, *Miscellaneous Reflections,* in *Characteristics,* ed. John M. Robertson (London, 1900), vol. 2, p. 169.

99. Aubrey L. Williams, "Pope and Horace: The Second Epistle of the Second Book," in Carroll Camden, ed., *Restoration and Eighteenth-Century Literature* (Chicago: University of Chicago Press, 1963), p. 314. The first of Williams's many examples is Pope's alteration of Horace's initial anecdote of the runaway slave boy which serves in both epistles as an excuse for a failure to write. In Horace, the boy's flaw is that he is a runaway; Pope "translates" this into stealing. Williams argues that Pope's early emphasis on thievery paves the way for the poem's final and grander metaphor of time as inexorable thief.

100. I am indebted to the conversation and writing of Richard Feingold for my thinking on Pope's satiric heroism in general and *Epistle II, ii* in particular. See his *Moralized Song: The Character of Augustan Lyricism* (New Brunswick: Rutgers University Press, 1989), pp. 23–51.

101. See Fabricant, "Pope's Cultural Combat," p. 168.

102. Morris, *Alexander Pope,* pp. 241–269. Morris discusses the relationship of Pope's physical deformity to his literary form; a relationship which his reading links to Pope's construction of Virtue in an age where vice is beautiful.

103. For documentation of this view of Horace as over-delicate and therefore politically craven, see Howard Weinbrot, *Augustus Caesar in Augustan England* (Princeton: Princeton University Press, 1978). While I want to complicate Weinbrot's characterization of Pope as "Juvenalian" in opposition to Horace here, what remains clear is that Pope puts a common contemporary cliché about Horace into "F.'s" untrustworthy mouth.

104. TE vol. 4, p. 299.

105. Pope to Fortescue, 31 July 1738, *Correspondence,* vol. 4, p. 114.

106. Swift to Pope, 26 November 1725, *Correspondence,* vol. 2, pp. 343–344.

107. Pope, *Essay on Criticism,* 71.

108. Pope thus exemplifies a crucial disjunction from the idea of classical representation defined by Michel Foucault in *The Order of Things* (New York: Vintage Books, 1973), p. 16, a definition which entails "the necessary disappearance of that which is its foundation—of the person it resembles and the person in whose eyes it is only a resemblance."

Index